Global Transformations in Media and Communication Research – A Palgrave and IAMCR Series

Series Editors

Marjan de Bruin
HARP, Mona Campus
The University of the West Indies
Mona, Jamaica

Claudia Padovani
SPGI
University of Padova
Padova, Italy

The International Association for Media and Communications Research (IAMCR) has been, for over 50 years, a focal point and unique platform for academic debate and discussion on a variety of topics and issues generated by its many thematic Sections and Working groups (see http://iamcr.org/) This new series specifically links to the intellectual capital of the IAMCR and offers more systematic and comprehensive opportunities for the publication of key research and debates. It will provide a forum for collective knowledge production and exchange through trans-disciplinary contributions. In the current phase of globalizing processes and increasing interactions, the series will provide a space to rethink those very categories of space and place, time and geography through which communication studies has evolved, thus contributing to identifying and refining concepts, theories and methods with which to explore the diverse realities of communication in a changing world. Its central aim is to provide a platform for knowledge exchange from different geo-cultural contexts. Books in the series will contribute diverse and plural perspectives on communication developments including from outside the Anglo-speaking world which is much needed in today's globalized world in order to make sense of the complexities and intercultural challenges communication studies are facing.

More information about this series at
http://www.springer.com/series/15018

Sergio Sparviero · Corinna Peil
Gabriele Balbi
Editors

Media Convergence
and Deconvergence

Editors
Sergio Sparviero
Department of Communication
 Studies
University of Salzburg
Salzburg, Austria

Gabriele Balbi
Institute of Media and Journalism
USI Università della Svizzera italiana
Lugano, Ticino, Switzerland

Corinna Peil
Department of Communication
 Studies
University of Salzburg
Salzburg, Austria

Global Transformations in Media and Communication Research – A Palgrave
and IAMCR Series
ISBN 978-3-319-51288-4   ISBN 978-3-319-51289-1   (eBook)
DOI 10.1007/978-3-319-51289-1

Library of Congress Control Number: 2017939100

Cover credit: Lincoln Allen/Photo650/Alamy Stock Photo

Printed on acid-free paper

This Palgrave Macmillan imprint is published by Springer Nature
The registered company is Springer International Publishing AG
The registered company address is: Gewerbestrasse 11, 6330 Cham, Switzerland

Acknowledgements

The authors are grateful to all the people that contribute to make the International Association of Media and Communication Research (IAMCR) an international, vibrant environment for the exchange of ideas, many of which are contained in the pages of this book. In particular, we would like to thank Claudia Padovani and Marjan de Bruin, co-chairs of the publication committee and editors of the *Global Transformations in Media and Communication Research* series, for their advice and support. Moreover, as this book is also the main outcome of the "Deconstructing Media Convergence" conference held in Salzburg in November 2013, we would like to thank the people that made it possible, from Josef Trappel, head of the Department of Communication Studies of the University of Salzburg, who sponsored the event, to Eva Gaderer, Alexandra Leitner, and Sanneke Tiesema who gave us the opportunity to focus on the content of the event by efficiently organizing everything else. We are also very grateful to Jim Rogers and Gianluigi Negro, well-informed academics on various topics covered in the book, and friends, who helped us when we needed them. We owe a debt of gratitude to Jana Büchner for the tedious work of subediting so many pages, to the editorial team at Palgrave, Felicity Plester, Heloise Harding and Sophie Auld for their patient support, and to the authors of the chapters of this book, who humbly accepted our suggestions and invested time in writing and revising their excellent contributions.

Finally, our special thanks go to our families and friends.

Contents

EDITORS AND CONTRIBUTORS

About the Editors

Sergio Sparviero is an Assistant Professor at the Department of Communication Studies of the University of Salzburg, Austria. His main field of research and teaching are: media economics; media management; and media innovation. In particular, he published research on the developments of the news, film and music industries. He is also the coordinator of the Erasmus + Joint Master Program "Digital Communication Leadership" (DCLead).

Corinna Peil is a Postdoctoral Researcher at the University of Salzburg's Department of Communication Studies, Center for Information and Communication Technologies & Society (ICT&S), Austria. Her research and teaching focus is on mobile communications, media (de)convergence, online publics, the use of media in everyday life contexts, and the mediatization of society.

Gabriele Balbi is Senior Assistant Professor at the Institute of Media and Journalism, Faculty of Communication Sciences, USI Università della Svizzera italiana, Switzerland. He is director of the China Media Observatory. His main areas of research are media history and history of telecommunications, with a focus on the relationships between analogue and digital media.

Contributors

Christopher Ali University of Virginia, Charlottesville, USA

Matthew Allen School of Communication and Creative Arts, Deakin University, Geelong, VIC, Australia

Gabriele Balbi USI Università della Svizzera italiana, Lugano, Switzerland

Luca Barra Università di Bologna, Bologna, Italy

Mark Eisenegger Department of Communication Studies, University of Salzburg, Salzburg, Austria; Research Institute for the Public Sphere and Society (fög), University of Zurich, Zürich, Switzerland

Angelo Gisler Research Institute for the Public Sphere and Society (fög), University of Zurich, Zürich, Switzerland

Uwe Hasebrink Hans-Bredow-Institut, Hamburg, Germany

Sascha Hölig Hans-Bredow-Institut, Hamburg, Germany

Kuo Huang English Service of China Radio International, Beijing, China

Fei Jiang School of International Journalism and Communication, Beijing Foreign Studies University, Beijing, China

Dal Yong Jin Simon Fraser University, Burnaby, Canada

Lothar Mikos Filmuniversität Babelsberg KONRAD WOLF, Potsdam, Germany

Kathrin Friederike Müller University of Münster, Münster, Germany

Paul Clemens Murschetz Alpen-Adria-University of Klagenfurt, Klagenfurt, Austria

Corinna Peil University of Salzburg, Salzburg, Austria

Jim Rogers Dublin City University, Dublin, Ireland

Jutta Röser University of Münster, Münster, Germany

Massimo Scaglioni Università Cattolica del Sacro Cuore, Milan, Italy

Mario Schranz Research Institute for the Public Sphere and Society (fög), University of Zurich, Zürich, Switzerland

Sergio Sparviero University of Salzburg, Salzburg, Austria

Yanran Sun Graduate School of Chinese Academy of Social Sciences, Beijing, China

Caja Thimm University of Bonn, Bonn, Germany

Hilde Van den Bulck University of Antwerp, Antwerp, Belgium

LIST OF FIGURES

LIST OF TABLES

PART I

Introduction

CHAPTER 1

Media Convergence Meets Deconvergence

Corinna Peil and Sergio Sparviero

MEDIA CONVERGENCE AS A CONCEPT

It is now more than thirty years since Ithiel de Sola Pool keenly observed a "convergence of modes" (Pool, 1983, p. 23), by which he referred to the increased connectivity between media and the erosion of formerly fixed boundaries. Ever since then, especially with the emergence and wide diffusion of the internet and online technologies, media convergence has been considered an overarching transition process and one of the major implications of digitization. As such, it has become a buzzword and a key issue in academic texts, policy documents and industrial papers (Diehl & Karmasin, 2013; Dwyer, 2010; Fagerjord & Storsul, 2007; Jenkins, 2006; Jensen, 2010; Jin, 2013; Lugmayr & Dal Zotto, 2016a, b).

The term convergence indicates a movement directed towards, or terminating in, the same point, a "coming together of things that were previously separate" (Meikle & Young, 2011, p. 2). In media and communications, where it has maintained unbroken popularity until today, it is used to describe a wide range of different developments and

We acknowledge the financial support of the Open Access Publication Fund of the University of Salzburg for the article processing charge.

C. Peil (✉) · S. Sparviero
University of Salzburg, Salzburg, Austria
e-mail: corinna.peil@sbg.ac.at

© The Author(s) 2017
S. Sparviero et al. (eds.), *Media Convergence and Deconvergence*, Global Transformations in Media and Communication Research - A Palgrave and IAMCR Series, DOI 10.1007/978-3-319-51289-1_1

3

transformations at the technological, industrial, cultural, social, spatial and political level (for example, Jenkins, 2006; Latzer, 2013; Miller, 2011; see also Balbi, Chap. 2 in this volume). An agreement concerning the existence of a media convergence at the level of technology stands out as the common denominator of different approaches. Although there have been forms of convergence in the pre-digitization era (see Balbi), contemporary appearances of a technological convergence have in common their being deeply rooted in the process of digitization. With the rise of a common digital standard, digitization has not only facilitated the recording, storage and transmission of data, but also enabled, for the first time, the decoupling of technologies and their respective media services: Digital media formats—be they voice, sound, text or film—were no longer restricted to one device only and, at the same time, almost all media devices were able to represent a plurality of different media formats and services. "This is the core of what is meant by technological convergence: all forms of media being increasingly stored and transferred on the same format and therefore becoming completely interchangeable" (Miller, 2011, p. 73).

Without adhering to a technological-deterministic view on media change, it seems safe to assume that, in the course of digitization, technological convergence has become a reality in today's media and communication landscape. Previously separate media technologies have indeed come closer together and lost their distinctive features; they are able to represent the same cultural forms and they provide similar functions and scopes of application. As all other forms of media convergence are linked to it, technological convergence can thus be considered an underlying feature of media convergence and a prerequisite for the emergence and development of other manifestations of convergence.

Taking technological convergence as a starting point, media convergence covers a set of different change processes at the macro, meso and micro level (Peil & Mikos, 2017). At the macro level, it can be located in the context of a series of socio-cultural and economic transformations commonly described with keywords such as commercialization, globalization, deregulation and market liberalization. More specifically, the convergence of media and communications markets indicates the opportunities that became available to information and communication technologies (ICTs), media, and telecommunication corporations to expand their activities by redesigning their value chains and becoming multimedia companies. As a result of this process former telephone and cable providers, television stations, and hardware and software providers offer nowadays a variety of services ranging from the delivery of content to communications and connectivity, often bundled in packages. The resulting emergence of large multinational corporations has not only advanced a cross-media concentration process, but also imposed permanent changes on market structures and dynamics in the media sector which have been the subject of numerous convergence studies (Meikle & Young, 2011, pp. 39–41; Miller, 2011, pp. 77–79) . At the meso level, media convergence mainly concerns the alteration of media texts as well as their production and distribution. Content, genres and formats have merged in multiple ways and they are distributed over a variety of platforms and channels. As it is widely known, much work in this vein has been done by Henry Jenkins (2006) who elaborated in great depths on transmedia storytelling, the expansion of media texts and the participatory behavior of the media users in convergence cultures. At the micro level, attention is shifted to the users' activities in converging media environments   (Peil & Mikos, 2017) . The latter are characterized by an extended ensemble of functional identical media technologies of which each affords a plethora of different applications, products and services. Convergent uses of media then refer to ways of access, to individual media biographies and interests and to related media repertoires (Hasebrink & Domeyer, 2012; Kim, 2016; Stark, 2014), or, in short, to "media life," as Mark Deuze (2012) has described the extensive pervasion and increased invisibility of media in today's everyday life and its consequences for the users.

All these processes, which are included under the generic concept of media convergence, are evolving dynamically and with close relation to each other. In a certain way, they all predict a movement towards the dissolution of former fixed boundaries and a unification of discrete elements merging into some greater whole. The emergence of the particular and somehow defined vision of media convergence delineated above can be explained with the concept of "social imaginary," which defines the existence of widely shared understandings that have achieved general legitimacy (Mansell, 2012, p. 6), and which are produced, accepted and then taken for granted as "people seek some consistency in their experience of the 'reality' of their lives in a world of rapidly changing technologies and cultural and social norms" (Carpentier, 2011 cited in Mansell, 2012, p. 31). Therefore, here we claim that there is a widely shared understanding of the imperative nature of media convergence, which has taken a particular pathway associated with assumptions such as efficiency, synergy, simplification, information abundancy, participation, availability and multimodality. The elements of reality of this vision are multimedia companies exploiting the combined transmission of images, texts and sounds to offer better and cheaper products and services that facilitate the existence of active and participating users. As these images have achieved general legitimacy, they render media convergence a powerful concept, serving, among others, to influence the political agenda or to legitimize and justify policy decisions.

Nonetheless, these privileged meanings of media convergence, which emphasize the inevitability of the once adopted direction, are increasingly challenged. Media convergence is not about a newly achieved status quo (Jenkins, 2006, p. 16); rather, it relates to the idea of a process, a continuous change characterized by several parallel running developments and not terminating in a designated endpoint. Therefore, a variety of imaginaries exist. Critical viewpoints, for example, stress that media convergence has been used as a buzzword for outlining the impact of digitization while oversimplifying the complexity of media and technological change and neglecting the possibilities of modifying or turning around paths that have once been taken (Fagerjord & Storsul, 2007; Storsul & Stuedahl, 2007; Silverstone, 1995; see also Balbi, Chap. 2 in this volume).

Alternative views on transformation processes in today's mediatized societies are essential for a balanced view on media innovations and their advancement. Competing visions of media convergence include some recent ideas of a divergence process complementing and going hand in hand with media convergence (Fagerjord & Stuehdahl, 2007; Lugmayr & Dal Zotto, 2016c). According to this perspective, it is not the integration of media technologies, markets, uses and content but their disintegration, multiplication and increased complexity that are believed to be central features of recent developments. In order to grasp these often underexplored tendencies we suggest comprehending current transformations in media and communication as interplay of media convergence and deconvergence.

Deconvergence is a term originally coined by Jin (2011, 2013) to describe the breaking apart of media and communications companies through spin-offs, split-offs and demergers. It defines a trend that is a reaction to, and departs from, the convergence of media and communication markets, yet it is not divergence because it also unfolds in parallel to the former. In fact, as detailed below, in reaction to the digitization of media and communications, many companies in these sectors have followed either the strategy of expanding their capital and market opportunities, or the strategy of refocusing their operations around core activities, or both of these strategies at different points in time. Here, the term deconvergence is applied more broadly to different facets of the still dominant media convergence narrative to emphasize the interaction of converging and diverging movements in the media and communication sector. Taking into account processes of diversification and fragmentation as well as unresolved ambiguities that accompany media convergence or are a part of it, deconvergence also stands for the refusal to recognize the ongoing changes as linear, connected processes leading to predictable solutions. The perspective on deconvergence embraced in this book can help shed light on the ambivalent nature of media convergence and the simultaneity of competing forces such as coalescence and drifting apart, or linearity and discontinuity. Its purpose is to provide alternative viewpoints, which are often overlooked in the dominant readings of the concept. While these sites of tension constitute a general focus of this book, two of them, which are the user's perspective and the convergence of markets, are analyzed more carefully in the following sections. They demonstrate the contradictory nature of technological change and illustrate the ways its consequences for society are met.

Media Convergence and Deconvergence from the User's Perspective

One distinct area of media convergence discourse concerns the media users as well as their scope of actions and their behavior in convergent media environments. To begin with, there is not even a consensus as to what is meant by convergent media use. Empirical research in this vein shares a common interest in the people's media activities within environments that are less and less characterized by standalone media and their respective contexts of reception. It takes into consideration the ubiquitous and time-independent availability of media technologies that have similar or identical range of applications. The media repertoire approach by Hasebrink and Domeyer (2012), for example (see Hasebrink and Hölig, Chap. 6 in this volume, for further explications), describes the specific combination of media and content. Media repertoires refer to relatively stable, transmedia usage patterns that are perceived as the outcome of numerous media contacts resulting from concrete selection decisions. The polymedia concept introduced by Madianou and Miller (2012, p. 125) supposes the existence of media-saturated environments in which media technologies gain significance in relation to each other. Against this background, it focuses on the meaning-generating user practices that determine the single media's role within the media ensemble. Herkman (2012), with his concept of "intermediality," emphasizes historical continuities and contextual differences between media while Terje Rasmussen (2014) sees the media increasingly personalized and integrated into everyday life leading to a "networked lifeworld." The "mediatized world" approach (Hepp & Krotz, 2014) also refers to a transmedia understanding of today's media environments, as it centers on the situations of media communication in the context of new technological possibilities. Taking into account the capacity of almost all media to provide similar content, communication modes and gratifications, the concept of "communicative figurations" (Hepp & Hasebrink, 2013) looks at patterns of communication processes that exist over a variety of different media. The point of departure of all these newer, user-oriented approaches to media convergence is the decoupling of device and services, which render ineffective conclusions on usage based on the selection of media technology. Rather, the whole media ensemble, as well as the media's overlaps, is considered in order to comprehend how the discrete devices are used, combined and put in relation to each other.

For the purpose of describing the interplay of convergence and deconvergence from the user's perspective and to shed light on processes that so far have often been overlooked, three different dimensions of media usage have been identified where these antagonisms show in a particular way: (1) the proliferation of devices and media-related practices; (2) the transmedia flow of content and the dissolution of distinctive usage scenarios; (3) the interconnection of media and the management of domestic infrastructures.

The Proliferation of Devices and of Media Related Practices

An early and central idea of media convergence touching the usage dimension has been the imagination of the "supermedium" (Jenkins, 2001; Herkman, 2012, p. 11) or the "Über-Box" (Fagerjord, 2002)— the emergence of an all-in-one device as single point of media contact where all media uses come together (see also van Dijk, 2012). This supermedium has in fact become a reality: Now, even the smallest media technology enables access to a great variety of functionalities and applications which were previously linked to standalone devices only. Highly personalized and portable online media like the smartphone integrate telecommunications, content and information technology, and thus represent in an almost paradigmatic manner one of the original notions of technological convergence. Yet this transformation of media into all-purpose devices is far from replacing the numerous technologies and boxes available in the home and offering a single solution for all the mediated activities of the users. In fact, almost every device has kept its unique place in the media ensemble. And since media have not only expanded their scope, but also specialized in terms of size, look and performance, households are now engaging with more devices than ever before. Described by Jenkins (2006, p. 14) as the "black box fallacy," the number and diversity of technologies has significantly increased in the last few years. And, equally, so have the standards, formats and practices of the users. Part of this convergence process is that the media have indeed moved closer together, as they are linked in manifold ways to one another. However, involving a high degree of disorder and complexity, the outcome of this development is not at all a streamlining of the media landscape. Rather than owning and making use of one personal all-round medium, users nowadays have to deal with an extremely sophisticated media environment and a multiplicity of media technologies, each of which comes with a specific focus or core competence and a broad range of functionalities. Traits of deconvergence thus appear in different forms of media access, in personalized media interests, in individualized media repertoires and in disparate media biographies.

The strong rise of media technologies, which is characteristic of convergent media environments, can be easily explained on the basis of the German long-term study Massenkommunikation (mass communication). In the response options of a question concerning the media equipment in the home, it listed only two electronic devices in the year 1970, but more than ten times as much in 2010 (van Eimeren & Ridder, 2011, p. 3). Several of these devices enable internet access and thus facilitate the use of various applications that are provided by other media as well. Ultimately, after 2010 even more devices including tablet computers have contributed to the increased variety of multipurpose technologies available to the average household (Engel & Breunig, 2015, p. 311). The users are thus able to make use of a certain media technology based on individual interests and demands. For any imaginable request they can select a specific device and assign a particular task to it. At the same time, the practices of media use have multiplied and diversified, too. Before digitization, one medium was usually related to only one form of activity (for example the radio was related to the practice of listening). Today, the above-mentioned study lists fifteen general online activities (for example, online banking, information seeking, forum discussions and so on) alone for the internet and seven activities linked to specific applications, like instant messaging or the involvement in photo communities (Frees & Koch, 2015, p. 372). In addition, more than twenty activities are allocated to just one single online application, such as the use of online communities (for example, watching videos, uploading photos, posting and so on) (Busemann & Gscheidle, 2012, p. 383). This variety of media-related activities exemplifies a fundamental shift of media communication which refers to a growing disparity rather than to a process of merging.

The Transmedia Flow of Content and the Dissolution of Distinctive Usage Scenarios

The interplay of media convergence and deconvergence becomes also apparent in the appropriation of media texts. On the one hand, media content, genres and modalities have grown together, most notably on the internet where written text, audiovisual content and interactive elements are regularly combined. On the other hand, the multiplication of distribution channels and the cost-effective production of digital content have led to the emergence of numerous platforms and to the differentiation of formats. As a consequence, the users have more options than ever to select the content they like while specialized interests can be met more easily by the producers. The convergence of media texts is thus likely to come along with greater individualization, fragmentation and deconvergence on the side of the users (Peil & Mikos, 2017).

One strategy to deal with the increasingly complex and disordered flow of content is the concept of transmedia storytelling (Jenkins, 2006), which has gained much attention in media and communications. It refers to a new form of narration that creates a textual universe and an overall media experience around a specific narrative. Jenkins himself (2006, p. 19) speaks of the "art of world making" where different media are organized around a starting point, such as a movie or a TV series, in order to let the narrative expand onto diverse platforms and to maintain a continuous audience flow. Transmedia stories have to be functioning both within a single medium and as a narrative puzzle piece within a transmedia cosmos, comprising classic media as well as computer or mobile games and merchandising products (Peil & Schwaab, 2014, p. 342; Peil & Mikos, 2017). They are considered highly participative, driven top-down by the producers and also bottom-up by the users, who can decide how deep they want to immerse themselves in a given story. While the migration of texts across different media is constitutive of convergent media environments, the relocation of usage practices onto different devices and platforms indicates tendencies of deconvergence. In the shifting reception of television from the home TV set to the small display of the smartphone, Max Dawson (2007, p. 233), for example, has detected an "unbundling" of media objects: Larger program packages like an episode of a TV series or a news show are shaped into smaller, more easily consumed segments which are able to promote a falling apart of media experiences and a fragmentation of media usage into diminishing units of signification. By emphasizing the coexistence of separate media, second screens similarly refer to disintegration and a "crisis of convergence," as Stauff (2015, p. 127) explains: "'Second screen' therefore points at a not only simultaneous, but also interrelated and supplementary use of different screens, thereby undermining the clear distinction between separate media." Fleeting forms of media consumption and shorter periods of attention as well as parallel, overlapping uses of different media are thus likely to characterize media use in convergent media environments. In contrast, with the emergence of additional distribution channels like DVD boxes and streaming services, new forms of concentrated and time-consuming media reception have arisen, too, for instance, in the form of binge watching (Mikos, 2016) or "media marathoning" (Perks, 2015).

The described processes are ambiguous, and they are not fully captured by the notion of convergent media use. In "Convergence Culture", Jenkins (2006) refers to an intensified experience of media texts that are enhanced and improved through transmedia storytelling. The stories are too broad and complex for being told in one medium only. The activities of the users who engage in the text are perceived as richer and more comprehensive compared with past forms of media reception (Schwaab,

2013). This association of an advanced condition or product is also part of the dominant social imaginary of media convergence. But rather than coming together or matching a harmonized textual universe, media usage is marked by overlaps of content, meaning and context (D'heer & Courtois, 2016; Stauff, 2015; Vukanovic, 2016). The convergence of media texts thus corresponds with different forms of deconvergence, as illustrated in the increased complexity of usage situations. These are reflected in opposing tendencies, such as elusive and extensive forms of media reception, and in nonlinear and multidimensional consumption modes resulting from the ubiquitous availability of media texts and their independence from former technological restrictions.

The Interconnection of Media and the Management of Domestic Infrastructures[1]

A seamless interconnection of different media and their smooth interplay is part of the dominant social imaginary of media convergence, since convergence is expected "to allow user experiences to move fluidly through multiple content and devices" (Tavares & Schofield, 2016, p. 246). While at the hardware level home networks need to be set up and maintained in order to establish the domestic infrastructures and manage the interrelations of convergent media technologies, cloud services are supposed to integrate media at the software level. In fact, cloud services seem to represent everything that convergence stands for: They integrate data, applications and personalized content, regardless of type or format, and make them available to users wherever they are and whenever they need them, thus supporting multi-device and cross-platform uses of media. In many respects, however, the idea of the unhindered interplay of media devices and the ubiquitous accessibility of content are inclined to conceal the disruptions and deconvergences that are involved in these processes.

First of all, unlimited interoperability and connection is not necessarily supported by the device manufacturers and service providers. Often, lock-in systems force users to receive content, services and applications from one brand only as switching to another brand goes with higher costs and inconveniences. "In digital cross-media culture, the specific affordances of each device or platform only unfold through interconnection with others; seamless connection, however, is guaranteed only by the 'walled garden' (the market power and proprietary technical standards) of one brand strongly constraining interoperability" (Stauff, 2015, p. 132). As a matter of fact, infrastructures are shaped by the market's need to be profitable and to strengthen customer loyalty; they are not automatically geared towards convergence at the side of the users. Deconvergence comes into play when connections fail or there is a lack of compatibility between content producers and distribution platform, or between services and devices.

More important, the users themselves are often compromising the fluent interplay of media since the work of connecting devices and bringing content and services together within the personal media repertoire lies mainly in their hands. Even though software solutions suggest compensating for some of these exercises, their simplifying potential tends to be overvalued. "Far from serving to realize the putative end of labour in the home, new technologies often require significant work" (Kennedy, Nansen, Arnold, Wilken, & Gibbs, 2015, p. 410). The labor of establishing media convergence includes diverse tasks such as setting up digital networks, storing, synchronizing and organizing data, and administering the media ensemble. In addition, with the increasing number of devices and shorter production cycles, regular and sometimes challenging updates, maintenance and coordination tasks become necessary. In light of the differentiation of almost each media device and given the permanent advancement of networked technologies these exercises can be demanding and frustrating (Montpetit, 2016). For a beneficial exploitation of convergent media environments, people need to have certain skills, they need to invest time, money and social capital in their media usage. This aspect of ability should not be underestimated as several studies point to the user's need for helpers and supporters who bring their technical expertise in order to connect media and make them work (Bakardjieva, 2005, p. 98; Courtois & Verdegem, 2016; Peil & Röser, 2014, p. 241). In this sense, media convergence can be perceived as some kind of challenge or even burden for the users with the potential to tire them out or overstrain them. The dominant social imaginary of media convergence, represented in the idea of the harmonized and interconnected infrastructure, should therefore be complemented by the notion of labor that comes into play when dealing with manifestations of deconvergence at the level of structures and interfaces.

THE CONVERGENCE AND DECONVERGENCE OF MEDIA AND COMMUNICATIONS MARKETS

The diversity and complexity of the media environment just described is nowadays fostered by networks of specialized and interconnected companies. Nonetheless, as explained in this section, in reaction to the emergence of technical convergence, many large media and communication companies first attempted to engage in mergers and acquisitions (M&As) in order to expand their capabilities and market shares of particular products. It is only in a later period that prioritizing the development of core competencies alongside the establishment of key partnerships became a more popular strategy to obtain these same goals. In this section, we review theoretical contributions and writings from business analysts and we attempt to explain these seemingly contradicting trends: market convergence and deconvergence.

The Rationale for Market Convergence

The main factors enabling the convergence of media and communications markets (in short, market convergence) were technological convergence and neoliberal globalization, defined as the process driven by policies designed and implemented to promote liberalization, deregulation, privatization and capital investment (Hesmondhalgh, 2013; Jin, 2013). In particular, the deregulation of the media and the telecommunication sectors, which is abundantly discussed in some of the chapters of this book, is the process that led to the removal of the existing barriers and the establishment of new comprehensive rules for competition in the emerging markets. These new rules, enacted in the US Telecommunications Act of 1996 and in the 1997 World Trade Organization Agreements, and supported by the 1997 EU Green Paper on Convergence, allowed corporations to own assets in different media and communication markets and to grow and expand their activities, not only domestically, but also internationally (Chon, Choi, Barnett, Danowski, & Joo, 2003; Jin, 2013).

Moreover, the dominant social imaginary of market convergence has certainly been shaped by new giants, like Google, Facebook or, in former days, America Online (AOL), which quickly emerged as providers of new services based on the new technological opportunities. Notably, their efforts to innovate have not always been produced internally, within their own organization; on the contrary, their innovation strategy (still) supports integrating emerging new companies with their ideas and products, or, as it was the case for AOL (see Johnson, 2000), joining forces with an established player providing complementary skills and assets. However, the strategy of adapting to the new digital paradigm by integrating existing ventures into their value chains was pursued not only by a few new or large media and communications companies. The wave of M&As that took place between the mid 1990s and the mid 2000s in the media, telecommunication and ICT sectors was indeed quite extensive and involved a variety of different organizations. While qualitative evidence is also provided by Jin and Rogers in their respective contributions to this collection, a quick illustration of the scope of this trend is provided elsewhere by Jin (2013, p. 112), who estimated the cumulative value of 103 mega-deals carried out between 1999 and 2008 to be 1326 billion dollars.[2]

Many mergers and acquisitions between media and communication companies were presented to the authorities, the press and the shareholders, as attempts to generate economic value through the realization of synergies. This rather loose concept embraces a large variety of case scenarios that are contingent to the sector, the industry or specific companies. Nonetheless, from a more theoretical viewpoint, the realization of synergies through conglomeration generally includes the following five objectives (Flew, 2011; Ozanich & Wirth, 2004): diversification (that is, spreading risks and opportunities across multiple industries and markets), the repurpose of media content over multiple platforms, the cross-promotion of media content across platforms, the creation of brands and the exploitation of subsidiary rights.

However, business innovation is a trial-and-error process driven by leaders that base their decisions not only on theoretical notions and on the information provided by (formal and less formal) research departments, but also on a generally accepted understanding of the current economic and business environments and of the technological trajectories of particular products and services. Notably, this happens in the case of M&As between public companies because, prior to the realization of any benefits, the business leaders involved have to sell the merger or acquisition to investors, small or institutional, with ideas that the latter understand and are likely to embrace. Therefore, in order to comprehend the rationale for M&As in this specific historical period, it is also useful to look into the specialized press, which refers to the opinions (mostly of them articulated simply through buzzwords) of analysts and of business leaders explaining their decisions.

So, writing in 2001 about the Majors, which are the companies that dominate the distribution of blockbuster movies owned by the largest media and communication conglomerates, Harmon (2001) explained that combining content and distribution was viewed as a smart paradigm and the strategy improving the efficient exploitation of assets. Such was the case during the Golden Ages of the Hollywood studios (see also Sparviero, 2014). Following this smart paradigm were, among others, AOL-Time Warner, which aimed at expanding the distribution of its content over the internet, as well as Viacom and News Corporation focusing, respectively, on cable markets and satellite distribution. Also, given that governments became more lenient on limiting the cross-ownership of assets in the media and communication sectors, many companies pursued the strategy of expanding their assets through M&As, simply because they were allowed and because many others did (Harmon, 2001). Finally, the large wave of M&As in the media and communication sectors of the late 1990s to the mid 2000s can also be explained by the pursuit of the personal interests of public companies' key leaders and stakeholders. As explained by Gaughan (2011) in a critical text about current practices in corporate governance, many CEOs received important financial benefits from carrying out M&As [Michael Cappellas, for example, received 14 million dollars in connection with the sales of Compaq to Hewlett-Packard, and, a few years later, 39 million dollars for the sale of MCI to Verizon (Gaughan, 2011, p. 490)]. Therefore, without necessarily doubting the good faith of the CEOs who earned important revenues for steering the process in favor of a merger or acquisition, one could nonetheless argue that these key stakeholders might also have been attracted by the amply available arguments explaining the benefits of integrating companies in the communication and media sectors because, finally, these helped them achieve personal goals.

The Rationale for Market Deconvergence

On the other hand, less attention is generally paid to the deconvergence of media and communications markets (or, in short, market deconvergence)—that is, the drastic slowdown of M&A activities in the communication sector since 2002, as well as the failure of 70% of the mega mergers carried out between 1998 and 2003 (as estimated in Jin, 2013) , which also included the breaking apart of the most representative companies of the smart paradigm, namely Viacom-CBS (in 2006),

AOL-Time Warner (in 2008), and News Corporation (in 2013), as well as the Financial Times (in 2015) (see Jin, Chap. 10 in this volume).[3]

Interestingly, this trend signals that, although M&As in the media and communication sectors are still frequent, the pursuit of a deconvergence strategy is emerging as a new paradigm (Jin, 2013), regardless of the fact that the enabling conditions for market convergence are still present and that the goals of media and communications companies are still the same (that is, the maximization of their value by expanding operations and market shares). In this section and in line with the main theme of the book, we briefly concentrate on those consequences of technical convergence that are less explored and mostly excluded from the social imaginary which justifies market deconvergence.

First, split-offs and spin-offs in the media and communications sectors became more frequent in the new millennium in absolute numbers because mergers, which were particular frequent in the previous decade, often failed (Gaughan, 2011). The main reason evoked to generally explain the failed marriage between two companies is the presence of (organizational) cultural differences. An organization's culture can be understood also as collective habits or ways of thinking that can be altered only gradually (Langlois & Robertson, 2002); these are indeed fundamental and believed to be a powerful force that determines priorities and decisions, influences behaviors and affects outcomes (Martin & Frost, 1996; Schein, 1992, cited in Mierzjewska & Hollifield, 2005). Therefore, a cultural clash in a company occurs when "two groups have different opinions about what really matters, what has to be measured, how to make better decisions, how to organize resources, how to supervise people, how to spread information and so on" (Ray, 2012, p. 40). These opinions, as the notion of organizational culture suggests, are embedded in the organization and they can evolve only slowly and arduously.

Hence, generally speaking, incumbent, traditional media companies, which have been established several decades before the digitization of media content and distribution, are based on different collective principles than the new media and IT ventures with which they merged. As a result, in many cases, distant organizational cultures have clearly been difficult to align and cultural clashes have certainly been the source of inefficiencies and obstacles to the realization of the promised synergies. Obviously, such a situation is particularly problematic for public companies that need to provide positive results in the short run. For example, as Ray (2012) explains, AOL, which was speedy and collaborative, focused and centralized, concentrated on the stock price and tight on spending, was far from being the perfect organizational match of Time Warner, a company described as slow and decentralized, diversified, focused on audience and costumer reach, and spendthrift. The lack of trust that was the consequence of these differences (Ray, 2012) hindered the development of an internet platform for the distribution of premium content produced by Time Warner while it was still merged with AOL.

Second, corporate focus, which has been a managerial buzzword since the 1980s and 1990s, is thought to be best served when the design of the organization, its control mechanism, the skills of the employees and the system of incentives are in line with the business of a company (Kirchmaier, 2001). Clearly, this alignment is simpler to achieve in smaller companies than in larger ones. Therefore, the volatile financial markets in the first decade of the new millennium brought in new perspectives and investors started to (re-)appreciate corporate focus and those companies that were prioritizing it before expanding in size. Thus, spin-offs were welcomed and seen as potentially value-creating when perceived as dispositions of assets outside of the core business (see Veld & Veld-Merkoulova, 2009).

Moreover, market deconvergence can also be interpreted in more abstract terms as a particular trend that belongs to, and is the consequence of, the social and technical changes associated with the diffusion of digital technologies. This viewpoint presented here stems from the literature of innovation studies concerning the dynamics of techno-economic paradigms (for example, Freeman & Louçã, 2001) or great surges of development (for example, Perez, 2010). Techno-economic paradigms are long-term cycles of capitalist societies and are driven by the emergence of new pervasive technologies, but also by innovation and organizational principles, which are introduced mostly by the industries that design the new pervasive technologies and by changes to the socio-institutional framework (see Perez, 2010).

The organizational principle of "the bigger the better" was applied successfully by the large manufacturer leading the previous techno-economic paradigm: the oil and the automobile industries, for example. The leading companies within these industries tend to be large, centrally and hierarchically managed and efficient in achieving economies of scope and scale in order to mass-produce standardized goods. Therefore, this principle is understandably part of the organizational culture of many established corporations, including the incumbent media organizations that emerged and/or developed between 1900 and the 1970s. However, to the contrary, the new industries that provided the technologies that digitized the economy are more likely to be organized as modular networks of interdependent activities, given that these organizational settings better suit the realization of a mass-customized production, the realization of economies of scope, increased specialization and the creation of niche markets (Perez, 2010), which are all factors providing companies with a competitive advantage.

There are many examples of goods and services that have emerged and diffused very quickly during the current techno-economic paradigm, that are indeed examples of innovations produced by modular networks. These include the personal computer, which merged audio, text and graphics by combining parts made by different companies (Campbell-Kelly & Aspray, 2004). Also, the digital distribution of music is an example of media convergence by the adoption of a modular network, as traditional media content is delivered to end-users through a value chain composed of interdependent activities: for example, musician, label, digital music provider, internet provider (see Rogers & Sparviero, 2011). According to Sturgeon (2002), modular production networks yield greater economic performance than other models, especially in the context of volatile demand, rapid technological change, and increasingly extensive and elaborate production geographies. Therefore, under these conditions, market deconvergence has created new performing companies that, through de-merger, spin-offs or split-offs, have opened up their value chains in order to integrate the products and innovations from a variety of stakeholders instead of focusing on realizing synergies with the activity of companies owned or controlled by the same corporation.

Aims and Scope of the Book

This book is to a large extent the main outcome of the conference "Deconstructing Media Convergence" that was held in Salzburg in November 2013. This 2-day meeting brought together scholars, who are regularly engaged in different sections of relevant international associations of communication: primarily the International Association for Media and Communication Research (IAMCR), then the European Communication Research and Education Association (ECREA) and others. This created a milieu of scholars coming from different research traditions and different disciplines including political economy, history and audience as well as communication policy and technology. Salzburg was the place where the authors had a chance to exchange ideas and reflect on the existence of critical viewpoints on the topic of media convergence in their respective fields of expertise. Based on these efforts, this edited collection gives alternative ideas of media convergence more visibility and a greater emphasis. By doing so, it explicitly takes a critical perspective, highlights the existence of opposing trends and explanations for these trends, and consequently distinguishes itself from existing collections and edited books on the same topic (for example, Diehl & Karmasin, 2013; Grant & Wilkinson, 2009; Jin, 2011, 2013; Lugmayr & Dal Zotto, 2016a, b; Meikle & Young, 2011; Nienstedt, Russ-Mohl, & Wilczek, 2013).

This book is structured in four main parts. Part I consists of two chapters by the editors of this book which are meant to introduce into the field. While this chapter by Corinna Peil and Sergio Sparviero sheds light on the interplay of different social imaginaries of (de)convergence, Gabriele Balbi provides a critical history of the concept and its related meanings in different phases of its adoption. Part II of the book is dedicated to the options, practices and realities of the users in convergent media environments. As described above, the users have always been a major point of reference for dominant imaginaries of media convergence, depicting them either as overactive prosumers effortlessly navigating through their sophisticated media ensembles or as unknown entities indistinctly accessing convergent media devices with blurring modes of reception and usage. In this sense, taking into consideration traces of convergence, as well as deconvergence in the use of media, is complicated by the discrepancies regarding what is actually considered converging at the side of the users. Thus in Part II each of the contributions discusses the users' actions in relation to a specific complement of media consumption, be it technological affordances (Thimm), content and its distribution (Barra and Scaglioni), social and situational contexts (Müller and Röser), or audience research (Hasebrink and Hölig). What these chapters have in common is not only their critical assessment of the status quo, but also their reconsideration of what is often taken for granted when it comes to media convergence from the perspective of the users. Being committed to exploring the complex processes of change, they share an interest in revealing the ambiguities and inconsistencies that are involved in the user's practices, especially as they are not necessarily reproducing the transformations in other dimensions of media convergence.

The non-linear and sometimes disruptive appropriation of convergent media technologies is clearly demonstrated by Kathrin F. Müller and Jutta Röser in their contribution about the media's interplay and domestic communication cultures in Germany. Based on their longitudinal, ethnographic study about the mediatization of the home, they show that the investigated households are far from replacing all "classic media" with online-capable convergent technologies. Rather, the situations and communicative settings of media consumption have proven to have a strong influence on media usage patterns in that they foster the use of already approved media. In most cases, convergent media use is something which is practiced in addition to established media routines while changes in the overall media setting have evolved only gradually. Luca Barra and Massimo Scaglioni provide a similar argument with regard to their research on the Italian television scenario. Considering media convergence both at the supply and at the user's side in their comprehensive study design, they come to the conclusion that audience practices are subject to constant changes and repeatedly shift between phases of deeper and more superficial convergence depending on technological innovations and program offers as well as on sociocultural and economic factors. Coming from a media logic perspective, Caja Thimm emphasizes the technological properties which come into play when using convergent media in today's digital environments. With the concept of media grammar she explains how technologies predefine a specific framework for the communicative practices of the users that are shaped by the possibilities and constraints provided. Along with the change of technological infrastructure, there has been an alteration of the public sphere by the formation of so called "polymedia media-publics" or "mini-publics." In this context, media convergence seems no longer an apt concept to describe current phenomena as it does not take into account the emergence of complex technological systems and related usage cultures. Uwe Hasebrink and Sascha Hölig then critically discuss how to overcome current challenges in audience research in order to grasp what media convergence actually means from the perspective of the users and how it translates into practices. They propose the two concepts of media repertoires and communication modes to explain how the media are put in relation to each other and how users, despite the complex and convergent media environments they inhabit, skillfully differentiate between a variety of distinctive media-related practices.

In Part III, the three chapters show some of the ambiguities of media convergence in the production and distribution of content. Thanks to digitization, previously distinguished media content (audio, video, text) is translated into binary language so that it can be produced, distributed and consumed more easily, rapidly and with minor costs. According to the mainstream research, looking rather positively at the potential of technological convergence, media texts can be centrally produced in order to be played out across different channels, platforms and networks, that is once they are developed, they can be readapted and flow through different media. On a closer look, however, the production and distribution of media content is far from being a standardized and linear process and, again, it is characterized by differentiations and disruptions. Another dominant media convergence narrative concerns new production dynamics of media texts: Digital and convergent media have often been interpreted enthusiastically, mainly because of their assumed ability to free audiences from the control of the one-to-many mass and analog media. Digital content can be easily generated, personalized, manipulated, actively changed and distributed through different channels: this brings consumers and producers closer (even linguistically with the concept of "prosumers") in the convergent media environment. Nevertheless, when researched, all these processes show some ambiguities.

Mark Eisenegger, Mario Schranz and Angelo Gisler focus their attention on the newsroom, comparing online and offline media content in Switzerland. They come to at least three counter-intuitive conclusions about media convergence: first, it has caused the concentration of media producers against the narrative of diversification in the digital world; second, at least in Switzerland, it seems to have led to a loss of quality, especially compared with traditional printed press reports; finally, convergence is based on an unprofitable strategy because of the audience unwillingness to pay for online content. This latter outcome goes against the narrative that media convergence would naturally produce new opportunities for revenues and would be profitable in general. Lothar Mikos' chapter deals with television and analyzes two media convergence strategies (transmedia storytelling and mega-narration) as the main answers given by TV producers and channels to the increasing market and audience fragmentation. Again, Mikos provides a critical perspective, claiming that these production strategies foster further audience fragmentation because of the personal and nearly infinite possibility of choice. Consequently, narratives indicating that transmedia storytelling and mega-narration are effective strategies to control audiences and to make a product easily successful need to be revised.

Matthew Allen's chapter is a reprint and a partial update of a paper published in the journal *First Monday* in 2008. Allen claims that, instead of seeing the internet and specifically the web as the main "product" of media convergence, some of the key elements of Web 2.0 are so incompatible with traditional mass media as to act against the convergence between old and new media technologies. This can be illustrated by four examples: Web 2.0 sites and services are more like a computer program than a TV program and they cannot be combined; advertising appeal of websites is again different from traditional media because it is not about consuming media products (and advertising with them) but about doing things; third, according to Allen, in the Web 2.0 users are primary producers of content instead of being consumers as in a traditional media environment; finally, Web 2.0 has often been seen as a vehicle for democratization, while traditional broadcasting has been often seen as an expression of established hegemony. In sum, Web 2.0 does not converge with traditional media in terms of production, but rather creates a different model.

Part IV of the book focuses on the changes brought about by digitization in the organization of the media industries, in the reconfiguration of media markets, and in the influence of policy and regulations. In these particular areas, the most popular images of media convergence predict the expansion of existing corporations and the emergence of new giants, a process that is enabled and sustained by a process of deregulation that removes the separation between communications, connectivity and media services. Notably, deregulation is assumed to be leading to free(r) markets. However, the alternative pictures that emerge from the critical analyses presented in this part of book show that media corporations have rediscovered the practice of enhancing the core competencies of their subdivisions, by engaging in split-offs, spin-offs and joint ventures in order to improve their value. In addition, these alternative pictures show that, although the process of deregulation has certainly affected the reconfiguration of media and communications markets, deregulated does not mean unregulated or less regulated. new tensions between stakeholders have emerged and new regulations have been established. Essentially this means that in the longer run, when the process of deregulation that in Western economies peaked in the late 1990s will be in a more mature stage, there will be different rules, but not necessarily fewer rules.

This part opens with the chapter by Dal Yong Jin, where he describes the coupling of convergence and deconvergence of media and communications markets, as well as the recent emergence of the latter as the main business paradigm. Interestingly, while he provides specific examples and the rationale for deconvergence, he also explains that nowadays M&As in this sectors tend to be horizontal, rather than vertical, stressing that the business strategy of investing in core competencies is nowadays at least as popular as attempting to create synergies between complementary activities. Next is the chapter by Jim Rogers, which focuses on the music industry and explains how the digitization of the distribution of media content have enabled the creation of new revenue streams, which, from the viewpoint of the whole industry, compensate for the loss in the sale of records. Nonetheless, while new players have emerged and value chains have been redrawn, the music business is still dominated largely by a handful of corporations.

The tensions between service providers and the struggle for the emergence of new regulations are the focus of the chapter by Hilde Van den Bulck, who supports her findings using three different case studies of media restructuring and policymaking in Flanders, Belgium. On the other hand, Paul Murschetz responds to the challenge of understanding the new complex media environment by exploring the applicability of the contingency theory of organizations, which he illustrates with the example of the evolution of the digital TV broadcasting environment in Germany. Finally, the chapter by Christopher Ali and that by Fei Jiang, Kuo Huang and Yanran Sun elaborate on the process of policymaking in two very different socioeconomic environments: the USA and China. Nonetheless, interestingly, parallel dynamics unfold: the coming together of different technologies and the potential for their exploitation is not matched by the coming together, or the full collaboration, of existing regulatory authorities, which are forced to review their own role in policymaking. In the USA, the user's prospects of accessing locally relevant content through cheaper and better connections are partly undermined by conflicts between federal, state and local authorities. Similarly, in China, besides the determination of the central government to enhance connectivity and to favor the establishment of new services, conflicts between two powerful departments, one governing telecommunications and the other governing the media, have so far hindered this plan.

NOTES

1. The expression *domestic infrastructures* refers to the networked media settings and technologies at home and thus slightly contrasts with the technical dimensions and material artefacts of national and transnational infrastructures that are discussed in, among others, Parks and Starosielski (2015).
2. A mega-deal is defined here as a merger or acquisition that is in the top 100 of the year in which it occurred and in terms of the new company's value (Jin, 2013).
3. The failure of an M&A is defined as the split-off of the companies prior the M&A, and/or the spin-off of some activities from the merged company, and/or the bankruptcy of the merged company.

REFERENCES

Bakardjieva, M. (2005). *Internet society. The internet in everyday life.* London: Sage.

Busemann, K., & Gscheidle, C. (2012). Web 2.0: Habitualisierung der Social Communitys: Ergebnisse der ARD/ZDF-Onlinestudie 2012. *Media Perspektiven, 7–8*, 380–390.

Campbell-Kelly, M., & Aspray, W. (2004). *Computer: A history of the information machine* (2nd ed.). Boulder, Colorado, USA: Westview Press.

Carpentier, N. (2011). *Media and participation: A site of ideological-democratic struggle.* Intellect Ltd. Retrieved from http://www.oapen.org/search?identifier=606390.

Chon, B. S., Choi, J. H., Barnett, G. A., Danowski, J. A., & Joo, S.-H. (2003). A structural analysis of media convergence: Cross-industry mergers and acquisitions in the information industries. *Journal of Media Economics, 16*(3), 141–157. doi:10.1207/S15327736ME1603_1.

Courtois, C., & Verdegem, P. (2016). With a little help from my friends: An analysis of the role of social support in digital inequalities. *New Media & Society, 18*(8), 1508–1527.

Dawson, M. (2007). Little players, big shows. Format, narration, and style on television's new smaller screens. *Convergence: The International Journal of Research into New Media Technologies, 13*(3), 231–250.

Deuze, M. (2012). *Media life.* Cambridge, UK, Malden, MA: Polity Press.

D'heer, E., & Courtois, C. (2016). The changing dynamics of television consumption in the multimedia living room. *Convergence: The International Journal of Research into New Media Technologies, 22*(1), 3–17.

Diehl, S., & Karmasin, M. (Eds.). (2013). *Media and convergence management.* Berlin, Heidelberg: Springer. Retrieved from http://www.springer.com/business+%26+management/media+management/book/978-3-642-36162-3.

Dwyer, T. (2010). *Media convergence*. Maidenhead, New York: McGraw Hill/ Open University Press.

Engel, B., & Breunig, C. (2015). Massenkommunikation 2015: Mediennutzung im Intermediavergleich: Ergebnisse der ARD/ZDF-Langzeitstudie. *Media Perspektiven, 7–8,* 310–322.

Fagerjord, A. (2002). Reading-View(s)ing the Über-Box: A Critical View on a Popular Prediction. In M. Eskelinen & R. Koskimaa (Eds.), *Cybertext Yearbook 2001* (pp. 99–110). Jyväskylä: Publications of the Research Centre for Contemporary Culture.

Fagerjord, A., & Storsul, T. (2007). Questioning convergence. In T. Storsul & D. Stuedahl (Eds.), *Ambivalence towards convergence: Digitalization and media change* (pp. 19–31). Göteborg: Nordicom.

Flew, T. (2011). Media as creative industries. In D. Winseck & D. Y. Jin (Eds.), *Political economies of the media: The transformation of the global media* (pp. 84–100). USA: Bloomsbury.

Frees, B., & Koch, W. (2015). Internetnutzung: Frequenz und Vielfalt nehmen in allen Altersgruppen zu: Ergebnisse der ARD/ZDF-Onlinestudie 2015. *Media Perspektiven, 9,* 366–377.

Freeman, C., & F. Louça. (2001). *As Time Goes by: From the Industrial Revolutions to the Information Revolution*. Oxford, New York: Oxford University Press.

Gaughan, P. A. (2011). *Mergers, acquisitions, and corporate restructurings* (5th ed.). Hoboken, NJ: Wiley.

Grant, A. E., & Wilkinson, J. (2009). *Understanding media convergence: The state of the field*. Oxford, New York: Oxford University Press.

Harmon, A. (2001, December 15). Hollywood's new force: The strategy; '01 media model: Content and distribution go together. The New York Times. Retrieved from http://www.nytimes.com/2001/12/15/business/hollywood-s-new-force-strategy-01-media-model-content-distribution-go-together.html.

Hasebrink, U., & Domeyer, H. (2012). Media repertoires as patterns of behaviour and as meaningful practices: A multimethod approach to media use in converging media environments. Participations. *Journal of Audience and Reception Studies, 9*(2), 757–779.

Hepp, A., & Hasebrink, U. (2013). Human interaction and communicative figurations. The Transformation of Mediatized Cultures and Societies. *Communicative Figurations, Working Paper No. 2,* 1–22.

Hepp, A., & Krotz, F. (Eds.). (2014). *Mediatized worlds: Culture and society in a media age*. Basingstoke: Palgrave Macmillan.

Herkman, J. (2012). Introduction: Intermediality as a theory and methodology. In J. Herkman, T. Hujanen, & P. Oinonen (Eds.), *Intermediality and media change*. Tampere: Tampere University Press.

Hesmondhalgh, D. (2013). *The cultural industries* (3rd ed.). London: Sage.

Jenkins, H. (2001). Convergence? I diverge: For all the talk about "convergence," multiple media will never coalesce into one supermedium. MIT Technology Review, 01 June 2001.

Jenkins, H. (2006). *Convergence culture: Where old and new media collide.* New York: New York University Press.

Jensen, K. B. (2010). *Media convergence: The three degrees of network, mass, and interpersonal communication.* London, New York: Routledge.

Jin, D. Y. (2011). De-convergence and the deconsolidation in the global media industries: The rise and fall of (some) media conglomerates. In D. Winseck & D. Y. Jin (Eds.), *Political economies of the media: The transformation of the global media* (pp. 167–182). London, UK: Bloomsbury.

Jin, D. Y. (2013). *De-convergence of global media industries.* New York: Routledge.

Johnson, T. (2000, January 10). That's AOL folks. Retrieved 25 May 2011, from http://money.cnn.com/2000/01/10/deals/aol_warner/.

Kennedy, J., Nansen, B., Arnold, M., Wilken, R. & Gibbs, M. (2015). Digital housekeepers and domestic expertise in the networked home. *Convergence: The International Journal of Research into New Media Technologies, 21*(4), 408–422.

Kim, S. J. (2016). A repertoire approach to cross-platform media use behavior. *New Media & Society, 18*(3), 353–372.

Kirchmaier, T. (2001). *Corporate demergers: Or is divorce more attractive than marriage.* CentrePiece, (Spring), 14–17.

Langlois, R. N., & Robertson, P. L. (2002). *Firms, markets and economic change: A dynamic theory of business institutions.* London: Routledge.

Latzer, M. (2013). Convergence, co-evolution and complexity in European communications policy: Working Paper of the Media Change & Innovation Division <mediachange.ch>. Zurich, Switzerland.

Lugmayr, A., & Dal Zotto, C. (Eds.). (2016a). *Media convergence handbook — Vol. 1: Journalism, Broadcasting, and Social Media Aspects of Convergence.* Berlin, Heidelberg: Springer.

Lugmayr, A., & Dal Zotto, C. (Eds.). (2016b). *Media convergence handbook — Vol. 2: Firms and user perspectives.* Berlin: Springer.

Lugmayr, A., & Dal Zotto, C. (2016c). Media convergence is NOT king: The triadic phenomenon of media "convergence-divergence-coexistence" is king. In A. Lugmayr, & C. Dal Zotto (Eds.), *Media convergence handbook — Vol. 2: Firms and user perspectives* (pp. 429–55). Berlin, Heidelberg: Springer.

Madianou, M., & Miller, D. (2012). Polymedia: Towards a new theory of digital media in interpersonal communication. *International Journal of Cultural Studies, 16*(2), 169–187.

Mansell, R. (2012). *Imagining the Internet: Communication, innovation, and governance.* Oxford: Oxford University Press.

Martin, J., & Frost, P. (1996). The organizational culturewar games: A struggle for intellectual dominance. In S. R. Clegg, C. Hardy, & W. R. Nord (Eds.), *Handbook of organization studies* (pp. 599–621). London: Sage.

Meikle, G., & Young, S. (2011). *Media convergence: Networked digital media in everyday life.* Basingstoke: Palgrave Macmillan.

Mierzjewska, B. I., & Hollifield, C. A. (2005). Theoretical approaches in media management research. In A. B. Albarran, S. M. Chan-Olmsted, & M. O. Wirth (Eds.), *Handbook of media management and economics* (1st ed., pp. 37–66). London: Routledge.

Mikos, L. (2016). Digital media platforms and the use of TV content: Binge watching and video-on-demand in Germany. *Media and Communication, 4*(3), 154–161.

Miller, V. (2011). *Understanding digital culture.* London, Thousand Oaks: Sage.

Montpetit, M.-J. (2016). The 2nd convergence: A technology viewpoint. In A. Lugmayr & C. Dal Zotto (Eds.), *Media convergence handbook — Vol. 1: Journalism, broadcasting, and social media aspects of convergence* (pp. 29–57). Berlin, Heidelberg: Springer.

Nienstedt, H.-W., Russ-Mohl, S., & Wilczek, B. (2013). *Journalism and media convergence.* Berlin: De Gruyter.

Ozanich, G. W., & Wirth, M. (2004). Structure and change: A communications industry overview. In A. Alexander, J. Owers, R. A. Carveth, C. A. Hollifield, & A. N. Greco (Eds.), *Media economics. Theory and practice* (pp. 69–84) Mahwah, NJ, London: Lawrence Erlbaum Associates.

Parks, L., & Starosielski, N. (Eds.). (2015). *Signal traffic. Critical studies of media infrastructures.* Champaign: University of Illinois Press.

Peil, C., & Mikos, L. (2017): Konvergierende Medienumgebungen. In L. Mikos & C. Wegener (Eds.), *Qualitative Medienforschung. Ein Handbuch.* (pp. 209–218). Konstanz: UVK.

Peil, C., & Röser, J. (2014). The meaning of home in the context of digitization, mobilization and mediatization. In A. Hepp & F. Krotz (Eds.), *Mediatized worlds: Culture and society in a media age* (pp. 233–249). Basingstoke: Palgrave Macmillan.

Peil, C., & Schwaab, H. (2014). Hello-Kitty-Konsum als Kommunikationskultur. Zur Ver-alltäglichung und Vergegenständlichung eines cute characters. In M. Mae & E. Scherer (Eds.), *Nipponspiration. Japonismus und japanische Populärkultur im deutschsprachigen Raum* (pp. 335–353). Wien, Köln, Weimar: Böhlau.

Perez, C. (2010). The Financial Crisis and the Future of Innovation: A View of Technical Change with the Aid ofHistory. The Other Canon Foundation and

Tallinn University of Technology. Working Papers in TechnologyGovernance and Economic Dynamics, 1–42.

Perks, L. G. (2015). *Media marathoning. Immersions in morality.* Lanham: Lexington Books.

Pool, I. de S. (1983). *Technologies of freedom.* Cambridge, Mass, London: Belknap Press of Harvard University Press.

Rasmussen, T. (2014). *Personal media and everyday life. A networked lifeworld.* Basingstoke: Palgrave Macmillan.

Ray, S. (2012). Cultural dimension analysis of AOL-time Warner Merger. *Journal of Applied Library and Information Science, 1*(2), 39–41.

Rogers, J., & Sparviero, S. (2011). Understanding innovation in communication industries through alternative economic theories: The case of the music industry. *International Communication Gazette, 73,* 610–629. doi:10.1177/1748048511417158.

Schein, E. H. (1992). *Organizational culture and leadership* (2nd ed., Vol. 356). New York: Wiley.

Schwaab, H. (2013). Transmedialität und Mediatisierung. Formen und Motive der Expansion serieller Welten und neuer Medienobjekte. *Navigationen, 13*(1), 85–103.

Silverstone, R. (1995). Convergence is a dangerous word. *Convergence, 1*(1), 11–13.

Sparviero, S. (2014). The creative destruction of the United States' audio-visual media ecosystem. In P. Wikstrom & R. DeFillippi (Eds.), *International perspectives on business innovation and disruption in the creative industries: Film, video, photography* (pp. 128–148). Cheltenham, UK: Edward Elgar Publishing Ltd.

Stark, B. (2014). Informationsverhalten im 21. Jahrhundert—eine repertoire-orientierte Analyse veränderter Nutzungsmuster. In K. Kleinen von Königslöw & K. Förster (Eds.), *Medienkonvergenz und Medienkomplementarität aus Rezeptions- und Wirkungsperspektive* (pp. 37–57). Baden-Baden: Nomos Verlag.

Stauff, M. (2015). The second screen: Convergence as crisis. *ZMK Zeitschrift für Medien- und Kulturforschung, 6*(2), 123–144.

Storsul, T., & Stuedahl, D. (Eds.). (2007). *Ambivalence towards convergence: Digitalization and media change.* Göteborg: Nordicom.

Sturgeon, T. J. (2002). Modular production networks: A new American model of industrial organization. *Industrial and Corporate Change, 11*(3), 451–496.

Tavares, T. A. & Schofield, D. (2016). Interaction design for convergence medias and devices: A multisensory challenge. In A. Lugmayr & C. Dal Zotto (Eds.), *Media convergence handbook — Vol. 2: Firms and user perspectives* (pp. 245–260). Berlin, Heidelberg: Springer.

van Dijk, J. A. (2012). *The network society.* London: Sage.
van Eimeren, B., & Ridder, C.-M. (2011). Trends in der Nutzung und Bewertung der Medien 1970 bis 2010: Ergebnisse der ARD/ZDF-Langzeitstudie Massenkommunikation. *Media Perspektiven, 1,* 2–15.
Veld, C., & Veld-Merkoulova, Y. V. (2009). Value creation through spin-offs: A review of the empirical evidence. *International Journal of Management Reviews, 11*(4), 407–420. doi:10.1111/j.1468-2370.2008.00243.x.
Vukanovic, Z. (2016). Converging Technologies and Diverging Market Trends of Internet/Web and Traditional Media. In A. Lugmayr & C. Dal Zotto (Eds.), *Media Convergence Handbook – Vol. 2. Firms and User Perspectives* (pp. 69–93). Berlin, Heidelberg: Springer.

Authors' Biography

Corinna Peil is a Postdoctoral Researcher at the University of Salzburg's Department of Communication Studies, Center for Information and Communication Technologies & Society (ICT&S), Austria. Her research and teaching focus is on mobile communications, media (de)convergence, online publics, the use of media in everyday life contexts, and the mediatization of society.

Sergio Sparviero is an Assistant Professor at the Department of Communication Studies of the University of Salzburg, Austria. His main field of research and teaching are: media economics; media management; and media innovation. In particular, he published research on the developments of the news, film and music industries. He is also the coordinator of the Erasmus + Joint Master Program "Digital Communication Leadership" (DCLead).

CHAPTER 2

Deconstructing "Media Convergence": A Cultural History of the Buzzword, 1980s–2010s

Gabriele Balbi

Introduction to a Confusing Term

The term convergence originates from the Latin word convergentia (gathering). Its use started in the 18th century in the field of the physics of rays. Then, particularly during the 19th century, mathematics (as in convergent series or fractions) and biology (as meaning "the tendency in diverse or allied animals or plants to assume similar characteristics") adopted it. Finally, beginning in the early 20th century, the term was used in meteorology, oceanography and, interestingly, in the social sciences and humanities such as anthropology, psychology, political science, economics and political economy (all these definitions were obtained from the Oxford English Dictionary Online, http://www.oed.com/view/Entry/40732?redirectedFrom=convergence#eid).

According to different authors, the idiom "media convergence" was first employed in either the late 1960s (Szczepaniak, 2013, p. 7; Gordon, 2003, p. 58) or the 1970s (Lind, 2004, p. 6). Since that time, it has

G. Balbi (✉)
USI Università della Svizzera italiana, Lugano, Switzerland
e-mail: gabriele.balbi@usi.ch

© The Author(s) 2017
S. Sparviero et al. (eds.), *Media Convergence and Deconvergence*, Global Transformations in Media and Communication Research - A Palgrave and IAMCR Series, DOI 10.1007/978-3-319-51289-1_2

had a variety of meanings and diverse media scholars have described the processes of media convergence using different terms. Convergence has been described as a technical, regulatory, financial, symbolic, economic, social, cultural, global, narrative, tactical, structural, static and evolving phenomenon (see, for example, Levasseur & Musso, 1993, p. 9; Flynn, 2000; Jenkins, 2001, p. 93; Gordon, 2003; Dailey, Demo, & Spillman, 2005; Dennis, 2006; Zhang, 2008, pp. 21–22; Infotendencias Group, 2012). As a macro-level phenomenon, it may involve single products, systems, apparatuses, networks, contents, services and markets (Flynn, 2000; Singer, 2004; Fagerjord & Sorsul, 2007; Infotendencias Group, 2012). The confusion in meanings has increased, even in the last decade, as explained in three books published in 2009 and 2010 containing "media convergence" in the title, all of which consider this topic using different perspectives (Staiger & Hake, 2009; Dwyer, 2010; Jensen, 2010). According to Espen Ytreberg (2011, p. 503 and 507), who reviewed the books, they "provide [an] illustration of just how diverse researchers' approaches to 'convergence'... seem almost to live in different worlds, each one seemingly unaware of the others' approach and traditions."

Given all these possibilities, media convergence is now considered by scholars to be a term that should be used more carefully. It has been described as "a dangerous word" (Silverstone, 1995, p. 11), an "unclear" (Fagerjord & Storsul, 2007, p. 132) and "ambigous" term (Latzer, 2013, p. 123), "one of those particularly hard-to-handle concepts" (Ytreberg, 2011, p. 502), an "umbrella concept" with a high degree of vagueness and intangibility (Marsden & Verhulst, 1999, pp. 3–5; Herkmann, 2012, p. 13), a "concept... so broad that it has multiple meanings" (Wirth, 2006, p. 445), "too nebulous to be used to identify specific variables, processes and media-related phenomena" (Grant, 2009, p. 15), and even "a hyped illusion" simply because of its attempt to encompass many concepts and to be "everything" (Noll, 2003, pp. 12–13).

This confusion does not mean that media convergence is a useless term, especially because it has become a buzzword in (new) media and communication studies in recent decades and it is often used as a rhetorical tool (Fagerjord & Storsul, 2007). Given its relevance, this chapter aims to deconstruct the historical meanings of the term, focusing on the emergence of different discourses and narratives regarding media convergence from the 1980s to the early 2010s and, at the same time, to understand how these discourses mutually reinforced each other and even affected how media developed in recent decades. Specifically, I intend to analyze the term using the following four historical and narratological dimensions: technological media convergence, which was the first way of examining convergence that emerged in the early 1980s; economic/market convergence, which characterizes firms' approaches from the late 1980s/early 1990s; political/regulatory media convergence, which appeared simultaneously in different countries during the 1990s; and, finally, cultural convergence, which was taken for granted in many discourses about the role of digital media in everyday life starting in the 2000s. This four-stage model was also adopted fully by Miller (2011) and partially by Grant (2009) and Dwyer (2010), but the different stages should not be considered mutually subsequent: on the one hand, they are interconnected and reinforce each other and, on the other, even if they emerged in different decades, their narratives are still there and influence the ways that we examine media convergence today. This chapter is based primarily on a revision of the academic literature on media convergence and partially on relevant political documents. In the conclusion, media convergence is also deconstructed using a quantitative perspective thanks to a search of the Factiva and Google NGram databases. These two tools are able to illustrate a type of diachronic evolution of this term in the last decades and provide insight to promote understanding of its peaks in popularity and unpopularity.

A Short Prehistory: Media Convergence Before Digitization

Before addressing the four different perspectives of media convergence, it is worth understanding if and how this idea emerged in media history before the 1980s. Most historical approaches that have reconstructed the term media convergence have considered digitization as a key prerequisite or the starting point of convergence. Nevertheless, even if the idea of media convergence was certainly boosted by digitization, the concept appeared much earlier in the analog world (Nieć, 2013, p. 19; Nguyen, 2007) meaning the blurring of different technologies and the integration of previously separated sectors.

Editorial contents/mass media and telecommunications started to converge in the 19th century when, for example, telegraph companies and press companies, which were not provided with a rigid distinction in the legislation at that time, found forms of synergies (Winsek, 1999). The same is true of the so-called "circular telephone," a new medium that was developed in the late 19th century in different countries that combined the point-to-point characteristics of the telephone and one-to-many press (later, broadcasting). This "radio before radio" (Balbi, 2010) brought entertainment into subscribers' houses through a telephone network and integrated editorial contents and telecommunication sectors again.

The movie industry was shaped by constant convergence with other media such as radio and TV and, subsequently, mobile phones and the internet (see, for example, the case of Indian cinema in Punathambekar, 2008). At the same time, wide-screen televisions and home movies represent a form of television and cinema convergence that occurred before digitization (Steward, 2014). More recently, informatics and telecommunications started to overlap during the second half of the 1970s, and many researchers realized it at the time. In 1977, Farber and Baran entitled one of their papers "The Convergence of Computing and Telecommunications Systems." A research project that was conducted at Harvard in the mid 1970s ("Information Technologies and Public Policy") identified an emerging overlap between voice telecommunication networks and data networks, introducing the term "compunications" (Oettinger, Berman, & Read, 1977). A more attractive and enduring neologism was coined by Simon Nora and Alain Minc (1978), who introduced the word "telematics" in a report addressed to the French government, to describe the process of the long-distance transmission of computer-based information (Richeri, 1982). This "convergence" can be considered to be only partially digital because telecommunication networks at that time carried analog signals exclusively.

These examples of media convergence that occurred prior to digitization can be viewed as initial attempts to deconstruct the term. Indeed, media convergence should be considered a long-lasting phenomenon that preceded digitization and was applicable to many media technologies and sectors, even in the 19th and early 20th centuries.

FOUR (HISTORICAL) DIMENSIONS THAT PROMOTE AN UNDERSTANDING OF CONVERGENCE

Technological Convergence from the Early 1980s

As previously mentioned, it was only with the macro-phenomenon of digitization that media convergence entered the academic discourse permanently. It is well known that media technologies have gone through a phase of digitization from the 1980s onwards that has shaped the contemporary media landscape (Balbi & Magaudda, forthcoming). The most significant feature of digitization is that text, fixed and moving images and sound (therefore, the media forms at the basis of the editorial contents sector) can be coded using the same language composed of simple strings of 0 and 1. Before digitization, text, images and sound were separate media forms. They were reproduced and transmitted by different devices (for example, phonographs, paper, telephones, radio and television). Furthermore, they had distinct markets that were regulated by politics in different ways (Zhang, 2008, p. 1). With digitization, the boundaries of different media forms have become blurred, as a single form of technology can transmit all the previous media contents.

As mentioned above, most media scholars have considered digitization to be the technological basis of media convergence. First, translating all media contents into a single language was a natural precondition of the introduction of a single and unique device that was able to decode these messages and called an überbox, telecomputer, teleputer, cellular phone, digital television or smartphone, depending on the decade (Kopecka-Piech, 2011, pp. 7–8). In reality, the überbox narrative was probably one of the most visible failed ideas of convergence. Henry Jenkins (2006, p. 14) called it "the black box fallacy," and Juha Herkman (2012, pp. 370–371) described it as "the great utopia of convergence" because "instead of coming together, as the term convergence suggests, today there is more variety than ever before in communication and media technologies, gadgets, devices, formats and standards."

Second, digitization sped up the process of network integration that started in the 1980s before networks were digitized. Thus far, communication networks historically have been designed to transmit a single type of information (voice or signs or data) and have often been managed by different organizations. Telegraph and telephone signals, for example, were transmitted through diverse cables and networks. At the beginning of the 1980s, a general phenomenon emerged in different European countries: monopolist telecommunication industries started to cable (parts of) nations, believing that new services would pass through these networks, most likely editorial contents. These companies reconfigured the networks to allow them to carry traditional television or traditional telephony without any difference; they therefore made cable networks naturally convergent (Pradié & Salaün, 1992, pp. 194–197). Then, when these networks were digitized, this process of integration reached its apex, and sound, text and images could flow and be transmitted in the form of bytes without any differences across diverse networks.

The technological basis of convergence was the most durable way in which convergence was imagined, not only because of digitization. Its popularity was probably due to the two founding fathers of convergence, both of whom imagined it in technological terms between the late 1970s and the beginning of the 1980s. The first "prophet" (Jenkins, 2006, p. 10) of media convergence was Ithiel de Sola Pool. In his famous book Technologies of Freedom he described the following:

> [C]onvergence of modes... blurring the lines between media, even between point-to-point communications, such as the post, telephone, and telegraph, and mass communications, such as the press, radio and television. A single physical means—be it wires, cables or airwaves—may carry services that in the past were provided in separate ways. Conversely, a service that was provided in the past by any one medium—be it broadcasting, the press or telephony—can now be provided in several different physical ways. So the one-to-one relationship that used to exist between a medium and its use is eroding. (de Sola Pool, 1983, p. 23)

The second founding father was Nicolas Negroponte, who depicted convergence at the MIT Media Lab using the famous figure of three overlapping circles in 1978. He claimed that the overlap between the "broadcast and motion picture industry," the "computer industry" and the "print and publishing industry" would become almost complete by the year 2000 (Brand, 1987, pp. 10–11).

Even if Negroponte and de Sola Pool neglected, respectively, the fundamental role of telecommunications and informatics in the process, their reflections helped to popularize the term during the 1980s and 1990s. Both generally understood media convergence as the "coming together of all forms of mediated communication in digital forms"

(Burnett & Marshall, 2003, p. 1) or even more generally as the coming together of different equipment, tools and media technologies. This narrative of media convergence as a technological phenomenon monopolized discourses for many decades (see, for example, Dennis, 1992; Baldwin, Stevens McVoy, & Steinfield, 1996; Watson & Hill, 1997, p. 65), and it is probably one of the most popular ways of examining convergence today.

Economic/Market Convergence from the Late 1980s/Early 1990s

A second and associated phenomenon of economic/market convergence started to emerge in Western cultures between the late 1980s and the early 1990s. Due to the rhetorical success of technological convergence and the various promises of cost reductions, many mergers and strategic acquisitions in telecommunications and media industries were tested and implemented, bringing a slow redefinition of the media market. Lind (2004) identified two waves of this type of economic/market convergence. The first wave began in the 1980s, when several equipment vendors in the IT and telecommunication sectors tried (and mostly failed) to enter each other's markets. The second and broader wave began at the beginning of the 1990s and was partially motivated by forecasts regarding the convergence of digital media and the IT/telecommunication industry (see also OECD, 1992). Specifically, during the 1990s, market convergence had two main surges. The first occurred in 1993–1994, when the vision of convergence carried many promises for business executives, although few of them knew exactly how to exploit and implement the new concept. Then, after a period of disillusion, the second wave started in 1997 and was driven by the fact that the internet had gradually made convergence strategies possible (Lind, 2004, pp. 10–11). It was during the 1990s, according to Lind, that the media convergence debate transitioned from being mainly internal to information and communication industries to "grab[bing] attention in the general media and business community" (Lind, 2004, p. 7). This was due to the growing dimensions of media industries and two other factors as follows: the economic and social rhetoric of the information superhighway introduced by US President Clinton's administration in 1993 and, in the second half of the 1990s, the rapid diffusion of the internet.

Furthermore, market convergence is often associated with the following two types of so-called integration: diagonal, which is when a firm in one sector expands to other sectors, and vertical, which is when a firm that is involved at one point in the production chain expands to another point in the production chain within the same industry (Doyle, 2013). Both types of integration have had significant relevance in recent decades. An example of diagonal integration is when telecommunication companies expanded into other sectors such as the editorial content industry: The merging of Viacom and CBS in 1999 or America Online (AOL) and Time Warner in 2000 are two famous cases of diagonal integration. This can also be considered an example of economic convergence because two media firms and, more generally, two market fields that were previously separated overlapped, realizing the so-called "economies of multiformity" or networks synergies (for instance, when a telephone company moves into the cable television industry, it can use its existing distribution infrastructure to sell two services instead of just one). Vertical integration can stimulate convergence in terms of contents. When, for example, a film production firm expands into film distribution, it aims to make contents flow through different and convergent channels that are owned by a single company. This occurred in 1994, for example, when Viacom bought Paramount, a film production company. In this way, when a new movie was released, it could be distributed through all the Viacom channels such as cinema chains, Blockbuster, and television stations.

In sum, media companies believed (and partially still believe) that they could exploit synergistic effects from their union, and politics encouraged them to follow this pattern. At the beginning of the 2000s, after having evaluated the real benefits and having discovered that they were overestimated, a complementary and reverse phenomenon of deconvergence started to emerge, which had a strong impact on media business and management. According to Albarran and Gormly (2004), fewer than half of the mergers involving media companies in the 1990s survived, and many of them ended in failure. Two relevant examples are the previously mentioned mergers between Viacom and CBS and America Online and Time Warner. Both mega groups started to deconverge and return to their past (separating into radically diverse companies) a few years after their integrations. These mega groups have changed their business model because they failed to obtain the promised benefits and they have embraced a type of deconvergence that is the basis of this book (see Jin, Chap. 10, and Peil & Sparviero, Chap. 1 in this volume).

Nonetheless, why did economic/market convergence occur? Beyond the desire to profit from the synergistic effects, there are other relevant reasons. Pradié & Salaün (1992) claimed that it was a natural expansion of the telecommunication industries that had cabled some nations in the 1980s and that, in the 1990s, aimed to merge with mass media companies to fill telecommunication networks with editorial contents and justify expenses associated with networks one decade earlier. According to Bernard Miège (1992, p. 23), one of the main motivators behind economic convergence was the fact that, in the early 1980s, both telecommunication and television industries experienced a moment of "saturation" in their respective markets and started to converge to search for new business opportunities and customers. Milton Mueller (1999) believed that market convergence, a phenomenon that, according to him, started long before the 1990s, was due to the declining cost of information processing power and by the development of open standards. Finally, the pervasive spirit of deregulation was crucial to enforcing media market convergence. This is one of the topics covered in the next section.

Political/Regulatory Convergence from the 1990s

European media were involved in a process of market liberalization and deregulation during the 1990s, which was one of the main effects of the long downturn that affected much of the world beginning in the late 1960s (Hesmondhalgh, 2002). Up to the 1990s, in Europe telecommunication companies have been regulated primarily as public monopolies or with a system of grants that were strictly controlled by state governments because administrators wanted to guarantee equal rights to access to their citizens (that is, "universal service"). Similarly, broadcasting was in the public's hands for a long time for civic reasons. Frequencies used to transmit radio and television messages were limited, and the state had to regulate them to prevent abuses of power and, again, to guarantee equal access. These narratives of regulation were progressively dismantled during the 1980s for many reasons. First, at the European level, there was a shared belief in creating a common, dynamic and competitive market to imitate the American model. Second, both telecommunications and broadcasting were widespread everywhere and no longer needed to be protected. Finally, especially in the case of broadcasting, new media increased the capacity to transmit information progressively; therefore, the argument relating to spectrum scarcity was no longer sustainable.

Consequently, neoliberal ideology identified telecommunications and broadcasting as the main sectors in which to intervene using a process of deregulation, liberalization from government intervention, and marketization. This occurred via three interrelated processes. First, the broadcasting monopoly was opened during the 1970s in Italy and the 1980s in the majority of other European countries, while telecommunications were gradually privatized in the first half of the 1980s in the UK and in the 1990s in other countries. The second process was an expansion of private ownership and company size, as partially described above. The third process was the dismantling of historical regulatory walls that were erected among telecommunications, broadcasting and new media companies. Under these conditions, Europe experienced what had occurred in the USA a decade earlier. In 1982, because of a decision by the Justice Department, AT&T, the dominant telephone company in the USA, was forced to divest in local business and engage in competition in the long-distance market. In return for agreeing to this divestiture, AT&T was allowed to enter the broadcasting and computer markets; consequently, traditional barriers between these sectors disappeared (Baldwin et al., 1996, p. 6). It was the first political and regulatory recognition of a phenomenon called media convergence.

From the late 1980s, the European community started to favor either privatization or the breaking up of regulatory walls among sectors. Early examples of this policy were the Green Books on television without borders and telecommunications in 1984 and 1987 as well as the directives on television and telecommunications in 1989–1990 (Levasseur & Musso, 1993, pp. 12–13).

During the 1990s, this wave sped up and a symbolic document on regulatory convergence, the EU Green Paper of 1997, was published. In the paper, the European Commission deeply discussed impacts, barriers, regulatory implications and future options for media convergence. This paper was likely influenced by another document released in 1996 by the US government to increase competition in the telecommunications market and to address the growth of the internet: "the Telecommunication Act". The EU Green Telecommunications ActPaper identified three stages of media convergence that had already occurred (technology and network platforms, industry alliances and mergers and services and markets) and the following three main options to regulate it in the upcoming future: (1) developing new regulations on current structures; (2) introducing a sector of new services that were separate from broadcasting and telecommunications; and (3) progressively introducing a new regulatory model to cover all services (European

Commission, 1997, pp. 34–35). Even if the Green Paper avoided taking positions, the third option was considered "the one which will minimize regulatory discrimination and market distortion in the converged environment" (Clements, 1998, p. 201). That is, in the second half of the 1990s, among European regulators, there was a general belief that new convergent technologies, industry alliances and mergers as well as new services and markets would bring major changes in policy and regulation (Latzer, 2014).

This change has not fully occurred, as an updated European Commission document (2013, p. 3) shows. The imminent arrival of a "fully converged ... world" is still a common belief, including the belief that "lines are blurring" and processes of "progressive merger of traditional broadcast services and the Internet" are being realized. In other words, as is the case with economic/market convergence, political/regulatory convergence seems to be a never-ending process and somewhat common and passpartout in the rhetorical language of media regulation.

Cultural Convergence from the 2000s

A third major figure in the area of media convergence added a "cultural layer" to this term and helped to popularize it. Indeed, after the publication of *Convergence Culture* in 2006, "a veritable wave of publications, conferences and debates over the issue" emerged (Szczepaniak, 2013, p. 8). Somehow contributing to the confusion surrounding the term, Henry Jenkins has viewed media convergence in many different ways, but he put at the center of his reflections a cultural perspective with a focus on users in particular.

> By convergence, I mean the flow of content across multiple media platforms, the cooperation between multiple media industries, the search for new structures of media financing which fell at the interstices between old and new media, and the migratory behavior of media audiences who would go almost anywhere in search of the kinds of entertainment experiences they wanted. Convergence is a word that manages to describe technological, industrial, cultural and social changes, depending on who's speaking and what they think they are talking about. (Jenkins, 2005, p. 2)

Again, he wrote the following: "[Convergence is] more than simply a technological shift. Convergence alters the relationship between existing technologies, industries, markets, genres and audience" (Jenkins, 2004, p. 34).

Cultural convergence can be observed as the fourth narrative of media convergence and involves numerous elements, especially media production and consumption. These two phases are not completely separated, but they are often self-reinforcing because audiences and media industries in the new environment can talk to each other and influence their behaviors just as cats and mice do (a metaphor provided by Barra and Scaglioni, 2013). Since the early 2000s, the rhetoric of cultural convergence has influenced the ways in which traditional media commodities are imagined and produced. Media products have become increasingly more "transmedial" (and therefore adaptable to different communication technologies). Then, they are often no longer singular products, but parts of series, flows and ideas that move from the media to reality and vice versa. This obviously changes the role and 'culture' of television production (Askwith, 2007) and mass media in general.

Consumption has been changed by convergence to a greater extent. Hynes (2003) argues that discourses on media convergence have often been surrounded by deterministic assumptions, including the fact that consumption has been irrevocably transformed by technological and economic convergence. In contrast, "consumption convergence," as she calls it, has occurred because of "the simultaneous use and consumption of media technologies" (Hynes, 2003, p. 3) in the home, as people have started to integrate and reuse previously separate devices and ideas, passing easily from one medium to another. In other words, both Hynes and Jenkins, despite holding different perspectives, focus on the role of users as relevant actors in stimulating media convergence.

First, in a convergent environment, "consumers are encouraged to seek out new information and make connections among dispersed media content" (Jenkins, 2006, p. 3), remixing pieces of culture taken from different media. This creates a new media experience, which is sometimes encouraged by media industries, in which the same story can cross different media platforms (Jenkins & Deuze, 2008).

A second narrative of cultural convergence is that media production and consumption are no longer separate and the line between amateurs and professionals is blurring (Deuze, 2007). Users enjoy participating in the co-construction of the message and even aim to become producers of media contents. This is the logic behind the so-called prosumer (a neologism indicating that the same person is the media producer and consumer), creating user-generated contents and spreading them through the convergent environment of the Web 2.0. This is the so-called participatory culture.

A third and related element of the convergence culture involves the increase in what Pierre Levy (1997) calls "collective intelligence," which refers to the fact that people in online environments can share information and resources and help each other to solve problems collectively. This would not be achievable through individual efforts. It is only possible because knowledge resides in the network and is collective.

These visions of the impact of media convergence are all optimistic and perhaps too simplistic. For this reason, in recent years, scholars have criticized them using at least three perspectives. Instead of being a widespread and commonsense phenomenon, user participation is limited (Nielsen, 2006). Rather than bringing about forms of collective intelligence, a great majority of users and consequently user generated contents are poor in quality; therefore, amateurization has a reverse and negative side (Keen, 2007; Fuchs, 2011, especially Chap. 7). Finally, instead of liberalizing and pluralizing media properties through multiple participation from below, digital and convergent media have undergone a progressive phenomenon of the concentration of power in the hands of a few large companies (Noam, 2015). Buzz terms such as "rich get richer" or "winner takes all" represent new metaphorical ways to express this prevalent narrative. The debate is ongoing, but the popular and utopian narratives of cultural convergence in the early 2000s are leaving space for negative and sometimes apocalyptic visions in which globalization, cultural homogenization and scarce interest in participation are emerging.

A Very Short Quantitative History of the Term

Media convergence increased in popularity during the 1990s and reached a peak at the beginning of the 2000s, as scholars focusing on technological, economic and regulatory convergence achieved the maturity of their reflections. Then, the term had a type of deflation, as shown in Figs. 2.1 and 2.2. Figure 2.1 resulted from a search among Factiva databases for the term "media convergence" from 1990 to 2015. Factiva provides access to a variety of media outlets. It contains thousands of articles in 22 different languages and provides full-text versions of products published by Reuters, Dow Jones and the Associated Press, as well as the Wall Street Journal and the Financial Times. Consequently, it represents a gateway to international economic and financial information and is crucial to understanding the evolution of the term in political, economic and business senses. The second graph resulted from a search

Fig. 2.1 Occurrences of the term "media convergence" in Factiva, 1990–2015. *Source* http://global.factiva.com/sb/default.aspx?lnep=hp

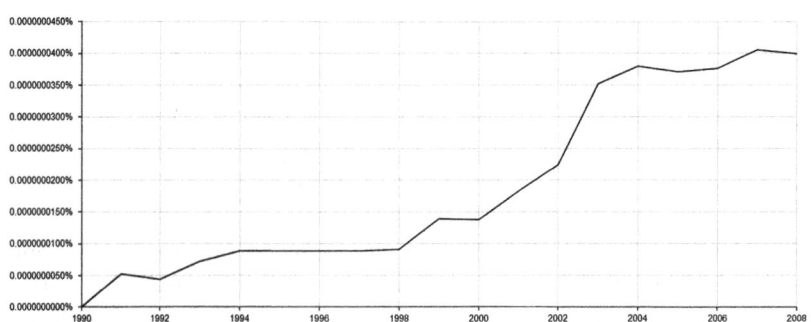

Fig. 2.2 Occurrences of the term "media convergence" in Google Books. *Source* The author, produced with Google Books Ngram Viewer: https://books. google.com/ngrams

of the same topic in Google NGram based on 30 million scanned books in the Google Books database from 1986 to 2008. Google NGram represents a valuable tool to understanding if and how a term has entered contemporary mentality though the frequency of its use in books scanned by Google.

Neither database is completely accurate, but I used them to show the *quantitative* frequency of the term without any reflection on its semantics, the ways in which it was used, or possible alternative terms that have emerged. Nevertheless, these figures can provide a historical overview of the rise and stagnation of the concept. Both tools show, for example, that its peak in popularity occurred in approximately 2000 and, since then, without disappearing, the term has become less relevant in contemporary culture (and probably contemporary media studies as well). This decline might have been caused by several factors, including disillusion after the explosion of the internet bubble at the turn of the century, the fact that it entered into the common mentality and therefore in some ways is taken for granted, or, again, the effect of all the criticisms, failures and doubts about convergence that have been raised during recent decades and that have brought about new (and apparently conflicting) terms such as media deconvergence. This is the one of the key questions in the book that you are reading.

Conclusion: A History of Change and Continuity

The term "media convergence" started to be used in the 1960s and 1970s, boomed in the 1980s, became widespread in 1990s and 2000s, and might be in crisis today. It has been conceived, theorized and analyzed by scholars using many perspectives over the years. This chapter wanted to reduce the confusion surrounding this topic, attempting to analyze the four key narratives that have been used to imagine and discuss media convergence in the scientific literature over time: media convergence as a technological, economic/market, political/regulatory and cultural phenomenon.

Each of these forms has shaped the approaches of media experts, businesspersons, politicians and, increasingly more, common people in different stages. Technological convergence was the first to appear and dominated the general discourse at least from the 1980s. Economic/market convergence became relevant owing to integrations among different media industries and reached its peak during the 1990s.

Consequently, politicians started to think about new ways to regulate convergent environments during the second half of the 1990s both in the USA and in Europe. Finally, starting from the 2000s, the phenomenon of cultural convergence seemed to be one of the most relevant trends in contemporary media.

The respective histories of these four layers of significance interrelate, and different meanings have overlapped during recent decades without deleting the previous one. Thus, media convergence currently conveys all these ideas together. It is likely that additional connotations will be added in the future and this perpetual change and instability, which is typical of any term, is the main reason why some scholars have proposed examining media convergence as a *continuous process* instead of a static *terminus ad quem* that is reversible, resistible and not necessarily moving from the past to the present. For example, Thorburn and Jenkins (2004, p. 3) claimed that

> [I]f we understand media convergence as a process instead of a static termination, then we can recognize that such convergences occur regularly in the history of communications and that they are especially likely to occur when an emerging technology has temporarily destabilized the relations among existing media. In this view, convergence can be understood as a way to bridge or join old and new technologies, formats and audiences. (Thorburn & Jenkins, 2004, p. 3)

In other words, this concept needs to be contextualized in history, which is why reconstructing and deconstructing the history of a term and the ways in which it is imagined and narrated can aid in its full comprehension and, in particular, in the understanding that partly it will remain stable and partly it will change again in the future. After all, doing (media) history often involves analyzing the relationship between change and continuity.

REFERENCES

Albarran, A. B., & Gormly, R. K. (2004). Strategic response or strategic blunder? An examination of AOL time warner and vivendi universal. In R. G. Picard (Ed.), *Strategic responses to media market changes* (pp. 35–45). JIBS Research Reports Series, no 2004–2. Sweden: Jönköping International Business School.

Askwith, I. D. (2007). *Television 2.0: Reconceptualizing TV as an engagement medium.* (Master Thesis). MIT, Boston.

Balbi, G. (2010). Radio before Radio: Araldo Telefonico and the invention of Italian broadcasting. *Technology and Culture, 51*(4), 786–808.

Balbi, G., & Magaudda, P. (forthcoming). *A history of digital media: An intermedial and global perspective.* London: Routledge.

Baldwin, T. F., Stevens McVoy, D., & Steinfield, C. (1996). *Convergence: Integrating media, information & communication.* Thousand Oaks, London and New Delhi: Sage.

Barra, L., & Scaglioni, M. (2013). Come il gatto e il topo. L'impatto della pirateria nei consumi televisivi e le reazioni dei broadcaster. In R. Braga & G. Caruso (Eds.), *Piracy effect: Norme, pratiche e studi di caso.* Milan and Udine: Mimesis.

Bohlin, E., Brodin, K., Lundgren, A., & Thorngren, B. (Eds.). (2000). *Convergence in communication and beyond.* Amsterdam: North Holland.

Brand, S. (1987). *The media lab: Inventing the future at MIT.* New York: Viking Penguin.

Burnett, R., & Marshall, P. D. (2003). *Web theory: An introduction.* London: Routledge.

Clements, B. (1998). The impact of convergence on regulatory policy in Europe. *Telecommunications Policy, 22*(3), 197–205.

Dailey, L., Demo, L., & Spillman, M. (2005). The convergence continuum: A model for studying collaboration between media newsrooms. *Atlantic Journal of Communication, 13*(3), 150–168.

de Sola Pool, I. (1983). *Technologies of freedom.* Cambridge, MA: Belknap Press of Harvard University Press.

Dennis, E. E. (1992). *Of Media and People.* Newbury Park, CA: Sage.

Dennis, E. E. (2006). Television's convergence conundrum. Finding the right digital strategy. *Television Quarterly, 37*(1), 22–27.

Deuze, M. (2007). Convergence culture in the creative industries. *International Journal of Cultural Studies, 10,* 243–263.

Doyle, G. (2013). *Understanding media economics.* (2nd ed.) Los Angeles, CA and London: Sage.

Dwyer, T. (2010). *Media convergence.* Maidenhead and New York: McGraw Hill/Open University Press.

European Commission. (1997). Green paper on the convergence of the telecommunications, media and information technology sectors, and the implication for regulation. COM (97) 623. Brussels: European Commission.

European Commission. (2013). Green paper. Preparing for a fully converged audiovisual world: Growth, creation and values. COM (2013) 231. Brussels: European Commission.

Fagerjord, A., & Storsul, T. (2007). Questioning convergence. In T. Storsul & D. Stuedahl (Eds.), *Ambivalence towards convergence* (pp. 19–32). Gothenburg: Nordicom.

Farber, D. J., & Baran, P. (1977). The convergence of computing and telecommunications systems. *Science, 195,* 1166–1170.

Flynn, B. (2000). *Digital TV, internet and mobile convergence developments and projections fro Europe.* Digiscope Report. London: Philips Global Media.

Fuchs, C. (2011). *Foundations of critical media and information studies.* New York: Routledge.

Gordon, R. (2003). The meanings and implications of convergence. In K. Kawamoto (Ed.), *Digital journalism: Emerging media and the changing horizons of journalism* (pp. 57–73). Lanham, MD: Rowman & Littlefield.

Grant, A. (2009). Dimensions of media convergence. In A. Grant & J. Wilkinson (Eds.), *Media convergence. The state of the field* (pp. 3–17). New York: Oxford University Press.

Herkman, J. (2012). Convergence or intermediality? Finnish political communication in the new media age. *Convergence: The International Journal of Research into New Media Technologies, 18,* 369–384.

Hesmondhalgh, D. (2002). *The cultural industries.* London and Thousand Oaks: Sage.

Hynes, D. (2003). Research report: Consumption convergence. *Irish Communications Review, 9,* 1–5. Available at http://www.icr.dit.ie/volume9/articles/Hynes.pdf.

Infotendencias group. (2012). Media convergence. In E. Siapera & A. Veglis (Eds.), *The handbook of global online journalism* (pp. 21–38). Chichester: Wiley.

Jenkins, H. (2001). Convergence? I diverge. *Technology Review,* June, 93.

Jenkins, H. (2004). The cultural logic of media convergence. *International Journal of Cultural Studies, 7*(1), 33–43.

Jenkins, H. (2005). Welcome to convergence culture. *Receiver,* 1–6.

Jenkins, H. (2006). *Convergence culture: Where old and new media collide.* New York: New York University Press.

Jenkins, H., & Deuze, M. (2008). Editorial: Convergence culture. *Convergence: The International Journal of Research into New Media Technologies, 14*(1), 5–12.

Jensen, K. B. (2010). *Media convergence: The three degrees of network, mass, and interpersonal communication.* London and New York: Routledge.

Keen, A. (2007). *The cult of the amateur: How today's internet is killing our culture.* New York: Doubleday/Currency.

Kopecka-Piech, K. (2011). Media convergence concepts. *Studia Medioznawcze, 46*(3), 1–19. Retrieved from http://sm.id.uw.edu.pl/Numery/2011_3_46/kopecka.pdf.

Latzer, M. (2013). Media convergence. In R. Towse & C. Handke (Eds.), *Handbook of the Digital Creative Economy* (pp. 123–133). Cheltenham: Edward Elgar.

Latzer, M. (2014). Convergence, Co-evolution and Complexity in European Communications Policy. In K. Donders, C. Pauwels, J. Loisen (Eds.), *The Palgrave Handbook of European Media Policy* (pp. 36–53). Houndmills: Palgrave Macmillan.

Levasseur, L., & Musso, P. (1993). Preface. *Reseaux, 11*(1), 9–16.

Levy, P. (1997). *Collective intelligence.* Cambridge, MA: Perseus.

Lind, J. (2004). Convergence: History of term usage and lessons for firm strategists. Online paper. Center for Information and Communications Research, at Stockholm School of Economics. Available at http://userpage.fu-berlin.de/~jmueller/its/conf/berlin04/Papers/1_LIND.doc.

Marsden, C. T., & Verhulst, S. G. (1999). *Convergence in European digital TV regulation.* London: Blackstone.

Miège, B. (1992). Des Convergences sont envisageables à terme. *Reseaux, 11*(1), 21–27.

Miller, V. (2011). *Understanding digital culture.* London: Sage.

Mueller, M. (1999). Digital convergence and its consequences. *Javnost-The Public, 6*(3), 11–27.

Nguyen, A. (2007). The interaction between technologies and society: Lessons learnt from 160 evolutionary years of online news services. *First Monday, 12*(3). Retrieved from http://firstmonday.org/issues/issue12_3/nguyen/index.html.

Nieć, M. (2013). A brief look at the history of media convergence. In R. Szczepaniak (Ed.), *Media convergence—Approaches and experiences.* Frankfurt am Main, Berlin, Bern, Bruxelles, New York, Oxford, Wien: Peter Lang.

Nielsen, J. (2006). *Participation Inequality: Encouraging More Users to Contribute.* Retrieved from http://www.nngroup.com/articles/participation-inequality.

Noam, E. M. (Ed.). (2015). *Who owns the world's media? Media concentration and ownership around the world.* Oxford and New York: Oxford University Press.

Noll, J. M. (2003). The myth of convergence. *International Journal on Media Management, 5*(1), 12–13.

Nora, S., & Minc, A. (1978). *L'informatisation de la Société.* Paris: La Documentation française.

OECD. (1992). *Telecommunications and broadcasting: Convergence or collision?* OECD Digital Economy Papers, 5, OECD Publishing. Available at doi:10.1787/237416285388.

Oettinger, A., Berman, P., & Read, W. (1977). *High and low politics: Information resources for the 80s.* Cambridge, MA: Ballinger.

Pradié, C., & Salaün, J. M. (1992). Synthese européenne. Réalité et illusions. *Reseaux, 11*(1), 173–205.

Punathambekar, A. (2008). We're online, not on the streets: Indian cinema, new media, and participatory culture. In A. Kavoori & A. Punathambekar (Eds.), *Global Bollywood* (pp. 282–299). New York: New York University Press.

Richeri, G. (1982). *L'universo telematico. Il lavoro e la cultura del prossimo domani.* Bari: De Donato.

Silverstone, R. (1995). Convergence is a dangerous word. *Convergence: The International Journal of Research into New Media Technologies, 1,* 11–13.

Singer, J. B. (2004). Strange bedfellows? The diffusion of convergence in four news organizations. *Journalism Studies, 5*(1), 3–18.

Staiger, J., & Hake, S. (Eds.). (2009). *Convergence media history.* New York: Routledge.

Steward, T. (2014). Wide-screen television and home movies: Towards an archaeology of television and cinema convergence before digitalisation. *View: Journal of European Television History and Culture, 3,* Retrieved from http://journal.euscreen.eu/index.php/view/article/view/JETHC070/170. Accessed September 14, 2016.

Szczepaniak, R. (2013). Editorial. In R. Szczepaniak (Ed.), *Media Convergence— Approaches and Experiences.* Frankfurt am Main, Berlin, Bern, Bruxelles, New York, Oxford, Wien: Peter Lang.

Thorburn, D., & Jenkins, H. (2004). Introduction: Towards an aesthetics of transition. In D. Thorburn & H. Jenkins (Eds.), *Rethinking media change: The aesthetics of transition* (pp. 1–16). Cambridge, MA and London: MIT Press.

Watson, J. D., & Hill, A. (1997). *A dictionary of media and communication studies* (6th ed.). London: Arnold.

Winseck, D. (1999). Back to the future: Telecommunications, online information services and convergence from 1840 to 1910. *Media History, 5*(2), 137–157.

Wirth, M. O. (2006). Issues in media convergence. In A. B. Albarran, S. Chan-Olmsted, & M. O. Wirth (Eds.), *Handbook of media management and economics* (pp. 445–462). Mahwah, NJ: Lawrence Erlbaum Association.

Ytreberg, E. (2011). Review article: Convergence: Essentially confused? *New Media & Society, 13*(3), 502–508.

Zhang, Y. E. (2008). Examining media convergence: Does it converge good journalism, economic synergies, and competitive advantages? *Dissertation Presented to the Faculty of the Graduate School at University of Missouri-Columbia,* May.

Author Biography

Gabriele Balbi is Senior Assistant Professor at the Institute of Media and Journalism, Faculty of Communication Sciences, USI Università della Svizzera italiana, Switzerland. He is director of the China Media Observatory. His main areas of research are media history and history of telecommunications, with a focus on the relationships between analogue and digital media.

PART II

Media Audiences and Usage

CHAPTER 3

Convergence in Domestic Media Use? The Interplay of Old and New Media at Home

Kathrin Friederike Müller and Jutta Röser

INTRODUCTION: CHALLENGES OF CONVERGENCE IN AUDIENCE AND RECEPTION STUDIES

Even though it has been more than twenty years since Silverstone labeled "convergence" as a "dangerous word" (Silverstone, 1995, p. 11), the term is still problematic. It is not only too broad to describe the multiple meanings that make up the phenomenon (Fagerjord & Storsul, 2007; Liestøl, 2007),[1] but it often refers to the idea that technical change leads to social change as well. In our current mediatized[2] societies with online-capable media everywhere, this monocausal concept suggests that the use of television (TV), radio or newspapers via the internet—along with content that is not produced by mass media—is regularly practiced. However, does this assumption apply to social life? We argue that media use is far more complex. In this chapter we discuss how the implementation of convergent media use has taken place in the domestic sphere and how it interrelates with the reception of classic media.[3] For this purpose,

K.F. Müller (✉) · J. Röser
University of Münster, Münster, Germany
e-mail: kathrin.mueller@uni-muenster.de

J. Röser
e-mail: jutta.roeser@uni-muenster.de

S. Sparviero et al. (eds.), *Media Convergence and Deconvergence*, Global Transformations in Media and Communication Research - A Palgrave and IAMCR Series, DOI 10.1007/978-3-319-51289-1_3

we will illustrate how online and classic media were used in average German households in 2013. Contrary to public and academic discourse (Kleinsteuber, 2009), we do not consider the implementation of convergent media use as an automatism or a radical process. We assume that the transformation of using online media instead of classic media is proceeding slowly but steadily. Our aim is to scrutinize and illustrate the interplay of technological change and media use in order to grasp the meaning of convergent media use in everyday life.

The findings on convergent media use which we present in this chapter are part of ethnographically oriented household studies of 25 couples. Referring to this qualitative panel study on the usage of old and new media, we show to what extent radio or TV programs and newspaper articles are used online via the internet in German households. Thus, we analyze convergence from a user-oriented perspective. We are interested in the question whether domestic media use is transforming from an activity that is not conducted online to a predominantly online-based practice. In this contribution, we discuss under which circumstances such processes are initiated and established. Based on these considerations, we define "domestic convergence" as the online reception of content that originates from linear TV, radio or newspapers—those media that were formerly used via standalone analog devices—with the help of digital devices which are able to transmit audiovisual and written content.[4] We reconstruct under which circumstances classic media technologies are replaced and followed by online-capable devices and how online media have become an integral part of everyday media use. We share with Hasebrink & Domeyer (2012) the idea of analyzing media repertoires to understand the interplay of different old and new media in the household and their unique meaning.[5] It is not altogether easy to identify indicators for convergence as an empirical phenomenon in the domestic sphere. This field of technological development is changing rapidly: In 2011 and 2013, when we conducted the empirical research this chapter is based on, we decided to use the definition of convergence as described. Meanwhile, technologies and content are more diverse and the definition of domestic convergence is, therefore, far more complicated.[6]

In this text, we demonstrate that, so far, we have not observed an extreme shift in average German households to using TV, radio or newspapers via the internet instead of via stand-alone analog devices. Convergent media use is still not common, but is developing.

THEORETICAL BACKGROUND: GRASPING CONVERGENCE AS A USER-DRIVEN PROCESS

Audience research on convergent media use has been a desideratum for a long time, even though Silverstone (1995) argued for an integration of the recipients' perspective quite early, stating that "consumers and producers" both shape convergence: "the futures of technologies are uncertain because the status of technology as culture is uncertain" (Silverstone, 1995, p. 13). As convergence was a new concept, the phenomenon did not gain much attention in academia until the late 1990s. Furthermore, the discussion about the implementation of online-capable media was often limited as it was dominated by "technological determinism" (Morley, 2006, p. 21). Media users were regarded as passively reacting to technological change and adopting new technologies without any of their own will (Wagner, 2011, p. 72). Therefore, research consisted primarily of quantitative studies on changes in media consumption, as this is one of the important research fields investigated by the "industry of audience measurement" (Hasebrink & Hölig, 2013, p. 191), in order to prove that digitization has an impact on media use. At that time, the idea that convergence might also be a user-driven phenomenon was simply not considered.

Two concepts of convergent media use: Cultural convergence and consumption convergence

Meanwhile, research on convergence has become more user-oriented as the qualitative field of audience and reception studies has also started to work on this topic (Hasebrink & Hölig, 2013; Hölig & Hasebrink, 2013; Wagner, 2011). We argue that concerning the current state of research, one can distinguish between two concepts to conceptualize convergent media use: cultural convergence and consumption convergence. Neither focuses on technology, but on changes that are initiated by the users. Nevertheless, they are aimed at different aspects of the phenomenon. The concept of "cultural convergence" (Jenkins, 2008,

p. 323) "means a shift in the logic by which culture operates, emphasizing the flow of content across media channels" (Jenkins, 2008, p. 323). Jenkins understands the appropriation of convergent content as an important aspect of convergence, as he is interested in "the migratory behavior of media audiences who will go almost everywhere in search of the kinds of entertainment experience they want" (Jenkins, 2008, p. 2). He analyzes how people use online media to network, to participate and to collaborate (Jenkins, 2008, pp. 251–270). Jenkins (2004) defines three different modes of convergent media use: (1) using corresponding content via diverse media (Jenkins, 2004, p. 37; Bolin, 2007, p. 244); (2) participating in interactive media such as weblogs (Jenkins, 2004, p. 36); and (3) connecting with others as collective intelligence in order to solve problems or to demand something (Jenkins, 2004, p. 35). All those aspects might add to the usage of online-capable instead of analog devices, as they offer more possibilities to switch between different kinds of content and to produce content on one's own. However, they do not explain completely why people decide to use online media instead of classic media, especially in the case where people do not use them as interactive, as described in Jenkins's texts, but more in the way they used classic media previously. Furthermore, recipients are not necessarily solitary media users who simply follow their own interests, but social beings who use media accompanied by others at home. The second term, "consumption convergence" (Hynes, 2003, p. 1) is closer to our research interest as it concentrates on the question of how the domestic media equipment is used against the background of technical convergence. It describes "the simultaneous use and consumption of media technologies" (Hynes, 2003, p. 3) and, therefore, is more oriented towards examining under which conditions people use new technological opportunities to appropriate two media via the same device at the same time[7] and, thus, develop media practices that are different from media use that is practiced with analogue media.[8] The concept of consumption convergence refers to the idea that the home is a hub for new modes and situations of media use. That also makes media use a spatial phenomenon, as the usage of different media texts "occurs in the same location" (Hynes, 2003, p. 4). Thus, "one location in the home has become a type of hub for competing and converging media" (Hynes, 2003, p. 4). Therefore, the concept stresses the idea that domestic consumption convergence implies negotiating how classic and online media are placed in relation to each other.

Analyzing convergence: From technological determinism to a user-centered perspective

We share with Hynes (2003) the intent to analyze how changes in reception patterns are linked to everyday life. In order to grasp media convergence—understood as the interconnection of different texts over several media or the merging of technologies—we need to examine the conditions that lead to changes or persistence in media use. As "online-media are more than technical artefacts" (Kolo, 2010, p. 288), we agree they are "constituted during social interaction by their usage" (Kolo, 2010, p. 288). We imply that media users would not use different media via the same device if that does not fit into their everyday routines, media habits or interests. Thus, we assume that the meaning of technology is constituted by the coming together of technological potential and the users during appropriation (Peil & Röser, 2012).

Therefore, the key question is how the media users act in converging media environments and how they handle technical change and new technical opportunities as well as new possibilities of media reception (Hasebrink, 2004; Hasebrink & Domeyer, 2012; Wagner, 2011, p. 70). Convergence might change media use and the domestic media repertoire fundamentally, but it might also have hardly any impact, as media users are "fractious" (Winter, 2001, p. 16). We consider the contexts in which online media are used in order to understand for which reasons media really converge in everyday life and why they are hindered.

Analyzing convergent media use against the background of the domestication approach

We refer to the domestication approach, as we are interested in the media users' role in establishing the routine of using media content online that was formerly distributed by classic media. We regard the home as a meaning-giving sphere, which forms the background for media use (Livingstone, 1992; Silverstone, Hirsch, & Morley, 1992). Everyday domestic life represents an important context of media appropriation.[9] It is about allocating technologies a physical and symbolic place within the domestic sphere (Peil & Röser, 2014, p. 331). We are interested in the (partial) replacement of classic media by online media. Given this research interest, we concentrate on the use of media at home, such as the TV set, the radio or newspapers (and also the internet) which are used predominantly alongside each other in the domestic sphere, where users create their specific media repertoires (Hasebrink & Domeyer, 2012, p. 758). The choice of one medium which is then used at a given moment is often made at home, where the whole range of media are available and used in relation to each other (Morley, 2003, p. 445). Thus, it makes sense to analyze the relatedness of watching TV, listening to the radio or reading the newspaper against the background of the home. Concerning the question of convergent media use, the home is assumed to be the place where people eventually decide to replace classic media by online-capable technologies, as most of the classic media devices like non-portable TV and radio sets are situated and have been used routinely for many years there. That does not mean that the home is the only place where convergent media use is performed, but it is the place where it is negotiated.[10] Thus, the home is an instructive environment for analyzing the circumstances under which people switch from classic media to a device that is connected to the internet in order to establish a media repertoire that perfectly meets their needs and purposes. The (potential) disappearance of classic media would become particularly visible in this sphere.

METHODOLOGY

All findings originate from a qualitative panel study on "The Mediatized Home," which analyzes how digitization changes the media repertoire which is in use in the common household (Peil & Röser, 2014; Röser & Peil, 2012). It refers to three stages of data collection in 2008, 2011 and 2013. The analysis is designed as an ethnographically oriented household study.[11] In this chapter, we concentrate on findings from 2011 and 2013.

We have interviewed 25 heterosexual couples in Germany who were living together in the same household. The sample is allocated by quota according to age and educational background. It includes three different age groups (the participants were between 25 and 63 years old in 2008, and therefore between 30 and 68 years in 2013) and two different educational groups (general/intermediate secondary school, high school graduation or vocational diploma). Therefore, the age span and educational levels of the participants are broad,[12] including a variety of different professions. On these grounds, the sample allows for an analysis of domestic media practices of the broad German middle class. In order to get to know more about domestic media use, we conducted qualitative interviews, each with both man and woman together as a couple, as we wanted to get an insight into the relationship and interactions concerning questions of media use.

The study reconstructs how media—online and classic—are used in the domestic sphere. Convergent media use is part of potential changes in domestic media use, but was not one of the main research interests. It was, however, included in two major research questions of the project:

1. How have media repertoires changed after the integration of the internet into the domestic sphere?
2. What meaning is ascribed to classic and online media in terms of a general mediatization process (Krotz, 2009)?

We asked the couple in each interview to describe how they use classic and online media at home. If it was relevant to them, the issue was also broached regarding convergent media use and the reception of multimedia content. The couples explained why they used certain media online or why they continued using the classic version. Additionally, home site inspections revealed where classic media had already been replaced in the household. We implemented home site inspections in all stages of data collection, which included taking pictures of the media devices mentioned for documentation purposes.

The evaluation is based on "ethnographic household portraits" (Röser et al. 2017, forthcoming). These portraits present a written text which comprises a structured analysis of interview transcripts based on guiding research questions. Those questions, for example, aimed at convergent media use. Portraits also include insights from memos and other empirical material, such as questionnaires and photographs. The households were grouped and typified in a second part of the analysis in order to name generalizable patterns of media use.

ANALYZING MEDIA REPERTOIRES: COEXISTENCE OF OLD AND NEW MEDIA

The empirical findings show that the media repertoires of the couples interviewed had not been transformed radically between 2011 and 2013. Even though plenty of new technologies and possibilities, such as tablets, online radios and smart TVs, which enable people to implement convergent media use in their homes, were on the market in 2013, we did not see a dynamic change concerning the media repertoires at that time compared with our findings in 2011. Classic media had not been removed from the domestic media repertoire by then; instead, old and new media were coexisting in the common household—a development that has been observed in other contexts in history before (Balbi, 2015, p. 242). Both classic and online media had specific meanings for the users and were used for defined benefits. No predominance of online media was found (Peil & Röser, 2014). Convergence—in the sense of replacing a classic by an online medium—was not a common phenomenon. It was only observed in a small group of 6 households in 2011 and 7 in 2013,[13] who had already started to use TV, radio or newspapers primarily on the internet, and its extent had remained stable between 2011 and 2013. We conclude that convergent media use in the domestic sphere is not established in a linear process at an enormous speed. Obviously, it is proceeding slowly and there are always phases of stagnation in which media convergence stays at the same level.

Three patterns of domestic media use

Nevertheless, the media repertoires in the households differed from each other, partly in a remarkable way. It was especially the status of the internet and, consequently, the combination of online-capable and classic media which led to the formation of different media repertoires in the homes. We identified three patterns of domestic media use altogether that allowed us to distinguish three types of households with regard to the internet's role within the media repertoire. Those groups varied according to the intensity of internet use and the spectrum of online activities (see Fig. 3.1).

Overall, we found out that the three types of households were not distributed equally. The group that had a focus on classic media was the smallest one. The largest group consisted of households that focused on classic media and on the internet. A third and rather small group had replaced classic media by online-capable devices and had stopped using some of the classic media they had accessed previously.

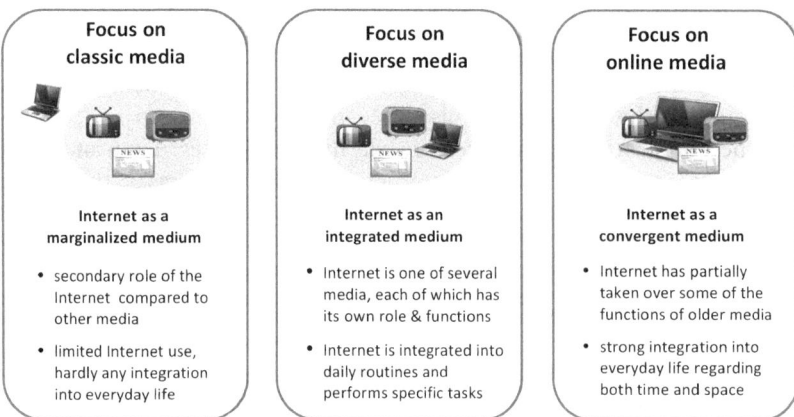

Fig. 3.1 Typology of households according to the status of the internet in domestic media use. *Source* The authors & Corinna Peil

Type 1: Focus on classic media
The first type is described as having a "focus on classic media." These households rarely used online media and concentrated on traditional media, such as newspapers, TV sets and radios. The usage of classic media had not been changed notably by the internet and the convergent use of media online did not play any role in these households. The internet had a minor significance in the media repertoire and its use was temporally limited. The integration of the internet into everyday life operates on only a low level. Those households used a stationary computer to go online which they set up in a workroom (Röser & Peil, 2014). Thus, the internet use was separated from everyday life inside the home and had only a minor significance compared with classic media. In these households, the internet was used for specific purposes and can be considered more like a kind of accessory than a necessary tool for managing domestic life. This type had become less prevalent since 2008.[14] In 2011, three elderly couples used media this way; in 2013, only two couples still belonged to this type.

Type 2: Focus on diverse media
The largest group consisted of 18 households in 2011 and the same number in 2013. These households formed the second type, which we

assume mirrored the average media use in German households. This type was characterized by the coexistence of classic media and the internet, which was integrated into the domestic sphere spatially and temporally. For example, the internet was also used in the living room and, whenever the couples needed it, accessed via mobile devices. First and foremost, these couples used the internet frequently for tasks that arose from everyday life, such as buying tickets for the cinema, concerts and public transport, and online banking, shopping or organizing vacations, to name but a few examples. In these households, going online had become a stable part of the domestic media practice. Nevertheless, convergent media use was practiced only sporadically. The couples had not replaced classic media in favor of their online-capable correspondents. Analog radio devices, TV sets or the printed newspaper page still formed the largest part of their media repertoire. However, some of the couples additionally used digital newspapers, online radios or multimedia resource centers from time to time if they wanted to deepen specific interests. The couples used the internet as one of many types of media while the "old" media had not lost their original role. Convergent media use was, therefore, an add-on to the reception of media content via classic media.

Altogether, both old and new media are of the same relevance in domestic media use for households of this type. All media have discrete meanings and are linked to specific requests and gratifications. The internet is as important as the classic media, but no more than them. It is used for defined tasks and functions that cannot be carried out via other media, such as the management of needs and desires that emerge in the context of everyday life. Hence, instead of substituting the purpose of classic media, such as radio, TV and newspapers, the internet has occupied a cultural sphere of organizing everyday life that has been managed previously without the help of media (Peil & Röser, 2014, p. 332).[15]

Type 3: Focus on online media
Seven of the households had replaced classic media and used online media instead in 2013. They formed type 3, "focus on online media." Those couples had transferred the functions and scopes of at least one of the classic media to the internet. Consequently, they had replaced older analog technologies and restructured their media repertoire in one or several of the following ways: instead of classic radio, they listened to audio streams, newspapers were read online, and any TV program was

appropriated via multimedia resource centers on the fixed personal computer or on network-compatible TV sets. The internet was integrated as a multifunctional and multimedia tool spatially and temporally in these households. It was used in almost every room of the household and at any time of the day. However, watching TV or listening to the radio via online media had not lost its former social meaning. It was still labeled as "watching TV" or "listening to the radio" and not regarded as an alternative kind of media use (Hasebrink, 2004, p. 70; Hölig & Hasebrink, 2013).

Interestingly, most of the households belonging to type 3 still possessed and used classic media, especially linear TV programs, and had not yet established a media repertoire which consisted fully of digital devices. Thus, again, convergent media use was combined with the reception of classic media and had not totally replaced it.

Reasons for the persistence of classic media

The descriptive overview of the three types underlines that the "focus on diverse media" (type 2) is the predominant variation of domestic media use. However, what is the reason for most of the households keeping classic media (in their media repertoire) and using the internet for specific, mostly organizational tasks? To understand this phenomenon, one has to take a closer look at the content and the symbolic meaning of TV, radio and newspaper.

Overall, we found out that each medium has specific functions in the common household which are linked to fields of everyday life and especially to living together as a couple. The households that regularly read a newspaper, for example, have subscribed to a local one to get information about their hometown. Newspapers are mostly read while having breakfast and reading is described as a sensory experience. For some of the couples, reading the newspaper together in the morning is a ritual between partners during which they share parts of the newspaper and show articles of interest to each other. The radio is used additionally while carrying out domestic work or other activities. The couples use it mostly by themselves during the day. The relevance of watching linear TV programs via a TV set becomes obvious in the evening: The TV reception is an activity that is used to spend time at home together and to feel community regardless of the television program. Couples "meet" at the TV set. Thus, the screen has a spatial function as it defines the place where to meet and sit together. Furthermore, couples prefer large TV sets to smaller online-capable devices because they are more comfortable to use together. Furthermore, watching linear TV programs has social functions. The practice of watching TV synchronizes different activities in the evening: "To us, it is just time we spent together frequently during the week" (Mr. Brinkmann, 55 years old, teacher). Communication is also a reason that people meet in front of the TV set. Couples talk about personal and organizational questions. For these purposes, the linear TV program remains important as it offers recreation and simplifies the decision about what is going to be watched.[16] Watching linear TV programs on a large screen is highly relevant to couples because they sense togetherness—on which their life is grounded—in front of it.

The findings show that the reception of these three classic media is strongly linked to rhythms of everyday life and to the constellation as a couple. Hence, TV, radio, newspapers and the internet coexist inside the homes. The specific character of the home promotes stability in media use. As everyday life contexts persist within the home and are not easily overturned, they shape how media are used and how new technologies are appropriated (Peil & Röser, 2014, p. 333). Couples repeat established practices of media use because they make sense in everyday life.

Factors promoting terminal convergence

Based on the insights into domestic media use of type 3 "focus on online media," we can name some factors which promote terminal convergence. Even though this group is not homogeneous at all, they share certain attributes. Firstly, convergent media use is practiced in households that have deeply integrated the internet into everyday life and are familiar with online media. But which socio-demographical or biographical characteristics form the background for such an appropriation? These couples are characterized by a high level of education. More than half of the households have a similar background: The interviewees were all students in the late 1990s and appropriated the internet at university during this period. Thus, most of them have been using online media for a long time. They are familiar with the internet and they have got used to online-capable technologies gradually. This is the reason that they adopt new online-capable technologies more easily and are more open to innovations[17] and convergent media use than other households.

All of these couples, aged between 30 and 40 years in 2013, share the same generational positioning regarding the domestication of the internet in Germany. However, referring to the whole group of households belonging to type 3, age is not a distinct factor for predicting terminal convergence.[18]

A second hint for convergent media use is the degree to which mobile devices are integrated into the households. All convergent households own such media. These mobile technologies promote convergent media use because their portability offers the possibility of using digital content comfortably anywhere in the home.

Thirdly, convergent media use is also linked to living alone. Three of the couples we interviewed separated between 2008 and 2013.[19] Consequently, the male partners in particular changed many of their media habits. They left their shared TV sets and radios at their former homes, where the female partners remained in each of our cases analyzed. Subsequently, they had to decide which media they wanted to purchase for their new home. Two of our respondents decided to use their laptops to watch TV and to listen to the radio, as they found it more convenient and due to financial reasons. These insights indicate that convergent media use is more suitable for people who live alone because it can be practiced more easily on one's own than in a couple constellation. As shown above, couples create community via media use during their leisure time. By contrast, people living alone do not have to create such a situational community. Therefore, they can use different media at the same time and do not mind having a small screen. The changes of media use caused by separation show that contextual necessities could change the sense that is ascribed to media in everyday life. This might lead to the initiation of new practices of media use and, therefore, to a more dynamic media convergence.

Convergence as an "add-on": Convergent media practices beyond the merging of devices

In addition to the findings concerning the replacement of classic in favor of online media, we came across three further examples of convergent media use regarding the entirety of our households. First, we observed that content, which was used formerly solely via classic media, is now used additionally via online media. The couples intensify the reception of their preferred media by using digital in addition to non-digital content. Households that generally like to watch TV add the reception of audiovisual content online to their media repertoire; the same happens to households that are keen on using the radio or reading newspapers. Thus, "fandom" for specific media is a motor for convergent media use. Secondly, the integration of mobile media, such as tablets, into the household leads to the use of second screens while watching TV, as the respondents are combining individual media interests, such as reading online (about their hobby) or communicating via social media, while experiencing community with their partners. It is also a strategy to use leisure time for the fulfillment of duties: mothers in particular use second screens (while watching TV) to purchase goods for themselves and their family, to search for holiday accommodation or to organize everyday life. That is how they balance the double burden which results from being a working mother. Thirdly, some couples use second screens to look up topics they came across while watching TV. As the internet and TV are used simultaneously, the reception of both media is also converging. Nevertheless, all these convergent media practices are foremost an addition to the use of classic media and have not yet caused a rearrangement of the media repertoires.

CONCLUSION

"Convergence is a dangerous word" (Silverstone, 1995, p. 11)—not just because of its complexity, but also because it suggests more dynamic media use than what can be observed in social reality. Our findings show that convergence from the side of the users proceeds slowly and not in a radical way. Online media have not replaced classic media in most of the households analyzed. The replacement of classic media is not common, but, from time to time, online-capable devices are used as an alternative to classical domestic media in average German middle-class households. We noticed an interplay of old and new media combined with convergent media practices in the majority of the households. Consequently, we observed an enormous differentiation of media practices. In other words, the domestic media repertoire did not converge to using a few media only, but became more diverse between 2011 and 2013, as more and more devices, like online media and/or mobile technologies, were integrated into the homes. Furthermore, as convergent media use is practiced additionally, rather than instead of classic media use, the established technologies also contributed to the diverse and manifold media repertoire that was used in the homes. Thus, in this context, we observed a form of divergence which became visible in a plurality of devices. We regard this development as an expression of deconvergence (see Peil & Spaviero, Chap. 1 in this volume). The various media technologies were used because they were all suited to special needs and tasks. At the time the study was conducted, old and new media continued to coexist and no predominance of online media or replacement of older media was found.

However, we came across variations of cultural convergence, such as the production and distribution of digital content and the practice of communicating with other users about it (Fagerjord & Storsul, 2007; Hölig & Hasebrink, 2013; Jenkins, 2008). Hence, we noticed changes and dynamics, but they proceed gradually and not abruptly.

Altogether, the findings underline that approved media practices make sense as long as the demands and practices of everyday life do not change. That is the reason why traditional mass media remain important and are not replaced by digital online media. The domestication theory underlines this insight by emphasizing the fact that new media are only integrated if their use fits into the routines of the common household. Convergence proceeds just as fast as the surrounding conditions in the common household and everyday life allow it to. If convergence makes sense in everyday life or in communicating with others, people develop practices of convergent media use. If not, the domestic media repertoires remain the same. Thus, convergence is a process driven by the media users.

NOTES

1. Convergence describes the merging of networks as well as of programs, devices, markets, rhetoric and regulatory regimes (Fagerjord & Storsul, 2007, pp. 20–26).
2. We follow Friedrich Krotz in defining mediatization as "a meta-process that is grounded in the modification of communication as the basis practice of how people construct the social and cultural world. They do so by changing communication practices that use media and refer to media. Hence, mediatization is not a technological driven concept, since it is not the media as a technology that are causal, but the changes in how people communicate when constructing their inner and exterior realities by referring to media" (Krotz, 2009, p. 25).

3. We define classic media as analog as well as digital media which distribute "conventional" content from mass media without using the internet for distribution. Such content is radio and TV programs that are broadcast by public or private companies or newspapers articles. By contrast, online media are understood as media which distribute audiovisual content or texts via the internet. This content may originate not only from broadcasting companies or publishing houses, but also from other sources, such as blogs, social media or streaming services.

4. This definition aims at describing convergence as a change in the distribution of media content via new channels and devices in the domestic sphere. Therefore, this process is similar to the merging of different media into one device, which is defined as "terminal convergence" (Fagerjord & Storsul, 2007, p. 21) as well as "service convergence", which enables the "transmission of all digital media services over the same network, and the use of different kinds of services on the same terminals" (Fagerjord & Storsul, 2007, p. 23).

5. A media repertoire is "the entirety of media" the person uses regularly (Hasebrink & Domeyer, 2012, p. 758). The authors distinguish "if they [the recipients] select media types, or genres, or topics or concrete brands, or if they rather select social contexts instead of certain media" (Hasebrink & Domeyer, 2012, p. 760).

6. There are devices such as digital radios and smart TVs that provide linear programs as well as other digital content. Thus, these devices are different from classic media and from laptops or tablets, which are not exclusively made for the distribution of media.

7. To illustrate simultaneous media use, Hynes (2003) gives the example of using the screen of a TV set to browse the internet while watching TV.

8. Consumption convergence is meant to be a concept of understanding technological change that differs from technological determinism. The perspective assumes "that consumers reject, shape, resist, reshape technologies according to the exigencies of their daily domestic life" (Hynes, 2003, p. 3). It "alludes to the notion that media networks are 'coming together', or becoming hybridised in the domestic sphere which has bought about a convergence in the consumption of media content" (Hynes, 2003, p. 3).

9. As the domestic context is understood as a meaning-giving sphere of media use, one has to take into account the surrounding situations, places, time, constellations and the integration of media use into different domestic practices when analyzing media reception (Morley, 2006; Röser & Peil, 2012).
10. Because of the ongoing saturation of everyday life with online media, convergent media use is also established in other spheres as a common practice of reception, for example in trains.
11. The long-term study "The Mediatized Home" has been part of the DFG-funded German Priority Program "Mediatized Worlds."
12. As the sample has aged since 2008, none of the respondents were younger than 30 years in 2013.
13. Six households belonged to this type in 2011. In 2013, seven household belonged to this type because one of the couples had split up in the meantime and husband and wife ever since were living in two different households. Both partners now use convergent media in separate households.
14. In 2006, the so-called "additionalists", who regard the internet as an accessory matter, have been dominant in Germany (Ahrens, 2009, p. 251). For further insights concerning this development, see Röser & Peil (2014).
15. With the exception of telephone books or catalogues, those organizational tasks have been done without media before.
16. Even though linear TV programs offer many options from which viewers can choose, its possibilities are limited, as only what is distributed at a given time can be watched.
17. This process of internet-adoption can be regarded as typical for internet users who were students in the late 1990s (Röser & Roth, 2015).
18. Two middle-aged men and an older couple belong to this group as well, whereas others of the younger and well educated couples do not belong to type 3.
19. After separation, we interviewed the partners individually at their households, where some of them had just moved.

References

Ahrens, J. (2009). *Going online, doing gender: Alltagspraktiken rund um das Internet in Deutschland und Australien.* Bielefeld: Transcript.

Balbi, G. (2015). Old and new media. Theorizing their relationship in media historiography. In S. Kinnebrock, C. Schwarzenegger & T. Birkner (Eds.), *Theorien des Medienwandels* (pp. 231–249). Köln: Herbert von Halem.

Bolin, G. (2007). Media technologies, transmedia storytelling and commodification. In T. Storsul & D. Stuedahl (Eds.), *Ambivalence towards convergence. Digitalization and media change* (pp. 237–248). Göteburg: Nordicom.

Fagerjord, A. & Storsul, T. (2007). Questioning convergence. In T. Storsul & D. Stuedahl (Eds.), *Ambivalence towards convergence. Digitalization and media change* (pp. 19–31). Göteburg: Nordicom.

Hasebrink, U. (2004). Konvergenz aus Nutzerperspektive: Das Konzept der Kommunikationsmodi. In U. Hasebrink, L. Mikos & E. Prommer (Eds.), *Mediennutzung in konvergierenden Medienumgebungen* (pp. 67–85). München: Fischer (Reihe Rezeptionsforschung, 1).

Hasebrink, U. & Domeyer, H. (2012). Media repertoires as patterns of behaviour and as meaningful practices: a multimethod approach to media use in converging media environments. Participations. *Journal of Audience & Reception Studies, 9*(2), 757–779.

Hasebrink, U. & Hölig, S. (2013). Conceptualizing audiences in convergent media environments. In M. Karmasin & S. Diehl (Eds.), *Media and convergence management* (pp. 189–202). Berlin: Springer.

Hölig, S., & Hasebrink, U. (2013). Nachrichtennutzung in konvergierenden Medienumgebungen. International vergleichende Befunde auf Basis des Reuters Institute Digital News Survey 2013. *Media Perspektiven, 11*, 522–536.

Hynes, D. (2003). Consumption convergence. Research Report. Irish Communication Review, 9. http://dit.ie/icr/media/diticr/documents/7%20Hynes%20ICR%20Vol%209.pdf (last download 04.09.14).

Jenkins, H. (2004). The cultural logic of media convergence. *International Journal of Cultural Studies, 7*(1), 33–43.

Jenkins, H. (2008). *Convergence culture: where old and new media collide.* New York: New York University Press.

Kleinsteuber, H. J. (2009). Convergence. Facts and fictions about a term and its political implications. *merz. medien + erziehung, 53*(6), 57–70.

Kolo, C. (2010). Online-Medien und Wandel: konvergenz, Diffusion, Substitution. In W. Schweiger (Ed.), *Handbuch Online-Kommunikation* (pp. 284–307). Wiesbaden: VS.

Krotz, F. (2009). Mediatization. A concept with which to grasp media and societal change. In K. Lundby (Eds.), *Mediatization: Concept, changes, consequences.* (pp. 19–38.). New York: Peter Lang.

Liestøl, G. (2007). The dynamics of convergence and divergence in digital domains. In T. Storsul & D. Stuedahl (Eds.), *Ambivalence towards convergence. Digitalization and media change* (pp. 165–78). Göteburg: Nordicom.

Livingstone, S. (1992). The meaning of domestic technologies. A personal construct analysis of familial gender relations. In R. Silverstone & E. Hirsch

(Eds.), *Consuming technologies. Media and information in domestic spaces* (pp. 113–30). London, New York: Routledge.

Morley, D. (2003). Where the global meets the local: notes from the sitting room. In L. Parks & S. Kumar (Eds.), *Planet TV: a global television reader* (pp. 286–302). New York: New York University Press.

Morley, D. (2006). What's "home" got to do with it? Contradictory dynamics in the domestication of technology and the dislocation of domesticity. In T. Berker, M. Hartmann, Y. Punie & K. Ward (Eds.), *Domestication of media and technology.* (pp. 21–39). Berkshire: Open University Press.

Peil, C. & Röser, J. (2012). Using the domestication approach for the analysis of diffusion and participation processes of new media. In H. Bilandzic, G. Patriarche & P. Traudt (Eds.), *The social use of media. Cultural and social scientific perspectives on audience research* (pp. 221–40). [ECREA- Book Series] Bristol/Chicago: intellect.

Peil, C. & Röser, J. (2014). The meaning of home in the context of digitization, mobilization and mediatization. In A. Hepp & F. Krotz (Eds.), *Mediatized worlds. Culture and society in a media age* (pp. 233–49). Basingstroke: Palgrave Macmillan.

Röser, J., Müller, K. F., Niemand, S., Peil, C. & Roth, U. (2017). Medienethnografische Porträts als Auswertungsinstrument: Techniken der kontextsensiblen Rezeptionsanalyse. In A. Scheu (Ed.), *Auswertung qualitativer Daten in der Kommunikationswissenschaft.* Wiesbaden: Springer VS. (to be published in autumn 2017).

Röser, J. & Peil, C. (2012). Das Zuhause als mediatisierte Welt im Wandel. Fallstudien und Befunde zur Domestizierung des Internets als Mediatisierungsprozess. In F. Krotz & A. Hepp (Eds.), *Mediatisierte Welten: Beschreibungsansätze und Forschungsfelder* (pp. 137–163). Wiesbaden: VS.

Röser, J. & Roth, U. (2015). Häusliche Aneignungsweisen des Internets: "Revolutioniert Multimedia die Geschlechterbeziehungen?" revisited. In R. Drüeke, S. Kirchhoff, T. Steinmaurer, M. Thiele (Eds.), Zwischen Gegebenem und Möglichem. Kritische Perspektiven auf Medien und Kommunikation, (S. 301–314). Bielefeld: transcript.

Silverstone, R. (1995). Convergence is a dangerous word. *Convergence, 11*(1), 11–13.

Silverstone, R., Hirsch, E. & Morley, D. (1992). Information and communication technologies and the moral economy of the household. In R. Silverstone & E. Hirsch (Eds.), *Consuming technologies. Media and information in domestic spaces* (pp. 15–31). London, New York: Routledge.

Wagner, U. (2011). *Medienhandeln, Medienkonvergenz und Sozialisation. Empirie und gesellschaftswissenschaftliche Perspektiven.* München: kopaed.

Winter, R. (2001). *Die Kunst des Eigensinns. Cultural Studies als Kritik der Macht.* Weilerswist-Metternich: Velbrück.

AUTHORS' BIOGRAPHY

Kathrin Friederike Müller is a Postdoctoral Researcher at the Department of Communication, Westfälische Wilhelms-University Münster in Germany, and a former member of the priority program "Mediatized Worlds." Her research interests are audience and reception studies, mediatization, cultural media studies, gender studies and qualitative methods in empirical social research.

Jutta Röser is a Professor in Communications at the Westfälische Wilhelms-University of Münster (Germany) and a former member of the priority program "Mediatized Worlds." Her research interests include audience and reception studies, the mediatization of everyday life, media and communication technologies in history and present, media sociology, cultural studies and gender media studies.

CHAPTER 4

Blurred Lines, Distinct Forces: The Evolving Practices of Italian TV Audiences in a Convergent Scenario

Luca Barra and Massimo Scaglioni

RESEARCHING CONVERGENT TELEVISION VIEWING PRACTICES: BEYOND THE IDEALIZATIONS

In characterizing television viewers in the age of media convergence (De Sola Pool, 1983; Jenkins, 2006; Szczepaniak, 2013; Meikle & Young, 2012), one is often at risk of ending up by simplistically and

---

The two authors conceived, planned and prepared this chapter jointly. The sections **"Researching Convergent Television Viewing Practices: Beyond the Idealizations"** and **"Mapping Convergent Viewers' Practices"** were written by Massimo Scaglioni, and **"Main Trends in Italian Television Convergent Television Consumption"** and **"Conclusions: A Doubly Mobile Pyramid"** by Luca Barra.

L. Barra (✉)
Università di Bologna, Bologna, Italy
e-mail: luca.barra@unibo.it

M. Scaglioni
Università Cattolica del Sacro Cuore, Milan, Italy
e-mail: massimo.scaglioni@unicatt.it

© The Author(s) 2017   75
S. Sparviero et al. (eds.), *Media Convergence and Deconvergence*, Global Transformations in Media and Communication Research - A Palgrave and IAMCR Series, DOI 10.1007/978-3-319-51289-1_4

systematically overturning the mass of negative rhetoric that has long permeated descriptions of media and television consumption from the outset. Thus, the viewer becomes correspondingly idealized: the abstract opposite of the previous passive-consumer stereotype, the couch potato who was often featured in the socially widespread discourse on the relationship between the audience and the small screen. In such depictions, contemporary viewers seem now to suddenly shake off all their passivity, their fragility and the communicative asymmetry that binds them to the mass communication media (what is more, this has been already questioned by British cultural studies since the late 1970s). Indeed, convergent consumers now rid themselves of the constraints imposed by the television offering, through their ability to fully personalize their schedule and their viewing habits. They become active, participative explorers; consumers have turned into "prosumers" : hyper-technological, digital, multimedia and multi-platform players in the media environment. Faced with this idealization, which somewhat simplifies the "real" convergent television and media consumption, a stratified research approach appears opportune—one which encompasses both the theoretical framework and the methodological aspect in order to better understand the evolving contemporary convergent television viewing practices.

The theoretical framework for conceptualizing "convergent consumption"—that is, the activities of television viewing taking place, in multiple forms, inside a convergent media scenario, with a stratified offer of multiple channels, platforms and devices, directly providing or indirectly helping each viewer with audio-visual content—should then primarily be what can be defined as a systemic perspective (Ortoleva, 2002; Scaglioni, 2011), taking into account both the different dimensions of the television medium and its role within the larger media system crossed by intermedial dynamics. Such a point of view is able to explain both the continuities and discontinuities in viewing practices, and the opportunities and the constraints involved both in a changing environment and in the audience reactions to these modifications. This conceptual frame needs to give due consideration to, in particular, all those external and internal limits that still affect contemporary viewers, albeit in a way different from that in the previous, pre-digital situation. One of the most important aspects is the typical rhythm of television programming, such as the temporal organization of shows and other audiovisual materials into a TV schedule, which remains central in orienting and synchronizing consumption, or at least a significant part of it, even when nonlinear, on-demand forms of viewing emerge (Ellis, 2000; Ytreberg, 2002; Van den Bulck, 2009; Barra, 2015). This approach should also be able to note and analyze the panoply of audience practices, which (now more than ever) cannot be distilled into a single or dominant model. Although some consumption practices can be connoted as particularly innovative, it is not to be forgotten that, especially in television, strong strands of continuity with the past and other forms of inertia remain (Spigel & Olsson, 2004; Lotz, 2007; Scaglioni & Sfardini, 2008). In sum, the rhetorical simplification of a consumption that is necessarily productive, active and interactive must be counterbalanced with a richer, more realistic vision that takes into account the varied mix of continuity and discontinuity that characterizes convergent consumption forms in a renewed television and media system.

To define a methodology able to develop such a systemic approach, the analysis of the convergent viewer requires an all-round series of methods including field research. This effort should focus at least on three aspects: on the media and television texts, seen currently as "extended" products; on the new branding and product-offering strategies enacted by the broadcasters and content producers to restore an "order" and to bring regimentation to more and more elusive consumption practices; and finally on those practices themselves, of course, via qualitative research methods that aim to reconstruct and "shadow" the several forms of convergent consumption. It is intended, therefore, as a process of systematic mapping of the relationships that link the increasingly open and expanded texts, the organizations' strategies to reshape their offering, and the ways in which consumption is multiplying along with the available technology platforms. This chapter then follows this research path, and presents part of the results of a multi-year qualitative study that examined the convergent television scenario in the Italian national context. The Italian case history looks particularly interesting because it follows some larger international developments of the television scenario (that is, digitization and convergence, conglomeration, transmedia storytelling and so on), while at the same time maintaining some peculiarities stemming directly from the shape of the national media and television system, its history and traditions, and the cultural, political and social factors involved (that is, a strong commercial and private sector with a mainstream approach to television programming, high average viewing times and so on).

The research has focused on several specific points regarding the broadcasters' strategies, the content ideation and production in several genres (fiction, entertainment and current affairs) and, naturally, consumption habits and practices. The study ran from 2008 to 2012, and it was structured around several lines of enquiry (Grasso & Scaglioni, 2010; Barra & Scaglioni, 2013). First, a corpus of 25 TV products (of different genres and origins, especially Italian original productions and US imported ready-made programming) has been examined with desk analysis tools, particularly scrutinizing their textual extensions, both institutional (top-down) and grassroots, and the patterns of their circulation. Second, a virtual ethnography of online practices, discourses and spaces has mapped and examined the spaces and the players of the peculiar web and mobile-based social interaction and discourse surrounding TV shows, networks and platforms. Lastly, a complex and articulated set of qualitative field research has been put into place, with a longitudinal panel of six households, monitored for a year with in-depth individual and group interviews and consumption diaries, and with a supporting field study comprising various focus groups and individual interviews.

From this complex research on the Italian television and media scenario, there clearly emerges the image of a renewed television supply chain, which can be described via three defining concepts: "extension," "access" and "brand." First, contemporary television products are no longer primarily closed texts confined to the television medium alone, expanding a trend partially present since the early years of the medium. They are now complemented by myriad ancillary products, or extensions, created both officially, by the broadcasters or production companies, and unofficially, by grassroots consumers and fans. Second, viewers today have often more than one means of consuming television products. Indeed, multiple forms of access to the content (and to all its possible extensions) are now constantly available, as technology platforms for distributing and circulating the programmes and the associated viewing devices have proliferated and multiplied. And third, building effective brands (associated as much with individual products as with a network, a broadcaster or a digital platform) becomes the main key to guiding, steering and "restoring order"—as far as is possible—to this unprecedented complexity and fragmentation of consumption. Therefore, it is inside this environment that the actual practices of Italian television viewers have at least partially changed, and are still changing.

Mapping Convergent Viewers' Practices

To understand and interpret contemporary convergent viewers' actual practices, it is necessary to take due account of the overall context. If television content cannot be encapsulated in a clearly delimited and stable text, it becomes also explorable in all its transmedia extensions (Jenkins, 2003, 2009; Jenkins, Ford & Green, 2013; Clarke, 2013; Evans, 2011; Ibrus & Scolari, 2012), as the story's endpoint is altered by the media and television industry's aptitude for generating storytelling forms that span different media and build "narrative ecosystems" (Pescatore & Innocenti, 2012). The "touchpoints" between viewers and television products (Askwith, 2007) have multiplied, as have the forms and methods of access. For some global genres, such as US television series, which are often distributed outside their country of origin, the modes of viewing and the wealth of extensions are becoming even more complex in the light of the process of "national mediation" (Barra, 2009) that the product undergoes in production and adaptation for the secondary market where it is localized. Where a US TV series is generally a highly expanded text with many ancillary products in the original North American context, this richness is only partially reproduced in the international editions, and that depends on the national distributor (be it a free or a pay network). Moreover, through forms of access that are actually completely or partially illegal (such as streaming and downloading), viewers can access the foreign content in distinct time patterns.

Given this increased complexity, which is rooted equally in the extended television products and in the broadcasters' means of distribution and promotion, consumption practices and the forms of viewing engagement have to adapt, and can be distinguished into definite, distinct categories. In attempting to construct a model to reflect the convergent practices' characteristics and their diffusion, based on findings from the empirical research, and mixing different methods and layers of analysis, these practices can be assembled in the form of an inverted pyramid. This model then defines three distinct areas that differ according to the practices' complexity and circulation (Fig. 4.1).

One area contains convergent-consumption practices that are very widespread and not particularly complex. This first type of more lightweight, "superficial" convergent consumption embraces not only, for example, the use of the web as a resource for gaining a broader picture and obtaining information on television contents, but also the simple

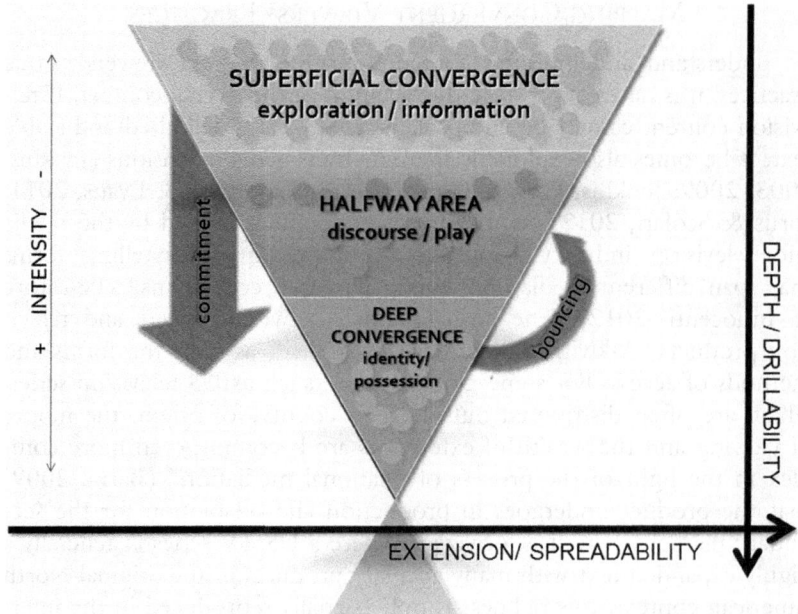

Fig. 4.1 The inverted-pyramid model of television convergent consumption practices. *Source* The authors

sharing of significant fragments of the series on viewers' personal social media pages (especially on Facebook). In general, the practices documented in this "superficial" area are mainly in regard to the viewers' attitudes to exploring and to finding information: The web, digital and social media, especially, become an increasingly "natural" and habitual digital complement to television watching, often via an ancillary second screen.

At the other end of the scale appears a set of decidedly more complex practices that are "deep" but much less widespread, associated with a group of highly motivated and engaged viewers. Downloading the subtitled episodes, soon after the original airing in another cultural and media context (as occurs very often with US TV series, and less with documentaries, factual programming or comedy shows), belongs to this area of great depth but limited breadth at the pyramid's base. Here, the convergent consumption practices acquire meanings associated more with (personal and group) identity and possession. Fandom, for instance, is frequently expressed through such deep consumption practices, in the sense both of defining identity (a fan of a US TV series usually synchronizes on the US scheduling time, without waiting for the Italian distribution window to broadcast the episodes) and of possession (for example, by collecting and keeping their favourite products, in physical or digital form, including the officially merchandized versions and objects).

Thus, there are two domains: of "superficial" and quite common but straightforward practices, on the one hand, and of "deep" practices that are much more complex and demanding for the viewer but also rarer, on the other. In the middle space between them lies a halfway area, an intermediate set of practices that are fairly frequent and of medium complexity for the television viewer. In this case, the television content becomes material for constructing a discourse or for playfully engaging with the text. By following a television series (legally or illegally) via streaming platforms, consumers not only avoid using the complex skills required for downloading, but they can also link up with a discourse community that anticipates the distribution timeframes or, more tritely, circumvents the time constraints of the schedule. Or, again, by sharing television use through social media, such as Facebook or Twitter, viewers can synchronize with a discourse community that comments on the shows in ironic, playful and irreverent vein (social TV).

The model sketched rapidly above, detailing three areas of convergent television audience practices classed by complexity and spread, also contains some elements of dynamism, thanks to the presence of several forces acting on it. Loyalty and commitment to a specific product may lead viewers, in fact, to "deepen" and extend their convergent consumption practices, as new devotees or fans of a TV series discover deeper and more complex new ways to engage and interact with their product of choice. In contrast, an opposing "bouncing" effect tends to make certain practices—and, above all, certain products often associated with a cult aura—less elitist, more visible and more widespread, thus producing lighter forms of fandom. Hence, certain viewing practices can rise from the bottom of the pyramid towards the top, and be more diffused. As will be clarified later, in fact, convergent consumption practices are always mutating; a snapshot taken in a single moment can categorize them only temporarily, as they are (probably) destined to evolve with time.

This inverted-pyramid model thus takes account also of "spreadability" and "drillability," respectively the expansive potential and the deep commitment of convergent media products explored by Henry Jenkins,

Sam Ford and Joshua Green (2013) or Jason Mittell (2015) across their widely influential works. On the one hand, content can go viral thanks to the audience's (often unexpected) grassroots activity. Jenkins et al. (2013, pp. 9–16) cite the video of Susan Boyle's singing performance on *Britain's Got Talent*, which spread on the web and social media well beyond the confines anticipated by the original broadcaster, thus clearly showing the importance of convergent practices in extending this content's popularity. In Italy, a similar episode with an international dimension unfolded with Sister Cristina, the singing nun on national *The Voice of Italy*. On the other hand, when viewers are interested in and passionate about a given product (like a TV series that they warm to and want to see all the way through as the plot unfurls), they are moved to adopt practices at greater depth, with a major involvement and engagement, closer to the pyramid's base.

Main Trends in Italian Convergent Television Consumption

In framing convergent television consumption within a model, however, we must not consider viewer behavior as stable and fixed, constant over the years, from television season to television season. Indeed, the development of the research over different television seasons enabled us to map a huge range of transformations, which fit into a temporal dynamic where the practices of TV consumption can change radically. Thus, trends, developments, changes and vanishing points in the Italian scenario can be identified that more clearly redefine the discontinuities, continuities and "returns to normality" after a first period of innovation or trial and error. The inverted pyramid then can become a useful arena to map the transformations, and to class them into general trends. Innovations affect the entire television and media landscape as a whole, and it is possible to divide them into four distinct (yet partially overlapping) categories, which emerge from the longitudinal study in the Italian context presented here but also indicate broader, more general trends.

A first category of television consumption practices, across the various genres, is connected to classic, broadcast, linear TV watching. Although the media offering is increasingly multifaceted and fragmented, content is still often channeled mainly through the traditional flows—free or pay models, on terrestrial or satellite distribution—built by networks, channels and schedules (Ulin, 2010; Barra, 2015).

The "generalist," mainstream output's power remains central, with its shows, its stars and its ability to create rituals and discourses. In fact, it endures as a "shop window for everyone," a place that is easy for many viewers to access for their first (more or less fortunate) encounter with a new show, which they will be able to start consuming only later via convergent practices on other platforms. Traditional television therefore remains a very important space which offers to audiences new content they do not know they like yet (but they might eventually love), through practices akin to so-called "showrooming" in physical shops before buying online. Programme viewing in this case may be more occasional and less continuous than with other means of consumption. Nonetheless, the loss of concentration on the single individual television text (replaced by a more general investment in the TV network, in its editorial policies, and in personal or collective viewing rituals and habits) is often compensated by a shared, participative consumption, whether in the residential and family unit, or with colleagues and friends, or via the forms of social TV.

In the mainstream arena, viewing choices are often made within a restricted roster of main networks and channels, a kind of personal, self-defined "walled garden" that seeks to reduce the complexity of a supply that is abundant even to excess. Despite the great and growing availability of platforms and content, viewers always congregate around a core of broadcasters, selected for their past reputation (that is, the youth-oriented programming of commercial network Italia 1 in the 1980s and 1990s), through each one's habits and traditions (that is, the favorite newscast, sportscast, or selection of prime-time recent movies), or for the clarity of their offering of shows, genres and prime-time appointments. Networks that carefully select and position procedural and crime series across their schedules, channels with talent or talk shows in their weekday evening slots, or stations with factual programming mainly intended towards female audiences in the afternoon, are just some of many possible examples of such a valorization through programming choices, as clearly emerged both in the analysis of online discourses and from the individual and group interviews.

In this framework, network branding is extremely important (Johnson, 2012; Grainge & Johnson 2015). For networks which cannot broadcast big, popular, high-budget TV shows, or in any case in a panorama where an oversupplied offering sometimes becomes indistinct or unnoticed, it is the broadcasters' brands (if they're well developed, positioned and established) that can build hype and interest—presenting, offering to national viewers, and sometimes imposing new (original or imported) shows. Through a strong historical tradition and/or effective promotion and communication, these channels can offer products that their viewers value on trust, "sight unseen." Networks' branding "animates" the programming, gives it space and visibility, and builds connections and engagement with the television audience. Thus, these operations add value to the most important programs of every network, as explicitly stated by television viewers, channeling interest in them and being able to turn them into success stories.

Only in this way can "classic" television, under certain conditions, act as a kind of "retaining wall" able to keep viewers interested in the small screen: a clear, consistent offering of content, brands and technologies (often in combination, as with the digital free or pay platforms) works as a brake on the "exodus" of fans and viewers from the broadcast TV universe. The ease and convenience of the available tools, the reliability of programming and the trust in a recognized brand are considered extremely important values by Italian viewers.

A second category of trends in convergent TV consumption practices that emerged from the research on the Italian context concerns the non-linear use of the medium—that is, the ability to isolate parts of the programming flow to watch (or watch again) via legal or illegal on-demand forms (Tryon, 2013), associated with new platforms and offerings presented by traditional TV operators, telecommunication companies and over-the-top players (including Netflix), or with forms of piracy.

Over the years, Italian consumers are progressively and visibly "mastering" all the digital tools provided by the networks or by other players in the audio-visual arena. Skills (both technological and practical, "operational") are gradually spreading, as are habits of using some of the available devices, with a choice of very simple and intuitive procedures. Examples include: the +1, +2 and +24 time-shifting of the channels, enabling viewers to cleverly manage their viewing time, and to catch up with already-started shows; the EPG, electronic programme guide, with the ability to "book" viewing times; and the automatic recording of unmissable programmes via a PVR (personal video recorder), or other actions on the broadcasting flow, including the pause function for live programming. The crucial variable here, more than a tool's actual potential, is how easy it is for it to be learnt and used, which gives some instruments an advantage over other options that may well be free of charge but are more cumbersome, such as illegal downloading. Therefore, the industry can win the battle against streaming and downloading when it provides easy access to content that is the same or better (including for its visual and sound quality). A further benefit then is flexibility: viewers can tailor their own schedules, using some tools and discarding the others, according to their specific needs and their particular emotional investment in the show.

With more decisive and permanent transitions to a nonlinear approach to programming, moreover, viewers do not turn back. Whatever tool they use to watch on the move or to escape from the constraints of the schedule, the shift towards on-demand is a real quantum leap, a step change for Italian audiences. After a first period of inevitable teething troubles and resistance—building a kind of momentum, in fact—it has become an established means of consumption. This development marks a major change in viewing diets and habits, and although it does not replace traditional television in its entirety, it does sometimes become the main viewing method for television and more generally audio-visual content, at least for some genres, such as TV series or feature films.

Lastly, recent years have also seen profound changes as regards illegal consumption, a quite diffused practice in Italy as in many other markets, such as an explicit trend towards what may jestingly be termed "mainstreaming." In other words, younger audiences, especially, but increasingly often mature adult audiences as well, are rejecting the (perceived) tedium and complications of downloading for a lighter, impulse-based form of viewing like illegal streaming, which requires no particular planning, even though the image quality is lower, the websites are rather unstable (with frequent changes of address, banners and pop-ups), and the video cannot be saved and stored.

A third category of changes in television consumption, exemplified by the research on Italian audiences, concerns viewing times and temporalities, which have become increasingly polarized. Indeed, the proliferation of the available television offering and of the opportunities to watch TV series and shows on multiple platforms tend to steer consumption towards two main temporal approaches at opposite ends of a continuum. That applies especially to scripted products (not only TV series but also factual programs, documentaries, animated cartoons and films).

On one hand, many viewers espouse the idea of synchronizing "to the extent that they can" to national or foreign programming times, following the Italian or the US schedule to the level that their language and other skills permit. Although audiences are still constrained by broadcasters' timings, they can follow several separate schedules—watching different products at different times—offered on free or pay national television or on US TV that they have somehow obtained via streaming, download or other forms of file exchange. For US TV series in particular, national viewers often transition from watching the first or the initial seasons on national TV networks, following the rhythms of broadcasting, to consuming the later seasons illegally (sometimes with fandom-produced subtitles in English or Italian; see Barra, 2009), in order to obtain them faster than the broadcasters are able to supply them, and to bridge the gaps and delays in the Italian schedules.

On the other hand, a different viewing pattern emerges that is quite entirely asynchronous, detached from specific screening times. Here, usually for some of their less favorite shows, viewers rely on the abundant repeats in the schedules and the availability on demand, hopping between channels or casually browsing the plentiful program offering. Repeats on the digital networks and the ever-available archive of nonlinear services form a sort of "infinite storage" of available shows to peruse in order to rediscover lost episodes, to watch recommended shows, to see a favorite episode again, or just to surf at random.

Lastly, habit is an important factor when choosing viewing times. Viewers tend to follow a program regularly and persistently over time when they come to settle on individual shows or a whole genre. For a crime series, viewing practices and times therefore may differ from those chosen for factual or quality television. Once established, however, they usually apply largely unchanged for years, including for new shows in the same genre or from the same network.

The fourth category of variations in convergent practices, emerging from the research, mainly concerns discourses, as television programs increasingly become a raw material for later reappropriation and reworking of both meaning and value.

A clear picture emerged, above all, of a progressive "dumbing down" and generalization of the information tools on television shows and networks. In this area, there is a strong tendency among TV viewers, especially in the mainstream, to more and more use non-specialist sources for information and other details and trivia about television programs. Individual series' forums, fan pages or specialized websites are no longer the main reference point they once were. Their place has now been taken by more "generalist," mainstream generic resources, such as Wikipedia, Yahoo! Answers, or (even more prosaically) a simple Google search.

In this respect, promotion and scheduling constitute often double-edged swords for TV series broadcasters. By raising a new show's profile and bringing it into the public eye, indeed, promotional discourses can both "persuade" viewers to watch the current series and "push" them to seek out the same series via illegal (or increasingly legal, for example, Netflix) means. Pay-TV programming, for instance, can "steer" people towards streamed or on-demand versions of more recent shows. Watching promos or the early episodes therefore "instils" a level of loyalty that TV cannot fulfill in the long term, and that may prompt viewers to move to various forms of illegal streaming, especially (and somehow paradoxically) for the most successful shows.

A last important trend is, then, the sharing of media discourses. On one hand, TV scheduling—of television series in particular, but also of other "intense" genres like talent shows or political talk shows—offers a broad corpus of content to tap. Consumers can share that material socially, both in real forums such as peer groups and in virtual environments as social networks (especially private ones, modeled on Facebook Messenger or WhatsApp). A clip, a song or photos of an actor or character help to define individual and social identities. On the other hand, the fragmented offering leads to a dearth of broadly popular shows, which lends greater value (partly through recommendations and word of mouth) to viewing choices asserted by individuals and groups. It is against this too often neglected but essential backdrop that public social-TV practices persist on Facebook or Twitter, often actively encouraged by broadcasters seeking to foster engagement (Barra & Scaglioni, 2014).

Conclusions: A Doubly Mobile Pyramid

It clearly emerges from the analysis of main trends happening in Italian television convergent consumption practices, as well as from the broadcasters' reactions to such an unstable and rapidly modifying environment, that the audience's convergent practices are continually evolving and changing direction, because of technological changes or programming innovations, cultural or social shifts, and economic and institutional factors. The sum of all these changes and variations is reflected in the television scenario as well as in the wider media arena, and impacts both at a national level and beyond, with the national responses to what is

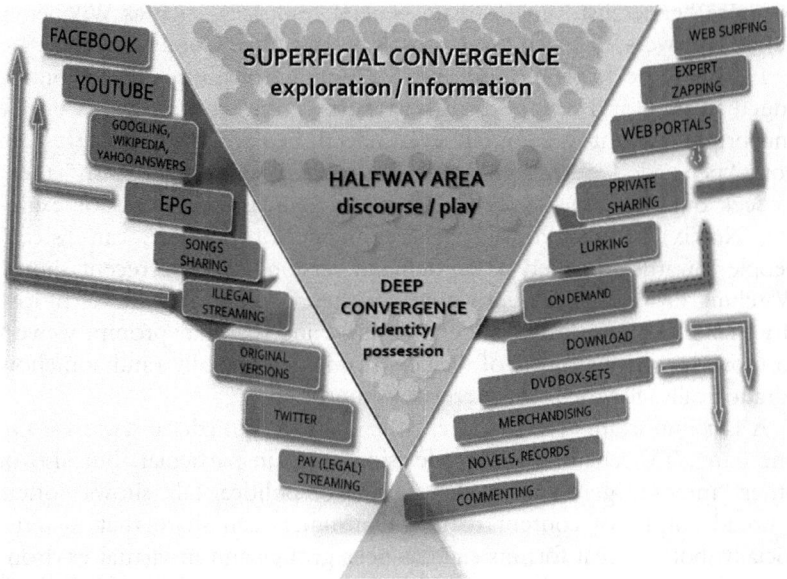

Fig. 4.2 Modifications of television convergent consumption practices on the inverted-pyramid model. *Source* The authors

happening abroad in foreign countries (that is formats, markets and so on) and at the same time with the participation of Italian television in larger global and transnational phenomena. The inverted-pyramid model of television convergent consumption practices proposed here (Fig. 4.2) emerges therefore as an especially useful tool at capturing these fluid, changing phenomena.

As shown before, the model is based on three dimensions of convergence (superficial, intermediate and deep), and three approaches corresponding to viewer program consumption. Although the model is stable, a wide scope remains for developments and for changing patterns, as some areas gain importance at the expense of others. In a few years, for example, downloading and DVD box sets of TV series have sunk into the depths of the pyramid, abandoned by the general public to remain the sole preserve of hardcore fans. Meanwhile, on-demand consumption, streaming, and the most sophisticated and complex uses of EPG have gradually risen to the surface, proficiently used by the mass audience. And new aggregations of practices have emerged, such as Twitter as a means of following a TV show's characters and actors, subtitling in a series's original language, and the extensive use of Facebook, Twitter social TV and second screens. Some practices rise and spread to broader audience strata, in some way penetrating the mainstream, while others lose importance or become the almost exclusive preserve of the fans and the most loyal viewers. In parallel with this fluidity, individual practices change meaning and value, signifying different things for different viewers.

As a consequence, the viewer's positioning and the depth of their convergent practices change generally over time, although they also alter in relation to the individual objects, to each program. In fact, the same viewer may adopt deep practices for one (favorite) show and quite superficial ones for many others. It is not right to believe that individual television users have a single constant attitude regarding the practices in the pyramid; rather, once again, their approach is somewhat variable and fluid. Based on one (more or less conscious) attribution of value to a single given show, to its genre or to the subjective "reservoir of meaning" in which it is set, indeed, a program is considered more or less suitable, more or less worthy of some convergent practices, at the expense of others that are nonetheless present in the toolbox.

Under the "umbrella term" of convergence (Marsden & Verhulst, 1999, pp. 3–5; Herkman, 2012, p. 371), it materializes a complex variety of evolving audience practices, different relationships with technologies and TV contents, new instruments and old habits, randomness, distinctions and overlapping. Single viewers can adopt contemporarily both convergent and de-convergent practices, according to their needs and desires. Each program (or genre, or network) is thus redefined by its consumption practices and lends itself to "naive" reworkings and original classifications, a fact that is not possible to ignore. And at the same time, the practices themselves constantly evolve, change form, hybridize and expand.

REFERENCES

Askwith, I.D. (2007). *Television 2.0. Reconceptualizing TV as an engagement medium*. Boston: MS thesis, MIT.

Barra, L. (2009). The mediation is the message. Italian regionalization of US TV series as co-creational work. *International Journal of Cultural Studies, 12*(5), 509–525.

Barra, L. (2015). *Palinsesto. Storia e tecnica della programmazione televisiva*. Roma-Bari: Laterza.

Barra, L., & Scaglioni, M. (2013). Risalite e discese. Le trasformazioni dei percorsi degli spettatori nell'ecosistema mediale. In C. Bisoni & V. Innocenti (Eds.), *Media mutations. Gli ecosistemi narrativi nello scenario mediale contemporaneo. Spazi, modelli, usi sociali* (pp. 165–174). Modena: Mucchi.

Barra, L., & Scaglioni, M. (2014). TV Goes Social. Italian broadcasting strategies and the challenges of convergence. *View. Journal of European Television History and Culture, 3*(6), 110–124.

Clarke, M. J. (2013). *Transmedia television. New trends in network serial production.* London: Bloomsbury.

De Sola Pool, I. (1983). *Technologies of freedom.* Cambridge (MA): Belknap Press.

Ellis, J. (2000). Scheduling: the last creative act in television? *Media, Culture and Society, 22*(1), 25–38.

Evans, E. (2011). *Transmedia television. audiences, new media, and daily life.* London: Routledge.

Grasso, A., & Scaglioni, M. (Eds.). (2010). *Televisione convergente La tv oltre il piccolo schermo.* Milano: Link RTI.

Grainge, P., & Johnson, C. (2015). *Promotional screen industries.* London: Routledge.

Herkman, J. (2012). Convergence or intermediality? Finnish political communication in the New Media Age. *Convergence, 18*(4), 369–384.

Ibrus, I., & Scolari, C. A. (Eds.). (2012). *Crossmedia innovations. Texts, markets, institutions.* Frankfurt: Peter Lang.

Jenkins, H. (2003). Transmedia storytelling. MIT Technology Review, 15 January.

Jenkins, H. (2006). *Convergence culture.* New York: NYU Press.

Jenkins, H. (2009). The revenge of the origami unicorn: Seven principles of transmedia storytelling. *Confessions of an Aca-Fan,* 12 December.

Jenkins, H., Ford, S., & Green, J. (2013). *Spreadable media. creating value and meaning in a networked culture.* New York: NYU Press.

Johnson, C. (2012). *Branding television.* London: Routledge.

Lotz, A. D. (2007). *The television will be revolutionized.* New York: New York University Press.

Marsden, C. T., & Verhulst, S. G. (Eds.). (1999). *Convergence in European digital tv regulation.* London: Blackstone Press.

Meikle, G., & Young, S. (2012). *Media convergence. Networked digital media in everyday life.* London: Palgrave.

Mittell, J. (2015). *Complex TV. The poetics of contemporary television storytelling.* New York: NYU Press.

Ortoleva, P. (2002). *Mediastoria. Mezzi di comunicazione e cambiamento sociale nel mondo contemporaneo.* Milano: il Saggiatore.

Pescatore, G., & Innocenti, V. (2012). Information architecture in contemporary television series. *Journal of Information Architecture, 4*(1–2), 57–72.

Scaglioni, M. (2011). *La tv dopo la tv. Il decennio che ha cambiato la televisione.* Milano: Vita e Pensiero.

Scaglioni, M., & Sfardini, A. (2008). *MultiTv. L'esperienza televisiva nell'età della convergenza.* Roma: Carocci.

Spigel, L., & Olsson, I. (Eds.). (2004). *Television after TV: Essays on a medium in transition.* Durham (NC): Duke University Press.

Szczepaniak, R. (Ed.). (2013). *Media convergence. Approaches and experiences,* Frankfurt: Peter Lang.

Tryon, C. (2013). *On demand culture. Digital delivery and the future of movies.* New Brunswick: Rutgers University Press.

Ulin, J. (2010). *The business of media distribution. Monetizing film, tv, and video content.* Burlington: Focal Press.

Van den Bulck, H. (2009). The last yet also the first creative act in television? *Media History, 15*(3), 321–344.

Ytreberg, E. (2002). Continuity in environments. The evolution of basic practices and dilemmas in northern television scheduling. *European Journal of Communications, 17*(3), 283–304.

AUTHORS' BIOGRAPHY

Luca Barra Luca Barra is Senior Assistant Professor at Università di Bologna, Italy, where he teaches Television and Broadcasting History and Digital Media. He is Senior Researcher at CeRTA (Research Centre on Television and Audiovisuals), Università Cattolica del Sacro Cuore, Milan. He is the author of the books *Palinsesto. Storia e tecnica della programmazione televisiva* (Laterza, Roma-Bari 2015) and *Risate in scatola* (Vita e Pensiero, Milan 2012), the co-editor of *Taboo Comedy. Television and Controversial Humour* (with C. Bucaria, Palgrave Macmillan, London 2016) and other two volumes, and he wrote various essays in edited collections and journals. He is Editorial Consultant for the Italian TV studies journal *Link. Idee per la televisione.*

Massimo Scaglioni Massimo Scaglioni is Associate Professor in Media History and Media Economics at Università Cattolica del Sacro Cuore, Milan, Italy. He is Head of Research at CeRTA (Research Centre on Television and Audiovisuals), and Editorial-Board Member of *VIEW. Journal of European Television History and Culture, Series* and *CS Comunicazioni sociali.* His publications include *Che cos'è la tv* (with A. Grasso, Garzanti, Milan 2003), *Tv di culto* (Vita e Pensiero, Milan 2006),*La tv dopo la tv* (Vita e Pensiero, Milan 2011) and *Il servizio pubblico televisivo* (Vita e Pensiero, Milan 2016). He has been Visiting Professor at Carleton University (Ottawa), Invited Professor at University of Nottingham (UK), and at Capital Normal University Beijing, Hong Kong Baptist University, Shanghai Theater Academy (China).

CHAPTER 5

Media Convergence and the Network Society: Media Logic(s), Polymedia and the Transition of the Public Sphere

Caja Thimm

Introduction

Few innovations have altered individual, social and political forms of communication and behavior as drastically as the internet. The net media's influence in almost every aspect of daily life is ever more visible, whether discussing how the internet serves as a tool for networking and real-time communication during the Arab Spring (Tufekci & Wilson, 2012), how computer games have revolutionized the very structures of entertainment, or how WikiLeaks has shaken international politics by introducing "leaking" as a new net-based option for transparency (Star & Keller, 2011).

Net media usage has become normality for an entire generation, who inhabit the internet as a true living space and regard this space as natural to them as a non-digital environment. This development can be retraced to the start of the millennium when text-based media and information exchange formed the core of digital social exchange in relatively static

C. Thimm (✉)
University of Bonn, Bonn, Germany
e-mail: thimm@uni-bonn.de

S. Sparviero et al. (eds.), *Media Convergence and Deconvergence*, Global Transformations in Media and Communication Research - A Palgrave and IAMCR Series, DOI 10.1007/978-3-319-51289-1_5

93

networks. The motives of today's "netizens," however, are no longer one-dimensional. The trend towards a dynamic-participatory medium can be described as a breakthrough in user empowerment. Digital networks and communities were born of social and communicative needs for interpersonal contact (Rheingold, 2000; Baym, 2010). Although the assumption that these networks give rise to a collective intelligence and a new culture of the "wisdom of crowds" is still much debated (Surowiecki, 2005), the idea of a pluralistic, deliberative public is intriguing. Some researchers characterize these changes within the public, political, secular, institutional and private spheres and in daily life as a pivotal "meta-process" (Krotz, 2007; Couldry & Hepp, 2013). One of the key observations on this type of mediated change is its character as a process over time (Lundby, 2009). The notion of process orientation is supported by models like the "phase model of mediatization" (Strömbäck, 2008), which conceptualizes mediatization as a multidimensional and inherently process-oriented concept. Hepp (2011), on the other hand, regards the media as a "molding force" for social change and describes the comprehensive process that shapes culture and society by medial communication, helping to explain social dynamics. The common baseline is that media have become so important because of how they are used in communicative behavior in society and how they help construct reality (Krotz, 2007). From this perspective, mediatization focuses on the increasing importance of the individual user, whose media activities shape social environments. So it is mainly the social factor of the media which influences societal change and is a driving force in the mediatization process.

As briefly described above, there is widespread agreement that one of the most viable forces behind this development is the internet, as technology has to be regarded a key issue for this process. Marked by characteristics like ubiquity (Thimm, 2004), user-generated content (Bruns, 2008), multimediality and portability (Chayko, 2008; Bächle & Thimm, 2014), the internet, and social media particularly, has gained increasing influence on people's lives. Whereas in the beginning these new media cultures were regarded by many either as ephemeral or transitory phenomena, today's media usage patterns clearly point to a profound change in society—the emergence of a digital society and a digital citizen (Mossberger et al., 2007).

Connected to these observations are manifold structural and individual changes, one of them being the profound transition of the public sphere. Regarding the new modes of participation as a central domain of societal change (Thimm, 2015), it is the option of user-generated publicity which can be regarded as a central manifestation for mediated change. These new usage cultures have also resulted in media adaption and technological development of almost uncountable platforms. This abundance of digital platforms has more recently been discussed as "platformization" (Helmond, 2015) or even as "platform society" (van Dijk, 2013).

This perspective opens up a more profound concept of the changes which are either caused by the media changes themselves or are accompanying the media changes from a societal perspective. For example, one of the most influential spheres for politics and democracy has been under particular pressure: the notion of the public sphere. Owing to the changing media technologies and their respective logics (more details below), which enable access and participation on a very different scale, the concept of the public sphere has been applied and linked to many issues and approaches in media and communication theory (Breese, 2011). The main underlying ideas, however, are based on the works of Habermas and his notion and conceptualization of the public sphere (Habermas, 1989). At the core of Habermas's work are the description of the evolution from opinion to public opinion and the socio-structural transformation of the latter. With the advent of the internet as a new driving force in society, the conceptualization of society as a "network society," characterized by "networks operated by information and communication technologies based in microelectronics and digital computer networks" (Castells, 2005, p. 32), lay the ground for an understanding of the public sphere as organized on the basis of media communication networks (Castells, 2008). In many works on the role of the internet in relation to the public sphere, authors have pointed at the potential or at the limits of the internet to advance political communication (for example, Dahlberg, 2007; Dahlgren, 2009; Papacharissi & De Fatima Oliveira, 2012). Less optimistic perspectives highlight possible downsides of political communication on the internet such as the fragmentation or polarization of society, the digital divide, the limited flow of information due to algorithmic power in the "filter bubble" (Pariser, 2011), and doubt the internet's participatory potential. However, in more recent works, particularly on social media, it has been argued that a more situated and contextualized approach is needed to assess the ways people engage and participate in specific online settings and for specific purposes (see contributions in Einspänner et al., 2014).

Taking up these first observations, this chapter tries to link the concept of convergence to a concept which specifically focuses on the role of technology and its embeddedness in interpersonal and institutional context: the concept of media logic. To demonstrate how media logic and the connected concept of media grammar play out in society, the notion of the digital public sphere will be discussed as an example.

NETWORK SOCIETY AND CONVERGENCE

The many social, political and cultural changes, which come along with such a transformation process are closely linked to the fact that the media are not isolated technologies anymore, but form a cohesive system in their own right. Based on this perspective, Castells formulated his concept of the "network society" (2005) and its consequences for politics and political participation (Castells, 2008). Taking up the notion of the network as a central metaphor for the twenty-first century, the concept of convergence needs to be reflected accordingly. For one thing, are social media just platforms "where different technologies converge" (Sacco, 2016, p. 365), or are they "converged media" by nature? If the term convergence is to be adapted in a sense-making way, we need to look at the many changes which have recently shaped media usage all over the world. It needs to be questioned, at least, whether the concept of a network society in the reading of Castells still entails a kind of convergence, as put forward by Jenkins (2006) or Hasebrink & Popp (2006).

In this chapter it will be argued that the phenomena which used to be described collectively as convergence have started to reach a level of complexity which can no longer be embraced by the convergence concepts alone. For one, convergence as a term implies a transition process, which for many new social media platforms does not seem to be applicable anymore: they are already polymediated (see below). Furthermore, the concept of convergence does not embrace the feeling of immersion, which is characteristic for today's media cultures in the digital age. Just looking at the millions of Pokémon-GO players, who stare at little screens without any awareness of their physical surroundings, gives a first taste of things to come.

Additionally, the societal embeddedness of digital activities, and the multiple social contexts which shape people's lives, frame this debate. With participatory digital media, citizens have the power to aggregate and filter news, post their own views online and remix media content, which is based on traditional media outlets. With increasing international connectivity enabled by the internet and social media networks, new civic duties and roles are emerging. On a global level, individuals can now actively monitor and comment on international affairs and engage in political issues irrespective of state boundaries, thereby becoming globally effective. Which way such new communication and activity options reshape the media development is another important question for a digital society. The notion of the public sphere, which is closely connected to political information and democracy, has come particularly under pressure. If everybody can produce news and participate in public—who determines the value of information and the role of public discourse?

Consequently we have to ask: If convergence does not grasp these digital worlds anymore and needs to be deconstructed, how do we explain media and societal change? Which approach could replace or substitute convergence?

In this contribution, the concepts of "polymedia" and "network media logic" are be introduced into the discussion, as they might add valuable insights into the rising demand for an explanatory model of media and societal change.

Convergence and Media Logic

The changes, which have been brought about by social media like Facebook, Twitter, Instagram or Snapchat, have started to change the conditions and practices of social interaction. There is an intricate dynamic between social media platforms, mass media, users and social institutions. In order to conceptualize the linkage between social practices and digital technologies as defining environments, Altheide and Snow developed what was described as "mass media logic" (Altheide & Snow, 1979). This approach was meant to identify the role of the media's powerful discourse outside their institutional boundaries. Altheide & Snow (1979) defined (mass) media logic as a set of principles or common-sense rationality cultivated in and by media institutions which penetrate every public domain and dominate its organizing structures. Their notion of media logic focused on an institutional perspective in which the distributed contents of mass media and their "bureaucratized media logic" transform and shape "the meanings of knowledge of social institutions, including politics" (p. 247). In a social environment, in which technologies influence our daily lives in many respects and in which media have turned into tools for participatory cultures of all kinds, it seems necessary to take a closer look at critical reflections on new media logics in the sense of multiple and interconnected media and their specific logic(s), or as Hjarvard (2008, p. 113) put it: "The term 'media logic' refers to the institutional and technological modus operandi of the media, including the ways in which media distribute material and symbolic resources and operate with the help of formal and informal rules." Until recently, the notion of media logics has primarily been used to describe the functions of mass media and in particular news media in relation to the logics of the political institutions. With the advent of many new forms of media, in particular various forms of digital and interactive media, the notion of media logics has been expanded and diversified to cover these new media as well as their influences in domains other than politics. We need to develop a concept of media logics in the age of new media, in particular social network media. This involves a careful examination of the different dimensions or layers of logics, including technological, commercial, social and semiotic dimensions. Furthermore, we need to develop an understanding of media logics that allows us to comprehend the functioning of media at the level of both societal structure and individual agency.

Overall, a variety of (overlapping) logics seem to be in effect—especially against the backdrop of digitalization and the ubiquity of the internet. For one, the internet requires a certain approach to media logics, for it is constructed and ruled by algorithms and filters, which are mainly programmed and controlled by commercial and/or institutional organizations. Besides that, users have the power to selectively use media to retrieve information, to connect with peers and to engage as consumers or politically active citizens, thereby changing the media environment by means of their individual actions. Not only does the ubiquitous availability of digital media influence people's communicative practices in their private and professional lives, but by its adoption in various social and cultural contexts media technology itself is changed, transformed and further developed.

Network Media Logic

Given today's digital network society (Castells, 2005), it seems reasonable to speak of "classical" media logic research (Altheide & Snow, 1979;

Altheide & Snow, 1992; Altheide, 2013), which at the time entailed the media logics of traditional media systems such as television. More recent approaches (Hjarvard, 2008) see media as reflexively acting institutions that construct (social) reality. Within this process, new research highlights a multitude of different angles (see Thimm et al., forthcoming). Particularly, the perspective of user activities on social media has led to the adaption of theoretical approaches, such as in Klinger & Svensson (2014). They conceptualize a "network media logic," comparing mass media and digital media in terms of dimensions of "producing content, distributing information and using media" (Klinger & Svensson, 2014, p. 1241). Van Dijk & Poell (2013), argued in the same direction, discussing a "social media logic" with four grounding principles: programmability, popularity, connectivity and datafication. Overall, it can be observed that finally technology has started to play an increasingly important role in the debate, beyond all fears of technological determinism (Katzenbach, 2012). More and more, algorithms are regarded as powerful players, which control data selection and determine user activities (Steiner, 2012). Some even see an "algorithmic turn" (Uricchio, 2011) or "automated media" (Napoli, 2014).

In times of a media system, in which a continuous stream of new evolving digital applications influences the individual and society, the concept of media logics can hence be regarded as an important approach for a better understanding of the relation between the users and their activities online. On the one hand, "the free web" is determined by algorithms and filter models, which are mainly programmed by commercial or institutional organizations. On the other hand, people selectively use media to retrieve information, to connect with others, and perform action. These activities are based more and more on social media logics and the polymedia affordances which come along with these platforms. From this perspective, convergence needs to be embedded as part of the media logic.

Converged Media and Polymedia

New technologies shed a different light not only on the process of convergence but also on the social and technical environment connected to it, or as Arango-Forero et al., (2016, p. 21) phrase it: "Convergence is not solely the way in which media contents are given new meanings by the users but the way itself in which they hold an interdependent narrative and technicality." Further down (p. 24) they specify: "In a sense, technological changes are more than just instrumental changes for communication; they are true transformations which slowly draw new boundaries to a communication culture which was before segmented by bound media."

To describe this transformation and dissolving of segmentation more precisely, the media logic of the platforms and their nature as "polymedia" (Madianou & Miller, 2013) are now discussed in more detail.

Most of the social media, which nowadays are the base for participatory online cultures, relate to other media platforms or the traditional media by cross-referencing in one way or the other: some by links, others by embedding media content automatically. Hence, they are based on techniques of convergent user cultures, or, as Madianou & Miller, (2013) described it more appropriately, are polymedial by nature. The concept of polymedia was introduced in 2012 (Madianou & Miller) in the context of intercultural media use. The authors define it as follows:

> [A]n emerging environment of communicative opportunities that functions as an "integrated structure" within which each individual medium is defined in relational terms in the context of all other media. In conditions of polymedia the emphasis shifts from a focus on the qualities of each particular medium as a discrete technology, to an understanding of new media as an environment of affordances of interconnected media. (Madianou & Miller, 2013, p. 170)

Under these conditions, so their argument goes, the media themselves change: "[T]he very nature of each individual medium is radically changed by the wider environment of polymedia, since it now exists in a state of contrast, but also synergy, with all others" (Madianou & Miller, 2013, p. 170). They point particularly to the social contexts which are implied by such connected media, and argue that the "first thing we need to understand about polymedia is how the media's functional propensities underpin their relational definitions and our understanding of them as an integrated structure" (Madianou & Miller, 2013, p. 183).

Consequently, social media platforms like Facebook or Twitter need to be conceptualized as "polymedia," because they no longer demand user activities of crossmedia activities, such as changing channels or platforms, but rather offer many different media in one. This is due to the network logics, which have shaped user activities since the advent of Web 2.0 technologies.

In order to describe more precisely what the authors regard as the "environment of affordances of interconnected media," it seems necessary to include the media logic and the technical affordances of the media as a category for polymedia. Most social media are converged platforms and thereby polymedia by nature, as they combine a group of media ("discrete technology") on their user interface and integrate diverse media, textual as well as visual.

This approach can be explained more clearly when looking at the interfaces of social media platforms. Twitter, for example, allows the combination of text, image and film in one tweet, without necessarily showing all the reference options on the screen. On Twitter there are only 140 signs open to the user, but the 140-character constraint does not foreclose a complex semiotic system. One can, for example, insert hyperlinks in a tweet in order to expand the 140-character limit. By adding multi-modal content (photos, videos and links to other websites) the user is able to substantiate statements by, for example, uploading a picture of proof of a particular newsworthy situation. Inserted hyperlinks to online articles or blog postings can provide additional background information. Hyperlinks are visually stimulating and can be seen as narrative elements within a discussion on Twitter. The function of embedding hyperlinks is one of four specific processes that contribute to the conceptualization of Twitter as a "discourse universe" (Thimm et al., 2011). The user is able to adapt the discursive system of Twitter language on multiple levels by the use of four signifiers: @ for addressing or mentioning, # for tagging, http:// for linking and RT for republishing, as depicted in the "Functional Operator Model of Twitter" in Fig. 5.1.

How one tweet can codify a whole political agenda can, for example, be seen in Fig. 5.2.

Regarding Twitter as a polymedia, which is based on converged discrete technologies, does not outrule the fact that polymedia environments can be dominated by a single media logic, such as in the case of Twitter, with its specific algorithms and technological options and limitations. In this context we need to ask how user perceptions and user cultures are reflected in social media logics. How this could be done systematically is now approached by introducing the concept of media grammar.

Fig. 5.1 Functional operator model of Twitter. *Source* The author and @ hadearkandil

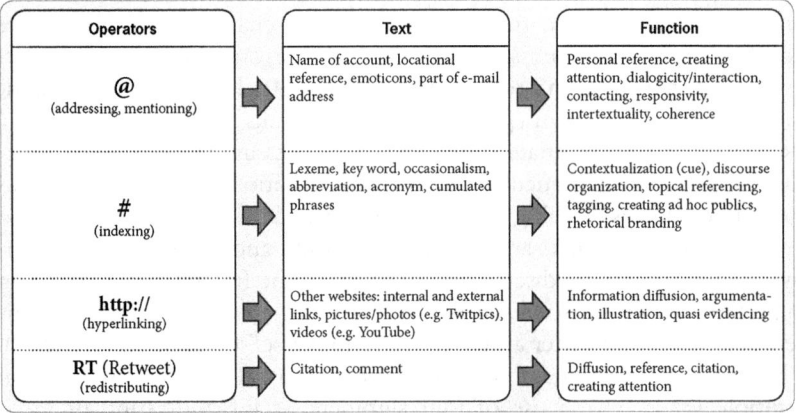

Fig. 5.2 Tweet operators in context. *Source* The author

Polymedia, Media Logic and Media Grammar

One of the most important aspects of the relation between polymedia, media logics and digital discourse is the fact that the logics of the technology in question can have formatting influences on the discourse itself. For example, on Twitter, the introduction of a hashtag can be regarded as the beginning of the formation of a discourse pattern. If the topic gets attention from a wider audience, the phenomenon of the formation of a "hashtag family" can be observed frequently. For example, in the case of the Paris murders at Charlie Hebdo in January 2015, a large variety of hashtags was created, such as #CharlieHebdo, #WeAreAllCharlie, #NousSommesCharlie, #JeSuisCharlie and others.

To better explain these usage cultures the concept of "media grammar" is now introduced briefly (for more details see Thimm, forthcoming). Media grammar refers to the within-media properties and property rules, which shape and constitute polymedia as a system. Central elements of the concept of media grammar are two different levels of grammar: (1) the "surface grammar," (2) the "constitutive property grammar."

Surface grammar (language, semiotic signs, sound, and so on) is visible and accessible to the users and (for some media) open to the creativity of the users (like in mash-ups, language creation, links, and so on). Surface grammar guides through the digital environment of the platform and is subject to usability and user acceptance.

Property grammar on the other hand is constitutive of the medium itself and determines the rules and the functional level of the surface grammar. Property grammar is ruled by algorithms, is not accessible to the users and cannot be modified by users either. As such, it is the basis for the network logics.

When focusing on network media (or social media) , media grammar points particularly to the interplay between the within-media properties, rules and regulations, which shape and constitute the media as a system on one hand and format content (media logic), and (partly) the communicative practices (agency) on the other. This perspective enables a more analytical assessment of the affordances and properties of the platforms themselves. When looking at the media practices, which means taking a user perspective, the approach of the media grammar also opens up categories for the differentiation of media platforms. One of the problems of many of the models on social media is the overgeneralization of these platforms. By no means do platforms like Snapchat, Twitter or Instagram work by the same functionalities, rules or mechanism. On the contrary, the more diverse the platform landscape gets, the more diverse are the user options regarding the respective platforms. Consequently, social media determine content and communicative practices via their specific logic, which can be understood as the implementation of a specific social media grammar. Communicative practices are performed within the framework of this specific social media grammar that allows for using functions and affordances, enabling certain communicative practices while constraining others.

From analyzing the options given in the property grammar, it becomes evident that the role of many platforms and their powerful owners, be it Google or Facebook, are relying on a non-transparent amalgamation of surface and property grammar. The allure, or rather illusion, of media literacy is often based on mastering the surface grammar and neglecting the lack of access to the underlying property grammar. Therefore the call for more transparency would have to include a more differentiated view on digital literacy.

This holds particularly true for the role of social media in the digital public sphere. It therefore seems necessary to reflect on the changes in media usage and media cultures based on the network logics which enable such new forms of participation.

CONSEQUENCES OF CONVERGED MEDIA AND POLYMEDIA PLATFORMS: MINI-PUBLICS

Media convergence has empowered users to produce and distribute their own content, with on-demand and mobile services open access to millions of websites, and users can engage with one another or with many others via peer-to-peer technologies. Polymedia platforms are enabling live witnessing and reporting such as is offered by Periscope on Twitter, with journalism undergoing massive changes due to the "convergence of news media" (Villi et al., 2016). All of these changes are contributing to the massive societal transition process of mediatization, which is not only relevant for the media themselves, but also entails an evolution of the public sphere towards a "digital public sphere" (Thimm et al., 2014).

Whereas in the pre-digital age mass media played a decisive role in formatting and influencing the public sphere, digital discourse networks do not have such widespread impact. Hence, it has been argued that agenda-setting processes have to be so reconceptualized as to include social media. Social media are perceived and experienced as assertive technologies, allowing users to expose their privacy, tastes, personality and convictions, without censorship. Consequently, postures of denunciation and protest find a renewed space for expression. One aspect of the social utility of social media relates to their possible use as "counter public spheres" (Downey & Fenton, 2003), especially for those otherwise devoid of access to the media sphere because of their low social visibility or their discourses considered extremist. For these internet users, the word of the authorities (media, politicians, intellectuals and moral authorities) is questioned, challenged, or even turned against.

More recently, there are particularly the socio-communicative functionalities of the big social networks, which have spawned new forms of mediatized publics (Bohman, 2004; Thimm et al., 2014). By going online, civic discourses expand and pluralize the existing systems of creating the public sphere, allowing the expression of socio-political concerns not only to political elites but to everyone. Such civic media activities have also started to shape the news agenda, circumventing the traditional gatekeepers such as TV or print media. Nowadays, many newspapers take up issues from the digital agenda set in social media environments, use social networking sites for their own news distribution, or develop their presence on social media platforms.

Overall, there can be no doubt that the transition of the public sphere in the direction of a digital public sphere marks an important societal change, as digital spaces can be a venue for the renewal of public discourses on all matters. Consequently, more and more media scholars call for a "rethinking of the public sphere" (Lunt & Livingstone, 2013).

In order to better understand the transition of the public sphere towards a digital public sphere from the perspective of polymedia platforms, smaller publics have to be included as important spaces for the digital presence. These smaller publics have been conceptualized as emergent "mini-publics." So far, mini-publics have been described as smaller circles of (better-) informed groups, which engage in information exchange processes and discourses (Bohmann, 2004; Goodin & Dryzek, 2006). Such a restricted perspective on mini-publics does not, however, offer a feasible approach for understanding the dynamics of online discourses, such as, for example, the outbreak of intense online debates on social networking sites. If we see opinion formation and debates as a central quality of new network cultures online, we have to regard smaller publics such as a Facebook discussion thread as a constitutive subset and element of the digital public sphere and not as a second-rate public, which has fallen "victim to fragmentation" (Webster & Ksiazek, 2012, p. 42). Second, the size of the group should not be limited to a number of persons "small enough to be genuinely deliberative," as demanded by Goodin & Dryzek (2006, p. 220). This condition does not reflect the online realities of many net-based groups, which are characterized by silent spectators or "lurkers," eclectically active "clicktivists," and highly engaged activists (Christensen, 2011).

Recently a first approach on a typology of mini-publics was put forward in Thimm (2015), and Einspänner-Pflock et al. (2015, p. 172). In this model a typology of mini-publics based on the categories "user-initiated mini-publics," "event-driven mini-publics," and "commercially launched mini-publics" was put forward. Additionally, other framing factors were isolated, such as the temporal perspective in "ad hoc mini-publics" and "over-time mini-publics" (p. 174). Another factor to include is the originator of each mini-public (institutional, private or organizational).

A variety of online mini-publics, as platform-based mini-publics, can be differentiated. These mini-publics exist on one media platform only and are based on the media logics of the digital environment (like YouTube mini-publics). On the other hand, mini-publics run across individual platforms and combine platforms, therefore contributing to the character of the digital public sphere as inter- and transmedial. Users not only engage on various polymedia platforms like Twitter or Facebook but also move between these social media and traditional media. Consequently, these mini-publics are characterized by a high intensity and frequent activities on all types of media and mostly engage a larger public.

Polymedia mini-publics can be regarded as important spaces for convergent user activities, particularly for political contexts. The easy cross-referencing options, which are enabled by the media logic of the platform involved, make distribution and participation much more convenient for the users. Citizens have started to take these options of the affordances connected to such participatory techniques for granted, and have developed various digital cultures based on these logics. This has led not only to the emergence of a growing diversity in social media usage, but also to creative appropriations of the respective media logics in order to further intensify interpersonal usage across single media. In particular the widespread usage of chat tools like WhatsApp has shown that polymedia environments, in which one platform offers simultaneous access to text, image and film, have become an essential for user adoption.

SUMMARY AND OUTLOOK: NEW UNIVERSES

In discussions of the understanding and conceptualization of convergence it has been pointed out repeatedly that convergence is used as a metaphor for a whole set of phenomena (see Balbi, Chap. 2 in this volume). But particularly the fact that technology and user cultures have become interwoven has shaped social contexts in a decisive way. Though these contexts have not been redirected to the technologies as a driving force, it does however seem particularly important to look at the interwoven system of technology and its respective logics to understand user cultures and the processes of media adoption in respect of the societal effects. In particular, developing a contextualized approach towards technology could open up important insights for convergent cultures as part of user cultures. Often technological frameworks are either not included or oversimplified in their role for social change, and often enough there is an underlying fear of being technologically determined (Katzenbach, 2012). This is particularly true for social media usage and its effects on the individual participants as well as on the role of politics and networks.

If convergence can be redirected to the changes in single media logics or, more convincingly, to network logics, the question still remains whether there is a plurality of media logics or if we can discover one underlying logic for all. Likewise, Couldry (2014) asks:

> First, do all media have a logic? Is it the same logic? ... Second, when media platforms and outlets change over time, do they acquire a wholly new media logic...? Third, if we limit the notion of media logic to media formats, does that capture enough of how media influence the social? (p. 55)

Such an approach towards media logics allows an understanding of creative appropriations such as mash-ups or cross-linking. Additionally, changes in media organizations as well as in mass media's technological affordances have rendered the explanatory power of media logic as a legitimizing force even more intriguing.

Linking this back to the question of whether or not the term and the concept of convergence still holds an analytical value, it could be argued that we need to consider the creation of "new universes" (Montpetit, 2016, p. 52) as results of new technologies, which are by definition already converged and need to be looked at as new narratives, since convergence in technology

> [h]as now moved the media discourse from the simple transposition of similar content from one platform to the next, [and] the notions of transmedia storytelling have opened a vast array of creative expressions in cable and web television, adding to the creations of app developers, authors and video game producers to create entire new universes. (Montpetit, 2016, p. 52)

It does seem necessary to better understand the system behind these narrations and how they are perceived—do users still perceive social media, for example, as different platforms? Which are the qualities, which are the affordances and logics behind online platforms that make them a "new universe"? The allure of such focus becomes particularly poignant when new technological and economic mechanisms emerge, transforming the character of the media landscape at large.

References

Altheide, D. L. (2013). Media logic, social control, and fear. *Communication Theory, 23*(3), 223–238.

Altheide, D., & Snow, R. (1979). *Media logic.* Beverly Hills: Sage.

Altheide, D. L., & Snow, R. P. (1992). Media logic and culture: reply to oakes. *International Journal of Politics, Culture, and Society, 5*(3), 465–472.

Arango-Forero, G., Roncallo-Dow, S., & Uribe-Jongbloed, E. (2016). Rethinking convergence: A new world to describe an old idea. In A. Lugmayr & C. Dal Zotto (Eds.), *Media Convergence Handbook* (Vol. 1, pp. 17–26)., Journalism, Broadcast and Social Media Aspects of Convergence New York: Springer.

Bächle, T. C., & Thimm, C. (Eds.) (2014). Mobile Medien—Mobiles Leben. Neue Technologien, Mobilität und die mediatisierte Gesellschaft. Münster: Lit.

Baym, N. (2010). *Personal connections in the digital age.* Chichester: Polity Press.

Bohman, J. (2004). Expanding dialogue: The internet, the public sphere, and prospects for transnational democracy. *The Sociological Review, 52*(1), 131–155.

Breese, E. B. (2011). Mapping the variety of public spheres. *Communication Theory, 21*(2), 130–149.

Bruns, A. (2008). *Blogs, Wikipedia, second life and beyond: From production to produsage.* New York: Peter Lang.

Castells, M. (2005). The network society: From knowledge to policy. In M. Castells & G. Cardoso (Eds.), *The Network Society: From Knowledge to Policy* (pp. 3–21). Washington, D.C.: John Hopkins University.

Castells, M. (2008). The new public sphere: global civil society, Communication networks, and global governance(s). *Annals of the American Academy of Political and Social Science, 616*(1), 78–93.

Chayko, M. (2008). *Portable communities. The social dynamics of online and mobile connectedness.* Albany: State University of New York.

Christensen, H. S., (2011). Political activities on the Internet: slacktivism or political participation by other means? *First Monday, 16,* 2–7 Retrieved from http://journals.uic.edu/ojs/index.php/fm/article/view/3336/2767.

Couldry, N. (2014). Media logic revisited. In A. Hepp & F. Krotz (Eds.), *Mediatized worlds: Culture and society in a media age.* London: Palgrave.

Couldry, N., & Hepp, A. (2013). Conceptualizing mediatization: Contexts, traditions. *Arguments. Communication Theory, 23*(3), 191–202.

Dahlberg, L. (2007). The internet, deliberative democracy, and power: Radicalizing the public sphere. *International Journal of Media and Cultural Politics, 3*(1), 47–64.

Dahlgren, P. (2009). *Media and political engagement: citizens, communication, and democracy.* Cambridge: Cambridge University Press.

Downey, J., & Fenton, N. (2003). New media, counter publicity and the public sphere. *New Media & Society, 5*(2), 185–202.

Einspänner-Pflock, J., Anastasiadis, M., & Thimm, C. (2015). Ad hoc mini-publics on Twitter: Citizen participation or political communication? Examples from the German National Election 2013. In A. Frame & G. Brachotte (Eds.), *Forms and Functions of Political Participation in a Digital World* (pp. 52–59). London: Routledge.

Einspänner-Pflock, J., Dang-Anh, M., & Thimm, C. (Eds.) (2014). Digitale Gesellschaft—Partizipationskulturen im Netz. Berlin: Lit.

Goodin, R. E., & Dryzek, J. S. (2006). Deliberative impacts: The macro-political uptake of mini-publics. *Politics and Society, 34*(2), 219–244.

Habermas, J. (1989). *The structural transformation of the public sphere: An inquiry into a category of bourgeois society.* Cambridge: Polity Press.

Hasebrink, U., & Popp, J. (2006). Media repertoires as a result of selective media use. A conceptual approach to the analysis of patterns of exposure. *Communications, 31*(3), 369–387.

Helmond, A. (2015). The platformization of the web: Making web data platform ready. *Social Media + Society,* 1–11. doi:10.1177/2056305115603080.

Hepp, A. (2011). *Medienkultur. Die Kultur mediatisierter Welten.* Wiesbaden: VS Verlag.

Hjarvard, S. (2008). *The mediatization of society. Nordicom review, 29*(2), 105–134.

Jenkins, H. (2006). *Convergence culture: Where old and new media collide.* New York: New York University Press.

Katzenbach, C. (2012). Technologies as institutions: Rethinking the role of technology in media governance constellations. In N. Just & M. Puppis (Eds.), *Trends in communication policy research: New theories, methods and subjects, intellect* (pp. 117–138). Chicago: Chicago University Press.

Klinger, U., & Svensson, J. (2014). The emergence of network media logic in political communication: A theoretical approach. *New Media Society, 17*(8), 1241–1257.

Krotz, F. (2007). The meta-process of mediatization as a conceptual frame. *Global Media and Communication, 3*(3), 256–260.

Lundby, K. (Ed.). (2009). *Mediatization: concept.* Changes, Consequences, New York: Lang.

Lunt, P., & Livingstone, S. (2013). Media studies' fascination with the concept of the public sphere: Critical reflections and emerging debates. *Media, Culture and Society, 35*(1), 87–96.

Madianou, M., & Miller, D. (2013). Polymedia: Towards a new theory of digital media in interpersonal communication. *International Journal of Cultural Studies, 16*(2), 169–187.

Montpetit, M.-J. (2016). The 2nd Convergence: A technology viewpoint. In A. Lugmayr & C. Dal Zotto (Eds.), *Media convergence handbook, Vol. 1: Journalism, broadcast and social media aspects of convergence* (pp. 29–58). New York: Springer.

Mossberger, K., Tolbert, C. J., & McLean, R. (2007). *Digital citizenship: The internet, society, and participation.* Boston: MIT Press.

Napoli, P. M. (2014). Automated media: An institutional theory perspective on algorithmic media production and consumption. *Communication Theory, 24*(3), 340–360.

Papacharissi, Z., & de Fatima Oliveira, M. (2012). Affective news and networked publics: The rhytms of news storytelling on #Egypt. *Journal of Communication, 62*(2), 266–282.

Pariser, E. (2011). *The filter bubble: What the internet is hiding from you.* New York: The Penguin Press.

Rheingold, H. (2000). *The virtual community: Homesteading on the electronic frontier.* Cambridge, MA: MIT Press.

Sacco, V. (2016). How does social media shape media convergence? The case of journalists covering war and conflict. In A. Lugmayr, C. Dal Zotto, (Eds.), *Media convergence handbook, Vol. 1.: Journalism, broadcast and social media aspects of convergence.* New York: Springer (pp. 363–87). Berlin: Springer.

Star, A., & Keller, Bill. (2011). *Open secrets: WikiLeaks, war and American diplomacy.* New York: The New York Times Company.

Steiner, C. (2012). *Automate this. How algorithms came to rule our world.* New York: Penguin Books.

Strömböck, J. (2008). Four phases of mediatization: an analysis of the mediatization of politics. *International Journal of Press/Politics, 2008*(13), 26–228.

Surowiecki, J. (2005). *The wisdom of crowds.* New York: Anchor Books.

Thimm, C. (2004). Mediale Ubiquität und soziale Kommunikation. In U. Thiedecke (Ed.), *Soziologie des cyperspace. Medien, strukturen und semantiken* (pp. 51–69). Wiesbaden: VS Verlag.

Thimm, C. (2015). The mediatization of politics and the digital public sphere: Participatory dynamics in mini-publics. In A. Frame & G. Brachotte (Eds.), *Forms and Functions of Political Participation in a Digital World* (pp. 167–183). London: Routledge.

Thimm, C. (2017, forthcoming): Media technology and media logic(s)—Introducing Media Grammar. In C. Thimm, M. Anastasiadis, & J . Einspänner (Eds.), *Media logic(s) revisited: Modelling the interplay between media institutions, media technology and societal change.* Basingstoke: Palgave MacMillan.

Thimm, C., Anastasiadis, M. & Einspänner-Pflock, J. (Eds.) (2017, forthcoming). *Media logics revisited.* Basingstoke: Palgave Macmillan.

Thimm, C., Dang-Anh, M., & Einspänner, J. (2011). Diskurssystem Twitter: Semiotische und handlungstheoretische Perspektiven. In M. Anastasiadis & C. Thimm (Eds.), *Social Media: Theorie und Praxis digitaler Sozialität* (pp. 265–286). Frankfurt/New York: Lang.

Thimm, C., Dang-Anh, M., & Einspänner, J. (2014). Mediatized politics—structures and strategies of discursive participation and online deliberation on Twitter. In F. Krotz & A. Hepp (Eds.), *Mediatized worlds: Culture and society in a media age* (pp. 253–269). Basingstoke: Palgrave Macmillian.

Thimm, C., Einspänner, J. & Dang-Anh, M. (2012). Politische deliberation online. Twitter als Element des politischen Diskurses. In A. Hepp & F. Krotz. (Eds.), *Mediatisierte Welten: Beschreibungsansätze und Forschungsfelder* (pp. 283–307). Wiesbaden: VS.

Tufekci, Z., & Wilson, C. (2012). Social media and the decision to participate in political protest: Observations from tahrir square. *Journal of Communication, 62*(2), 363–379.

Uricchio, W. (2011). The algorithmic turn: Photosynth, augmented reality and the changing implications of the image. *Visual Studies, 26*(1), 25–35.

Van Dijck, J. (2013). *The culture of connectivity: A critical history of social media.* New York, NY: Oxford University Press.

Van Dijk, J., & Poell, T. (2013). Understanding social media logic. *Media and Communication, 1*(1), 2–14.

Villi, M., Matikainen, J., & Khaldarova, I. (2016). Recommend, tweet, share: User-distributed content (UCD) and the convergence of news and social networks. In A. Lugmayr & C. Dal Zotto (Eds.), *Media convergence handbook* (Vol. 1, pp. 289–306)., Journalism, Broadcast and Social Media Aspects of Convergence New York: Springer.

Webster, J., & Ksiazek, T. (2012). The dynamics of audience fragmentation: Public attention in an age of digital media. *Journal of Communication, 62*(1), 39–56.

AUTHOR BIOGRAPHY

Caja Thimm is Professor for Media Research and Intermediality at the University of Bonn in Germany, where she is Head of Department. Her main areas of research are digital media theory, humans and machines and digital ethics.

CHAPTER 6

Deconstructing Audiences in Converging Media Environments

Uwe Hasebrink and Sascha Hölig

INTRODUCTION

Audiences have always been a highly risky and volatile component of mediated communication. The "people out there" perform a wide range of highly individualistic practices of media use that are dependent on social context and situational conditions. Thus audiences are hard to control. In order to gain control media companies are—as Ien Ang put it as early as 1991—"desperately seeking the audience." This desperate search has led to a specific conceptualization of audience that helped to construct audiences as countable and tradable commodities. In the second half of the twentieth century, a powerful research industry has developed that focuses on providing evidence on what people do with the media. The media industry has an existential interest in finding out how many people use their products; it is exactly this kind of audience data

U. Hasebrink (✉) · S. Hölig
Hans-Bredow-Institut, Hamburg, Germany
e-mail: u.hasebrink@hans-bredow-institut.de

S. Hölig
e-mail: s.hoelig@hans-bredow-institut.de

© The Author(s) 2017   113
S. Sparviero et al. (eds.), *Media Convergence and Deconvergence*, Global
Transformations in Media and Communication Research - A Palgrave and
IAMCR Series, DOI 10.1007/978-3-319-51289-1_6

that media companies can sell to the advertising industry. The challenge for this kind of research is that mass media audiences cannot be regarded as a concrete and countable group, like for example the audience being present in a theatre or cinema. Instead, it is necessary to construct media audiences by certain operational definitions and methodological procedures. All over the world, the media and advertising industries have developed similar mechanisms to construct the "mass audience" as the dominant model of research on exposure to media (Ang, 1991; McQuail, 1997; Webster & Phalen, 1997).

The theoretical and empirical core of this model can be characterized along the following premises

- Audience measurement focuses on contacts between users and specific media; thus the respective research is mainly based on behavioral measures such as frequency and duration of use.
- Audiences are described as aggregate behaviors, for instance as the percentage of users that have been reached by a specific medium.
- Audiences refer to single media, so the particular research constructs television audiences or radio audiences or newspaper audiences.

In this chapter we will discuss how this dominant model of audience research is challenged by the ongoing process of media convergence. Starting from the observation that it is quite unclear in which respect the process of (de)convergence affects the media practices of individual users, we will present two concepts for audience research that can help to adapt to the changing media environments.[1] First, the concept of media repertoires can help to better understand how audiences combine different kinds of media. Second, the concept of communication modes can help to distinguish media practices by which the users fulfill specific functions and produce specific meanings. Finally we discuss some implications for the role of audiences in times of converging media.

How Does Convergence Affect Audience Behaviors?

The concept of audience as described so far is under pressure. This is not a new phenomenon: Many researchers have questioned the industry's "dominant model" of constructing audiences as a controllable and tradable commodity since the early beginnings of audience research (for example, Ang, 1991; Webster & Phalen, 1997; Napoli, 2011). However, today, owing to the process of increasing media convergence, the concept is challenged on a more fundamental level.

As outlined in more detail in other contributions to this volume, the term convergence refers to several parallel developments. First, as indicated by the earlier keyword multimedia, today's media services increasingly combine and integrate different forms of presentation, that is pictures, moving images, sound, written text. Second, the concept of convergence refers to the fact that, as a consequence of digitization, any media content can be distributed by using different networks and platforms. Third, convergence refers to the development of new technical devices, which integrate formerly separated functionalities, for example, telephone, TV screen and games console. And fourth, it refers to the merging of at least three industry branches, that is information technology, media and telecommunication; this process is partly the condition of the other three developments and partly the consequence of them.

From the users' perspective the process of convergence is linked with several consequences. Different technical functionalities and services get merged and are made available on the same device. At the same time a single service may be used via different technical platforms. Thus a service is no longer coupled rigidly with a certain device, and neither are forms of media use and communicative activities bound to a certain technical equipment or distribution platform. It is not possible to decide at first glance what a user is actually doing when he or she uses a certain device—for example, a laptop, a mobile phone or a TV set. And, with regard to the overall topic of this volume, it remains an open question whether media practices converge into an integrative type of activity or, alternatively, they deconverge or differentiate into an increasing number of specific activities. Below, we will introduce the concept of communication modes that meets the challenges of this development.

While these aspects challenge the previously unproblematic definition of the medium that has been used and the specific practice related to this medium, another consequence of current changes in media environments follows from the increasing role of cross-media strategies on the supply side. Again, the fact that people use not just one medium but combine different media and different kinds of content is all but new; as Kim Schrøder (2011) has put it, media use has always been inherently cross-media. However, as shown above, this has not been reflected in the composition of media audiences. Today, with media content being distributed on different platforms and with new forms of transmedia storytelling being developed, approaches to the analysis of audience behaviors have to consider these aspects in order to provide meaningful results on current patterns of media use and to understand if these patterns may be interpreted as (de)converging practices. This challenge will be taken up in the next section.

CROSS-MEDIA REPERTOIRES: HOW DO USERS COMBINE DIFFERENT MEDIA?

Conceptual Considerations

Research into media use traditionally focuses on the use of single media types such as television or newspapers or the internet, or of single genres such as news or daily soaps, or of specific topics or products; in doing so the entirety of different media that an individual uses and the interrelations among these different media are often ignored. At the same time, we see a growing need for transmedia approaches in research on media use because of the processes of differentiation and convergence of media technologies and media products and the increasing importance of cross-media strategies for media industries (Bjur et al., 2014).

Research into media use is also characterized by a conceptual gap between two paradigms (for a recent overview see Nightingale, 2011): On one hand, there is the large industry of audience measurement and sometimes also academic studies that aim at providing an accurate picture of people's media related contacts and behaviors (Napoli, 2011; Webster & Phalen, 1997); this kind of research relies mainly on large standardized representative surveys that allow for solid descriptions of aggregate audience behaviors. On the other hand, there is a broad mainstream of academic, mostly qualitative research on audiences and reception processes that aims at reconstructing individual media use as meaningful practice within social contexts (Jensen & Rosengren, 1990; Livingstone & Das, 2009). Although both paradigms share both individual and aggregate patterns of media use as their main object of investigation, there is no productive cooperation; as a consequence, results of large-scale audience measurement studies are generally highly descriptive and far away from people's everyday practices and thus "meaningless," while results from qualitative receptions studies have limited capacity to generalize their concepts and empirical findings to broader populations.

In order to help to overcome these two gaps of research on media use, we have proposed the concept of media repertoires (Hasebrink & Popp, 2006; Hasebrink & Domeyer, 2012): The media repertoire of a person consists of the entirety of media he or she uses regularly. While the transmedia aspect is quite obviously an inherent characteristic of this concept—this way it provides a conceptual basis to overcome the above-mentioned single-media bias of audience research—the concept of media repertoires also offers a potential to productively combine the two research paradigms and to link findings on aggregate patterns of behavior and their distribution among the population with results of qualitative work on the meaning of media practices. From the perspective of a repertoire-oriented approach these two paradigms and their corresponding methodologies are regarded as the two sides of a coin—taken together they allow for a more insightful analysis of transmedia practices.

Figure 6.1 characterizes the two areas of research on media use as sketched above. Media repertoires as we conceive them can be regarded as a relevant issue for both areas: they may contribute to both kinds of research questions, since they are understood as patterns of behavior—as such they are compatible with audience research—and at the same time they are understood as meaningful practices—as such they are compatible with research on media use as social practice.

The concept of media repertoire refers to the entirety of media that a person regularly uses. Media repertoires can be regarded as relatively

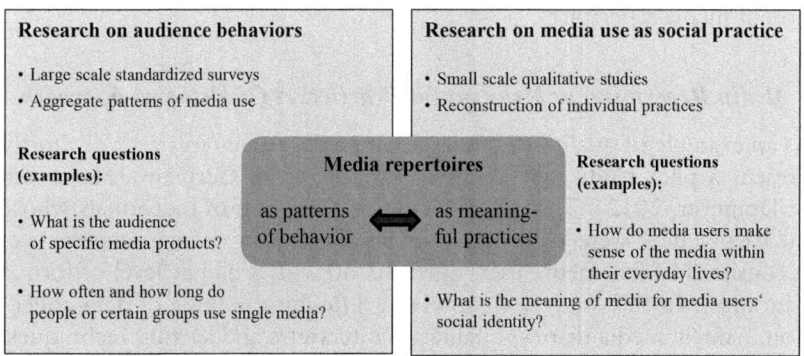

Fig. 6.1 Media repertoires as conceptual link between two areas of research on media use. *Source* Hasebrink & Domeyer (2012, p. 759)

stable transmedia patterns of media use. A repertoire-oriented perspective on media use is characterized by the following principles:

- User-centered perspective: The concept of media repertoires moves the media user into the focus; rather than taking the media-centered perspective that asks which audiences a particular medium reaches, this concept emphasizes the question of which media a particular person uses.
- Entirety: The repertoire-oriented approach stresses the need to consider the whole variety of media regularly assembled by a person; this helps to avoid misinterpretations resulting from approaches to single media.
- Relationality: Within a repertoire-oriented approach the interrelations and specific functions of the components of a media repertoire are of particular interest since they represent the inner structure or coherence of a media repertoire; this reflects our basic assumption that the media repertoire of a user is not just the mere sum of different media he or she uses, but a meaningfully structured composition of media. In our understanding this structure will reflect the social contexts or communicative figurations (see Hepp & Hasebrink, 2014) that a user is involved in.

In order to demonstrate the fruitfulness of a repertoire-oriented approach to audiences in converging media environments we will present examples of qualitative and of quantitative approaches to the investigation of media repertoires.

Media Repertoires as Meaningful Practice: A Qualitative Approach

As an example of qualitative research on media repertoires we will shortly present a pilot study that has been conducted in Germany (Hasebrink & Domeyer, 2012). This study focused on a group of individuals whose media practices were most likely to be affected by media convergence: it consisted of five media users aged 20–30 with a higher level of formal education. In this study we combined different methods of data collection, namely media diaries, qualitative interviews and sorting techniques. Participants were asked to keep a semi-structured diary for one week recording all their media activities. The completed diary was then used as a stimulus in a semi-structured interview. In order to facilitate speaking about the complex and often unconscious matters related to the description of media repertoires, sorting methods were included in the interviews. Figure 6.2 provides an example of the kind of data we got from the sorting procedure.

In a first step, participants were given a set of cards and asked to write each of the main elements of their media repertoire on one of these cards. They were completely free as to how many cards they used and which kinds of media they referred to. The participant documented in Fig. 6.2 first wrote four cards (laptop, television, radio, books); when the interview went on she added a fifth card (internet/SNS) and linked it with laptop, arguing that the new card indicates what she actually does with her laptop. As the outcome of this step we identified the relevant components of the participants' media repertoire.

In a second step, participants were asked to sort the cards on a large board with concentric circles with "Me" in the center according to the

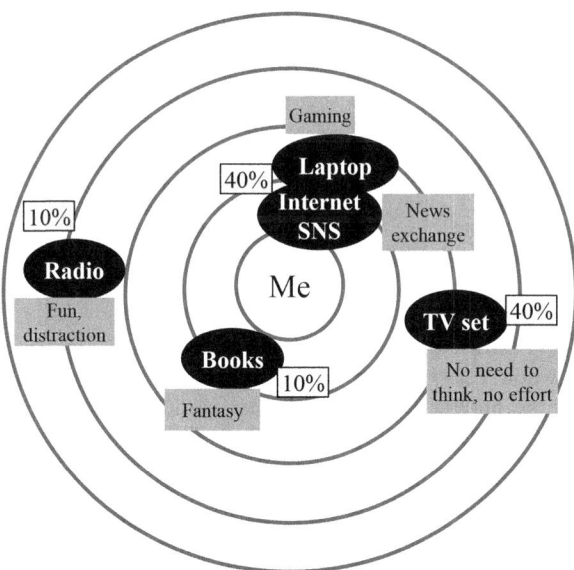

Fig. 6.2 Example of the visual reconstruction of a media repertoire. *Source* The figure displays a summary and translation of the results of the four steps of sorting cards by a selected participant of the study presented in Hasebrink & Domeyer (2012, p. 767); the original steps have been documented by photos

personal relevance of the respective component of their media repertoire. The example in Fig. 6.2 shows the highest relevance for internet/web. de/SNS, followed by books, television and radio.

In a third step, participants were given a number of tokens and asked to distribute them among the—in the case of Fig. 6.2, four—elements according to the relative time budget for each of the components they had mentioned. This distribution can be registered in terms of percentages of the overall time budget for media. One important finding for this example is that the amount of use is not fully consistent with the perceived relevance; thus these indicators are conceptually as well as empirically distinct aspects of media repertoires.

In a last step, participants were given another set of cards in different colors and asked to write down the main functions of the components they had mentioned or the roles that they play in their everyday lives.

The main function of these methods was to facilitate talking about media repertoires during the interview. While writing the cards, placing them on the board and attributing functions, the participants kept talking and reflecting on their decisions. Thus the main data for the analysis were the verbal comments (similar to think-aloud protocols), while the results of the sorting method were saved by taking photos and served as helpful additional indicators for the reconstruction of the respective media repertoire.

All the data collected were then analyzed by means of qualitative content analysis with regard to their overall subjective meaning. We cannot here go into details of the findings (for more details see Hasebrink & Domeyer, 2012).

In order to illustrate our general argument that media repertoires are a structured whole that is mainly shaped by the social contexts of the user, we present the findings for one particular participant whose description of her media repertoire explicitly referred to different contexts. Although still a young student, this participant already has a good professional position linked with a promising career. She seems to successfully combine two worlds, the life of a young sociable student enjoying the flexibility and lightheartedness of the student milieu on one hand and the life of a career-oriented professional on the other. It is with a high degree of self-confidence that she describes her corresponding media repertoire, which includes a combination of "girlie"-like television series on one hand and regularly reading a subscribed quality newspaper and watching television news, particularly for information on politics, economics and finance.

In our terms, this repertoire is clearly structured along the two communicative figurations that shape her everyday life.

Media Repertoires as Patterns of Behavior: A Quantitative Approach

The empirical basis of our example for a quantitative analysis is the German study Mass Communication, which has been run every 5 years since 1964; we have used the respective surveys of the years 1980, 1985, 1990, 1995, 2000, 2005 and 2010 (see Reitze & Ridder, 2011). The surveys are based on representative samples of the German population (14 + years). The questionnaire includes a broad range of indicators for media use, for example, the frequency and duration of use of television, radio, newspaper, internet (since 2000), magazines, books, video/DVD and CD/records. In addition, there are some items asking for evaluations and opinions regarding the respective media. At this point, we now present three steps of analysis that can serve as examples for different approaches to the empirical investigation of media repertoires.

Describing Relative Proportions of Media Within People's Time Budget

The first and rather simple approach to an analysis of media repertoires is to take the proportion of time that is devoted to different media and to present the findings as a transmedia time budget (see Fig. 6.3). General descriptions like this can be used as an indicator of the aggregate media repertoire of the population and of the relative importance of the single media that have been investigated. The findings indicate a substantial increase of the overall repertoire in terms of the time devoted to all media between 1980 and 2010, reaching a level of 9 to 10 h per day in the years 2005 and 2010. As to the relative importance of single media, Fig. 6.3 shows that almost all media have increased the absolute duration of use except newspapers and magazines. In relative terms, the percentage of television has slightly increased (1980: 36%, 2010: 38%); starting with a first reliable measure of 3% for the year 2000, the internet increased its share up to 14%. The clearest decrease can be observed for newspapers (1980: 14%, 2010: 4%).

Investigating Correlations Between Different Media

While the kind of analysis in the previous paragraph is quite familiar, it is only a first step towards the description of media repertoires. A second repertoire-oriented approach to this kind of data is an analysis of

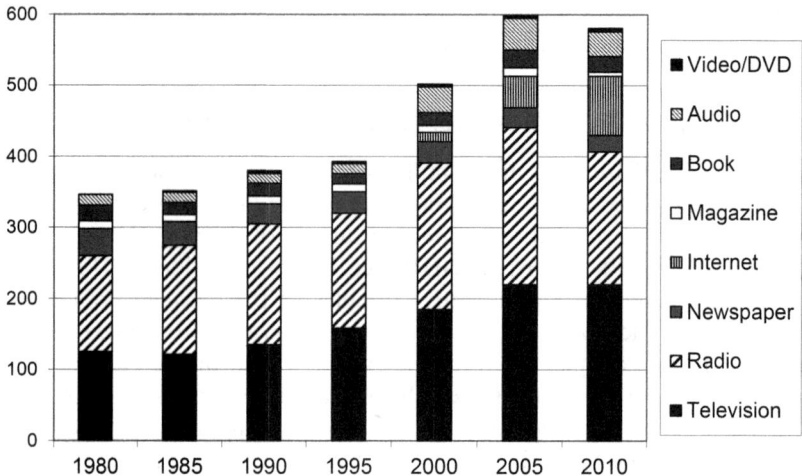

Fig. 6.3 Time budget for eight types of media in Germany 1980–2010 (minutes per day)

Source Hasebrink & Domeyer (2012, p. 772)

Note: Representative samples of the German population 14 years and older. 1980–1985: *n* = 2000; 1990–1995: *n* = 6000; 2000: *n* = 5017; 2005–2010: *n* = 4500. 1990 has been the first survey that included the area of the former GDR. Until 1995 data were collected by means of face-to-face interviews; since 2000 data are based on telephone interviews

the correlations between different kinds of media or content. When we calculate bivariate correlations between the amount of use of two media, for example, television and internet, a negative coefficient would indicate a certain tension between these two media, so that, say, they do not seem to fit to each other, and using one of them comes at the expense of the other. As a consequence of this, there should be few people who combine heavy use of both media. A positive correlation, on the other hand, between the frequencies of use of these two media would indicate that they are likely to be combined within media repertoires. Finally, a zero correlation between the two media would suggest that we can find any combination of them within different media repertoires. Thus, we regard the bivariate relations between different media or kinds of media content as one important indicator for media repertoires.

As an example for this kind of analysis we take up the ongoing discussion about how the increasing role of online media might affect the use of traditional media. The data provided by the above-mentioned study allow for the calculation of correlations between the frequencies of use of different media.

Table 6.1 shows the extent to which the frequency of online use correlates with the frequency of use of seven other media in 2005.[2] For the whole population the findings show that there are small but (owing to the big sample size) highly significant negative correlations between television and newspapers and moderate positive correlations between listening to audio media and watching videos or DVDs. This finding could be read as follows: The more people use the internet for accessing content or communicating, the less they watch television and read newspapers—an interpretation quite in line with the public debate on the consequences of online media on traditional media. However, as detailed analyses for more specific groups—for illustrative reasons we selected adolescents, middle-age/middle-class people, and pensioners—demonstrate, this interpretation does not hold at the more particularized level. Within the group of adolescents the correlation between online and television is zero, and for newspapers there is a moderate and highly significant positive correlation. For young people these data indicate that the more they use the internet the more they read newspapers, which is clearly against common assumptions on the relationship between the internet and newspapers.

Table 6.1   Correlation between the frequency of online use and the frequency of use of other media in 2005 (Pearson correlation coefficients)

	Total population	Selected subgroups		
		Adolescents	Middle age, middle class	Pensioners
Respondents	n = 4500	n = 444	n = 915	n = 1052
Television	−0.15	0.02	−0.03	0.00
Radio	0.00	0.22	0.02	0.11
Newspaper	−0.06	0.22	0.02	0.09
Magazines	0.03	0.21	0.09	0.06
Books	0.02	0.06	0.05	0.11
CD/records	0.20	−0.03	0.12	0.13
Video/DVD	0.33	0.20	0.15	0.17

Source Hasebrink & Domeyer (2012, p. 774)

The lesson to be learnt from this empirical example is twofold: First, the patterns of how people compose their media repertoire are more complex than often expected. Research on media use has to analyze systematically the relationships between different media as they are reflected by patterns of exposure. Second, it is crucial to consider the role of demographic and other contextual variables. At first glance there is a negative correlation between the internet and television. However, when we look at specific groups there is not one to verify this finding. Thus, the correlation for the total sample can be fully explained by demographical factors—in this case the fact that older people watch a lot of television and are less likely to use the internet compared with young people.

Identifying Patterns of Media Use and Types of Media Users

The principal idea of media repertoires obviously goes beyond the level of bivariate correlations between pairs of media. Media repertoires are conceived as comprehensive patterns of media use. Empirical approaches to the analysis of patterns are, for instance, configuration frequency analysis, or, most important in the field of lifestyle research, cluster analysis. The rationale of these approaches is to identify cases which share the same attributes and as such can be regarded as one cluster of media users that can be clearly distinguished from other clusters of media users with different attributes of media use. Thus, to identify clusters of media users on the basis of their overall pattern of media use is the third empirical approach of the proposed repertoire-oriented research perspective.

The rationale of this step has been the assumption that people's media repertoires differ with respect to their favorite medium; the survey used above included the respective variable, which was used as a categorical variable in a two-step cluster analysis together with eight variables indicating the frequency of use of eight media (see Table 6.2). This procedure led to five clusters; four of them are mainly characterized by one of the media as favorite; however, the analysis also reveals significant differences between the clusters with regard to the frequency variables, indicating that the five repertoires differ with regard to both the favorite medium and the frequency of use of the other media. Cluster 1, for instance, includes users who say TV is their favorite medium and who watch TV more often than respondents in any of the other groups; they combine this TV-oriented pattern with high frequencies in terms of using radio and VCR, and low frequencies in terms of internet use and, particularly, reading books. Thus, this repertoire is characterized by

Table 6.2 Clusters indicating five media repertoires in Germany 2005

Cl.	%	Favorite medium	TV	Radio	News-paper	Inter-net	Maga-zine	Book	Video	Audio
1	35	TV	++	+		−		−	+	−
2	10	Various	−	−	−	+	−			
3	11	Newspaper			++	−		++	−	−
4	24	Radio		++		−		−		
5	21	Internet	+	+	−	++			++	+

Source Hasebrink & Domeyer (2012, p. 775)
Note Massenkommunikation 2005; $n = 4500$; result of a two-step cluster analysis with one categorical variable (favourite medium: TV or radio or newspaper or internet) and eight continuous variables (frequency of use of the eight media). +/-: higher/lower than average, $p < .05$; ++/--: higher lower than any other cluster, $p < .05$

a clear preference for audio-visual content. Those who regard the internet as their favorite medium (Cluster 5) have quite a rich media repertoire with regard to all electronic media, while they are less frequent readers of newspapers. The only cluster that includes users with different favorite media (Cluster 2) is characterized by the lowest use of the traditional news media (TV, radio and newspapers) and an above-average frequency in terms of internet use. Compared with the other cluster with high internet use (Cluster 5, see above), this repertoire indicates a generally low interest in media.

To our understanding, such analytical approaches to media audiences meet the challenges linked with converging media environments. Instead of characterizing media users by single indicators, a repertoire-oriented approach takes a holistic view on media-related practices. Thus, it takes into account that today's media users face a rich media environment and it allows researchers to investigate which of the available offers they select and combine with which other kinds of media offers

COMMUNICATION MODES: WHAT ARE PEOPLE ACTUALLY DOING WHEN THEY USE A MEDIUM?

The repertoire-oriented perspective as presented above provides a conceptual framework for the description and explanation of media users' stable and often habitualized patterns of cross-media behavior. The second perspective, on audiences in converging media environments, sets out to solve another problem that today's audience research has to face: Owing to multifunctional devices and forms of digital content that are distributed through different platforms it is increasingly difficult to decide what an individual is actually doing with a certain media service. Are people who watch a TV newscast on their mobile phone watching television? And what kind of activity is it if they download TV news from YouTube? Do users of social networking sites or micro blogs look for information in order to build an opinion on current issues? Or do they rather manage their personal networks?

Traditional approaches of audience research have been aligned to devices and services: The assumption was that each media device is linked with a specific media activity. People sitting in front of a TV set were regarded as watching television; and a similar assumption was made about listening to the radio or making a phone call. Current media devices, however, are no longer limited to one specific function; rather, they provide many options of usage. At the same time, any media-related activity can be realized with different devices. The same is true for media services. A specific website offers a wide range of functionalities. Thus, the structural link between a device or a service and its specific use is repealed. The consequence of this decoupling of apparatus and media service on one hand and communicative activities on the other is that audience research cannot infer a specific communicative action just from the device or service that has been used; instead we have to take a user-centered perspective.

In order to meet these challenges, we propose the concept of communication modes, which refers to how users define themselves and their current activity in a specific situation of media use (see Hasebrink, 2004; Hölig, 2014). To think in terms of communication modes includes a user-centered perspective: It is the user who defines her or his communicative situation, for example, as "watching TV," "reading a newspaper," or "chatting with a friend" and so on. Nevertheless, it is assumed that communication modes are linked to the respective communication services. While a specific communication service cannot determine the communication mode of its users, it defines the range of modes which can be realized by using the respective service. Communication services are defined on the basis of externally ascribed, "objective" criteria referring to technical and economic features and to the content and presentation of the service. In dealing with a specific communication service users realize a particular part of the given functional potential; this is what we call the communication mode (see Fig. 6.4). Following this conception,

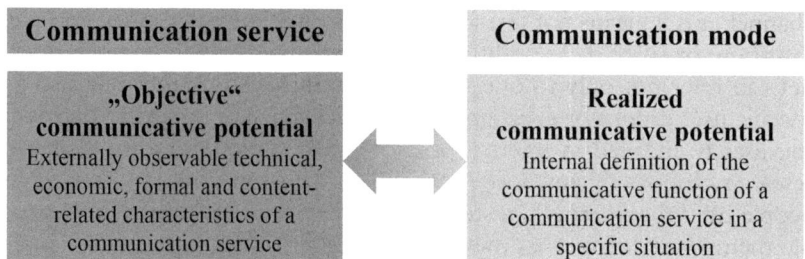

Communication service	Communication mode
„Objective" **communicative potential** Externally observable technical, economic, formal and content-related characteristics of a communication service	**Realized** **communicative potential** Internal definition of the communicative function of a communication service in a specific situation

Fig. 6.4 Communication services and communication modes as interrelated concepts. *Source* Hasebrink & Hölig (2013, p. 198)

communication services and communication modes are mutually related; the theoretical status of this relationship is similar to the discourse on media genres: By using certain genre-specific indicators the service triggers certain genre-related schemata, which help the users to make sense of the respective story; however, the producers as well as the recipients can also play with the genre conventions and thus open a wide spectrum for interpretations.

Communication modes refer to the situational level of analysis: A communication mode is the concrete form of using a communication service in a given situation. It is the situation-specific result of functional expectations and the way of handling the respective service. Furthermore, it is assumed that in any situation the users are in exactly one communication mode and that they know what they are doing—for example, which communication mode they are in. This does not mean that they explicitly or consciously reflect their current mode; instead, the knowledge might be rather implicit—it becomes particularly obvious when there is a dismatch between the mode and the respective service: As soon as the on-going interaction does not suit the current expectations, the user will re-evaluate the situation and change the service (according to the function he or she would like to realize) and/or redefine the communication mode (according to the features offered by the respective service).

At this point we will exemplify these conceptual considerations by asking what people are doing when they use the internet for information. The range of functionalities that are part of what we are used to call "the internet" seems to be interminable. The internet not only represents a source of content, but at the same time it is a communication channel; it is a means not just to receive information but also to produce, distribute or share it. In addition, communicative activities on the internet can refer not only to one single communication partner but also to specific user groups or even large publics. This makes it hard to decide if the user is engaged in interpersonal or mass communication. Audience research cannot rely anymore on the plain question of if and how often people use "the internet"; instead it is necessary to investigate how people themselves define what they do with the internet, that is which communication modes they realize.

Following this argument, Hölig (2014) investigated how media users deal with the internet in order to realize a range of information needs located on the spectrum between interpersonal communication and mass communication. The first research question was which characteristics media users apply in order to distinguish different information services on the internet: What are the relevant criteria that make a meaningful difference? This information is crucial for understanding which communication modes can be identified between mass and interpersonal communication and where the tipping points between them are. In order to answer this question an open card sorting method was applied: Subjects got a set of 31 cards each indicating a specific internet service—for example, reading a newsletter, watching live stream television, chatting and so on—and were asked to sort them according to their similarities and differences. The core data of this step were collected by recording think-aloud protocols of subjects' explanations why they felt that a specific service differs from the others. These arguments have been analyzed with a focus on the spectrum between mass and interpersonal communication; the following criteria were identified as characteristics that are used to distinguish between different internet services:

- Users' Activity: Users distinguish usage situations according to their own activity. The distinction is made between being active (for example, producing, sharing or distributing), passive (for example, reading, listening, watching) or interactive (dialogic communication).
- Communication Partner: Users make clear distinctions concerning their communication partners and evaluate if the source or the assumed recipients of the service correspond with their expectations. Whether an information source is eligible or not depends strongly on the given needs. Sometimes, for example, the wisdom

of the crowd will be sufficient and sometimes it will not. In this example the user is rather in the role of a recipient and the factual level is paramount. In another situation, the distance between the involved communication partners is not that large. It is more personal when a user is giving an advice to a single person in a more private situation. The given constellation is crucial for the interpretation frames of a communicative situation. Applied categories are: friends or relatives, interested anybody, expert or authority, mass media respectively journalism. Co-Audience: Additionally, the audience size and access possibilities, as perceived by the internet user, are relevant. Differences are made between individuals, closed groups, public but focused group, and a mass audience.

- Temporal Distance: The common differentiation between synchronous (real-time) and asynchronous (with time delay) communication is supplemented by quasi-synchronous communication (not real-time communication but near-term) and communication without any reference to the present point in time, such as searching in an archive.

Any particular combination of these four criteria characterizes a specific communication mode. Thus, these criteria can be used as an instrument to assess the mode of specific communicative actions.

In order to validate this instrument, a second research phase was based on the following considerations: In a given situation, the salient information needs, and thus the specific gratifications sought, influence the communication mode that is applied. The argument here is that the activities performed on the internet are not determined by the internet as the platform or by a certain internet service, but to a considerable extent by the interests and needs of the user.

The research design simulated different information scenarios. With regard to either political or health-related issues, respondents were asked to imagine one of four basic types of information needs: (1) general orientation on the respective field; (2) specific interest in a concrete issue; (3) knowledge of what the relevant peer group thinks about these issues; (4) individual problem-oriented issues. The hypothesis was that depending on the respective information need, users would realize different communication modes. Subjects were asked to search on the internet for the information they needed. They were completely free to choose any service they wanted, be it an online newspaper, Wikipedia or a direct message to a professional or a friend on a social networking platform. When they felt they had reached their aims they were asked about what they had done on the internet with regard to the four criteria that were identified in the first step. The analysis showed that only very few out of the logically possible combinations of these four criteria appeared significantly more often than expected. These combinations can be interpreted as typical communication modes:

- Journalistic Mass Communication: Passive reception of content from journalistic sources within a small temporal distance and a dispersed mass as co-audience.
- Public Expert Communication: Passive reception of content from specialized sources within a small temporal distance and a public, but thematically focused co-audience.
- Private Expert Communication: Non-public, real-time conversation with a topic-related specialized communication partner.
- Personal Communication: Non-public, real-time conversation with friends, relatives and so on.

These communication modes have been meaningfully linked with the different information needs: public expert communication is significantly linked with concrete thematic interests, while the mode of private expert communication is applied if there is an individual problem to be solved. The mode of personal communication is closely connected with peer-related information needs, and mass communication with undirected information needs for general orientation. The findings support the assumption that the communication mode, which is applied in a given situation, is strongly related to the salient information or communication need. While this statement might seem rather trivial, it clearly emphasizes the fact that users' media-related practices cannot be inferred from the specific media platform or service they use—as audience research often does. The observations in this study demonstrate that even single services or websites, for example, a specific social networking platform or the portal of a newspaper publishing house, are used for different communication modes, depending on the respective information need of the user.

Beyond the above example the concept of communication modes can be applied to a wide range of communicative practices. It has been applied to identify different modes between the poles of "linear" and "non-linear" television (Hasebrink, 2012) and modes of multi-screening—that is, forms of combining two or more screens at the same time (Siebenaler & Hasebrink, 2016).

CONCLUSION

This chapter has started from the established model of audience research, according to which audiences are constructed on the basis of the number of people reached by the respective medium or service, the frequency and duration of use, and the structure of this group in terms of specific target groups. As we have shown, this approach is under pressure. The consequences of the current process of media convergence question many of the premises of former audience research. We have discussed two of the challenges that arise.

On one hand, people's manifold media-related activities cannot be understood appropriately on the basis of contacts with single media. Each user uses different media, they combine different platforms, genres and kinds of content, and he or she thus composes an individual media repertoire that makes sense to them within their everyday life. Research on audiences in convergent media environments has to deal with these media repertoires in order to understand the role of specific media offers within these repertoires. On the other hand, the former link between a certain technology or a certain device and the users' activities has substantially eroded. Today we cannot know what a user is doing when he or she watches a TV screen or a mobile phone or visits a social networking site. Research has to ask users for their own definition of the current situation. As we have shown, this insight does not mean that there are no regularities or patterns of user behavior; the concept of communication modes refers to certain culturally established practices that users realize when they use the media. For audience research that sets out to deliver relevant theoretical and empirical evidence this concept can help to identify these patterns and regularities even in converging media environments.

Last but not least we would like to stress that the two concepts we have proposed can also help to investigate empirically to what extent we can actually speak of "convergent" media practices. In this respect, both concepts emphasize aspects that are not in line with the assumption of a general process of convergence: Repertoire-oriented research investigates how media users combine different media services and media content;

from this we learn about the diversity of individual media practices. The concept of communication modes starts from the assumption that technical, organizational and content-related convergence does not necessarily lead to convergent media practices; instead we stress the fact that media users make a difference between different media practices.

NOTES

1. These thoughts and findings are based on Hasebrink & Hölig (2013).
2. Raw data for 2010 were not available; therefore we took data for 2005 in order to illustrate our argument.

REFERENCES

Ang, M. I. (1991). *Desperately seeking the audience*. London: Routledge.

Bjur, J., Schrøder, K. C., Hasebrink, U., Courtois, C., Adoni, H. & Nossek, H. (2014). Cross-media use—unfolding complexities in contemporary audiencehood. In N. Carpentier, K. C. Schrøder & L. Hallett (Eds.), *Audience Transformations. Shifting Audience Positions in Late Modernity* (pp. 15–29). New York: Routledge.

Hasebrink, U. (2004). Konvergenz aus Nutzerperspektive: Das Konzept der Kommunikationsmodi. In U. Hasebrink, L. Mikos, & E. Prommer (Eds.), *Mediennutzung in konvergierenden Medienumgebungen* (pp. 67–86). München: Reinhard Fischer.

Hasebrink, U. (2012). Any time? Modi linearer und nicht-linearer Fernsehnutzung. *Medien und Zeit, 27*(2), 44–53.

Hasebrink, U., & Domeyer, H. (2012). Media repertoires as patterns of behaviour and as meaningful practices. A multimethod approach to media use in converging media environments. *Participations, 9*(2), 757–783.

Hasebrink, U., & Hölig, S. (2013). Conceptualizing media audiences in convergent media environments. In S. Diehl & M. Karmasin (Eds.), *Media and Convergence Management* (pp. 198–202). Berlin: Springer.

Hasebrink, U., & Popp, J. (2006). Media repertoires as a result of selective media use. A conceptual approach to the analysis of patterns of exposure. *Communications, 31*(3), 369–387.

Hepp, A., & Hasebrink, U. (2014). Human interaction and communicative figurations: The transformation of mediatized cultures and societies. In K. Lundby (Ed.), *Mediatization of Communication* (pp. 249–272). Berlin/New York: de Gruyter.

Hölig, S. (2014). *Informationsorientierte Kommunikationsmodi zwischen Massen- und interpersonaler Kommunikation*. Baden-Baden: Nomos.

Jensen, K. B., & Rosengren, K. E. (1990). Five traditions in search of the audience. *European Journal of Communication, 5*(2–3), 207–238.

Livingstone, S., & Das, R. (2009). *The end of audiences? Theoretical echoes of reception amidst the uncertainties of use.* Paper presented at Transforming audiences 2, 3–4 September 2009, University of Westminster. Retrieved from http://eprints.lse.ac.uk/25116/.

McQuail, D. (1997). *Audience analysis.* Thousand Oaks, CA: Sage.

Napoli, P. M. (2011). *Audience evolution. New technologies and the transformation of media audiences.* New York: Columbia University Press.

Nightingale, V. (Ed.). (2011). *The handbook of media audience.* Oxford: Wiley.

Reitze, H., & Ridder, C.-M. (Eds.). (2011). *Massenkommunikation VIII. Eine Langzeitstudie zur Mediennutzung und Medienbewertung 1964–2010.* Baden-Baden: Nomos.

Schrøder, K. C. (2011). Audiences are inherently cross-media: Audience studies and the cross-media challenge. *Communication Management Quarterly, 18*(6), 5–27.

Siebenaler, A., & Hasebrink, U. (2016). Modi der Multiscreen-Nutzung. Eine Untersuchung von Praktiken der Kombination verschiedener Bildschirme. In U. Göttlich, L. Heinz & M.R. Herbers (Eds.), *Ko-Orientierung in der Medienrezeption: Praktiken der Second Screen-Nutzung.* Wiesbaden: Springer (Forthcoming).

Webster, J. G., & Phalen, P. F. (1997). *The mass audience: Rediscovering the dominant model.* Mahwah, NJ: Lawrence Erlbaum.

Authors' Biography

Uwe Hasebrink is Director of the Hans Bredow Institute for Media Research and Professor for Empirical Communication Research at the University of Hamburg, Germany. He has been involved in several international research networks and projects, e.g. *EU Kids Online* and the COST Action *Transforming Audiences, Transforming Societies.*

Sascha Hölig born in 1976, studied communications, sociology and philosophy at the Friedrich-Schiller-Universität Jena, Germany. In his doctoral thesis at the University of Hamburg he identified information-oriented communication modes in the Internet. He works as senior researcher at the Hans Bredow Institute for Media Research in Hamburg, Germany.

PART III

Production and Distribution of Media Content

Convergent Media Quality? Comparing the Content of Online and Offline Media in Switzerland

Mark Eisenegger, Mario Schranz and Angelo Gisler

INTRODUCTION

This chapter examines the effects of the convergence of the online and offline news offerings in the digital age on the diversity of the media market, its financial resources and its journalistic quality. This leads us to the important socio-political question of whether an increasing media convergence contributes to a more efficiently functioning public sphere of the media.

The chapter centers on the following research questions: Does the convergence of the news media lead to a more diversified media offer or

M. Eisenegger (✉)
Department of Communication Studies,
University of Salzburg, Salzburg, Austria
e-mail: mark.eisenegger@sbg.ac.at; mark.eisenegger@foeg.uzh.ch

M. Eisenegger · M. Schranz · A. Gisler
Research Institute for the Public Sphere and Society (fög),
University of Zurich, Zurich, Switzerland

A. Gisler
e-mail: angelo.gisler@foeg.uzh.ch

© The Author(s) 2017
S. Sparviero et al. (eds.), *Media Convergence and Deconvergence*, Global
Transformations in Media and Communication Research - A Palgrave and
IAMCR Series, DOI 10.1007/978-3-319-51289-1_7

to more media concentration? What are the effects of digitalization and media convergence on the financial basis of information journalism? And what quality of content characterizes media reporting? Is the quality of the online news offer better or worse than the contents of the printed press?

Under the influence of the euphoria surrounding the internet, many authors stressed the advantages of online journalism over its conventional counterpart. In view of new technical innovations, research bodies also initially developed strongly positive expectations on news journalism as a result of the internet. They welcomed the merging of diverse, formerly separated media contents (text, audio, video) resulting from such processes of technical convergence. As opposed to this, the findings of this study imply a more critical view. In the first section that follows, the relevance of such a comparison will initially be discussed, and the central findings of research into online journalism will be presented. In the next section, the methodical foundations of the study will be briefly described. A third section will examine the differing framework conditions for online and press journalism on the basis of advertising revenues and usage figures as well as the qualitative differences between online and offline reporting. Finally, a compilation of the results will be presented.

CONSEQUENCES OF CONVERGENCE AND DIGITALIZATION ON JOURNALISM

The convergence of media types and technologies and its effects on the production, consumption and financing of news journalism has been a topic of increasing research in recent years (Lugmayr & Dal Zotto, 2016; Wilczek & Nienstedt, 2013). However, there is no unanimity about this term, which is used to describe numerous aspects of the media transformation, often apparently in highly inconsistent ways (see Balbi, Chap. 2 in this volume). The digitalization of the information media is leading to an increased convergence of the various media types. This has an impact on media production (for example, new forms of organization for elements such as newsrooms and professional roles within journalism) and usage (like the trend toward mobile use) as well as the financing and ownership/influence structures in the media industries (notably the free-bie culture, the globalization of media markets, the encroachment of the techno giants onto the news business, novel forms of cooperation, and the increasing significance of new industry segments such as the digital media market). Although digitalization is by no means a new phenomenon, the process of digitalization has intensified in recent years to reach a new stage. Both scientific analyses and practical applications indicate that an incisive break has occurred which not only has changed the production, distribution and consumption of news but also has quite fundamentally challenged the previous business model of the news media (Picard, 2011) and also has serious consequences for democracy (Lutz & Du Toit, 2014; Levy, 2010) and society (Couldry, 2012; Morozov, 2012).

Various phenomena must be examined in order to describe and explain this trend toward convergence. First, the accelerated rate of technological change must be noted. The widespread introduction of a powerful broadband internet and the fast-growing dissemination of mobile devices among the population allowed the online information offerings to reach maturity and with changed patterns of use to become a strong alternative to the traditional press and radio offerings. In the course of this process, the media markets have also become more strongly globalized and convergent. Global techno companies such as Facebook, Google, Microsoft and Apple have consequently appeared as new players on the scene who are increasingly squeezing the information media on the advertising market and pushing them onto the periphery. And, not least, the growing importance of the social networks has led to the appearance of new channels and forms of communication which are decisively changing the presentation and distribution of the news—for example, the proliferation of channels, increased interactivity, and the growing significance of a logic of discourse based on community values and everyday life experiences with feedback effects on information journalism. The consequent technical convergence on online platforms has reconfigured the information markets by bringing together the traditional actors within information journalism who had worked in separate sectors for decades: The media titles of traditional press publishers now encounter the traditional providers of the private and public radio and TV (such as the BBC) sector as well as new actors in the information business from outside the industry (such as bluewin.ch, Google and Facebook). This also means that actors who have hitherto focused on text-based communications are now also obliged to create (or publish) their products in audio and video formats, and also that radio and TV providers on digital platforms are additionally investing in text reports.

Many researchers have welcomed this convergent trend from the aspect of the relevant contents. In view of the new technical possibilities, scientific researchers also initially expressed strongly positive expectations—for example, they primarily highlighted the opportunities that would arise for information journalism on the internet. They argued that digitalization would lead to more offerings and greater diversity, that the quality of public discourse would improve thanks to the opportunities for greater interactivity, feedback loops to the public and the multimedia experience, and that the possibilities of citizens' journalism on the internet would go hand in hand with a democratization of public communications (see Huang et al., 2004; Quandt, 2008; Kretschmar, 2009). Many authors welcomed the development towards a democratization of the public discourse: they claimed that the digitalization of the information media would lead to a breakup of the traditional monopoly of opinion between political, business and media elites (Picard, 2014) and of the long-prevailing "elitist" top-down structure of information distribution (Jarren, 2015) in our society.

On the other hand, other authors have contested this view by pointing out that some effects of convergence and digitalization have a negative impact on the quality of the reported contents (La Piscina et al., 2015). They implicitly criticize a purely technological perspective (Steensen, 2010) and suggest that the availability of material (such as funding, advertising revenues and technology) and immaterial resources (hiring conditions, research time) would play a key role in deciding whether the quality of online journalism could ever reach a comparable level (Puppis et al., 2014; Barnhurst, 2010; Fenton, 2010; Trappel, 2008; Keel et al., 2010). They observe that the even greater scarcity of resources in the online sector of information journalism—for example, financing problems, a scarcity of well-educated journalists as well as a lack of time consequent to the accelerating growth of online journalism—make it highly unlikely that the euphoric expectations on online journalism will be fulfilled in the near future.

METHODOLOGY

The following section describes the method used to approach these various research questions. The Swiss media market is small and highly fragmented, subdivided into a relatively large German-language media market, a smaller French-language market in the west, and a very small

Italian-language market in the south of the country (Künzler, 2011; Puppis & Künzler, 2013). In order to answer the questions raised in this chapter, the news media titles with the broadest reach in the French and German parts of Switzerland were selected. The analysis considers both press titles and news sites of the following types: daily newspapers, tabloids and free media. The following media were examined: Aargauer Zeitung, Basler Zeitung, Berner Zeitung, Corriere del Ticino, Le Temps, Neue Luzerner Zeitung, Neue Zürcher Zeitung, Südostschweiz, Tages-Anzeiger, Blick, Le Matin, Le Matin Dimanche, Sonntagsblick, 20 Minuten, 20 min, 24 heures, 24heures.ch, nzz.ch, tagesanzeiger.ch, blick.ch, lematin.ch, 20 minuten.ch and 20 min.ch.

The analysis of media use and the development of the information offer are based on comparable coverage data. The companies WEMF AG for media research and NET-Metrix AG provide comparable coverage figures for the Swiss press and online information media on a daily, weekly and monthly basis. The data of the Total Audience study 2015–2 were used for the following analysis, notably the key figure of "daily use," as this offers the most valid indicator for how many people regularly use a particular medium.

In the question of funding, our main source was the advertising data of Media Focus Schweiz GmbH. This company has for many years made data available at the level of individual media titles on gross advertising revenues for both print media and online editions.

The data used to measure the contents-based convergence, for example, the media quality of the press and online titles, was drawn from the media-quality yearbook entitled Qualität der Medien—Schweiz, Suisse, Svizzera (for a fuller description of the method applied and a detailed derivation of the quality indicators see fög, 2015, pp. 217–226). In view of the rapid transformation of the media in recent years, the significance of media quality as an indispensable normative basis of the public debate in a functioning democracy has increasingly become a topic of research (Strömbäck, 2005; Wessler, 2008; Jandura & Friedrich, 2014; Weiss et al., 2016). This insight into the normative standards of public communications is often associated with the historical movement of the Enlightenment. The conviction that "a public enlightens itself... if it is given the freedom to do so" (Kant, 1912 [1784]) implies a corresponding development in the demands made on the quality of public communications. These are reflected in the statutory regulations of these communications, especially in the demands made on the public radio service, in journalistic paradigms, editorial guidelines, the rules issued by advisory media bodies, the expectations of the public and the quality analyses of social science. The canon of these quality standards invariably consists of claims for universal validity, balance, objectivity and relevance, all of which have their roots in the philosophy of the enlightenment (see also Karmasin, 2002; Wyss, 2002; Bucher & Altmeppen, 2003; Weischenberg, 2006; Arnold, 2009; Grossenbacher & Trebbe, 2009). This section focuses mainly on the following study variables:

- Relevance of Reporting: The quality dimension of relevance is based on the premise that public communications should give greater weight to the general interest than to private and particular interests—for example, from this perspective, the information-centered topics relating to politics, business and culture are classed as of higher quality than entertainment-based soft news topics such as human interest and sports reporting. The higher the share of hard news topics, the more relevant is the reporting of a particular medium.
- Objectivity of Reporting: The parameter of objectivity measures the degree of rationality of the reporting, and distinguishes between a cognitive-argumentative and an ethical-emotional style of discourse. Whereas the former is characterized by a rational, argumentatively discursive way of addressing the topic, the latter is more strongly focused on emotions, polemics and escalating ethical claims. The exchange of arguments receives a higher qualitative weighting than communications based more strongly on the exchange of emotions and feelings (see Imhof, 2012; Strömbäck, 2005).
- Contextualization of Reporting: Finally, the contextualization achieved by the reporting is measured. On the basis of the differentiation introduced by Iyengar (1991) between an "episodic frame" and a "thematic frame," the weighting of episodic news—oriented only to the topicality of direct events—is determined in comparison with contextualized reporting, which also brings in background aspects. In addition to the presentation of news, it is essential for information journalism to produce longer reflective reports that include contextualized assessments of events. The greater the share of contextualized reporting in a media title, the more highly will its quality be estimated.

The three indicators of relevance, contextualization and objectivity were finally summed to produce a quality score that can be represented and interpreted over time (for this calculation see fög, 2015, pp. 223–226). The higher the quality score of a media title, the better is its reporting quality considered to be. In order to compare the quality of the press and online offerings, the quality scores of the individual titles were aggregated and a mean value was calculated.

EMPIRICAL ASPECTS

The main empirical findings are presented below. In a first step, our interest centers on the effects of the convergence of the media on the diversity of the offer. On the basis of the various usage figures of the press and online offers, we analyze the extent to which the diversity of the convergent media offer exceeds that of the printed press. It is shown how this convergence has changed the structure of the offerings provided by the information media in the Swiss online sector. Does the online sector really offer greater diversity? Are there more high-coverage media offerings in the online information media than in the offline world?

In a second step, we examine how the digitalization of information journalism and media convergence affect the financing basis—for example, advertising revenues as a central source of funds of the news media. The advertising revenues of the press titles and news websites will be compared for this purpose.

Finally, the consequences of this convergence for the quality of the contents presented by the information media offerings will be shown in a third step. Do the better opportunities now available to online journalism really lead to more relevance and contextualization and thus to better quality of the contents?

Digital News Offerings: Traditional Press Still Dominates the Online Sector

The readership figures for Swiss newspapers in the press and digital sectors (WEMF: MACH Basic study, Total Audience Study; NET-Metrix: Profile study) show that the usage of the print versions of information media has shown a tendency to decline for many years. The classical subscription newspapers such as Tages-Anzeiger and Neue Zürcher Zeitung in particular have recorded strong declines: thus both these quality papers have lost about a third of their circulation (as measured by print runs) since 2001. The print versions of the tabloid media (for example, Blick) are also losing readers. Thus the print run of Blick has been practically halved since 2001. And after the exorbitant growth rates of the free papers (for example, 20 Minuten) in the first decade of this century, they can now at best merely maintain the current size of their respective readerships. On the other hand, the readership figures for most news sites of the Swiss information media show significant gains (NET-Metrix: Profile study). However, clear differences are apparent between the various types of online media (Schranz & Gisler, 2015): Whereas the news sites of the free and tabloid media recorded steep user growth in recent years, only low growth rates were observed for the news sites of the subscription media. Despite these opposing trends between online and offline information offerings, which have been observed for many years, we are not yet seeing a widespread replacement of print offerings by their online counterparts. These findings had previously also been prominently introduced into the debate by Bocowzki (2005). In fact, the "Total Audience" (WEMF, 2015) study published regularly by the WEMF since 2014 shows for the year 2015 that the print edition of a title is still as a rule (in some cases considerably) more frequently consulted than the corresponding online edition of the same title (see Table 7.1): thus, for example, the 1.665 million readers of 20 Minuten (print title) contrast with only about 680,000 online users of 20 minuten.ch (with about 425,000 dual users).

For Tages-Anzeiger the ratio is even more significantly in favor of the printed edition (420,000 vs. 168,000 exclusive unique online users per day). Only for Blick is the number of exclusive unique users between press and online editions already pretty much in balance (562,000 vs. 555,000 exclusive users).

In order to assess this transformation in terms of diversity and quality, the extent to which digitalization is leading to new high-coverage offerings that compete with the traditional press and radio providers must also be analyzed. The latter have dominated the information market for many decades, the press even for centuries. The digitalization of information journalism was also associated with the hope of achieving an overall more diverse information offer: the entry of new providers onto the information market (for example, online portals or pure players such as watson.ch) would lead—it was claimed—to a quantitative and qualitative

Table 7.1 Readership data for newspaper titles in Switzerland (daily use) shown separately for "exclusive print users," "exclusive digital users" and "dual users" for the period from 9 April 2014 to 29 March, 2015

	Readership print/exclusive (in tousand)	Readership print and digital	Readership digital/exclusive (in tousand)	Exclusive print/ overall reach (in %)
Neue Luzerner Zeitung	284	10	21	90
Le Temps	100	2	12	88
Corriere del Ticino	117	9	10	86
Berner Zeitung	321	17	41	85
Le Matin	268	28	93	69
Basler Zeitung	121	17	41	68
Tags-Anzeiger	420	37	168	67
Neue Zurcher Zeitung	259	128	15	64
20 Minuten	1665	425	680	60
Blick	562	101	555	46

Source WEMF, 2015

extension of the overall offerings by the professional information media. However, a glance at the most widespread offerings on the Swiss online information market shows a significantly less encouraging picture. The online sector is dominated by the same providers that have already characterized the press and radio sectors for many years. In fact, the media titles and news formats of well-funded media companies such as Tamedia AG, Ringier AG, the NZZ media group and SRG also serve most users in the online information segment. Thus the WEMF circulation figures for 2014 show that 20 Minuten was the front runner ahead of Blick am Abend (or Blick), Tages-Anzeiger, Neue Zürcher Zeitung and Aargauer Zeitung (without Sunday papers) in the press sector. The online data of NET-Metrix show a similar pattern. Here too, the news site of 20 Minuten had the largest readership, ahead of blick.ch, srf.ch, bluewin.ch, tagesanzeiger.ch and nzz.ch, in that order. This shows that the hierarchy of the highest-circulation press titles corresponds closely to the online sector.

Compared with the press, however, the online information media market differs in two ways. First, the news portals of the public-service

SRG SSR have a high coverage in the online sector; and second, purely external players such as bluewin.ch and gmx.ch, which also offer news on their portals, currently (still) reach a large public.

Although the press landscape does include other publishers who offer competitive products in addition to the large providers, namely Tamedia AG, Ringier AG and the NZZ media group, the high-coverage offerings on the online sector are essentially restricted to the three large press publishers as well as the providers SRG and Swisscom. So the diversity of professional information providers in the online sector is even more restricted than in the press sector. In addition, the sector of professional online information providers is characterized by greater cooperation of the media titles than in the offline sector. Thus the Newsnet network further restricts the offer of diverse topics and opinions in both German and French-speaking parts of Switzerland. For example, the website contents of Basler Zeitung or indeed Berner Zeitung are very similar to the offering of tagesanzeiger.ch, whereas these titles are still significantly more independent in the press sector. The NZZ group also contributes to a further reduction of diversity with its network (NZZ-Netz). By the same token, the online contents of the new Luzerner Zeitung and of St. Galler Tagblatt are very strongly influenced by the online contents of Neuen Zürcher Zeitung.

Even though digitalization initially allowed new high-coverage providers originating from outside the field of information journalism to become established (including bluewin.ch, gmx.ch and msn.ch), their development has recently been significantly regressive (see Fig. 7.1).

Long-term developments show that the importance of the pure players on the Swiss online market is not increasing but rather declining over time. A relatively new offering, namely watson.ch, is the only one able to buck the trend and grow on this market. In contrast, the email service providers whose websites include an information offer (for example, gmx.ch, bluewin.ch) show a great decline in their use as email services have been increasingly superseded by the social networks. So it must be noted that online information use in Switzerland is still concentrated among relatively few professionally operated online titles offered by the traditional press publishers and radio service operators despite the presence of new providers. This runs counter to the trend seen abroad, where pure brands such as the Huffington Post, Buzzfeed and Vice are among the highest-coverage titles at all (see Newman et al., 2015). In Switzerland in contrast, independent news offerings on the online sector

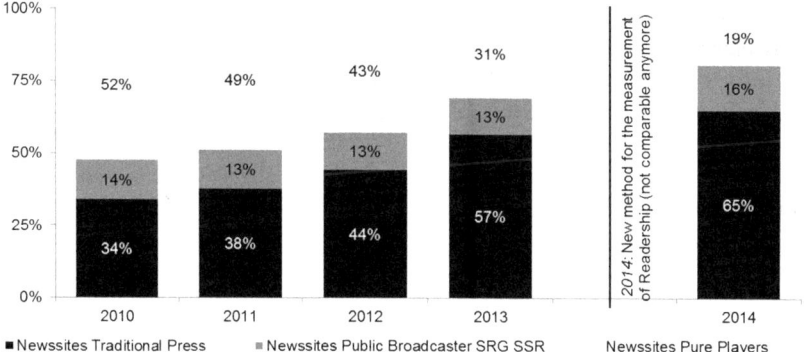

Fig. 7.1 Readership trends for various newspaper types. *Source* The authors, based on data from NET-Metrix (daily use). *Note* Due to a change in the method used, the figures for 2014 are no longer directly comparable with older data

such as infosperber.ch, journal21.ch and even tageswoche.ch essentially represent niche products with relatively low user numbers.

As regards the utilization of information offerings under the impact of digitalization, therefore, the following interim conclusion may be drawn: Although the general readership of online information offerings is increasing and most print offerings have shown, in comparison, (strong) declining user levels for many years, printed information is as a rule still used significantly more widely than information provided via online channels. In other words, the loss in users of the print editions has so far not been compensated by the gain in users of online information media.

News Media—Advertising Revenues

Sheer economics plays a key role in setting up a successful online information offering. The problem is that advertising funds, which have always been a central pillar for financing information journalism, do not flow in the online sector to a degree sufficient to compensate the funds lost in the press sector, and in addition the willingness to pay for online news is very low. The sales revenues of Swiss print products have been declining continuously since 2006. Although people in Switzerland spend more and more money on the media in general (see Verband Schweizer Medien, 2015), ever fewer of them are still prepared to pay for information journalism (Newman et al., 2015). In recent years, more and more Swiss media titles have introduced paywalls to their online offerings. Despite this development, however it still remains completely unclear to what extent these paywalls will actually lead to a substantial improvement of the financial situation, as information providers in the online sector face a readership who are essentially (no longer) willing to pay for news: A survey carried out in several countries (but excluding Switzerland until 2016) by Reuters Institute (2016) showed that in Great Britain, for example, 75% of the respondents would never pay for online information contents. A freebie culture has become increasingly established in Switzerland since the end of the 1990s, with the advent of commuter newspapers, and this soon spread to printed information in general. However, this culture was additionally promoted by the publishers, who made free information available on online channels for many years which had to be paid for in its printed form, and is once again significantly more marked for the online information offerings.

Neither has this earnings deficit so far been compensated by (additional) advertising revenues from the online information media, as the online titles can in no way offset the strongly declining revenues of the press titles. The gap between press losses and online gains was US$3.86 billion worldwide in 2014. Data from the World Association of Newspapers and News Publishers show that this gap has widened successively since 2010, and that the underlying dynamics did not come to a standstill until 2014. Most of the information offerings from the print sector have been (continuously) losing advertising revenues for many years, including in Switzerland. Thus the national net advertising revenues of the Swiss daily and Sunday press were practically halved from 2007 to 2014 (see Stiftung Werbestatistik Schweiz, 2015).

The same gloomy picture may be seen at the level of individual media titles (see Table 7.2): Advertising revenues in the online sector are still considerably lower than in the press sector. The relevant data for the Swiss print and online media originate from Mediafocus: They show the gross advertising revenues for the Swiss online and offline titles in CHF. As combined systems for marketing advertising revenues have also developed in the online sector, the relevant data can in many cases no longer be assigned to specific titles. This problem arises in particular for the advertising revenues of the Newsnet system. Accordingly, the data shown

Table 7.2 Gross advertising revenues for selected media titles in the press and online sectors in Switzerland, 2012–2014

Ad revenues (in tousand CHF)	Ad revenues 2012–2014			Development (2014 compared to 2012)		
	Press	Online	Online(%)	Press	Online	Online(%)
20 Minuten	821.698.323	89.246.033	10,86%	−20.180.182	12.104.926	−8.075.257
Blick	145.703.632	50.442.548	34,62%	6.765.551	5.326.297	12.091.847
Le Temps	66.404.473	7.814.872	11,77%	−2.971.838	215.661	−2.756.117
Neue Zurcher Zeitung	160.344.353	31.190.613	19,45%	−2.000.723	2.658.712	657.989
Newsnet-Network (incl. Tages Anzeiger)	669.486.652	70.708.801	10,56%	−46.981.829	1.170.393	−45.811.436

Source Authors' presentation based on Media Focus (2015)

in Table 7.2 compares the total advertising revenues of all the online titles included in Newsnet (Tages-Anzeiger, Berner Zeitung, Der Bund, Basler Zeitung, Le Matin, Tribune de Geneve, 24 heures) with the corresponding figures for all print editions of the corresponding media titles. For the other media titles shown in Table 7.2, it was possible to assign the online and offline revenues at the level of individual titles.

The share of online advertising among the individual media titles varies between 11 and 35%. Even for a media brand with high advertising impact such as 20 Minuten, the greater part of its advertising revenues still originate from the press sector. Approximately CHF 821 million for the press titles contrasts with CHF 89 million in the online sector (figures Media Focus).

Although revenues on the online advertising market are also increasing continuously in Switzerland, the expert assessments of Media Focus (Media Focus, 2015, p. 5) show an increase of the total online advertising market from CHF 674 million to CHF 848 million for the period 2012–2014, equivalent to 26% growth. However, only a small part of this advertising growth actually accrues to the information media, which in the first instance benefit from the revenues of display advertising, but scarcely at all from the other significantly faster-growing sectors of online advertising such as search engine advertising and online classified headers.

The fact that the online sector has so far failed to fulfill expectations on the generation of advertising revenues can be explained on the basis of two circumstances: First, a large part of the revenues for online advertising flow to the global techno giants such as Facebook and Google. These (American) companies have become established as providers which are opening up new dimensions for the advertising industry as regards coverage even without the provision of information. Thus over 95% of the revenues accruing to Facebook come from online or mobile advertising. The latest figures from the State of the News Media 2015 study (Pew Research Center, 2015a) show that 61% of the online advertising revenues in the USA are already accounted for by the five largest providers. Google (38% of total revenues) and Facebook (10%) were the market leaders in 2014, and there were no longer any traditional news providers among these top five. Although no figures are available for Switzerland, the current Swiss discourse on media policy also assumes that about 50% of online advertising revenues in Switzerland flows abroad (Polynomics, 2016, p 13). Second, advertising in the online sector shows a significantly lower level of acceptance than is the case for print advertising.

Trends in the Reporting Quality of Press and Online Titles

Against the background of the current framework conditions imposed by digitalization, a final question arises, namely how this situation might correspond to the quality of the contents. Does digitalization of the media titles lead to a higher quality of reporting, or is online news of lesser quality than that of the press editions? For this purpose, the contents quality of the press titles was compared with that of the online information sites in the period 2010–2014 (see the section "Methodology" above for data on the methods used and on the media sample). The online–offline quality comparison came to the following conclusions:

First, the quality of reporting in the online information media is on the whole lower than that of the printed media (see Fig. 7. 2). These differences can be seen in the entire study period from 2010 to 2014. Whereas the quality scores of the media titles range between the values

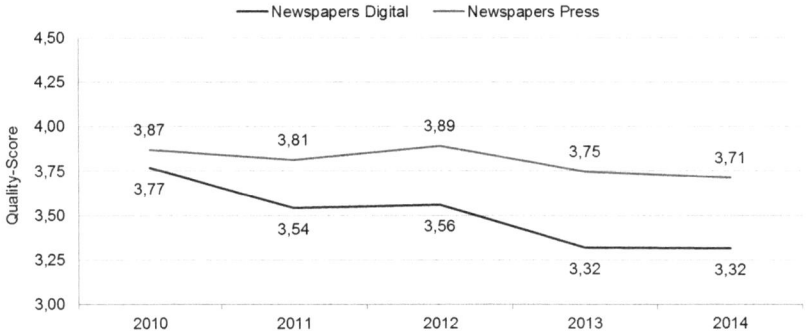

Fig. 7.2 Development of the quality score of press and online titles in Switzerland, 2010–2014 (n = 46,963). *Source* The authors, as described in the text

of 3.7 and 3.9, the online media titles score significantly lower (range: 3.3–3.8). This finding applies not only to the aggregated level, but is in most cases also seen in a direct comparison between the respective online and offline counterparts of a media title. Thus the quality score of the nzz.ch news site in all five study years is significantly poorer than the printed edition of NZZ; the same applies to Tages-Anzeiger and the large-subscription media from French-speaking Switzerland (for example, 24 heures).

The heterogeneous nature of the scores for the various types is naturally relatively marked. Great differences in media quality can be seen within the groups of both online and press media titles. The media titles of the tabloid and free types show fundamentally lower quality values than the titles of the regional and supra-regional subscription media. Thus online titles of the subscription type (including nzz.ch, tagesanzeiger.ch, 24heures.ch, Le Temps Online) score better on quality than the printed editions of the tabloids (Blick and Le Matin) and those of the free and commuter newspapers (20 Minuten and 20 min).

Second, the data for the years 2010 to 2014 show a (continuously) declining quality of reporting in both the print and online sectors. A particularly striking note is that the quality of the online information media has declined more quickly than that of the press editions. The online quality has declined by 0.4 score points (from 3.8 to 3.4) since 2010, whereas a loss in quality was also observed (−0.2) for the press types, but this was less marked and occurred at an overall higher initial level (from 3.9 to 3.7).

What factors can explain these differences between the press and online titles? Against the background of the convergence strategies adopted by most publishers, this finding of a quality gap needs to be explained, as the commitment to convergent editorial structures (such as establishing newsrooms) would rather lead us to expect a quality gradient. First, a decline in reporting relevance can be observed for the online websites. Thus the reporting in the print editions is on the whole not only more relevant than on the corresponding news sites, but the qualitative difference has tended to shift (further) toward the printed editions after 2010. So compared with the news sites, the print editions report significantly more frequently about relevant hard news from the fields of politics, business and culture. They also report much more extensively about overall social and organizational contexts than about narrowly specific and personal matters. Second, the sector of online information media is characterized by a significantly lower level of contextualization of the reporting. In view of the faster rate of news production—which is reflected to a much higher degree on the online channels—the time resources for contextualized and integrative reporting are fast diminishing. The placing of current events in larger (for example, social) contexts requires time, which is available to an ever lessening extent with a mode of reporting that aims for maximum topicality and is oriented to click rates.

CONCLUSIONS

Some voices within the scientific and public discourse have highlighted the benefits of the media convergence for the news media markets and focused on the associated diversity. Our analysis shows that this finding does not hold for Switzerland. Undesired effects of this convergence appear in various sectors. Indeed, the convergence of the media in the digital age appears to have particularly negative consequences with regard to the financing capability and contents quality of the news media.

Growing Media Concentration: The online market offer is characterized by a few news providers from the traditional private press and public radio. Purely digital brands such as watson.ch are still very rare and do not have such a wide range as the providers mentioned above. In addition, various news brands such as bluewin.ch, gmx.ch or msn.ch have suffered a contraction of their range in recent years. In Switzerland, digitalization and the convergence in the sector of professional information journalism have produced not less but more media concentration.

Growing Financing Problems: Whereas the media offers in the online sector are gaining strongly in importance, and their user figures are also growing strongly in many cases, there continue to be major differences between the financial health of the classical offline and new online news offerings. Press titles still generate very much more advertising revenues than their online counterparts. The share of online advertising revenues in the total figure (online and press) is between 10 and 20% in Switzerland. In addition, the digital news media have to struggle with the great problem of advertising acceptance, especially among younger users. In addition, the willingness to pay for online content is generally low in Switzerland, as it is throughout the world (see Newman et al., 2016).

Growing loss of quality: with few exceptions, the relevance of the press reports is far higher than that of the online titles which focus much more strongly on human interest and sport reports than on political topics and economic issues. The online titles also differ from their printed editions as regards the main criteria of professionalism, namely objectivity and contextualization. With few exceptions, the reports carried by the printed press are more objective and are supplied more fully with contextual background than the online reports.

REFERENCES

Arnold, K. (2009). *Qualitätsjournalismus: Die Zeitung und ihr Publikum.* Konstanz: UVK Verlagsgesellschaft.

Barnhurst, K. G. (2010). The form of reports on US newspaper internet sites, an update. *Journalism Studies, 11*(4), 555–566.

Boczkowski, P. J. (2005). *Digitizing the news: Innovation in online newspapers.* Cambridge, MA: The MIT Press.

Bucher, H.-J., & Altmeppen, K.-D. (2003). *Qualität im Journalismus Grundlagen—Dimensionen—Praxismodelle.* Wiesbaden: Westdeutscher Verlag.

Couldry, N. (2012). *Media, society, world: Social theory and digital media practice.* Cambridge, Malden, MA: Polity Press.

de La Piscina, T. R., Gorosarri, M. G., Aiestaran, A., Zabalondo, B., & Agirre, A. (2015). Differences between the quality of the printed version and online editions of the European reference press. *Journalism, 16*(6), 768–790.

Fenton, N. (Ed.). (2010). *New media, old news: Journalism and democracy in the digital age*. Los Angeles: Sage Publications Ltd.

Fög—Forschungsinstitut Öffentlichkeit und Gesellschaft/Universität Zürich (Ed.). (2015). Jahrbuch 2015 Qualität der Medien. Schweiz—Suisse—Svizzera. Basel: Schwabe Verlag.

Grossenbacher, R., & Trebbe, J. (2009). *Qualität in Radio und Fernsehen. Die inhaltsanalytische Messung konzessionsrechtlicher Vorgaben für die Radio und Fernsehprogramme der SRG SSR idée Suisse*. Zürich/Chur: Rüegger Verlag.

Huang, E., Rademakers, L., Fayemiwo, M. A., & Dunlap, L. (2004). Converged journalism and quality: A case study of the Tampa Tribune news stories. *Convergence: The International Journal of Research into New Media Technologies, 10*(4), 73–91.

Imhof, K. (2012). Die Krise des Informationsjournalismus. In W. A. Meier (Ed.), *Gehen in den Leuchttürmen die Lichter aus? Was aus den Schweizer Leitmedien wird* (pp. 69–80). Münster: LIT Verlag.

Iyengar, S. (1991). *Is anyone responsible?*. Chicago:University of Chicago Press.: *How television frames political issues*.

Jandura, O., & Friedrich, K. (2014). The quality of political media coverage. In C. Reinemann (Ed.), *Handbooks of communication science* (Vol. 18, pp. 351–374), Berlin: de Gruyter Mouton.

Jarren, O. (2015). Journalismus—unverzichtbar?! *Publizistik, 60*(2), 113–122.

Kant, I. (1912 [1784]). Beantwortung der Frage: Was ist Aufklärung? In E. Cassirer (Ed.), Kants Gesammelte Schriften, Bd. 8, Berlin: B. Cassirer.

Karmasin, M. (2002). *Medien und Ethik*. Stuttgart: Reclam.

Keel, G., Wyss, V., Stoffel, A., Saner, & Saner, M. (2010). Auswirkungen des Internets auf die journalistische Praxis und berufskulturelle Normen. Winterthur: IAM Institut für angewandte Medienwissenschaften. Retrieved from https://www.zhaw.ch/no_cache/de/forschung/personen-publikationen-projekte/detailansicht-publikation/publikation/6506/.

Kretzschmar, S. (2009). Journalismus to go. In C. Neuberger, C. Nuernbergk, & M. Rischke (Eds.), *Journalismus im internet. Profession, Partizipation, Technisierung* (1st ed., pp. 335–52). Wiesbaden: VS Verlag für Sozialwissenschaften.

Künzler, M. (2011). *Mediensystem Schweiz*. Konstanz: UVK Verlagsgesellschaft.

Levy, D. A. L. (2010). *The changing business of journalism and its implications for democracy*. Oxford: University of Oxford, Reuters Institute for the Study of Journalism.

Lugmayr, A., & Dal Zotto, C. (Eds) (2016). *Media business and innovation. media convergence handbook—Vol. 1: Journalism, Broadcasting, and Social Media Aspects of Convergence* Berlin, Heidelberg: Springer Verlag.

Lutz, B., & Du Toit, P. van der P (2014). *Defining democracy in a digital age: Political support on social media*. Basingstoke: Palgrave Macmillan.

Media Focus (2015). Media focus—online werbestatistik report. Zürich. Retrieved from www.mediafocus.ch.

Morozov, E. (2012). *The net delusion: The dark side of internet freedom.* New York: PublicAffairs.

Newman, N., Levy, D. A. L., & Kleis Nielsen, R. (2015). *Reuters institute digital news report 2015: Tracking the future of news.* Oxford: Reuters Institute for the Study of Journalism.

Newman, N., Richard, Fletcher, Levy, D. A. L., & Kleis Nielsen, R. (2016). *Reuters Institute digital news report 2015.* Oxford: Reuters Institute for the Study of Journalism.

Pew Research Center (2015). State of the News Media 2015.

Picard, R. (2011). Digitization and media business models. Mapping digital media. Open Society Institute. Retrieved from https://www.opensocietyfoundations.org/sites/default/files/digitization-media-business-models-20110721.pdf.

Picard, R. G. (2014). Twilight or New Dawn of journalism? *Journalism Studies, 15*(5), 500–510.

Polynomics (2016). Beurteilung des geplanten Joint Ventures zwischen: Staatsnahe Unternehmen mit neuem Geschäftsmodell für den digitalisierten: Olten.

Puppis, M., & Künzler, M. (2013). Private television in small european states: Ireland, Austria and Switzerland. In K. Donders, C. Pauwels, & J. Loisen (Eds.), *Private television in western europe: Content, markets, policies* (pp. 85–101). London: Palgrave Macmillan UK.

Puppis, M., Schönhagen, P., Fürst, S., Hofstetter, B., & Meissner, M. (2014). Arbeitsbedingungen und Berichterstattungsfreiheit in journalistischen Organisationen. Universität Freiburg.

Quandt, T. (2008). (No) News on the World Wide Web? A comparative content analysis of online news in Europe and the United States. *Journalism Studies, 9*(5), 717–738.

Schranz, M., Gisler, A. (2015). Online: Qualitätsvalidierung. In fög—Forschungsinstitut Öffentlichkeit und Gesellschaft/UZH. Qualität der Medien. Schweiz - Suisse - Svizzera. Jahrbuch 2015 (pp. 191–209). Basel: Schwabe.

Steensen, S. (2010). Online journalism and the promises of new technology. *Journalism studies, 12*(3), 311–327.

Stiftung Werbestatistik Schweiz (2015). Werbeaufwand Schweiz 2015. Zürich. Retrieved from http://www.werbestatistik.ch/index.php?pid=81.

Strömbäck, J. (2005). In Search of a Standard: Four models of democracy and their normative implications for journalism. *Journalism Studies, 6*(3), 331–345.

Trappel, J. (2008). Online media within the public service realm? Reasons to include online into the public service mission. *Convergence: The International Journal of Research into New Media Technologies, 14*(3), 313–322.

Verband Schweizer Medien (2015). Medienbudget 2014. Zürich: Verband Schweizer Medien. Retrieved from http://www.schweizermedien.ch/branchendaten/studie-medienbudget.

Weischenberg, S. (2006). Medienqualitäten: Zur Einführung in den kommunikationswissenschaftlichen Diskurs über Maßstäbe und Methoden zur Bewertung öffentlicher Kommunikation. In S. Weischenberg, W. Loosen, & M. Beuthner (Eds.), *Medien-Qualitäten. Öffentliche Kommunikation zwischen ökonomischem Kalkül und Sozialverantwortung* (pp. 9–34). Konstanz: UVK Verlagsgesellschaft.

Weiss, R., Magin, M., Hasebrink, U., Jandura, O., Seethaler, J., & Stark, B. (2016). Publizistische Qualität im medialen Wandel—eine normativ begründete Standortbestimmung. In P. Werner, L. Rinsdorf, T. Pleil, & K.-D. Altmeppen (Eds.), *Verantwortung—Gerechtigkeit—Öffentlichkeit. Normative Perspektiven auf Kommunikation* (pp. 27–50). Konstanz, München: UVK Verlagsgesellschaft.

WEMF (2015). Total Audience 2015. Retrieved from http://www.wemf.ch.

Wessler, H. (2008). *Investigating deliberativeness comparatively. Political communication, 25*(1), 1–22.

Wilczek, B., Nienstedt, H.-W., & Russ-Mohl, S. (Eds.). (2013). *Media convergence/ Medienkonvergenz: volume/band 5. Journalism and media convergence.* Berlin, Boston: De Gruyter.

Wyss, V. (2002). *Redaktionelles Qualitätsmanagement: Ziele, Normen, Ressourcen.* Konstanz: UVK Verlagsgesellschaft.

AUTHORS' BIOGRAPHY

Mark Eisenegger is a Full Professor at the University of Salzburg's Department of Communication Studies, Organizational Communication Unit, Austria. He is also President of the Research Institute for the Public Sphere and Society (fög) at the University of Zurich, Switzerland. His main areas of research are: organizational communication/PR; business communication; sociology of the public sphere; media change; quality of the media.

Mario Schranz is Head of the Research Institute for the Public Sphere and Society (fög) at the University of Zurich, Switzerland. His main areas of research are media change and quality of the media; corporate reputation; and business communication.

Angelo Gisler is a Research Associate at the Research Institute for the Public Sphere and Society (fög)/University of Zurich, Switzerland. His main areas of research are organizational communication/PR, business communication, sociology of the public sphere and quality of the media.

CHAPTER 8

Transmedia Storytelling and Mega-Narration: Audiovisual Production in Converged Media Environments

Lothar Mikos

In the past three decades the media landscape has undergone a unique transformation. Digitalization and the integration of traditional media and telecommunication have allowed films and television programs to be marketed and used on other technical platforms besides conventional cinema and television.

The concept of convergence has a crucial importance on several levels in contemporary media culture (see Balbi, Chapter 2 in this volume). With Roger Silverstone (1995, p. 11) we can consider that convergence is "a dangerous word," because it means different things to different people. One can also assume what Anders Fagerjord and Tanja Storsul (2007, p. 28) mentioned some years ago, namely that the term convergence is used as a "rhetorical tool." The term is used to describe significant and complex changes in the contemporary media landscape initiated by digitalization. They state: "The current media developments are diverse. What we see are several parallel developments resulting in a

L. Mikos (✉)
Filmuniversität Babelsberg KONRAD WOLF, Potsdam, Germany
e-mail: l.mikos@filmuniversitaet.de

© The Author(s) 2017
S. Sparviero et al. (eds.), *Media Convergence and Deconvergence*, Global Transformations in Media and Communication Research - A Palgrave and IAMCR Series, DOI 10.1007/978-3-319-51289-1_8

159

higher level of complexity, with new alignments of networks, terminals, services and markets." (Fagerjord & Storsul, 2007, p. 27) Convergence is used as a metaphor to describe these changes in a simple way—in other words, to reduce complexity. Nonetheless, we can maybe speak of a converged media environment in which we all live. This converged media environment includes developments and changes on various levels and in various areas: (1) technology, (2) economy, (3) politics, (4) culture, and (5) social developments. Politics, industry and audiences/consumers are undergoing significant changes in convergent media environments.

The processes of convergence go hand in hand with processes of deconvergence (Jin 2013, pp. 111–126). It is a dialectical process. Technological change leads to a multiplicity of channels and platforms which deliver audiovisual content. The fragmentation of film and television leads also to fragmented audiences. Diverse audiences use different media platforms to get films and television shows whenever and wherever they want. Producers face several challenges and develop strategies to deal with media and audience fragmentation. For instance, there are two goals for television in converged media environments: "first, to stimulate emotional investment and generate audience loyalty, and second, to use this to create new revenues" (Simons, Dhoest, & Malliet, 2012, p. 26).

The following paragraphs will deal with two parts of the consequences of digitalization in converged media environments: the level of cultural developments in textual production, namely transmedia storytelling as an industrial practice to engage audiences with television drama series as multi-layered media texts, driven by technological and economic changes; and what I will call "mega-narration" as an industrial practice to engage audiences with a story universe as a global brand. The chapter will argue that transmedia storytelling is a consequence of media convergence and deconvergence in multi-platform media environments. Film studios, production companies, networks and other TV channels attempt to involve viewers via transmedia storytelling in a fragmented media market with a fragmented audience in creating a 360° experience. Furthermore, the chapter will systematize transmedia outlets of television drama series and use the example of the Marvel Cinematic Universe to shed light on mega-narratives in converged media environments. The chapter will thus deliver some critical insights into the production and distribution of contemporary film and television texts in an era of convergence and deconvergence.

Transmedia Storytelling and the Building
of Narrative Worlds

In a convergent media environment, film franchises and television formats are established as global transmedia brands. The story in the viewers' minds is no longer created by just one film or television show. Rather, all of the various offerings associated with a film or television text contribute to it. A media franchise distributes the same text and the same story on different platforms; it is a cross-media activity accompanied by consumer products that are related to that specific multimedia text. Derek Johnson, who has analysed the history of media franchising, argues that:

> [T]he media franchise of the late twentieth and early 21st century has constituted and been constituted by the shared exchange of content resources across multiple industrial sites and contexts of production operating in collaborative but contested ways through networked relations to one another (frequently across boundaries of media platform, production community, and geography). (Johnson, 2013, p. 7)

Media franchises are changing the way of both media consumption and cultural consumption. Based on technological developments that are initiated by digitalization, media franchises and media brands offer the possibility of new ways of storytelling. Media franchises are convergence and deconvergence at work. Franchise is an economic concept which tries to keep audience loyalty as long as possible to a cultural product as brand, by selling symbolically loaded goods to consumers. Transmedia storytelling is not necessarily part of franchises; they can work without transmedia outlets. Instead franchises such as the Marvel Cinematic Universe create a mega-narration over a series of movies that are based on comic books and extended by computer games.

From a production point of view, transmedia storytelling is the systematic planning of a story throughout different platforms—and not one story on different or multiple platforms (see Evans, 2011; Simons et al., 2012). From the beginning the diverse narrative and aesthetic possibilities of different media outlets are part of the development of the story. Transmedia storytelling offers a 360° experience for audiences:

> A transmedia story unfolds across multiple media platforms, with each new text making a distinctive and valuable contribution to the whole. In

the ideal form of transmedia storytelling, each medium does what it does best... Each franchise entry needs to be self-contained so you don't need to have seen the film to enjoy the game and vice versa. Any given product is a point of entry into the franchise as a whole. Reading across the media sustains a depth of experience that motivates more consumption. Redundancy burns up fan interest and causes franchises to fail. Offering new levels of insight and experience refreshes the franchise and sustains consumer loyalty. (Jenkins, 2006, pp. 95–96)

To make consumers enthusiastic participants in the market that creates "streamed content" for multiple media (Murray, 2003, pp. 13–14), producers must give their media products ideological and demographic characteristics that are specific enough to get consumers to invest emotion in the "brand content." The commercial success of television drama series with an independent brand identity, such as Heroes or True Blood, is therefore explicable not least by the fact that specific psycho-social profiles are mapped in them, and precisely enough to appeal across multiple media formats to consumers who hold a loyal attitude to the content.

This requirement determines to a great extent the aesthetic quality that producers must give to the brand content. To facilitate the transferability of brand content over multiple media platforms and at the same time to ensure sufficient emotional involvement of the consumers for them to form a lasting bond with the content, the techniques of transmedia storytelling have increasingly evolved away from the linear dramaturgy of suspense, towards the immersive forms of an "art of world-making":

More and more, storytelling has become the art of world building, as artists create compelling environments that cannot be fully explored or exhausted within a single work or even a single medium. The world is bigger than the film, bigger even than the franchise—since fan speculations and elaborations also expand the world in a variety of directions. (Jenkins, 2006, p. 114)

In the context of such an art of designing complete, consistent and hence plausible worlds, the acoustic and visual form—the "aesthetic design"—takes on greater importance in contrast to purely narrative resources (see Cubitt, 2004, p. 217; Evans, 2011, pp. 28–31; Jenkins, 2006, p. 115). Konzal (2012) labels these tendencies of multiplatform world building as "entertainment architecture," because a comprehensive process of planning is necessary to produce a transmedia text.

Among the advantages of transmedia storytelling, in terms of narrative economy, is the fact that individual characters do not have to be completely introduced in the first episode of a television drama series. A brief reintroduction is often sufficient, since the characters can be presumed to be familiar from other sources, for instance on related websites to television series as in the case of Game of Thrones or Lost, both drama series where a huge cast is involved. The examples illustrate how additive understanding as a mode of reception is apt to fill gaps in individual texts from prior knowledge.

According to Ryan (2013, p. 89) there are two poles of transmedia storytelling. At one pole are adaptations, prequels and sequels, and at the other pole there are projects such as television drama series in which a story is conceptualized from the beginning to evolve on different media platforms. But also in this case there is a core text mainly in television from which the story unfolds on the other platforms. Each story on each platform contributes to a narrative world that is constituted by the different media outlets, not around a text but around the story world of a drama series. Every piece of the story on the various platforms "interacts with the others to deepen the whole—but it is capable of standing on its own—giving the audience the choice as to how deep into the experience they go" (Weaver, 2013, p. 8). That is the main challenge for transmedia storytelling, to create every piece of the story as part of a whole story world, but every piece has to be a story in its own right (Harvey, 2014, p. 278). This challenge of transmedia storytelling is clearly linked to processes of convergence and deconvergence. The combination and interplay of different media platforms is a process of convergence, whereas the production of different media texts for every platform that should build a unified narrative world as well as several stories in its own right is linked to processes of deconvergence. Therefore Elizabeth Evans (2011, p. 31) has claimed a "unified author" for the production of transmedia texts. This does not mean that there is a single author for all platform outlets of a story world, but there should be a kind of "authorial coherence" that becomes manifest, for example, "through the branding of each transmedia text" (Evans, 2011, p. 33). Coherence in production practices and additionally in broadcasting services is also necessary.

According to Evans (2011) a third and most important form of coherence is part of transmedia texts. Beside narrative and authorial coherence there should be a temporal coherence, because transmedia stories can use "the temporal windows inherent in the television schedule" (Evans, 2011, p. 37). Most of the transmedia texts are related to television series, which are almost always the core or kernel of a transmedia world—there are only very few examples whereby transmedia stories are based on other media outlets than television, for example, the Marvel Cinematic Universe. A transmedia story is able to extend the television text onto other platforms. In general there are two approaches to transmedia storytelling: "[Y]ou either create a story that can only be told across multiple platforms or you take a story from one medium and add other media to it to deepen the world created in the focus medium" (Weaver, 2013, p. 8). Therefore Weaver makes a distinction between "native transmedia" and "additive transmedia" (Weaver, 2013, p. 11). For example, Pokémon is created as a native transmedia story, whereas most of the television series have created additive transmedia story worlds for another medium. TV drama series like Game of Thrones, Sherlock and The Walking Dead have added a lot of multiplatform experiences, from graphic novels to augmented reality games to extra episodes for mobile phones (Clarke, 2013, p. 137; Evans, 2011, p. 85; Hills, 2015; Klastrup & Tosca, 2014).

> A transmedia television episode can ultimately be seen as a story that is engaged with across a range of audio-visual platforms, during a limited timeframe and defined by shared episodic-specific narrative codes and either personal or corporate authorship. (Evans, 2011, p. 38)

Audiences can enter a transmedia world from different access points. In the presence of aesthetic convergence, transmedia storytelling thus presupposes three categories of viewers or users with paradigmatic attitudes of reception which are characteristic of media products in the digital age: first, "the actively engaged real-time viewers who must find suspense and satisfaction in each single episode"; second, "the more reflective long-term audience who look for coherent patterns in the story as a whole"; and third, "the navigational viewer who takes pleasure in following the connections between different parts of the story and in discovering multiple arrangements of the same material" (Murray, 1999, p. 257). But still the majority of viewers do not actively participate in the narrative worlds. Therefore, most of the transmedia outlets are successful only with engaged fans and not with "ordinary" audiences. And as viewers can access transmedia stories from different access points and choose how deep they want to go into the story world, transmedia storytelling is fostering audience fragmentation even if the intention of producers is to keep audiences connected to the audiovisual brand on every platform.

TYPES OF TRANSMEDIA STORYTELLING AND TELEVISION DRAMA SERIES

Principally it is important to distinguish different types of transmedia storytelling related to television drama series. They can be categorized by the purposes the transmedia outlets serve. The categorization is an analytical one; in practice the different types overlap. The purposes of transmedia television drama series are to keep the branded narrative universe alive and bridge the gaps between seasons, to make a drama series more attractive to different target audiences, to give more character information than possible in the television show and to engage audiences extensively in the experience of the drama series. For these goals producers use different forms of transmedia extensions: viral marketing and advertisement, graphic novels, web series, mobile apps, web pages, computer games, online games, alternative reality games and role-playing games.

Viral marketing is one type of transmedia narration that should introduce a drama series brand or keep it alive. For instance, viral marketing was very important in the case of the vampire series True Blood:

> For the first series a cross-media marketing campaign for True Blood was developed using the iconography of an adult drink, with taglines such as "Real blood is for suckers" "All flavor. No bite." Videos spread virally some three months before the series aired explaining how True Blood enabled vampires to "come out," while faux TV spots appeared on cable and late-night network TV advertising vampire-targeted products. (Hardy, 2011, p. 11)

A website was created (www.trubeverage.com) where viewers could get more information about the drink Also a website for vampires went online that was allegedly created by the American Vampire League. The organization promoted equal rights for humans and vampires in the USA. Short videos were shown online in which delegates of the American Vampire League joined TV morning shows to advertise their concerns. In another short video a White House spokesman announced that the President will take the concerns of the vampires very seriously. Also supporters and opponents of equal rights for vampires were interviewed. These video clips were shown on the Facebook site.

To bridge the gap between two seasons of TV drama series producers often launch web series which are an extension of the serial story world. 24 Conspiracy was an extension of 24 and Torn Apart an extension of The Walking Dead. While 24 Conspiracy paralleled the fourth season of 24 (Evans, 2011, p. 119), Torn Apart filled the gap between the first and second season of The Walking Dead. Some producers use web series or apps to introduce new characters of a drama series during a season break. In 2012 during the summer break of the Dutch soap Goede tijden, slechte tijden (Good Times, Bad Times) an app for mobile devices was published. The app Wie is Tim? (Who is Tim?) delivered diary entries of a mysterious character who was introduced as a cliffhanger in the final episode of the last season. Audiences could uncover the secrets of the character little by little. At a final event some of the users of the app could meet the character. The show was able to increase ratings after the summer break because of the popularity of the app. A total of 17% of all viewers of the soap downloaded the app (Wouda, 2013). Beside authorial and production coherence, the temporal coherence of transmedia storytelling is extremely important for viral marketing, the bridging of season gaps and the targeting of younger audiences. Otherwise the extension would not work well with viewers and audiences.

Some television drama series use apps and web series to provide more character information than is possible in the TV show itself. Therefore some aspects and/or actions of characters become a central part of web series. Little Monk is a web series in which the main character of the crime series Monk is shown as a child. Audiences are able to watch how some of his attitudes and idiosyncrasies emerged and how even as a child he was already solving the problems and small-time crimes of his schoolmates. Also the minor characters of a drama series can become somewhat more famous as the hero in a web series or "appisodes" for mobile devices. The web series Nurse Jeffrey shows how the male nurse Jeffrey comments on the actions of Dr. House and disses him. Jeffrey's commentaries are published as "Bitch Tapes." The web series gives audiences a perspective on the drama series other than the actions of the main hero. It enhances the story world of the drama series through another narrative perspective.

One of the main purposes of producers is not only to attract audiences, but to engage viewers in the overall transmedia experience of a drama series by connecting an alternative reality game to the story world. The fiction of the drama series and the reality of viewers collide. Audiences can solve the secrets and mysteries of the drama series by playing the game and extending it to social reality. The success in gaming might also unlock or activate other transmedia extensions of the series. The most famous example is The Lost Experience which started during the gap between the second and third season of Lost (Mittell, 2015, p. 301). The first European television drama series that was combined with alternative reality games was Sanningen om Marika (The Truth About Marika) produced by Swedish public service broadcaster SVT and the company P. It achieved success with critics and scholars, but "it was also fairly unsuccessful among viewers" (Bolin, 2010, p. 77). The construction of Marika's story world combined classical linear television (faked debate programs and a five-episode fictional drama series), a web site Conspirare (www.conspirare.se), mobile apps and the Entropa Universe, a Swedish multiplayer virtual universe, to create what SVT's head of drama Christian Wikander called "fiction without limits" (cited in Bolin, 2010, p. 77). The story was about a girl who disappeared without a trace. The case drew attention before the drama series was aired. In her blog a young woman is looking for hints that could provide information about her best friend who has disappeared. The case was linked to real criminal events in Sweden. Audiences could participate in playing an alternative-reality game and in playing the Nordic version of a live-action role playing game (LARP) that expands the fictional world to social reality. The fictional universe consists of two fictional layers: the Conspirare website and the TV debate on one hand and the TV drama series on the other (see Waern & Denward, 2009). In participating in the games the viewers were able to expand the fictional universe. But the whole experience lacks some authorial and production coherence. The example of Sanningen om Marika provides some evidence that the transmedia story world of a television drama series should not be too complex. Instead of gaining audiences they lose the part of the audience that is not willing to participate in online worlds. However, the majority of audiences are still passive and want to watch a television show in a classical linear manner. Only some parts, mainly of younger audiences, are active in an engaging way. They try to get every piece of a transmedia story on every platform and go deep into the story world, as well as participating in fan fiction and other activities related to the branded story. In the end these fan audiences are niche markets which can be exploited more intensely than ordinary audiences. Interestingly, these "converged" audiences arise out of the deconvergence of the media and communication industry.

MEGA-NARRATION IN THE MARVEL CINEMATIC UNIVERSE

Marvel comic books had already created an own fictional world to compete on the market when superheroes from one comic book appeared in other books. That way Marvel created a shared story world that facilitated faithful readership and manifold consumption (Johnson, 2013, p. 74). In 1993, Marvel Entertainment founded Marvel Films, which in 1996 was renamed Marvel Studios, and expanded into the film industry. They gave licenses for movies to other film studios. 20th Century Fox bought the rights to produce the X Men movies, and Sony bought the rights to produce the Spiderman movies. Because the revenues from selling license rights to other studios were relatively small, Marvel Entertainment was thinking about starting to produce its own movies. In 2008, Iron Man premiered as the first film of the Marvel Cinematic Universe produced on Marvel's own authority. "Marvel launched a unique model for cinema production in the age of convergence: an independent company with expertise in a different media industry drove blockbuster film content" (Johnson, 2012, p. 1). Marvel also revealed their cross-media strategy, in announcing the production of several movies which all should be part of the Marvel Cinematic Universe (see Johnson, 2012, p. 5; Weaver, 2013, p. 194). Marvel started to keep the creative control on their fictional universe. This was made possible by a credit line from Merrill Lynch. "The deal provided budgets of between $50 million and $165 million per film, the profits from which could be reinvested, allowing Marvel to project the production of ten films over eight years with this funding" (Johnson, 2012, p. 11). The first films of the Marvel Cinematic Universe were very successful, so Marvel could increase their revenues from $343 million in 2007 up to $6 billion in 2011. The very success attracted Disney and they bought Marvel for a price of $4 billion. But Marvel was able to keep the creative control. The deal makes clear that "brands rather than products now drive the entertainment industry business model" (Santi, 2015, p. 206).

Having the financial resources and the creative control, Marvel started the ambitious project of the Marvel Cinematic Universe: Phase

One—Avengers Assembled (see Johnson, 2012, 5), which is made up of six films: Iron Man (2008), The Incredible Hulk (2008), Iron Man 2 (2010), Thor (2011), Captain America: The First Avenger (2011) and Avengers (2012). One year after the last of these, Marvel commenced with Phase Two of the Cinematic Universe which consists also of six films: Iron Man 3 (2013), Thor—The Dark Kingdom (2013), Captain America—The Winter Soldier (2014), Guardians of the Galaxy (2014), Avengers: Age of Ultron (2015) and Ant-Man (2015). In April 2016, Marvel started the third phase of the Cinematic Universe with Captain America—Civil War (2016). Another thirteen films are announced to be produced until 2020. All these films share a common narrative universe that consists of a huge ensemble of characters. "The Marvel Studios motion pictures seem to all exist within the same storyworld" (Dowd et al., 2013, p. 42), but at the same time each of the films or film series must exist by its own. Therefore, the film series "are built around a particular set of key story elements that distinguish them from each other, elements such as their own variations on story/theme, plot, characters, setting, style and tone" (Dowd et al., 2013, p. 42). But all the characters are part of a shared narrative universe. Therefore, the Marvel Cinematic Universe can be qualified as mega-narrative. In addition it has expanded to television with drama series such as Marvel's Agents of S.H.I.E.L.D. (2013–, ABC), Daredevil (2015–, Netflix), Jessica Jones (2015–, Netflix), Agent Carter (2015–, ABC), Luke Cage (2016–, Netflix), and nine other series are announced.

Marvel's authors and directors use several creative tools to connect one film to the bigger story universe. There are several hints in the setting of the films (for example, the shield of Captain America in the background of a scene in Iron Man), and some characters are mentioned in the dialogues of films in which they do not appear. Also some after- and midcredit scenes enlarge the narrative world of a single film. Already in the first film of the Marvel Cinematic Universe, Iron Man, an after-credit scene tells the audience to be aware that there will be more. When Tony Stark as Iron Man comes home after his fight with the evil Stane, a guy appears out of the dark, wearing an eyepatch and a leather coat. It is Nick Fury, leading agent of the S.H.I.E.L.D. organization, who says addressing Stark: "You think you're the only superhero in the world? Mr. Stark, you've become part of a bigger universe. You just don't know it yet." Agents of the S.H.I.E.L.D. organization appear in nearly every film, because they have to collect the different superheroes and assemble them in the Avenger films. An after-credit scene of Iron Man 2 shows S.H.I.E.L.D. agent Phil Coulson in a desert where he has discovered Thor's hammer. The fictional universe opens up a new story that will be told in the Thor films. Most of the hints to other superheroes, villains or agents come up in dialogues between characters. These pieces of information are not necessarily important to understanding the story of the single film, but they are indications of the bigger narration and of other events as part of the mega-narration.

The films of the Marvel Cinematic Universe highlight how transmedia stories offer numerous intertextual and transtextual references, but every single film creates a story in its own right. Even when the superheroes assemble in The Avengers, they open up new possible stories. Film scholar Jasmina Kallay (2013, p. 95) has identified The Avengers as

> a prime example of a cinematic resistant to closure or an end point. Based on the fictional universe provided by the Marvel comic books, it gathers characters from preexisting comics and films... deepening the sense that all of these heroes' and heroines' paths intersect, and setting the foundation for more cross-pollination among the different superheroes, ensuring a potentially endless narrative engagement and endless narrative configurations.

Audiences get involved in the narrative universe. The attraction of The Avengers is the "felt perception of the movement of the commodity across a personalized, and yet collectively acculturated space" (Isaacs, 2014, p. 220). Audiences and superheroes share a common space within the mega-narration of the Cinematic Universe.

There is no chronologic continuity, because the films are placed in different historical times and they can be consumed in an order different from the chronology of their release dates. But the narration of every single film offers audiences access points or touchpoints that can be used individually. Transtextual references establish a connection to the mega-narration of the Marvel Cinematic Universe. The S.H.I.E.L.D. agents in particular are responsible for building connections, because they appear in every film. This way every single character—Tony Stark/Iron Man, Bruce Banner/Hulk, Thor, Scott Lang/Ant-Man and Steve Rogers/Captain America—exists in a story world of its own right, while at the same time they exist in the mega-narration of the Marvel Cinematic Universe, in a universe together with the S.H.I.E.L.D. agents such as Nick Fury, Phil Coulson, Hawkeye, Peggy Carter and Natasha Romanov/Black Widow. It is up to the viewers how deeply they want to participate in the fictional universe that is built up not only by the films of the Marvel Cinematic Universe and its expansion into television drama series, but also by the comic books and computer games.

CONCLUSION

Transmedia storytelling and mega-narration is the answer of producers and television channels to the increasing fragmentation of the market and of audiences. The extension of core texts such as films or television drama series is the attempt to engage audiences in more than one way and to offer audiences a 360° experience with films, TV shows, web series, graphic novels, alternative reality games, computer games, role play games, apps for mobile devices and social network sites. These production strategies foster further audience fragmentation, because it's up to audience to decide how deep they go into the story world.

The process of digitalization has created multiple ways of creating, producing and distributing texts such as television drama series. In a digital convergent media environment it is possible to create transmedia narrative worlds much more extensive than before where, for instance, the story of a TV show like Twin Peaks with its cinematographic aesthetics was extended only by print material like The Secret Diary of Laura Palmer (Desmet, 1995; Lavery, 1995). They exist as part of a textual universe in which transmedia storytelling is playing an important role. The new technologies do not change texts so much as the social and cultural contexts, the "reading formations" (Bennett & Woollacott, 1987) that influence the creation of meaning in co-production between text and audiences. These formations enter into a mutual relationship with the text as an aesthetic object, one which, in the case of a transmedia text, has a narrative, authorial and temporal coherence.

The consequences for audience studies are grave, since "under these contemporary conditions of media culture it has therefore arguably become impossible to clearly isolate out what the meaning of a single, specific, bounded text would be" (Hills, 2005, p. 26). Consequently, audience studies are no longer concerned simply with investigating the meaning of television shows for different audiences, but rather with investigating the processes that have contributed to making television drama series a part of the circulation of meanings in cultural and social contexts. Classical text analysis can expose how the dramatic, narrative and aesthetic structures of a television drama series and its transmedia extensions involve the viewers in the co-production of meanings. Moreover, it must also focus on the institutional conditions in the global media market, the intertextual frames, the social and cultural conditions of the audiences' life-worlds and their everyday lives, as well as on the social discourses with which the co-production of meanings shares a mutual relationship.

Films and television drama series continue to supply symbolic material with which audiences in their sociocultural contexts carry on the meaningful construction of their life-worlds. But these series are also increasingly bound up in a network of multiple media. This sets media studies the task of developing more complex methods of analyzing television drama series and their transmedia extensions. The digital multimedia environment offers new ways of distribution for films and television drama series.

Audience engagement is becoming more and more important for producers in digitalized multimedia environments. The content has to be available on all media platforms so that the audience can find the TV drama series brand wherever they are. Transmedia extensions of television drama series strengthen the awareness of the branded content in the present "marketplace of attention" (Webster, 2014). Audiences have the chance to decide how deep they want to go into the fictional story worlds of transmedia television drama series. Television drama series and their transmedia extensions are of economic importance for producers, TV channels and video-on-demand platforms because, in their view, audience engagement contributes significantly to economic success.

The examples discussed make clear that not every transmedia extension leads to success among audiences. Whereas the combination of television drama series with alternative reality games is only successful among younger audiences, bridging the gap of seasons and keeping the drama series brand alive is able to increase the awareness and the success on television. Transmedia narratives are successful when they fulfill specific purposes, but they are not successful as experiments in which an online world is combined with the story of a drama series without targeting specific audiences. Interestingly, the transmedia extensions of popular US television drama series were applied in Europe to productions of public service broadcasters more or less successfully (see Simons et al., 2012). To succeed with transmedia drama series it is necessary to have in mind that transmedia narratives need authorial, production and temporal coherence. Therefore they must address specific audiences that are available in time and space. Mega-narrations such as in the Marvel Cinematic Universe seem to be more successful with audiences than some transmedia extensions of television drama series. Even if every single superhero film has different success with audiences, all of the films of the Marvel Cinematic Universe together are a huge success and generate huge revenues for Disney and the Marvel Studio.

In fragmented converged media environments producers try to keep their audiences and catch them wherever they are. Audiences are independent in what they are doing, where they watch films or drama series, on which technical device they watch, and finally they decide how deep they want to go into a transmedia story world. Transmedia storytelling and mega-narration are attempts of the media industry to keep the audience flow over all platforms where they are present with their film or drama series brand. Nevertheless they facilitate audience fragmentation, because it's up to audiences to experience transmedia story worlds and mega-narrations and to decide whether transmedia storytelling will be a success story or not. Further research should focus on the audience perspective and investigate which kind of audiences engage and/or participate in which type of transmedia storytelling of television drama series or mega-narration of a fictional film universe. But even a transmedia story universe and a mega-narration will not attract huge audiences if the story and the characters are unattractive. Storytelling with complex characters will always be the core element in the digital future of film and television in a converged media environment.

Mega-narration and transmedia storytelling are production practices that should accept the challenges in a fragmented media market with fragmented audiences. Digitalization of media resulted in technological and economic converged media environments with deconverged media outlets and media use. The development of media industries and the production of audiovisual media products in the 21st century see convergence and deconvergence at work simultaneously.

References

Bennett, T., & Woollacott, J. (1987). *Bond and beyond. The political career of a popular hero*. Basingstoke: Macmillan.

Bolin, G. (2010). Digitization, multiplatform texts, and audience reception. *Popular Communication, 8*(1), 72–83.

Clarke, M. J. (2013). *Transmedia television. New trends in network serial production*. New York: Bloomsbury.

Cubitt, S. (2004). *The cinema effect*. Cambridge and London: The MIT Press.

Desmet, C. (1995). The canonization of Laura Palmer . In D. Lavery (Ed.), *Full of secrets. Critical approaches to twin peaks* (pp. 93–108). Detroit: Wayne State University Press.

Dowd, T., Fry, M., Niederman, M., & Steif, J. (2013). *Storytelling across Worlds. Transmedia for creatives and producers*. New York & London: Focal Press.

Evans, E. (2011). *Transmedia television. Audiences, new media and daily life*. New York and London: Routledge.

Fagerjord, A. & Storsul, T. (2007). Questioning convergence. In T. Storsul & D. Stuedahl (Eds.), *Ambivalence towards convergence. Digitalization and media change* (pp. 19–31). Göteborg: Nordicom.

Hardy, J. (2011). Mapping commercial intertextuality: HBO's true blood. *Convergence, 17*(1), 7–17.

Harvey, C. B. (2014). A taxonomy of transmedia storytelling. In M.-L. Ryan & J.-N. Thon (Eds.), *Storyworlds across media. Toward a media-conscious narratology* (pp. 278–94). Lincoln and London: University of Nebraska Press.

Hills, M. (2005). *How to do things with cultural theory*. London: Hodder Arnold.

Hills, M. (2015). Storyselling and storykilling: affirmational/transformational discourses of television narratives. In R. Pearson & A. N. Smith (Eds.), *Storytelling in the media convergence. Exploring screen narratives* (pp. 151–73). Basingstoke: Palgrave Macmillan.

Isaacs, B. (2014). *The orientation of future cinema. Technology, aesthetics, spectacle*. New York: Bloomsbury.

Jenkins, H. (2006). *Convergence culture. Where old and new media collide*. New York and London: New York University Press.

Jin, D. Y. (2013). *Deconvergence of global media industries*. New York and London: Routledge.

Johnson, D. (2012). Cinematic destiny: marvel studios and the trade stories of industrial convergence. *Cinema Journal, 52*(1), 1–24.

Johnson, D. (2013). *Media franchising. Creative license and collaboration in the culture industries*. New York and London: New York University Press.

Kallay, J. (2013). *Gaming film. How games are reshaping contemporary cinema*. Basingstoke and New York: Palgrave Macmillan.

Klastrup, L., & Tosca, S. (2014). Game of thrones: transmedial worlds, fandom, and social gaming. In M.-L. Ryan & J.-N. Thon (Eds.), *Storyworlds across media. Toward a media-conscious narratology* (pp. 295–314). Lincoln and London: University of Nebraska Press.

Konzal, W. (2012). Entertainment architecture: constructing a framework for the creation of an emerging transmedia form. *Journal of Cultural Science, 5*(2), 120–152.

Lavery, D. (1995). The semiotics of cobbler: twin peaks' interpretive community. In D. Lavery (ed.), *Full of secrets. Critical approaches to twin peaks* (pp. 1–21). Detroit: Wayne State University Press.

Mittell, J. (2015). *Complex TV. The poetics of contemporary television storytelling.* New York and London: New York University Press.

Murray, J. H. (1999). *Hamlet on the holodeck. The future of narrative in cyberspace.* Cambridge, MA: The MIT Press.

Murray, S. (2003). Media convergence's third wave. *Convergence, 9*(8), 8–18.

Ryan, M.-L. (2013). Transmediales storytelling und Transfiktionalität. In K. N. Renner, D. von Hoff & M. Krings (Eds.), *Medien—Erzählen—Gesellschaft. Transmediales Erzählen im Zeitalter der Medienkonvergenz* (pp. 88–117). Berlin and Boston: De Gruyter.

Santi, A. (2015). *Selling the silver bullet. The "Lone Ranger" and transmedia brand licensing.* Austin: University of Texas Press.

Silverstone, R. (1995). Convergence is a dangerous word. *Convergence, 1*(1), 11–13.

Simons, N., Dhoest, A., & Malliet, S. (2012). *Beyond the text: producing cross- and transmedia fiction in flanders* (pp. 25–40). Northern Lights: Film and Media Studies Yearbook.

Waern, A., & Denward, M. (2009). On the edge of reality: reality fiction in sanningen om marika. In *Proceedings of Breaking New Ground: Innovation in Games, Play, Practice and Theory—Digital Games Research Association (DiGRA).* London: Brunel University, 1–4 September 2009. http://soda.swedish-ict.se/4033/1/SOM-DIGRA-Final_%28kopia%29.pdf. Retrieved November 27.

Weaver, T. (2013). *Comics for film, games, and animation. Using comics to construct your transmedia storyworld.* New York and London: Focal Press.

Webster, J. G. (2014). *The marketplace of attention. How audiences take shape in a digital age.* Cambridge MA and London: The MIT Press.

Wouda, E. (2013). Contact is king. Paper presented at the workshop "Digital Strategies. Financing, Marketing and Distribution 2.0" of Erich Pommer Institute in Berlin, December 5.

AUTHOR BIOGRAPHY

Lothar Mikos is Professor of Television Studies at Filmuniversität Babelsberg Konrad Wolf in Potsdam, Germany. He is the former Director of the Erich Pommer Institute of Media Law, Media Economy and Media Research. His main research interests are: digitalization of the audiovisual media industry, comparative studies of popular television formats, popular culture, audience studies, and legal and economic contexts of audiovisual media production.

CHAPTER 9

Web 2.0: An Argument Against Convergence

Matthew Allen

Introduction

A decade ago, Web 2.0 was the "in thing" in the heady re-emergence of software and internet investment after the dot.com crashand before the far more dramatic upheavals of the global financial crisis. One of the persistent themes in discussion at this time was the ongoing insistence by some that convergence—a coming together of all media and computing businesses—was an inevitable consequence of the internet's technological development and business exploitation. In this context, I suggested in the paper which re-appears as this chapter that Web 2.0 was not an argument for convergence but, in fact, further revealed how the underlying dynamics of code and networking were contradictory to the business imperatives behind "big media" and that the next "big thing" was computer corporations taking over the media's natural field or, at least, diverging into new forms of corporate consumer business.

This chapter was first published in 2008 as a paper in First Monday and reappears partially updated in this collection with the kind permission of the publishers.

M. Allen (✉)
School of Communication and Creative Arts, Deakin University,
Geelong, Victoria, Australia
e-mail: matthew.allen@deakin.edu.au

© The Author(s) 2017
S. Sparviero et al. (eds.), *Media Convergence and Deconvergence*, Global Transformations in Media and Communication Research - A Palgrave and IAMCR Series, DOI 10.1007/978-3-319-51289-1_9

177

This takeover is the "future" which has now eventuated. But, hindsight, I admit I failed to see how "telephony" (both in the sense of service provision and devices) would return to the fray, trumping media as the natural ally of the code industries, through the next wave of internet development, the "app." As I explain below, the history of Yahoo! can be understood through the success of its creation; the disaster of its attempt to become a media company; and its failure to return successfully to the code business. Now its future is clear: bought by Verizon, a telecommunications provider in search of a way inside the domination exerted by Apple and Google over the capacity of the new internet of the 2010s and beyond to generate vast profits from ubiquitous consumer use.

YAHOO! AND THE DANGERS OF CONVERGENCE

The bid by Microsoft in 2008 to acquire Yahoo! in a hostile takeover provided stark evidence of the continuing complexity of the intersection of computing and media businesses battling for dominance in the global market. Just as in the case of Time Warner and AOL (Klein, 2003), the proposed Microsoft–Yahoo! deal was about convergence. The big difference, however, was the new context of threats and opportunities which led to Redmond attempting to deploy its legendary financial muscle in pursuit of corporate goals of market domination. This difference became clear from changing conditions of networked media-computing which are in part associated with the rise of Web 2.0 and which provide an essential clue to understanding why Web 2.0 occupies such an important position in contemporary thinking about the internet. As I explain in this chapter, Web 2.0 can itself be understood fully only by locating its emergence and significance within the broad movement of convergence of old and new media forms.

To introduce this topic, consider why Yahoo! was vulnerable to, or perhaps even welcoming of, a takeover by its long-time internet competitor. This vulnerability came about because of decisions, taken in the first years of this century, that reoriented Yahoo! away from being an internet search and portal company to attempting to promote new channels to market for traditional media products via the internet, or supported by the internet (see for example, Koman, 2006). This change was clear in the appointment of media industry heavyweight Terry Semel as CEO in 2001 and in subsequent appointments and business planning that prioritized the relationship of Yahoo! to television and film producers.[1] It can be argued that the problems Yahoo! had with its underlying network technologies (affecting the utility of its search-advertising connection, but also its Messenger service and "360" profile/networking service) were a consequence of this shift in organizational focus. Yahoo! suffered from its efforts to change from being a dot.com innovator (which had made Yahoo! such a significant internet business by the time Semel arrived) to also providing online media services. Notably, Semel's departure in mid 2007 was greeted with relief by many internet analysts and commentators precisely because it was thought to signal a return to a focus on core networked computing functionality. One summed up the change: "The valley [Silicon Valley] will take over Hollywood. Not the other way around" (Arrington, 2007).

The weakness of Yahoo! could have been ascribed to an ill-conceived ambition to be a media company, rather than internet company. Microsoft's primary goal in the proposed takeover was to strengthen itself against Google, the most obvious competitor for its global dominance of computing services and the most successful Web 2.0 business to date. The legacy of Yahoo!'s media strategy was unlikely to have been be of much appeal to Microsoft, which had its own largely unhappy history of attempts to "converge" with media provision. Indeed Yahoo!'s vulnerability resulted from its failure to understand the relationship between the internet and traditional media, just as was the case in the failure of AOL–Time Warner. Convergence, it seems, has not been quite as simple or obvious as we might first believe. Equally, Yahoo!'s vulnerability for takeover reflects the company's relative failure to move successfully into the era of Web 2.0, for the concentration on media partnerships left Yahoo! struggling with technological approaches and assumptions about the internet that dated from the 1990s (Koman, 2006). And, with this in mind, let me now turn to the main focus of this chapter: what Web 2.0 means and what it tells us about the adoption and development of the internet more generally.

WEB 2.0—WHAT DOES THAT MEAN?

Web 2.0 is a curious term, laden with uncertainty. As I have explored elsewhere (Allen, 2007), this situation results largely from the way the term was initially promoted by Tim O'Reilly via his Web 2.0 conference in 2004, as well as the influence of the internet itself in hosting and spreading debate about Web 2.0 (see especially Graham, 2006, and Doctorow, 2006, for interesting views on O'Reilly's role). It is not the case, however, that there are competing definitions for the term: rather,

Web 2.0 is a shorthand term for many different things, some in conflict, some overlapping but marked especially by the fact that they are onto-logically non-compatible. In short, Web 2.0 is about ideas, behaviors, technologies and ideals all at the same time. Moreover, its distinctive assertion of a change in state, from Web 1.0 (a term that was never used in any case) to Web 2.0, begs the question of the degree to which this change has actually occurred or may be occurring because of something new, or simply involves a re-expression of things previously understood as 'the web', but placed in a new arrangement or seen in a new light.

I would argue that while many current internet developments, activi-ties, applications and the like can be understood as examples of Web 2.0, they do not themselves constitute it. Rather, Web 2.0 is a conceptual frame, within which we can correlate and make sense of those diverse events even as we use it as a convenient shorthand. What then are the main elements to this frame, the pieces whichtogether create the bound-aries around the picture of the current state of the World Wide Web? There are four—technology, economy, users and philosophy—and I will outline each in turn, drawing on both the originating material for the idea of Web 2.0 and on subsequent debates (O'Reilly, 2005; Musser, 2006; Madden & Fox, 2006; and see Allen, 2007 for further details).

Firstly, Web 2.0 is a term applied to approaches to the design and functionality of websites and the services they offer that have emerged in recent years, and essentially describing technological implementations that prioritize the manipulation and presentation of data through the interaction of both human and computer agents. One example would be a mash-up of data from one website with data from another site, which is then seamlessly presented to users through a third site, in which users can control how and what data combinations occur. Another example might be the automated collation of data about one user of a website which is then utilized to enable other users to contact or interact with that first user. The concepts behind these technologies are not new, but their application to the web has become significant in recent years, thus justifying a description—Web 2.0—that implies a different kind of World Wide Web from that of the 1990s.

Second, Web 2.0 refers to a business model for financial success in using the internet to put people and data together in meaningful exchanges. At its simplest, Web 2.0 business approaches are those in which web companies offer services that allow advertisers to reach con-sumers with marketing communications that are precisely targeted to the specific users most likely to engage with that marketing and at a time when the advertising will have its greatest effect (for example, when a purchasing decision is about to be made). By offering a free and attractive service to users, these web companies will create an audience that can be addressed very effectively by advertisers who will, in return, provide the revenues necessary for financial success. The attention economy was often proposed as the basis for business success for the web in the 1990s (Goldhaber, 1997 among others); but Web 2.0 is presumed to be a radical advance in that it involves more sophisticated technologies to permit acquisition of detailed data about users, the delivery of more precisely targeted advertisements, and a closer integration between online behavior and marketing communication.

Third, Web 2.0 attempts to describe services and activities that permit or create a new kind of media consumer who is more engaged, active and a participant in the key business of the internet: creating, maintaining and expanding the "content" which is the basis for using the internet in the first place (Hinchcliffe, 2006). Once again, as with the other two approaches to defining Web 2.0, this situation is not entirely new: Internet users have always been thought of as "different" from traditional media consumers, as being users and not audiences. However, Web 2.0 implies a significant acceleration in the number of active participants and the quality and attractiveness of their contributions to the point where provision of services to these "produsers" (see Bruns, 2008), rather than delivery of content, is the key element in harnessing the technologies to achieve the successful implementation of the business approach outlined above.

Fourth and finally, Web 2.0 is a political statement of a kind of libertarian capitalism that appears to suit an era in which societies are more and more intensely "mediated" by all forms of entertainment and information media, particularly in the economic First World nations such as the USA who are driving internet development but elsewhere as well. The politics of Web 2.0 are expressed in traditional democratic terms, emphasizing freedom of choice and the empowerment of individuals through what O'Reilly (2005) has termed the "architecture of participation." However, crucially, this freedom and empowerment relates to a more democratic form of media consumption and production, of making the internet itself "democratic." Web 2.0, it is claimed, positions users of the internet, both large and small, as relatively equal and equally engaged participants. Of course, there have been similar claims of the democratizing potential of the internet for many years (for example, Raab et al., 1996, pp. 283–285) well prior to even the emergence of the World Wide Web; what is different now, however, is that, within Web 2.0, the focus is on "democracy" as a state of affairs within the internet itself, rather than as a term suggesting ideals of equality in society as a whole, that might be achieved through the democratizing possibilities of networked communications.

And what ties all four of these elements together is that their current valence and application depends on articulating the renewed relevance of longer-established elements and principles of the internet, despite the apparent decline caused by the dot.com crash at the turn of the century. Thomas (2006, p. 389), for example, concludes that

> Web 2.0 has galvanized some sectors of the digital community to philosophize about wired-ness [sic] in a way that was notably missing for quite some years, ever since the initial euphoria of pre-web internet cultures was damped down by the dotcom boom-and-bust in the rush to monetize every pixel.

More prosaically, O'Reilly identified that Web 2.0 seemed to make sense for him in 2004 because "a lot of programmers were out of work, and there was a general lack of interest in web applications … [but] we saw a resurgence coming …" (O'Reilly, 2007, np). Indeed, O'Reilly's founding assumption, as he came to formulate and promote Web 2.0, was that many internet companies had survived and prospered despite the crash; thus, the crash provided a brutal but very accurate assessment of the kinds of approaches and business thinking that would work and these should drive the next phase of internet development (O'Reilly, 2005).

Proponents of Web 2.0 variously claim it to be a continuation of the World Wide Web but in a better way, or a return to the approaches and the possibilities of the internet before the World Wide Web, or even a second attempt at what the web was originally trying to achieve. In many ways, all of them are correct, because there is no clear logical path of development that can be followed here. As noted above, all four key elements to Web 2.0 do refer directly to approaches and behaviors before 2004; they all also claim to be providing something which breaks with the assumed first version of the web. This contradiction, of course, is precisely what makes Web 2.0 a marketable meme and, for some, a compelling statement of the direction of web development—it is the past, present and future, all at once. O'Reilly, the father of Web 2.0 as much as Berners-Lee was the father of the World Wide Web, has consistently used the term (as have many others) to reinvigorate our collective enthusiasm for the "web," recognizing both current and past explorations and initiatives, and harnessing the validity of them in a clarion call for the future.

Web 2.0 emerges from 2004 onwards, rapidly—though not with criticism—moving to become a "given" in debates and discussions of the internet, so much so that people now use the rhetoric of Web 3.0 if they are attempting to look into the future (for example, Martin, 2008).[2] Web 2.0 is, as I have demonstrated above, a concept that, by framing many individual elements, allows for the development of a general and coherent picture of the web that highlights "good" web practice (where good means one or more of profitable, useful, technologically clever, and socially valuable). In this manner, Web 2.0 fulfils the original aim of its chief promoter, Tim O'Reilly, who wished to find a way to "sell" the internet by reinventing the web for a new round of investment and development. This selling process came at a time of continued weakness in the internet industry, as it recovered from the crash, and when it was believed that, without the kind of proselytizing inherent in Web 2.0, there was a risk that society may not have the kind of sustainable, useful data networking services which had been the promise of the boom in the 1990s.

Convergence—Where Web 2.0 Sits

What I wish to consider now is the way in which the general picture of the web as proposed by Web 2.0 can be related to the broader field of internet and media development. In doing so, I attempt to show how Web 2.0 is a quite specific challenge to some orthodox assumptions about the general state of the internet, media and telecommunications that is framed by the equally conceptual term, convergence. It may seem odd to imagine that Web 2.0 can be an argument against convergence. Surely Web 2.0, just like the World Wide Web in the 1990s and pre-web internet services before then, is part of the overall convergence of media and information? This approach fails to account for the fact that convergence is not simply a vague delineation of broad assumptions about the likely shape of info-media futures, but is a highly significant, historically located struggle for control over the particular form of that info-media future, a struggle being waged by various competing elements seeking to shape that future primarily for their own profit.

Much has been written about convergence (both as part of the process of creating convergence and as critical commentary upon it) and I do not wish to rehearse these debates here. However, it is a reasonable summary to say that convergence has come to mean the process by which various instantiations of human behavior involving information transfers and exchanges, previously separate, come together to be provided in a comprehensive, interlinked manner. Convergence would break down the boundaries between distinct worlds of electronic media (both broadcast television and radio, and their subscription equivalents), print media (both newspapers and magazines), screened movies (both in cinemas and at home), computer gaming (both games as normally understood and also gambling), multimedia (as understood in its 1980s form) and last but not least, voice and text telecommunications (both electronic and print-based forms such as the fax). More significantly, and as implied by the term itself, however, convergence would involve the confluence of several different activities, unified within a single new converged form. Thus, at one level, convergence might be thought to mean the delivery of movies once available only in cinemas over the same communications links used for voice communication; but, in the end, convergence would be combinations such as watching a "television" program while chatting, internet-style, to other viewers at the same time, while also playing games with those viewers involving the content of that program, all via the same system of reception and transmission.

Convergence is best thought of as a reorganization of the economic structures and social practices for the provision and consumption of a broad range of communication and information services enabled by technological advances that lead to the digitization of data, and its circulation at ever-increasing speeds over computer-based networks involving direct connections through telecommunications links. While these technologies provide the conditions for the possibility of convergence, they do not determine its particular forms because the technologies only come to be applied in ways that, in a predominantly free-market global economy, serve the needs of private corporations and their financial interests in the media and information industries.

Those needs are not necessarily coherent. Not only is there competition between various corporations, with different kinds of convergence suiting different interests, but they must also take account of the behavior of media users, even as corporations attempt to shape that behavior so it better suits their profit-oriented needs. Convergence is, therefore, a site for the ongoing struggles within capitalism for the harnessing of technological advance in pursuit of private profit by exploiting the desires of consumers (essentially making media consumers "work" for capital investment in the media). However, the particular characteristics of the technologies which drive convergence undermine this process by creating opportunities for capital investment outside of established structures and by empowering consumers/users so they are much less readily shaped to suit established corporate goals.

Convergence, while often promoted, praised and assumed, is not however a straightforward process; it is as much a source of confusion about the future of media and information in society as it is a clear guide to intended outcomes. Why is this? First of all, while we popularly date convergence as a phenomenon of the late 1990s, there is no doubt that the industries associated with all of the media and information activities which might "converge" were already involved with convergence before this time. Thus, while the internet, as it emerged in the 1990s, was characterized as the harbinger of convergence, it also disrupted existing assumptions about the trajectory of convergence and interrupted efforts already underway to achieve convergence. Equally, the ability to debate and define sensibly the relationship between convergence and the internet was hampered by the fact that "internet" could mean variously (and simultaneously) the underlying protocols for interconnection; the infrastructure of computerized switches, routers and cable or wireless networks by which the internet worked; the services that it provided; and the culture and experience of using the internet.

While the ambiguity of the word internet has led to contradictory approaches to convergences, the underlying reason for that ambiguity also provides a way to analyze and understand why Web 2.0 is an argument against convergence. The internet is both the infrastructure by which data services are possible and also those data services; these two aspects of the internet are owned and controlled by different entities in the struggle of convergence, and involve different possibilities for economic exploitation, not least because, while the web as a data service requires that infrastructure, the infrastructure can (and is) put to other purposes. Moreover, while some elements of the internet's architecture enable convergence in a theoretical sense (for example, interconnection of disparate networks and devices and equal treatment of data packets), those elements can also inhibit the actual occurrence of convergence by complicating the degree of control which convergence competitors can exert.

The dot.com crash has already been noted for its importance in generating both the need for, and some of the underlying logic of, the development of Web 2.0. It was also significant for exposing the significant oversupply in data network data traffic capacity, representing a very large sunk investment for telecommunications providers from which they were unable to profit or even cover costs (Schaff, 2002). As a result, after the crash, one of the key tasks facing the owners of this infrastructure was to find ways to make it profitable. At the same time, there were continued pressures to extend, develop and improve the network—especially at the consumers' end—so as to create a true broadband internet. These pressures were in part a reflection of the rhetoric of government policy makers pursuing rather idealistic goals of information economies and increased citizen engagement through high-speed networks (Allen, 2006). The pressures also stemmed from demands by consumers for higher-speed and always-available internet access. Yet, at base, the business of telecommunications infrastructure providers remained the same: to invest money in creating networks that would allow those companies to extract significant surpluses from the use of the networks by others.

In this environment, the focus for predictions and developments began to rest more on the provision of voice and audio-visual program services, two traditional media and communications forms that had long preceded the internet, but now could be refashioned, utilizing internet infrastructure. In this moment of convergence, which involved both traditional telephone-service-oriented telecommunications companies as well as newer, subscription television corporations (which, in some countries were one and the same), there emerged a necessary struggle over the real meaning of the internet. The owners of network infrastructure, while promoting the internet and claiming to be its pioneers, sought to emphasize the particular uses (voice and video communication; and television and movie presentation) which would suit their position as controlling the infrastructure, because they would be the ones to benefit from and arbitrate the uses of this kind of internet. The future of converged telecommunications was thought to lie in the so-called "triple-play" of internet telephony (or VOIP), internet television, and general internet access (see for example, OECD, 2006).

However, in this triple play, the last use was the least significant for those wishing to promote investment in high-speed networking. The web was not an opportunity here, but a threat—a kind of internet use which excluded the providers of the infrastructure, and which also threatened the audience base of the media organizations which might partner those providers in the delivery of audio-visual content. Moreover, because the web of this era had been designed for largely lower-speed connectivity, it did not appear to offer a compelling reason for the investment in, or purchase of, the high-speed networks which the telecommunications providers wished to build. Essentially, since the internet had come to be popularly equated with the World Wide Web, a data service that did not require broadband (even though such access made it more usable), after the crash, telecommunications providers saw the need and an opportunity to reorient the marketable and consumable internet away from this form, to one more suitable to their long-term plans and ambitions.

THE HISTORY OF DATA SERVICES—THE ORIGINS OF WEB 2.0?

To understand how this situation came to be requires us to consider the long-running history—from the 1970s at least—of the engagement with networked data services by telecommunications providers (see Carlson, 2007). Technologically speaking, this history runs in parallel with the development of the internet, up until the mid-1990s, with the possibilities of packet-switched data services delivered over telecommunications infrastructure being explored by two groups who, while overlapping, had distinctly different approaches. Existing telecommunications providers and partners in traditional media were just as interested in data services via telecommunications as the computer scientists and engineers who are normally understood to be the heroic originators of the internet, whether from public research institutions or other non-profit initiatives, or in the emerging commercial data-services world.

By the early 1990s, there had emerged several different kinds of data services which pre-figure the World Wide Web (see Kyrish, 1996; Abbatte, 1999; Hauben & Hauben, 1997; Hafner & Lyon, 1996; Rheingold, 2000; Grossmann, 1997; Herndon, 2007; *Wikipedia* also provides good summaries of these developments as does Carlson, 2007). There were, variously, hobbyists and enthusiasts providing bulletin board services, some of which were marginally commercial while others were a private, but free service (most famously, WELL in California). Activists were developing and using services such as Pegasus. There were a small number of relatively successful commercial services, such as Prodigy and CompuServe and AOL. Libraries offered online searching and other data services. The internet (collectively describing numerous national networks such as AARNET in Australia and NSFNET in the USA) was established within universities but increasingly with availability to, or interconnection with, other kinds of users. Local public government initiatives were underway as well, bringing services to people within a particular community. UUNET provided a kind of networked service via USENET newsgroups. There had also been efforts to provide online text media—primarily newspaper content—via commercial services such as ViewTron in the USA and Prestel in the UK, though many were no longer in operation by this time. And of course there were emerging possibilities for new kinds of data services of which the last and equally unsuccessful was the Microsoft Network concept which was briefly implemented in Australia, for example, as "OnAustralia," in partnership with the monopoly telecommunications company Telstra.

This complex array of competing, overlapping and duplicating data services, all of which existed side by side and were largely concerned with networking a specific group of people, who formed a collective either based on interest or locality, soon gave way to the world of the web. Berners-Lee and others provided the technical breakthrough of HTTP and HTML (Berners-Lee, 1999), enabling the internet to become much more usable and scalable, for both developers and users, as well as mimicking the graphical interfaces which had dominated personal computing. Equally, the public became conscious of the web through the combined, if competing, efforts of Microsoft in attempting to sell the Windows 95 operating system and of Netscape in establishing its web browser and server software as the "must-have" applications. However, this was not ordained, nor inherent in those earlier developments. Long-time data services proponent John Quartermain used the term "Matrix" to define the emerging pattern of network services, of which the internet, and indeed the World Wide Web, was just one component (see Kitchen, 1998, p. 4; and Salus, 1998). While retrospectively, the internet appears to encompass all of these lines of development, it was by no means inevitable that we would end up with a largely free, publicly oriented and highly distributed data network service of the kind which the web represents.

Whatever the technical similarities among these developments, there were two different sets of assumptions about the business of delivering these services. First, telephone companies understood data exchange via telecommunications as an opportunity to sell different services to subscribers, utilizing their existing infrastructure. Data services allowed telephone companies, in partnership with media organizations—particularly newspapers that were threatened by increasing use by consumers of broadcast electronic media and who were already moving into computer-based content production—to extract additional revenues from the phone services they already provided and maintained with little further investment in hardware. Indeed, in the largely unsuccessful deployment of these services, consumers were expected to cover the cost of the specialized equipment as well as pay both for the data and for the communications costs. Media organizations, who had invested in producing the news and related content in the first place, also saw these services as a mechanism to generate increased returns on that initial investment. In other words, data services were not a radical break with current practice for these commercially oriented organizations but, instead, a new field for capitalization and profit. Crucially, for telecommunications providers, the profit was to be made by exploiting their existing network. Notably, too, in their partnerships with media organizations, the focus fell upon content delivery, rather than the more diverse array of data services which have played such a central role in the popularization of these services.

Developers working outside of telecommunications industries took a different approach. As well as being more open to the possibilities that data services such as email might supplement or even replace traditional communications, these developers treated the existing telecommunications infrastructure as a given, a service that was already provided and could be repurposed. The internet as we know it emerged because the presumption about the purpose and use of the infrastructure by those who were more interested in connectivity over existing networks won out over the plans and aspirations of those who actually owned the infrastructure. And that success was due in part to the fact that providers who, because they were not in the business of providing voice and related communications, and emphasized email, chat and other computer-based communication, were more successful than those who emphasized pay-per-view content that was essentially the same as was available in print, but simply delivered in a different form.

The rapid emergence of the World Wide Web in the 1990s as a popular, public mechanism for data interchange, drawing on existing internet applications and creating new uses, meant an end to the few existing data services that, using the same infrastructure, provided pay-per-use content with limited or no interconnection between systems. Moreover, the particular way in which the web became, effectively, the sole public data service established two assumptions about such services that challenged the profitability of any future development that might attempt to return to the plans of telecommunications and media providers for pay-per-use systems. First, the academic origins of the internet, which privileged non-proprietary interconnection and largely uncontrolled data exchange, made it all but impossible for telecommunications providers to utilize their network ownership to continue with, or reintroduce, proprietary access arrangements that would monetize the actual content rather than the service. Second, internet consumers had come to presume that the services to be found online were, largely, there for free, once the costs of the initial connection were met. Aside from exceptions involving unusually high-demand, low-availability content, internet content and applications providers also operated on the assumption that users would not pay and, instead, embraced an advertising model (as found in free-to-air television) rather than a pay-per-use model (as was normal in telecommunications).

Thus the internet of the 1990s, through the dominance of the World Wide Web, challenged the capacity of the owners of both content and, more importantly, infrastructure, to make any significant exploitation of that ownership. At first, telecommunications providers were more than happy to promote and support the Web, accessed mainly via dialup internet access. For these companies, additional revenues could be earned from the provision of additional fixed telephone lines, timed calls to internet service providers (ISPs) in many countries, and of course the wholesale charging of ISPs themselves. While the emergence of the Web had undone some of their plans for different kinds of data services, it was obviously a source of unexpected short-term profits. However, the economics of this provision were largely based on exploiting the existing public-switched telephone network in new ways, without the need for additional investment, effectively layering the internet on top of existing voice services.

At the same time, while traditional media companies were caught up in the enthusiasm for online media generated by the World Wide Web, there was a fundamental incompatibility between the old and the new. In the form of the World Wide Web, the internet seemed likely to draw attention (and thus advertising revenue) away from traditional media consumption; and, through file-sharing programs, actual content might escape from the control of the major media providers in a manner that would prevent them fully exploiting the profit-making capacities of their ownership of that material. Moreover, in some countries, media organizations had come to own infrastructure not dissimilar to that of telecommunications providers by which to provide subscription television services. While this infrastructure was, soon enough, turned to the task of giving internet access to consumers (and at speeds much higher than those available through dialup), the content being provided over this infrastructure was not in almost all cases actually monetized by the companies concerned. Efforts (notably by Excite) to create internet content services for cable subscribers failed, leaving those media companies involved in subscription television services in a similar position to the large telecommunications companies: their ownership of the network infrastructure was simply a means by which their customers could access other products and services, providing a revenue stream to companies offering web services, rather than being a source of significant financial advantage.

The result of this situation, in recent years, has been a very strong emphasis by providers of network infrastructure on the importance, future significance and general relevance of services other than the web. In doing so, they have argued strongly for convergence, of a kind in which traditional owners of media content, along with traditional owners of infrastructure, create partnerships for an internet dominated by high-bandwidth circulation of audio-visual products, including communications. They have, also, been very active in emphasizing that future investment in network development—to achieve the kind of broadband networks which policy makers have claimed to be necessary for future economic prosperity—can proceed only if there is a clear mechanism by which that investment can be recouped. In America, this insistence has found expression through the arguments for and against network neutrality. In this debate, essentially, infrastructure owners claim that they deserve a share of the profits earned by web-based companies (via their advertising revenues). These owners are also attempting to create arrangements for additional payments from users (both providers and consumers) for the content transmitted over that network above and beyond the normal connection charges, based on the proposed quality of service guarantees and the like.

The first few years of this century therefore saw a different kind of argument for convergence than that proposed, loosely, in the 1990s. This argument returns to the origins of the telecommunications sector's interest in exploiting their ownership of infrastructure but, instead of emphasizing data services, now, they focus on voice and video communication because the possibility of monetized data services was lost when the World Wide Web emerged. The network neutrality debate has brought into stark focus the underlying conflict between telecommunications, on one hand, and the kind of web-based industries that have prospered via the former's infrastructure, on the other. Convergence is now defined by the harmonizing of interests between those telecommunications providers and the media corporations who wish to utilize that infrastructure for financially sustainable content delivery.

In this situation, we can see that Web 2.0, as it emerged in 2004 and since, is not just a marketing move designed to return investment to the internet industries, but exists also to propose and promote those industries and their role in networked society in the face of threats from the traditional giants of media and telecommunications who see convergence as implying the centrality of their approaches, to the cost of the internet as a distinct industrial sector. Web 2.0 addressed the perceived weakness of the web, as the least significant element in the discourse of the triple-play of voice, video and data which dominated the past several years of debate about the future of the internet.

WEB 2.0 AS AN ARGUMENT AGAINST CONVERGENCE

The surrounding context I have just discussed starts to make clear the significance of the timing of Web 2.0's emergence as a conceptual frame by which to promote and make sense of the web as an internet-delivered data service. Web 2.0 is, in this sense, a general proposition that the web is not just one of many components of the convergence of media and internet. Otherwise, telecommunications and media corporations would greatly increase their ability to regain control over the trajectory of development of integrated, interactive media as anticipated in the 1980s, but severely disrupted by the World Wide Web in the 1990s, by sidelining the web and focusing instead on internet applications that were not the web. To demonstrate the importance of Web 2.0 in this respect, I want to conclude by returning to the definition that I advanced above, and examine again the relationship between the four key elements of Web 2.0 and show how each constitutes a specific critique of, and argument against, convergence where that term is understood to mean the domination of the internet by media and telecommunications providers.

First, Web 2.0 emphasizes technologies for the creation and operation of web sites and services that make the web more and more like a computer program, rather than a collection of media channels or forms. Rather than making a web that is based on the precepts of print and electronic media, Web 2.0 emphasizes that the web involves cybernetic programs that offer and take input from the world and process it so as achieve the goals of users. Sites might involve programming in the computer-science sense of the word and thus they are not at all like television "programs"; nor can they be understood by those whose business is to create such programs.

Second, Web 2.0 declaims the significance of the targeted advertising model as the basis for successful profit, claiming implicitly to be far superior to traditional media advertising by creating a climate in which the advertising is part of the activities of users, rather than simply being collocated with their media consumption habits. In this respect, Web 2.0 claims that the internet, far from converging with traditional media, offers a significantly superior kind of advertising appeal precisely because it is not about consuming media products (and advertising with them) but about doing things which are directly connected to marketing communications (such as searching for information on products).

Third, Web 2.0 promotes an understanding of the user of computer networked services that is completely different from the traditional notion of media audiences. Within Web 2.0, users are primary producers of content. Web 2.0 therefore emphasizes applications development, rather than content development, undercutting the power of the media corporations who dominate the creative content industries. It also proposes that the model of ideal "media" behavior is in producing one's own content, rather than consuming someone else's unless that other content has been produced by users like oneself.

Finally, Web 2.0 is also about the politics of networked services and claims to be the vehicle for increased democratization. It legitimizes this claim by favorably contrasting the equality and engagement of users and service providers within Web 2.0 with the apparently undemocratic relations between audiences and producers/broadcasters in the traditional media that create a kind of hegemony in which the latter come to choose for those audiences. Of course, Web 2.0 limits its understanding of democracy to the freedoms we might wish for in using "the media," but nevertheless it can claim considerable authority through this easy contrast. Further, the particular politics of Web 2.0 helps bring together the elements of technology, economics and culture of use already outlined— privileging the fusion of humans and technologies in ways that promote users' liberation from the media as a corporate monolith, in harmony with the freedom of web businesses to profit from those users through their technological engagement.

Web 2.0, in its promotion of these features of internet use, is itself open to significant criticism for the way it validates a kind of advanced, promotional entrepreneurial capitalism that binds users to profit-making service providers via the exploitation of those users' immaterial labor. Web 2.0 also serves as an ideology for the creation of new forms of dependence between individual humans and corporations who, by monopolizing and controlling the network activities through which key forms of human sociality becomes possible, can therefore benefit disproportionately from that dependence. As an argument against convergence, Web 2.0 also suggests that, in the struggles for corporate domination and control over technologies that circulate information through our cultures, and make meanings from that information, there is no unanimity of interests between those who see themselves as old media making new, and those who—by adopting and working within the frame of Web 2.0, seek to make media something else altogether.

NOTES

1. One sign of that change, for example, was the partnership in Australia between Yahoo! and television network Channel Seven that created a new, television-oriented version of Yahoo! Australia (Yahoo7); many other arrangements were put in place to tie Yahoo! to specific audio-visual content linked with the traditional providers of that content in the television, movie and music industries.

2. At the moment at least this use of Web 3.0 is purely a rhetorical move whose significance lies more in what it says about the prevalence of its predecessor term.

REFERENCES

Abbatte, J. (1999). *Inventing the internet.* Boston: MIT Press.

Allen, M. (2006). Broadband technologies and techno-optimism and the hopeful citizen. In J. Weiss, J. Nolan, J. Hunsinger, & P. Trifonas (Eds.), *International handbook of virtual learning environments* (pp. 1525–1548). Dordrecht: Springer.

Allen, M. (2007). Web 2.0: Discursive entrapment, empowerment or both? *Internet Research 8.0—Let's Play!* Annual Conference of the Association of Internet Researchers, Vancouver, CA, October 2007. Available from the author.

Arrington, M. (2007). Breaking: Yahoo's Terry Semel quits. *TechCrunch.* June 18 2007. Retrieved from http://www.techcrunch.com/2007/06/18/yahoo-ceo-terry-semel-resigned/. Accessed Feb 1, 2008.

Berners-Lee, T. (1999). *Weaving the web.* San Francisco: Harper-Collins.

Bruns, A. (2008). *Blogs, Wikipedia, second life and beyond: From production to produsage.* New York: Peter Lang.

Carlson, D. (2007). The online timeline *David Carlson's virtual world.* Retrieved from http://iml.jou.ufl.edu/carlson/timeline.shtml. Accessed Jan 18, 2008.

Doctorow, C. (2006). Can Anyone own "Web 2.0?" *BoingBoing.* May 26, 2006. Retrieved from http://www.boingboing.net/2006/05/26/can-anyone-own-web-2.html. Accessed Oct 10, 2007.

Goldhaber, M. (1997). The attention economy and the net, *First Monday,* 2 (4). Retrieved from http://www.firstmonday.org/issues/issue2_4/goldhaber/index.html. Accessed Feb 3, 2008.

Graham, P. (2006). *Interview about Web 2.0.* Retrieved from http://paulgraham.com/web20interview.html. Accessed Oct 1, 2007.

Grossman, W. (1997). *net.wars.* New York: NYU Press. http://www.nyupress.org/netwars/contents/contents.html. Accessed Feb 10, 2008.

Hafer, K., & Lyon, M. (1996). *Where wizards stay up late: The origins of the internet.* New York: Touchstone.

Hauben, M., & Hauben, R. (1997). *Netizens: On the history and impact of Usenet and the internet.* Los Alamitos, CA: IEEE Computer Society Press.

Herndon, K. (2007). The history and hype of early online media endeavors. *Internet research 8.0—Let's Play!* Annual Conference of the Association of Internet Researchers, Vancouver, CA, October 2007.

Hinchcliffe, D. (2006). The state of web 2.0. *Social computing magazine* Apr 2, 2006. Retrieved from http://web2.socialcomputingmagazine.com/the_state_of_web_20.htm. Accessed Jan 4, 2008.

Kitchen, R. (1998). *Cyberspace: The world in the wires.* New York: Wiley.

Klein, A. (2003). *Stealing time: Steve Case, Jerry Levin, and the collapse of AOL Time Warner.* New York: Simon & Schuster.

Koman, R. (2006). Should Semel go? Is Yahoo a media company? Is that a good thing to be? (Yes, Yes, No.). *SiliconValleyWatcher,* December 10, 2006. Retrieved from http://www.siliconvalleywatcher.com/mt/archives/2006/12/should_semel_go.php. Accessed Feb 1, 2008.

Kyrish, S. (1996). *From Videotex to the Internet: Lessons from Online Services 1981–1996.* Melbourne: La Trobe University Online Media Program. Retrieved from http://www.latrobe.edu.au/teloz/reports/kyrish.pdf. Accessed Jan 13, 2008.

Madden, M., & Fox S. (2006). *Riding the Waves of "Web 2.0": More than a buzzword but still not easily defined.* Washington: Pew Internet Life Project. Retrieved from http://www.pewinternet.org/pdfs/PIP_Web_2.0.pdf. Accessed Oct 10, 2007.

Martin, R. (2008). Web-volution. *Catapult: Making ideas happen*, Australian Broadcasting Corporation. Retrieved from http://www.abc.net.au/catapult/indepth/s2091002.htm. Accessed Feb 12, 2008.

Musser, J. (2006). *Web 2.0—Principles and practices [Executive Summary]*. *O'Reilly Media*. Retrieved from http://www.oreilly.com/catalog/web2report/chapter/web20_report_excerpt.pdf. Accessed Oct 10, 2007.

O'Reilly, T. (2005). *What Is Web 2.0: Design patterns and business models for the next generation of software*. *O'Reilly Group*. Retrieved from http://www.oreilly.com/pub/a/oreilly/tim/news/2005/09/30/what-is-web-20.html. Accessed Oct 1, 2007.

O'Reilly, T. (2007). *Today's Web 3.0 Nonsense blogstorm O'Reilly radar October 4, 2007*. Retrieved from http://radar.oreilly.com/archives/2007/10/web_30_semantic_web_web_20.html. Accessed Feb 1, 2008.

OECD (2006). *Multiple Play: pricing and policy trends. Report from OECD working party on telecommunication and information services policies*. Retrieved from http://www.oecd.org/dataoecd/47/32/36546318.pdf. Accessed Dec 10, 2008.

Raab, C., Bellamy, C., Taylor, J., Dutton, W. H., & Peltu, M. (1996). The information polity: Electronic democracy, privacy, and surveillance. In W. H. Dutton (Ed.), *Information and communication technologies: Visions and realities* (pp. 283–300). Oxford: Oxford University Press.

Rheingold, H. (2000) (revised edition). *The virtual community: Homesteading on the electronic frontier*. Boston: MIT Press. Retrieved from http://www.rheingold.com/vc/book/. Accessed Feb 3, 2008.

Salus, P. (1998). *Casting the net: From ARPANET to INTERNET and Beyond*. New York: Addison-Wesley.

Schaff, W. (2002). Taking stock: Oversupply and competition keep telecom equipment stocks down. *Information Week, March 18, 2002*. Retrieved from http://www.informationweek.com/story/showArticle.jhtml?articleID=6501412. Accessed Feb 1, 2008.

Thomas, S. (2006). The end of cyberspace and other surprises. *Convergence: The International Journal of Research Into New Media Technologies, 12* (4), 383–391.

AUTHOR BIOGRAPHY

Matthew Allen is Professor of Internet Studies, and Head of School, Communication and Creative Arts, Deakin University, Geelong, Australia. He is a former president of the Association of Internet Researchers, author of more than 50 articles and papers, and an award winning online educator.

PART IV

Regulation and Media Markets

The Deconverging Convergence of the Global Communication Industries in the Twenty-First Century

Dal Yong Jin

INTRODUCTION

The global communication industries have undergone a process of structural transformation in the twenty-first century. Already since the late 1990s, communication industries and, in particular among these, telecommunications and broadcasting corporations, have pursued media convergence between old media and new media. Media convergence in the form of mergers and acquisitions (M&As) has consequently become one of the central developments taking place across the media, telecommunications and information branches of the communication industries. However, media convergence, which has grown swiftly based on neoliberal policies and digitization, has been controversial because it has often failed to produce the promised synergy effects, such as increasing profits, revenues and stock prices. The strategy of media firms that had acquired too many companies in too many unrelated lines of business became impossible to manage and began to unravel (Jin, 2013).

D.Y. Jin (✉)
Simon Fraser University, Burnaby, Canada
e-mail: djin@sfu.ca

© The Author(s) 2017
S. Sparviero et al. (eds.), *Media Convergence and Deconvergence*, Global Transformations in Media and Communication Research - A Palgrave and IAMCR Series, DOI 10.1007/978-3-319-51289-1_10

199

Consequently, deconvergence has replaced convergence in the global communication industries. For example, while the deconvergence trend—as a dis-integration of corporations by either selling parts of the shares to other companies or the splitting-off and/or spinning-off of their companies—is not new, as the Viacom-CBS (2006), AOL–Time Warner (2008) and News Corporation (2013), as well as Financial Times (2015) cases exemplify, media deconvergence has rapidly become a norm in the media industries. Corporate spin-offs, break-ups and asset sales are bound to increase (Gomes-Casseres, 2015), although deconvergence does not mean that media convergence is over.

This chapter discusses the recent trend of media deconvergence, and documents this dramatic change in the global communication industries. It investigates the ways global media corporations have changed and developed the business paradigm and its implications in the global media markets. It then maps out the major characteristics of media deconvergence, which has become a new trend in the media industries. We expect that this contextualization of the recent developments of media deconvergence will shed light on our debates on the fall of media convergence and the emergence of media deconvergence as a new business model.

MEDIA CONVERGENCE AMID MEDIA DECONVERGENCE

Convergence has often been considered as a technology-driven phenomenon; however, "convergence is more than simply a technological shift," because convergence fundamentally alters the relationship between technologies, industries, markets and audiences (Jenkins, 2006, 15; Jin, 2013; Evens, 2014). Concerning the global media industries, convergence is a commercial integration between media content companies, such as television and radio networks, and transmission channels such as those dealing with telephone cable networks. Therefore, media convergence can be viewed as consolidation through industry alliances and mergers, the combination of technology and network platforms, and the integration between services and markets (Baldwin et al., 1996; Jin, 2013).

Convergence is key "for firms wishing to remain profitable and successful when everyone is spending less and cutting costs and looking for greater, lasting impacts" (Goodson, 2012). This indicates that convergence cannot be done without the integration of production between the old and new media, but at the same time, convergence cannot be done without structural integration in the market. As several previous works (for example, Chan-Olmsted, 1998; Noll, 2003; Chambers & Howard, 2005; Flew, 2011) point out, global media companies have pursued convergence in large part for the maximization of profits through the concentration of media companies. Media corporations believed that mergers and acquisitions would bring synergy effects. By the end of the 1990s, concentration and conglomeration had been common (Herman & McChesney, 2001). Digitization and the convergence of media corporations required media firms to develop a range of interests across different media, information and telecommunications operations. The digitization of information means that the space of communication is increasingly consolidated into one network constituted by telecommunications, the internet and the mass media (Jenkins, 2006, cited in Arsenault & Castells, 2008, 710), while beforehand a multitude of media and communication networks operated in parallel, sometimes jointly, sometimes independently.

However, in many cases media convergence has failed to produce the promised synergy effects (Jin, 2013). As Manuel Castells already pointed out (2001, pp. 188–190), "the business experiments on media convergence carried on since the early 1990s have ended in failure." Stephanie Peltier (2014, p. 271) also stated that "it became obvious that the attempt to build media giants through M&As undoubtedly failed, because many media firms after M&As did not improve economic performance measured by profit margins." Peltier (2004, cited in Alexander & Owers, 2009) argued that neither size, simultaneous presence in different media industries, nor complementary assets led to better economic performance. As Terry Flew (2011, p. 93) aptly put it:

> [I]t is often the case that media conglomerates that grow through takeovers and mergers bring together management teams that lack compatibility or have expertize [sic] in related fields. The merger of AOL and Time Warner was the most conspicuous case of this; it created an entity whose combined value was estimated at US$350 billion, but it ultimately proved almost impossible in practice to achieve the much-vaunted content synergies across the two very distinct corporate entities.

Consequently, there has been a recent trend, known as deconvergence, emerging as a new business paradigm. Although we cannot deny that there is a general trend toward larger media firms by way of M&As, an industrial reorganization that partially offsets this trend has emerged

(Alexander & Owers, 2009). Deconvergence is an emerging catchword in the communication industry. In Fidler's book Mediamorphosis (1997, cited in Appelgren, 2004, p. 243), deconvergence is said not to lead to fewer forms of communication nor to established traditional media becoming extinct. "A recent media publishing trend is the creation of niche publishing channels focusing on a certain topic or a specific target group."

Deconvergence can be identified as a disintegration of corporations by either selling parts of the shares to other companies or splitting-off and/ or spinning-off of their companies. Deconsolidated companies through spin-offs and/or split-offs are operating as independent corporations separated from a parent corporation in the market; therefore, they are not part of the parent company anymore, although in many cases the parent company still controls or at least holds some shares of these companies (Jin, 2013, 10). Media corporations have pursued deconvergence with several motivations, and they commonly implement the deconvergence business model in order to reverse those transactions that have not produced synergy effects. "Many large media corporations have had to address dysfunctional organizational structures resulting from previous acquisitions," and the best strategy is to deconverge the units that do not fit well with other parts of the company (Alexander & Owers, 2009, 104). Deconvergence can create value if the businesses are worth more separately than they are together:

In popular terms, convergence makes sense when $1 + 1 = 3$, when the combination has the potential to create more value than the parties can on their own. By the same language, deconvergence makes sense when $1 = 0.5 + 0.8$, or some other set of fractions that add up to more than one: the parts are more valuable separately than bundled together. (Gomes-Casseres, 2015, para. 8)

Deciding what not to include in the scope of the business or what to drop can be just as important as deciding what to include. Many vertically integrated companies have divested pieces of their portfolios to focus better on core areas that are more crucial for their growth. This refocusing is often the other side of the coin in an acquisition strategy. (Ibid., para. 3)

The deconvergence business model does not mean that media convergence disappears, because convergence always occurs in the global media industries. However, the nature of media convergence has fundamentally shifted in the early twenty-first century, as the old form of convergence—the integration between old media and new media sectors—has mostly failed. Therefore, it is crucial to understand how media convergence and deconvergence work together.

DECONVERGENCE OF MEDIA INDUSTRIES IN THE 2010S

Media corporations in many countries have pursued deconvergence strategies in the 2010s. Several top-tier media corporations, such as News Corporation, Time Warner, Pearson, Garnett and Liberty Media have split off or sold out parts of their media corporations in order to develop their own unique media contents, while pursuing standalone strategies. Of course, most often, financial matters dictate deconvergence. When media corporations need to reallocate capital, because a certain unit is not performing as desired, it can be sold off and the proceeds reallocated to other units within the corporation (Alexander & Owers, 2009).

While there are several different patterns in deconvergence strategies, several major mega media corporations have separated previously merged new media companies. In the 1990s, the internet was one of the most significant new media technologies for media corporations, and therefore many media firms, both small and big, purchased into the internet sector to generate synergy effects. As one of the driving forces of media convergence was digitization, the companies purchasing internet-related firms believed firmly that these would bring unprecedented profits. However, the promised synergy effects were not realized for several reasons, including different corporate cultures, financial uncertainty, and severe competitions among media companies embedded in the internet. Several mega giants, such as AOL-Time Warner, CBS-Viacom and AT&T had no choice but to separate their integrated companies into a few independent divisions. The major deconvergence trend primarily started in the mid 2000s, but it continues to be one of the primary business norms even in the 2010s (Jin, 2013). Taking examples from very recently deconverged media corporations, from audio-visual entertainment corporations, including NewsCorporation, to print-focused corporations, such as Garnett, they continue to break up or split off their companies.

Among these, Rupert Murdoch divided News Corporation in two companies—separating newspapers like The Wall Street Journal, The New York Post and The Times of London from the fast-growing entertainment unit (Chozick, 2012). In a news release distributed in 2012, Murdoch stated:

News Corporation's 60-year heritage of developing world-class brands has resulted in a large and unparalleled portfolio of diversified assets. We recognize that over the years, News Corporation's broad collection of assets have become increasingly complex. We determined that creating this new structure would simplify operations and greater align strategic priorities (Chozick, 2012, para. 3).

Murdoch cited the company's "spirit of innovation" in the decision, which he viewed as an opportunity to free his newspapers from their ugly-stepchild status within the giant corporation. "Our publishing businesses are greatly undervalued by the skeptics," he wrote. However, Murdoch also said, "through this transformation we will unleash their real potential, and be able to better articulate the true value they hold for shareholders" (Chozick, 2012, para. 8). As this statement clearly proves, News Corporation decided to divide the corporation primarily to give shareholders what they wanted. News Corporation, a media conglomerate born from newspaper publishing, purchased Myspace as part of its desire to become involved in the internet sector, in particular with a digital platform, as Google purchased YouTube; however, the result was disastrous. Although this was not the only reason, News Corporation recalculated its business strategies and pursued the deconvergence business model, resulting in the separation of its publishing activities from the media and entertainment businesses, leading to two distinct publicly traded companies.

In fact, News Corporation believed that a separation of the businesses into distinct public corporations with their own identities and strategies would enhance overall shareholder value and allow each company to: (1) focus on and pursue distinct strategic priorities and industry-specific opportunities that would maximize their long-term potential; (2) benefit from greater financial and operational flexibility and better position each company to compete, (3) respond and react more quickly to rapidly evolving technology and global market opportunities, and (4) tailor its capital structure, and allocate and deploy resources in a manner consistent with its strategic objectives that best enhances value for its respective shareholder group. With more focus devoted to each business's financial and operational structure, investors would be able to evaluate more clearly the inherent value of both portfolios of assets and invest in each company accordingly (News Corporation, 2012).[1]

While stakeholders' confidence is not negligible during the deconvergence process, mega media corporations certainly understand that they are able to fulfill their plan when they focus on core business areas. In June 2014 when Time Warner Inc. announced that it had completed the previously announced spin-off of Time Inc. from Time Warner, commenting on the spin-off, Time Warner Chairman and Chief Executive Officer Jeff Bewkes clearly said:

The spin-off of Time Inc. completes the process we began several years ago to position Time Warner as the world's leading video content company. Our strategy reflects our commitment to delivering strong returns to our shareholders as we light up the world with the best storytelling. The spin-off gives Time Warner even more focus as we continue to deliver on this strategy. (Time Warner, 2014, para. 3).

Time Warner, formerly AOL-Time Warner temporarily, became the largest media corporation after the merger; however, it did not create the expected synergy effects. When shareholders asked to change its direction after firing several CEOs, the once largest media corporation had to pursue its new business paradigm, which was media deconvergence. In line with the strategy of these media corporations, Liberty Media Corporation also completed the spin-off of Liberty Broadband Corporation (Liberty Broadband) in 2014. As a result, Liberty Media and Liberty Broadband are now separate publicly traded companies (Liberty Media, 2014).

A media deconvergence strategy was also adopted by media groups whose core activity is newspaper publishing. In August 2015, Pearson in the UK, for example, sold its Financial Times to Japanese media group Nikkei for $1.3 billion, putting one of the world's premier business newspapers in the hands of a company influential at home but little known outside Japan (Holton, 2015). For years, London-based Pearson—which generates about 60% of its sales in North America and three-quarters of its revenue from education—had rejected talks on the sale of its salmon-colored, business-focused title (Zekraia, 2015). However, Pearson chief executive John Fallon said that after nearly 60 years of ownership,

we've reached an inflection point in media, driven by the explosive growth of mobile and social. In this new environment, the best way to ensure the FT's journalistic and commercial success is for it to be part of a global, digital news company. (Zekaria, 2015, para. 4)

Since June 2015, as one of the most recent examples in the USA of the deconvergence trend, Gannett also split into two companies. Gannett spun off its publishing business from its broadcasting and digital operations. It followed the Tribune Co. and News Corporation in breaking off print media from its rapidly expanding broadcast and digital operations. The spun-off publishing company, which adopted the name Gannett, owns newspapers in 92 markets, including USA TODAY, while TEGNA owns or provides services to 46 TV stations nationwide (Yu, 2015). They believed that the transformation would give the publishing company and the broadcasting and digital company enhanced strategies and operating, financial and regulatory flexibility to pursue growth and consolidation opportunities in their respective markets, while delivering strong cash flow to build further upon Gannett's long-standing traditions of award-winning journalism and service to local communities, as president and CEO Gracia Martore said in a statement (Associated Press, 2014; Yu, 2015).

As these cases exemplify, global media corporations have strategically developed deconvergence for several different reasons. On one hand, some media corporations had to pursue deconvergence in order to resolve their financial stress and regain investor confidence. Many media corporations, including AOL-Time Warner and Vivendi, after convergence through M&As, lost their stock values, and thereafter, investors left. In order to soothe major stakeholders, they had to sell off or split off their merged corporations. By selling off or splitting off non-core areas, they were able to refocus on their core areas, which regained stakeholders' confidence. General Electric (GE) sold its 49% share of NBC Universal to Comcast in 2013, which made Comcast America's largest cable TV provider and the largest global media corporation. For GE, the deal accelerated a transition to a more purely industrial company, something that investors had been wanting for a long time (Associated Press, 2013). As AOL-Time Warner, CBS-Viacom and News Corporation have focused on core areas after deconvergence, Vivendi strategy also focused solely on the cash-rich telecommunications business (Alexander & Owers, 2009). Deconvergence has led to a newfound emphasis among major media corporations on their core businesses, particularly content. With clear evidence that convergence often fails, media corporations are fixing their strategy on horizontal consolidation, where core competencies can be strengthened (Jin, 2011, 2013). For these media corporations, being a media conglomerate has not been attractive anymore, and they believe that they can be much better off as small units.

Until the early twenty-first century, the emphasis in the global media market was on the production of media content, such as films, music and television programs, under the slogan "content is king," as Steinberg (forthcoming) aptly put it. In January 1996, Microsoft CEO Bill (Gates, 1996) himself wrote an essay titled "Content is King," which was published on the Microsoft website and said, "Content is where I expect much of the real money will be made on the Internet, just as it was in broadcasting." His statement has become a mantra repeated over and over again by CEOs of media corporations and internet experts. Needless to say, content is what has been driving the internet—unluckily, sometimes to the point where it has lost all meaning, because digital platforms, including social networks, search engines and smartphones, as explained below, have rapidly come to control contents.

IMPLICATIONS OF MEDIA DECONVERGENCE

Media deconvergence has deeply influenced global media industries because there are tangible shifts in the global media markets. To begin with, media deconvergence has changed the lineup of major players in media markets. Over the past 10 years, the communication market has witnessed the rise of sprawling media giants of the likes of Time Warner, Disney, News Corporation, NBC-Universal and CBS-Viacom that have dominated domestic and global media markets. However, we now witness the emergence of new players in the global media market as these former mega giants have deconverged their media corporations (Jin, 2013). According to Fortune, Time Warner was the largest media corporation in 2005; however, in 2015, Comcast became the largest media corporation in the global media market. As AOL-Time Warner had continued to separate its units into four major parts, Time Warner's total sales decreased from US$42.8 billion in 2005 toUS$28.1 billion in 2015 (see Table 10.1). Among the top 10 largest media corporations, 50% disappeared from the chart, while new players entered.

Current trends suggest that these media empires are pursuing a strategy of deconvergence not because of protests by civic groups, or on account of government regulations that place a premium on the maximum disposal of media power as a key factor in creating a healthy democracy, but on account of economic imperatives and changing

Table 10.1 Big 10 global media companies (US$ Billion)

2005	Sales	2015	Sales
Time warner	42.8	Comcast	68.8
Walt disney	30.7	Walt Disney	49.8
Viacom	27	Twenty-fist Century Fox	32.6
News corp	20.8	Time Warner	28.1
Comcast	20.3	Direct TV	33.3
Direct TV	11.9	Time Warner Cable	22.8
Omnicom	9.7	WPP	19
Clear Channel	9.4	CBS	14.1
Liberty Media	8.6	Viacom	13.9
Gannett	7.3	British SKY Broadcasting	13.4

Source the author, based on Forbes (2005) and Le (2015)

business fashions. Deconvergence changes the ownership and organizational structure of the media industry, from concentration to deconcentration, at least for a while, but fundamental changes in terms of the total shift of the trend to the media still remain far off in the distance (Jin, 2013).

Meanwhile, media corporations' strategies in tandem with new media have shifted from internet-focused to platform-technologies-focused, which means that instead of seeking convergence with internet firms, including AOL, they have pursued it with platform corporations, in particular, primarily between platform and platform corporations. As discussed, when it sold off the Financial Times, Pearson chief executive John Fallon argued (Starkman, 2015, para. 3) that "an inflection point in media had been reached and that this was driven by the explosive growth of mobile and social." In other words, we need to understand that social media and smartphone technologies have partially caused the recent setbacks of many media corporations, resulting in the separation of their companies. On the flip side, owing to the significance of digital platforms, media corporations have sought platform corporations. They continue to pursue convergence; however, the nature of convergence is much different, as new media corporations primarily pursue the convergence of digital platforms, such as social network sites, search engines and smartphones and their operating systems. "These digital platforms are known as digital intermediaries, and they have greatly changed and influenced people's daily lives" (Jin, 2015, 5).

In fact, in February 2014, Facebook acquired WhatsApp, a rapidly growing cross-platform mobile messaging company, for a total of approximately $16 billion, including $4 billion in cash and approximately $12 billion worth of Facebook shares. The agreement also provided for an additional $3 billion in restricted stock units to be granted to WhatsApp's founders and employees that will vest over four years subsequent to closing (Facebook, 2014). "WhatsApp has built a leading and rapidly growing real-time mobile messaging service, with over 450 million people using the service each month" (Carlson, 2014). The acquisition supports Facebook and WhatsApp's shared mission to bring more connectivity and utility to the world by delivering core internet services efficiently and affordably. The combination will help accelerate growth and user engagement across both companies. "WhatsApp is on a path to connect 1 billion people. The services that reach that milestone are all incredibly valuable," said Mark Zuckerberg, Facebook founder and CEO (Carlson, 2014, para. 8). "Google Inc., founded in 1998, started off as a simple search engine company and went on to establish its proprietary search technology as a foundation for navigating the internet." Google continues to extend and promote its platform. Google also purchased YouTube in 2006 (Gawer & Cusumano, 2008, 5).

Korea's largest mobile messaging service Kakao Talk also bought Daum Communication in 2014 (Kim & Kang, 2014). Korea's dominant mobile-messaging service company agreed to buy domestic internet portal operator Daum Communications in an all-stock deal, hoping to boost its presence in Web and mobile services (Lee, 2014). The deal is the latest in a series involving makers of online-messaging apps, which have been in the spotlight globally because of their explosive growth as many users shift from texting to less-expensive instant messaging on their smartphones. The same month Rakuten, a Japanese internet firm, paid $900 million for Viber—an instant messaging and Voice over IP (VoIP) app for smartphones—founded by Israelis but based in Cyprus. In March 2014, Alibaba, a Chinese online giant, paid $215 million for a slice of the Silicon Valley firm Tango, a free mobile messaging appmaker (The Economist, 2014).

While there are several reasons for the recent convergence with mobile messaging service corporations, one of the most significant is the role of platforms of this new service engine. After the integration of Daum and Kakao, Sir-goo Lee, co-CEO of Daum Kakao alongside Sae-hoon Choi, clearly stated, "Mobile, life, platform and connection are the four keywords that represent Daum Kakao's directions. We are aiming at becoming a mobile lifestyle platform leader" (Bahk, 2014, para. 19). In their own press release in October 2014, Daum (Kakao, 2014) announced that they finalized the merger to form a new company.[2] of course, Koreans do not just use the app to chat: it is also a popular platform for mobile games, from which Kakao makes most of its money, and for sending both digital and physical gifts.(The Economist, 2014, para. 3).

Naver, the largest internet portal in Korea, also owns a messaging app, Line, with 400 million users; however, it is headquartered in Japan and the major subscribers are Japanese (The Economist, 2014). As such, media convergence in the 2010s proves that media corporations simply pursue deconvergence strategies. Unlike the 1990s when they wanted to own everything from content to the internet, media corporations now focus on their core areas, while pursuing convergence between platform corporations. In sum, the emergence and use of platform technologies, in particular social media, have certainly become a critical reason for media convergence.

DISCUSSION AND CONCLUSION

This chapter has discussed continuity and change in the global communication industries, primarily by focusing on the emerging new business model. In the early twenty-first century, the main trend in communication industries shifted from convergence to deconvergence as a form of deconsolidation of the media sector. While many media corporations still pursue media convergence, several others have differentiated their business model. Among these are many mega media firms that have no choice but to pursue deconvergence since the outcomes of communication M&As have been disappointing from an acquirer's shareholders' perspective.

Moreover, it is certain that the deconvergence trend is a response to the limited success of the mega mergers that characterized the late 1990s, as the deconvergence business model was embraced by those firms that were quickly becoming lumbering dinosaurs, and whose chances for survival were put under pressure by their crumbling economic models and stock market valuations. Therefore, "forced by this turn of events, they tried to morph into small or middle-sized companies" (Jin, 2012, 128).

Driven by both neoliberal policies and digitization, media convergence, once one of the most popular business models, has now mostly lost its authenticity due to overcapacity and to the attempt by communication industries to find a new business paradigm. The deconvergence strategy has been the new business model that global media corporations had to take up. Also, several mega media giants, such as AOL-Time Warner, CBS-Viacom, GE-NBC Universal and News Corporation, have pursued a deconvergence strategy in order to regain stakeholders' confidence and profits. Unlike convergence, emphasizing synergies through the integration of old and new media sectors, deconvergence focuses on core-business areas. This new trend, therefore, shifted the structure and dynamics of the media industries in several ways.

The fall-off in convergence does not mean that the dominant paradigm will disappear, because many media companies still seek consolidation—in particular, in the realm of platform sectors, such as social network sites, smartphones and search engines. Deconvergence itself sometimes supplements convergence in another sense: For example, when GE finished its sale of NBC Universal in 2013, the broadcasting network was acquired by Comcast. Therefore, they are often on both sides of one complex transaction (Gomes-Casseres, 2015). Media corporations are able to change their industrial organization in different ways.

To get larger,

> they can either grow internally or acquire other firms to accelerate their rate of growth. Conversely, firms can decrease in size by reducing operations or take the discrete step of divesting the strategic business units, which would change their industrial organization. Thus, both convergence and de-convergence are frequently part of overall ongoing strategies to change the set of the strategic business units that a firm encompasses. (Alexander & Owers, 2009, p. 103)

What we are witnessing is deconvergence becoming another core business trend, competing with convergence strategies. Media convergence as a form of integration of media firms is still strong, but deconvergence will continue. As business models, convergence and deconvergence do not permanently replace one another. Instead, they now go hand-in-hand in the global media market.

Unlike in the earlier part of this century, in the 2010s media corporations have pursued limited media convergence either between new media and new media sectors, or between one content production corporation and another, instead of between the old and the new, which is not the norm anymore. In particular, platform corporations have fiercely invested in other platform corporations because these function as digital intermediaries and control digital contents. While media convergence in the late twentieth century focused mainly on convergence in order to control the whole media sector, from the production to the distribution of content, the contemporary media convergence strategy has shifted its focus to platform technologies due to their increasing significance.

Finally, what we have to contemplate is that the major goal of deconvergence is to create substantial value for media corporations in several different contexts, which means that both convergence and deconvergence consider financial value as the most significant factor for restructuring. Regardless of severe protests by several parts of society because of the concerns about the effects on diversity, ownership and democracy, media corporations have been pursuing convergence. Likewise they conduct deconvergence not because of the concerns raised by media critics and protestors but because of the lack of synergy effects. To the extent that it undoes conglomeration, the new deconvergence business model has important policy implications. Deconvergence represents a countervailing force to the concentration associated with M&A. It is of interest to note that when deconvergence is anticipated to create value, corporations may voluntarily undertake such transactions without prompting from regulatory authorities (Alexander & Owers, 2009, p. 111). However, media corporations must understand that, even when they focus on profits, they also generate social benefits. It is also necessary for them to contemplate the changing nature of the media environment, which asks for diversity, small media—even personal media—and public good, which means that media deconvergence is one of the best business strategies to achieve both financial profits and the fulfillment of social needs.

NOTES

1. The new global media and entertainment company that would be created through the proposed transaction would consist of News Corporation's highly profitable cable and television assets, filmed entertainment, and direct satellite broadcasting businesses, including Fox Broadcasting, Twentieth Century Fox Film, Twentieth Century Fox Television, Fox Sports, Fox International Channels, Fox News Channel, Fox Business Network, FX, Star, the National Geographic Channels, Shine Group, Fox

Television Stations, BSkyB, Sky Italia and Sky Deutschland, among others. As a pure-play content producer and distributor, the company would build on its deep heritage in developing incredibly strong, premium content for distribution on screens of all sizes by leveraging its leading content across its entertainment and cable news verticals, as well as its unparalleled collection of regional sports networks, and the industry's leading movie and TV production and distribution company. In addition, the entertainment company would benefit from its rapidly growing, high-margin cable network and pay-TV assets, and the distribution capabilities and opportunities associated with its unrivaled global footprint with significant scale across North and South America, Europe and Asia (News Corporation, 2012).

2. Kakao had 140 million users of its KakaoTalk instant messaging service application as of May 2014, and KakaoTalk was on 93% of smartphones in Korea and the company has invested in Southeast Asia—mainly, Indonesia, the Philippines and Malaysia—as it seeks growth (Song, 2014).

References

Alexander, A., & Owers, J. (2009). Divestiture restructuring in the media industries: A financial market case analysis. *The International Journal of Media Management, 11,* 102–114.

Arsenault, A., & Castells, M. (2008). The structure and dynamics of global multi-media business networks. *International Journal of Communication, 2,* 707–748.

Associated Press. (2013, February 13). *Wall street: Comcast got a steal on NBC Universal.* Accessed August 8, 2016. http://www.usnews.com/news/technology/articles/2013/02/13/wall-street-comcast-getting-great-deal-on-nbcu.

Associated Press. (2014, August 5). *Media company gannett is splitting into 2 companies.* Accessed August 8, 2016. http://www.businessinsider.com/gannett-to-split-in-two-companies-newspaper-broadcast-2014-8.

Appelgren, E. (2004). *Convergence and divergence in media: Different perspectives.* Paper presented at the Proceedings of the 8th ICCC International Conference on Electronic Publishing, Brazil.

Bahk, E. J. (2014, October 1). Daum Kakao faces more challenges than Naver. *The Korea Times.*

Baldwin, T. F., McVoy, D. S., & Steinfield, C. (1996). *Convergence: Integrating media, information, and communication.* Thousand Oaks, CA: Sage.

Carlson, N. (2014, February 19). Facebook is buying huge messaging app Whatsapp for $19 billion! *Business Insider.* http://www.businessinsider.com/facebook-is-buying-whatsapp-2014-2.

Castells, M. (2001). *The internet galaxy.* New York: Oxford University Press.

Chambers, T., & Howard, H. (2005). The economics of media consolidation. In A. B. Albarran, S. M. Chan-Olmsted, & M. Wirth (Eds.), *Handbook of media management and economics* (pp. 363–386). Mahwah, NJ: Lawrence Erbaum.

Chan-Olmsted, S. (1998). Mergers, acquisitions, and convergence: The strategic alliance of broadcasting, cable television, and telephone services. *Journal of Media Economics, 11*(3), 33–46.

Chozick, A. (2012, June 28). Murdoch, announcing news corp. *Split, Calls Newspapers 'Viable' and 'Undervalued' The New York Time*. http://mediade-coder.blogs.nytimes.com/2012/06/28/news-corporation-makes-it-official-two-companies/?_r=0.

Daum Kakao. (2014, October 1). Daum kakao launches as a mobile lifestyle platform company. *Press Release*.

The Economist. (2014, May 31). Daum and Kakao merge getting the message.

Evens, T. (2014). (De)convergence in TV: A comparative analysis of the development of Smart TV. *European Media Management Association (EMMA) Conference, Proceedings*. Presented at the European Media Management Association (EMMA) Conference.

Facebook. (2014, February 19). Facebook to acquire Whatsapp. *Press release*.

Fidler, R. (1997). *Mediamorphosis: Understanding new media*. Thousand Oaks: Pine Forge Press.

Flew, T. (2011). Media as creative industries: Conglomeration and globalization as accumulation strategies in an age of digital media. In D. Winseck & D. Y. Jin (Eds.), *The political economies of media: The transformation of the global media industries* (pp. 84–100). London: Bloomsbury.

Forbes. (2005). *Top global 100 companies*. Accessed May 2007.

Gates, B. (1996, January 3). Content is king. Retired from the original website but available online at http://www.craigbailey.net/content-is-king-by-bill-gates/.

Gawer, A., & Cusumano, M. (2008). How companies become platform leaders. *MIT Sloan Management Review, 49*(2), 28–35.

Gomes-Casseres, B. (2015, December 3). A Yahoo break-up could be the start of lots of splits. *Harvard Business Review*. https://hbr.org/2015/12/a-yahoo-break-up-could-be-the-start-of-lots-of-splits.

Goodson, S. (2012, March.1). Convergence is the future of marketing. *Forbes*. http://www.forbes.com/sites/dailymuse/2015/08/12/3-everyday-words-that-make-you-sound-pretty-rude-in-emails/.

Herman, E., & McChesney, R. (2001). *Global media: The new missionaries of global capitalism*. London: Bloomsbury.

Holton, K. (2015, July 23). Japan's Nikkei buys Financial Times in $1.3 billion deal. *Reuters*. http://www.reuters.com/article/2015/07/23/us-pearson-m-a-financialtimes-idUSKCN0PX0YM20150723.

Jenkins, H. (2006). *Convergence culture*. New York: New York University Press.

Jin, D. Y. (2011). Deconvergence and deconsolidation in the global media industries. In D. Winseck & D. Y. Jin (Eds.), *The political economies of media: The transformation of the global media industries* (pp. 167–182). London: Bloomsbury.

Jin, D. Y. (2013). *De-Convergence of global media industries.* New York: Routledge.

Jin, D. Y. (2015). *Digital platforms, imperialism and political culture.* London: Routledge.

Le, V. (2015, May 22). The world's largest media companies of 2015. *Forbes.* http://www.forbes.com/sites/vannale/2015/05/22/the-worlds-largest-media-companies-of-2015/#3bbef2f72b64.

Lee, M. J. (2014, May 26). South Korean Messaging-App maker kakao to buy web portal Daum. *The Wall Street Journal.*

Liberty Media. (2014, November 4). Liberty Media Corporation announces completion of Liberty Broadband Corporation spin-off. *Press Release.*

Kim, R. & Shinhye, K. (2014, May 26). Kakao corp agrees to buy Daum to spur growth, Cain Seoul listing. *Bloomberg Business.*

News Corporation. (2012, June 28). Separation would create two category-leading public companies. *Press Release.*

Noll, M. (2003). The myth of convergence. *The International Journal of Media Management, 5*(1), 12–13.

Peltier, S. (2004). Mergers and acquisitions in the media industries: Were failures really unforeseeable? *Journal of Media Economics, 17*(4), 261–278.

Song, J. A. (2014, May 26). S. Korea's Kakao to merge with Daum. *Financial Times.*

Starkman, D. (2015, July 23). Pearson sells the Financial Times to Nikkei Inc. for $1.3 billion. *Los Angels Times.*

Steinberg, M. (forthcoming). Converging contents and platforms: Niconico video and Japan's media mix ecology. *Asian Video Cultures.* In Neves & Sarkar (Eds.) forthcoming.

Time Warner. (2014, June 9). Time Warner Inc. Completes spin-off of Time Inc. *Press Release.*

Yu, R. (2015, June 29). TEGNA, Gannett go separate ways as print spin off is completed. *USA TODAY.*

Zekaria, S. (2015, July 23). Pearson inks deal to sell Financial Times to Nikkei in jettisoning the FT, its flagship newspaper, publisher will focus on education. *The Wall Street Journal.* http://www.wsj.com/articles/pearson-in-talks-to-sell-the-financial-times-1437646601.

AUTHOR BIOGRAPHY

Dal Yong Jin is Associate Professor in the School of Communication at Simon Fraser University, Canada. His major research and teaching interests are on social media and platform technologies, mobile technologies and game studies, media (de)convergence, globalization and media, and the political economy of media. He is the author of several books, such as New Korean Wave: *Transnational Cultural Power in the Age of Social Media* (University of Illinois Press, 2016), *Digital Platforms, Imperialism and Political Culture* (Routledge, 2015), *De-Convergence of Global Media Industries* (Routledge, 2013), and *Korea's Online Gaming Empire* (MIT Press, 2010). He has also edited several volumes, including *Mobile Gaming in Asia: Politics, Culture and Emerging Technologies* (Springer, 2016) and *The Political Economies of Media: The Transformation of the Global Media Industries* (Bloomsbury, 2011).

CHAPTER 11

Deconstructing the Music Industry Ecosystem

Jim Rogers

INTRODUCTION

The core task of this chapter is to critique and explain the form and nature of the relationship between technological convergence and market convergence as it has developed in the context of the music industry's evolution in a digital environment since the late 1990s. The chapter highlights the value of music industry analysis to understanding fundamental institutional and organization reconfigurations in media companies with the spread of digital technologies.

At headline level, the concept of convergence relates to the melding of what have hitherto been considered separate communication services and functions (de Sola Pool, 1983). Over the past two decades, technology convergence trends have consistently been conceived of in negative terms in the context of the music industry. Hence, at the outset, we recognize how the established music labels have frequently found themselves to be the first media actors confronted by the problems and demands emerging with ever-maturing digital media innovations. The

J. Rogers (✉)
Dublin City University, Dublin, Ireland
e-mail: jim.rogers@dcu.ie

© The Author(s) 2017
S. Sparviero et al. (eds.), *Media Convergence and Deconvergence*, Global Transformations in Media and Communication Research - A Palgrave and IAMCR Series, DOI 10.1007/978-3-319-51289-1_11

evolution of cost-free models and illicit file-sharing practices are widely deemed to have sabotaged the capacity of the industry to generate revenue from the content it distributes. With the profound decline in global record sales revenues since the turn of the century, media (and much academic) discourse around the music industry has largely been preoccupied with images of stagnation and collapse.

However, as Jenkins (2006) and others have emphasized, beyond the technological, more pertinent "convergences" relate to the flow of content across the entire media system and enhanced cooperation between different media industries (Jin, 2012, p. 761). Here, we are concerned with how, in response to a changing and challenging technological context, major music labels are reconceptualizing their own roles and practices (and modifying their core structures) so as to maximize revenue-generating opportunities available to them across the range of (traditional and new) media platforms and other "real-space" sites where their copyrights and brands can be exploited.

As such, our analysis of the unfolding relationships between the core music industry subsectors (recording, publishing, live) and the network of ancillary services surrounding this core, points to a fundamental reconfiguring of the music industry's structure and organization per se so as to materialize a fresh range of opportunities and potential revenue streams. Here, we critique and assess the implications of evolving patterns of ownership in the music industry, and we examine how its traditional core power structures have been sustained through (1) the exploitation of content across a proliferating range of platforms and spaces; and (2) courtesy of an ongoing process of ongoing mergers, joint ventures, acquisitions and partnerships.

While some commentators (for example, Jin, 2012) highlight an evolving trend for demergers and spin-offs across the broader media industries—and not withstanding that there have been some notable breakups and "sell-offs" in the music industry—recent developments indicate that convergence is not simply an "old paradigm" in this context. Mergers, alliances and acquisitions continue to form core aspects of the strategies adopted by the music industry's biggest actors in accommodating themselves through the "digital turn."

Arguments relating to contracting markets as a result of technological convergence are frequently used to justify such consolidation strategies. Such an approach to analyzing the evolving character of the music industry demonstrates how concepts such as concentration and commodification remain crucial to a more comprehensive understanding of how this particular media sector has responded to the challenges posed by technological convergence.

This forces us to acknowledge the distinctive if not unique features and characteristics of music as a form of media content, with music crucially demonstrating how it adapts itself to and embeds itself within a vast range of other forms of media content, both traditional and new.

Ultimately, the chapter will interrogate the changing nature of the relationships between the music industry's key subsectors and music's increasingly dense and complex relations with other media sectors, hence emphasizing the continued relevance of vertical and horizontal integration as key frames for understanding music industry dynamics. In essence, we illustrate how market convergence characterizes a core response mechanism of the established actors in the music industry to the threats and challenges posed by the digital innovations that are widely perceived as having driven illicit file-sharing on the net.

This chapter draws significantly upon two earlier studies by the current author both of which examined processes of change and continuity in the music industry across the digital era and which combine to comprise more than sixty in-depth ethnographic interviews conducted with a range of music industry personnel and key informants at different points between 2007 and 2015. The arguments advanced are informed by the critical perspectives arising from these interviews with individuals which span the spheres of music management services, live music promotion, record production, manufacturing, music retailing and music journalism, as well as personnel from both major and independent recording and music publishing companies. This has been complemented by additional (extensive) desk research. The results of this research, parts of which are summarized for the purpose of this chapter, have earlier been published in a series of academic journal articles and chapters (for example, Rogers & Sparviero, 2011; Preston & Rogers, 2010, 2012; Rogers, 2014a, b; Rogers & Preston, 2016; Rogers & Cawley, 2016), and also a book (Rogers, 2013). While only highly select quotes or accounts from specific interviews are detailed in this chapter (given the limitations of space), the perspectives arrived at, courtesy of analyzing and critiquing these recorded interviews and discussions, inform everything that follows below.

THE MUSIC—DIGITAL CONVERGENCE: A MARRIAGE MADE IN HELL?

Across the 21st century to date, the methods and manners by which music is circulated and ultimately accessed by its end-users have evolved beyond recognition. Fundamental developments in the realm of digital technology have seen the evolution of successive waves of illicit file-sharing platforms, but also licensed "cost-free-to-consumer" models emerge, all of which are widely perceived to have undermined the willingness of the consumer to pay for music content. For example, authors such as Leyshon et al. (2005) point to a "quasi-gift economy of music" evolving in the wake of digital distribution (cited in Giletti, 2012, p. 11). While Geisler (2006) and Baym (2011) essentially see illicit file-sharing networks as "gift giving" systems, other studies (for example, Giletti, 2012) indicate that while a significant majority of licensed streaming users express satisfaction with the ad-supported (free-to-consumer) service they avail themselves of, most do not proceed to paid subscription. Giletti thus concludes "that the consumer perception is that it is not worth paying for subscription services" (Giletti, 2012, p. 23).

In numerous journalistic accounts the music economy in the era of digital distribution is characterized by a profound decline in the fortunes of the record industry as a result of such technological innovations that forcefully impair traditional economic models around which the music industry operates (see Rogers, 2013, pp. 4–8 for a detailed overview of such commentary). Similar sentiments can also be found in much academic writing on the subject (for example, Liebowitz, 2006, 2008; Hughes & Lang 2003; Dubosson-Torbay, Pigneur, & Usunier, 2004), and equally in popular literature (for example, Barfe, 2004; Knopper, 2009).

For many of our interviewees, Napster marked a very significant turning point. As one international record industry executive advances:

> That was when the genie was out of the bottle irretrievably… Virtually overnight we saw music being devalued in ways that had never occurred before. All of a sudden its value went down to zero. The basic market mechanism that you've got in place to make sure that the industry can invest and artists can get paid, suddenly shifted. (Personal interview.)

The subsequent proliferation of file-sharing technologies leads some interviewees to question not only the long-term viability of music as an industry, but as a cultural form per se. According to one Irish based music publisher:

> If you keep robbing music off the internet, why would anybody make any music? Why would anyone ever write a new song if no one is ever going to pay for it? How are songwriters going to make money? (Personal interview.)

Much of the evidence driving such pessimistic accounts has emanated from press releases and reports issued by the record industry, which throughout the 20th century established itself as the dominant and most lucrative sector of the wider music industries. The International Federation of Phonographic Industries (IFPI) argue that the "constant and ever-changing challenge" of digital piracy continues to constitute the "biggest single threat" to the development of the global industry, with an estimated 20% of internet users "regularly" accessing unlicensed digital services (IFPI, 2015a). The Recording Industry Association of America (RIAA) contend that the US economy is losing $12.5 billion in total output annually as a result of online music piracy, with more than 71,000 consequent job losses (RIAA, 2015).

Moreover, other commentators (for example, Scholes, 2014) advance the argument that "piracy" in the music sector has produced a "ripple effect on the global economy" with the broader entertainment industry losing approximately $80 billion within the USA alone. For Scholes, by the turn of the century some 60 million Napster users generated sufficient damage to drive music revenues on a downward spiral that would continue for more than a decade.

The apparent stark turn in fortune for the record industry in the 21st century is frequently drawn upon to support injurious claims against the realm of digital distribution. While the final decade of the 20 century saw the record industry enjoy a boom on the back of the blossoming CD market, the 16 year period from 1999 to 2014 (inclusive) saw the trade value of global record industry revenues drop from $26.6 billion to $14.9 (IFPI, 2000, 2015b). While the 2010–2014 period (inclusive) has seen this decline significantly decelerate—falling by a relatively modest 5.7% across these years, the overall drop in trade revenues since 1999 has, at time of writing, been almost 44%. While within this, the value of the digital music market grew to almost $7 billion by 2014 (IFPI, 2015c), this does not come close to offsetting the losses resulting from a depleted physical market.

So, on the face of it, the shift to digital distribution has dramatically transformed how we access music, and undermines the scope of the industry to monetize its output. As such, the digital–music convergence is often characterized by notions of stagnation and crisis.

That said, there are a few (for example, Napier-Bell, 2008) who celebrate the "effects" of digital innovations, emphasizing how artists and consumers alike are now more free than ever from the shackles of a corporate music industry that is no longer perceived as a necessary middleman in the music producer–consumer relationship. In keeping with the prophesies of such information age "gurus" as Negroponte (1995) and Kelly (1999), digital is perceived as the great liberator, rendering obsolete conventional "arrangements" around corporate control and music market concentration.

Thus, in the recent history of the music industry, technological convergence is simultaneously portrayed as both hero and villain, but more commonly villain. However, irrespective of whichever worldview we choose to subscribe to, the conventional wisdom is that digital technological innovations have radically transformed the music industry sphere, rendering obsolete the traditional power structures along with the established roles and practices of the major music labels.

Here, it is also worth reflecting on the lack of consensus that exists among scholars in the field of earlier research that specifically focuses on the economic dimensions of file-sharing. Some reports and studies (for example, Blackburn, 2004, 2007; Liebowitz, 2006, 2008; Zentner, 2006) conclude that the illicit online sharing of music files inflicts significant losses on the music industry. Other studies are more ambivalent in their findings regarding the effects of file-sharing activities. For example, Oberholzer-Gee and Strumpf conclude that the "empirical evidence on sales displacement is mixed," and while "some studies find evidence of a substitution effect, other findings, in particular the papers using file-sharing data, suggest that piracy and music sales are largely unrelated" (2010, p. 25). Furthermore, Van Eijk, Poort and Rutten find that only a small percentage of music exchanged on peer-to-peer file-sharing networks "comes at the expense of industry turnover" (2010, p. 51). Furthermore, a study conducted by the research agency The Leading Question concludes that active file-sharers spend four and a half times more money on legal music purchases than consumers who only download from licensed sites (Billboard, 2011).

Moreover, Sterne (2012) points to "conduit" industries benefiting significantly from file-sharing activities. Sterne describes how, for example, the suppliers of various hardware products (such as hard drives, playback devices and so on) grew their revenues on the back of free, illicit content.

INSTITUTIONAL AND ORGANIZATIONAL RESPONSES TO TECHNOLOGICAL THREATS

On one hand, the major music labels have sought recourse to the courts as a mechanism through which to address the unauthorized sharing of their copyrights. This strategy has been three-pronged, with waves of lawsuits being issued against the producers and suppliers of file-sharing technologies, individual music fans and internet service providers (ISPs). However, here, we are less concerned with such actions that are designed to hinder or combat file-sharing activities. Rather, we contend that fundamental ways in which these same labels have modified their practices and reconfigured their core structures in order to more fruitfully exploit their catalogues, artists and brands is much more significant in arriving at a thorough understanding of how the industry has evolved in the digital era.

Below, we first consider how the music industry has sustained itself through a climate of technological change in the 21st century by increasingly shifting its focus from music as a "good" to sell to a "service" to be licensed via the exploitation of copyrights and trademarks across the broadest possible range of spaces and outlets in both real space and cyberspace, and encompassing traditional and new media alike. We then describe how, over the past decade, the major music labels have been reconfiguring their core structures in order to ensure maximum benefit from these evolving revenue streams. As such, we illustrate how the major labels have reimagined themselves as fully rounded "music" labels, as opposed to the traditional conception of a record label. Not only has power within individual music sectors (for example, recording, publishing, live, merchandising) remained concentrated, but power across the music industries per se has become increasingly concentrated with mergers, takeovers, joint ventures and alliances involving actors across the industry's main subsectors coming to characterize recent developments regarding ownership trends, and ultimately seeing the industry's biggest "record" labels successfully maneuvering control of other sectors, and the revenue streams that come with them.

Understanding how music operates as an intellectual property industry requires that we consider how music possesses key characteristics and features that distinguish it from other forms of media and cultural industry content. As previous authors (for example, Kassabian, 2001, 2002, 2004; Rogers, 2013) have indicated, music has become ubiquitous, and this omnipresence makes it distinct as a media and cultural form. Music is everywhere. It colonizes our private worlds and public environments. It possesses the ability to access places and spaces that other forms of media cannot reach. Moreover, aside from existing as a standalone media form, music also forms a core constituent element of almost all other forms of audio-visual media, both traditional and new. We find it on radio, television, films, advertising, digital games and a plethora of mobile and online platforms (such as social networks, streaming services and so on). As such, music's value as a commodity to be licensed to such an array of spaces and sites offers the owners of the most popular and well-established music copyrights immense potential for revenue generation. In the space of this short chapter it is not possible to go into significant detail on the various platforms and spaces new and old, in cyberspace and real space, that offers sources of revenue to music. However, a headline-level overview now follows.

First, we must acknowledge the vast and widening spectrum of online and mobile platforms and formats that have evolved since the early noughties. Beyond the digital music store model (dominated by Apple iTunes), we have seen the emergence and spread of ad-supported streaming services, subscription-based sites, social networks and others among a wealth of licensed online services. The sheer range of formats now available for recordings is evidenced by Beyoncé's I Am Sasha Fierce album from 2009 which was released across no fewer than 260 different formats including ringtones, mobile full-track downloads, video and bundled album digital store downloads (IFPI, 2010). The past dozen years have seen the global digital music market grow to a (trade) value of almost US$7 billion which accounts for 46% of overall recording revenues (IFPI, 2015). Within that, 2014 saw overall subscription revenues alone grow by 39%. Moreover, ad-supported streaming services saw a

38.6% increase, with video streaming outlets such as YouTube and Vevo at the heart of this expansion (IFPI, 2015c).

YouTube itself claims to have paid out €3 billion to date to the music industry, with user-uploaded videos generating some €2 billion for rights owners since its "Content ID" system was introduced (Google, 2016). Midia Research indicate that music video streams on YouTube rose by 170% across 2015 (cited in Ingram, 2016). While the BPI point to the number of online video streams rising by 88% in 2015, they highlight that revenues from these activities have only increased by less than half of 1% across the same period (Dredge, 2016).

Offline too, the spaces for music to occupy have burgeoned. Film, TV and radio, media that have long enjoyed a symbiotic relationship with music, have become more important to its financial health. And we can also put video games into this equation. Not just in terms of the promotional value they bring to music and artists, but in terms of the direct revenues generated through licensing across these platforms. With the rapid deregulation and privatization of the broadcasting sector that occurred across Europe since the early 1990s, radio and television outlets have proliferated, and in turn driven a vast increase in music licensing revenues from these sectors. As record sales have declined, synchronization to audio-visual media (for example, the use of music in film, TV, advertising, computer games and so on) has been pursued much more assiduously by labels and artists. As the manager of one major international recording artist argues:

> [S]yncs are now a huge part of the business, huge. They can provide that real adrenaline. It's the one thing that managers, record companies, publishers are desperate for. (Personal interview.)

Another interviewee advances:

> There are so many new outlets and platforms… It's become so much more sophisticated in recent years… Music to sell a film. Music to sell television. Music to sell advertising. Music to sell a brand… Music revenues are more and more generated by the application of music in other things. It's music as a secondary factor. Music used as an emotional hook to attach you to other brands. (Personal interview.)

Overall, global synchronization revenues grew by 8.4% across 2014, with markets such as Germany, Japan and France showing the largest increases (IFPI, 2015). Such trends have been central to the growth of performing rights revenues. The International Confederation of Authors and Composers Societies (CISAC) estimate the global value of this sector to be $6 billion (CISAC, 2012).

Within this, adverting has become a very significant source of revenue for the music industry. Marketing executives in the major labels that were interviewed by this author in 2014 describe the development of commercial teams within their organizations aimed primarily at forging relationships between music and products/brands. For one such major label employee based in the UK, "[O]pportunities for engaging with brands are more prevalent and have become more key in the last 5 years" (personal interview). Such "opportunities" have meant that songs by folk and rock artists that until recently would not have been conceived in such a context, now often find themselves used to sell various commodities. For example, Woody Guthrie's Car Song has been used in an Audi campaign; the songs of Bob Dylan have been adopted by lingerie brand Victoria's Secret; the music of Lennon and McCartney sells hardware and electronic products (Target) and banking services (The Halifax); John Fogerty's Fortunate Son, an anti-Vietnam-War protest song, has been used by Wrangler.

The live music industry has also experienced phenomenal growth in the 21st century. Data produced by Statistica (2015) indicate that the revenues from concert ticket sales in the USA increased sixfold across the quarter century 1990–2014 (inclusive). Valued at just over US$1 billion in 1990, this market was worth $6.2 billion by 2014. Such trends are reflected worldwide, with Laing (2012) estimating the global value of the concert industry to have reached $25 billion by 2010. A new development in recent years has seen major labels negotiate a percentage of their artists' live revenues courtesy of multi-rights recording contracts.

As an increasingly important site of revenue generation, the music merchandising sector has witnessed an accelerated level of takeovers, mergers and joint ventures in recent years involving established music labels, independent merchandising companies and players in the e-commerce market.

Signaling their intent to expand in this area, the Universal Music Group (UMG) acquired Bravado International Group Merchandising Services as part of its takeover of the Sanctuary Records Group in 2008, a move which saw Bravado expand its operations to include some 46 countries around the globe. This secured UNG rights to such vintage acts as the Rolling Stones and the Beatles, and Bravado currently boasts some 800 international recording acts (current or defunct) on its roster. Having already developed its own merchandise outlet through collaboration with the US fashion brand Thread Shop, 2013 saw Sony expanded its merchandising operation in the North American market courtesy of a joint venture with Band Merch—the merchandising arm of the Anschultz Entertainment Group's concert promoter AEG Live. Equally, the Warner Music Group's own merchandise production arm provides a range of touring, retailing and direct-to-consumer services to artists on WMG labels and beyond.

The Convergence of Music Industry Sub-Sectors

Within the context of all the trends outlined above, the major labels have also fundamentally reconfigured their core structures so as to optimize their revenue-generating capabilities in all of these areas. No longer does the recording artist sell records and perform concerts; nowadays the figure of the music artist represents an all-encompassing bundle of rights that can be simultaneously exploited across a range of platforms.

Often, the music artist is positioned as a universal source of revenue for one central rights holder who controls and administers all rights on behalf of that artist. This is exemplified through the evolution of 360-degree deals whereby all revenues generated through the exploitation of artist copyrights, trademarks, patents and other are funneled back to the same corporate entity., Thus, 360-degree deals see artists sign contracts with one company, assigning to them the handling of all facets of the artist's career including recording, publishing, merchandising, endorsements, all aspects of image rights, and all other artists' related rights. Moreover, as indicated above, the record label can also generate direct revenue from their artists' live concert tours. As the marketing manager of the Irish arm of one of the major labels said in his interview, his label will seek 20% of live revenues in their multi-rights contract with an artist. He contends that:

> [I]t would be commercially naïve of us not to do that. Because the amount of time, money, effort that we spend on these acts to get them to that

level and then to reap none of the rewards for them as a touring entity just doesn't make sense. (Personal interview.)

Another interviewee (the manager of an internationally successful singer-songwriter) explains:

The labels are obviously very keen to get their share of every aspect of an artist's income, from recording to publishing to merchandising to live to whatever. That's very much one way that they look at the future, one sort of big umbrella organization with everything under the same roof. (Personal interview.)

Perhaps unsurprisingly, the major labels argue the benefits of this to the artists on their rosters. For example, a London-based executive at one of the majors:

The words collaboration and integration are buzzwords that are around, and I think record labels becoming multi-rights companies is working in a way that allows more opportunities for both artist and label. You look at the strengths of what the business can deliver in each territory around the world. (Personal interview.)

However, elsewhere, a music industry lawyer asserts that multi-rights deals make it harder for an artist to earn income from the royalties they generate for the label. This is because the label will usually cross-collateralize the various revenue streams as to ensure all of their investments across all facets of the artist's career are recouped before the artist themselves can start to earn. She argues: "[F]or a band signing up to a 360-degree deal, you are dealing with Goliath" and unless the band is already an established brand with a successful catalogue, "they will have very little to bargain with" (personal interview).

In essence, the major music label's embrace of multi-rights deals effectively serves to mitigate any downturn in recorded music sales revenues. For copyright owners, recorded music sales now form the source of just one set of potential revenue streams alongside a host of others. This development has effectively seen heretofore discrete music industry sub-sectors more comprehensively integrated under the umbrella of a corporate label.

So what have all of these developments meant for overall music industry revenues in recent years? Contrary to the dystopian accounts telling of the collapse of the music industry in the digital era, the processes outlined above have combined to enable the major music labels to sustain themselves and offset the downturn in physical record sales since the turn of the century. According to media industry consultancy Midia Research, the global music industry has effectively remained stable across the 21st century, contracting by just 3% between 2000 and 2013 (Resnikoff, 2014). Drawing on sales data for recording, publishing, live performance and merchandise, this reports illustrates a dramatic drop of more than 40% in the value of the recording sector over this period, matched by an even more dramatic mushrooming of the live performance sector, which it estimates rose by 60% over the same timeframe. As a result, overall industry revenues have fluctuated very moderately, resting at approximately $56 billion in 2013.

In terms of the three major labels, it is first crucial to recognize them as "music" labels as opposed to simply "record" labels. As such, their performance over the past decade has been relatively stable. Over the 11 years to 2014, full-year revenues for the Universal Music Group fluctuated mildly year on year, dropping overall from $4.8 billion in 2004 to $4.6 billion in 2014 (Vivendi, 2008, 2009, 2010, 2011, 2013, 2014, 2015; Business Wire, 2006). Over the same period, the Warner Music Group (WMG) saw its overall revenues drop from $3.4 billion to just in excess of $3 billion (WMG, 2005, 2007, 2008, 2009, 2010, 2014), while Sony Music Entertainment saw its overall revenues marginally dip from ¥523 billion to ¥520 between 2009 and 2014 (Sony, 2011; Ingham, 2015). Also, despite the promises that the internet brought for dismantling the power of the major labels, these three corporations still account for more than 70% of the recording market and 65% of the music publishing market worldwide. As such, music markets remain highly concentrated.

In short, the internet has not radically disrupted power relations in the music industry. Rather, it has seen the major companies mutate to bolster and maintain their oligopolistic dominance.

OLIGOPOLISTIC TRENDS IN MUSIC MARKETS

In all core sectors of the music industry, an evolving pattern of mergers and takeovers characterize the recent evolution of the business with ownership remaining highly concentrated across the board. Here, let us briefly make a headline-level examination of the current composition of the recording, music publishing and live music spheres.

The market for recorded music—albeit a declining market in recent years—continues to remain highly concentrated. Over the past number of decades, a small handful of major labels have consistently accounted for more than 70% of the global market in any given year. In some smaller national markets—such as Ireland, where the current author is based—this figure has on occasions risen to more than 90%. Moreover, contrary to the "long tail" predictions of Shirky (2003) and Anderson (2006), wealth in the 21st-century music economy is also concentrated among the few, with just 1% of the top earning artists accounting for 77% of income in the global recording sector in 2013 (Mulligan, 2014).

Since the late 1990s, when the internet first emerged as a major platform for the circulation of music, this "small handful" of distinct major players has halved from six to three, with Universal, Warner and Sony now combining to monopolize the terrain.

Following its takeover of the lion's share of EMI in 2011, Universal firmly established itself as the biggest record company in the world. It currently comprises a family of some 31 labels. While the EMI takeover saw it acquire Capitol and Virgin-EMI, its earlier acquisition of Polygram (as part of Vivendi's takeover of Seagram's entertainment division) saw Polydor, Mercury, Def Jam, Interscope, A&M, Island and Vertigo all brought under the UMG umbrella.

Sony entered the recording industry in the early 1990s following its acquisition of CBS Records. After Universal, Sony Music Entertainment (SME) is currently the world's second-largest label. Having entered a joint-venture arrangement with Bertelsmann's BMG Records in 2004, Sony ultimately acquired full control of the operation in 2008. The Sony-BMG marriage saw Columbia, Epic and RCA brought together as the core labels/groups under one corporate overlord. As with other labels, the blurring of distinction between major and independent recording sectors is epitomized through the ongoing integration of indie networks with Sony infrastructure. With independent distribution network RED already under its administration, 2009 saw SME announce that it was partnering with the International Online Distribution Alliance (IODA) to deliver digital distribution and services for independent rights holders. This network was subsequently rebranded as The Orchard and was fully acquired by Sony in 2015, the same year that saw them purchase German-based Century Media Records.

Warner stands as the third major corporate entity dominating the record industry landscape. Once part of the Time Warner corporation, the USA-based Warner Music Group (WMG) is currently owned by British billionaire Len Blavatnik. It comprises four main "umbrella" labels—Warner Bros. Records, the Atlantic Records Group, Rhino Records and Parlophone—and also holds significant interests in the sphere of independent distribution. As part of the afore-mentioned break-up of EMI, various national EMI operations have come under the ownership and administration of WMG since 2011. Its core record groups in turn carry more than eighty labels internationally. Beyond this, WMG has also continued to secure or enter joint ventures with some of the most successful independent companies over the past two decades (including Sub Pop, Hardly Art, Nonesuch and Rykodisc). It currently distributes recordings for approximately 140 such labels through Alternative Distribution Alliance, Warner's independent music and film distribution company.

The domain of music publishing shows similar trends. With Sony/ATV Music Publishing acquiring EMI Music Publishing from Citigroup for a reported US$2.2 billion in 2011, the sector is now dominated by just three major actors: Sony/ATV, the Universal Music Publishing Group and Warner Chappell. In 2014, these three combined to account for 65% of the global music publishing market, leaving 35% to independents (Music & Copyright, 2015).

Within the independent music-publishing sector, the two biggest players have significantly increased their prominence over recent years, with BMG Rights Management (an arm of the Bertelsmann conglomerate) growing their share of the global market from 5.1 to 5.4% in 2014, and Kobalt doing likewise from 3.5 to 3.9% (Music & Copyright, 2015). The extent of concentrated power in this market is further emphasized when we realize that combined, the two biggest independent players account for just under 10% of global revenues. While Kobalt's expansion has been "organic," the strides made by BMG have been aided primarily by acquisitions. Recent years have seen them acquire

Virgin Music and Famous Music UK from Sony/ATV as well as a plethora of independent publishers including the Chrysalis Music Group, Crosstown Songs, Cherry Lane Music Publishing (whose print publishing portfolio comprises such artists as Metallica, The White Stripes and Barbara Streisand), Primary Wave (a company founded by former Virgin and Arista executive Lawrence Mestel and whose catalogue includes Kurt Cobain, John Lennon and Def Leppard) and Talpa Music (who carry songs of The Rolling Stones, AC/DC, will.i.am, Take That and Bruno Mars among a host of others).

So, the two biggest independent publishing entities, along with the three major companies, all combine to account for approximately 75% of the global music publishing market.

Despite the ongoing trends of alliances and mergers outlined here, it is nonetheless important to acknowledge in the bigger media industries ownership picture, major music companies have divorced from their parent media groups. For example, by late 2001, AOL-Time Warner found itself with debts well in excess of $20 billion. Following a "corporate record-breaking" writedown of $54 billion in the first quarter of 2002, the shares in the company were valued at $10 whereas Time Warner's shares had traded at $71 prior to the merger (Bettig & Hall, 2012, p. 46). A range of assets were subsequently sold off in order to reduce AOL-Time Warner's debt, with its CD and DVD manufacturing operations (which were purchased by Cintam International for more than $1 billion) among the first to be offloaded (Time Warner, 2003). Later, the Warner Music Group was sold to Edgar Bronfman Jr. for approximately $2.6 billion.

In the concert industry, the past decade has seen one brand, Live Nation, grow to dominate this vista at global level. Initially growing a predominantly USA-based portfolio of venues (through, for example, its acquisition of the HOB chain of music venues, and other), its alliance with entertainment venue management company SMG in 2008 saw it significantly extend its operations internationally (predominantly in Europe and North America). In addition, Live Nation acquired key promotions companies in many territories around the globe such as Milano Concerti (Italy), Gunnar Eide Concerts (Norway), EMA Telstar (Sweden) among numerous others. Then, in 2009, Live Nation's merger with Ticketmaster bound together the world's biggest touring agent and concert promoter with the largest ticketing retailer. Subsequently rebranded as Live Nation Entertainment (LNE), the company owns, operates or retains an equity interest in hundreds of theatres and arenas around the globe.

As the global concert industry has mushroomed over the past decade, so too have LNE revenues. In 2014 they promoted approximately 23,000 events around the world for some 2700 artists which were attended by almost 59 million fans (LNE, 2015). LNE's concert business was worth $4.73 billion globally by 2014, an overall rise of 28.5% over the proceeding 7 year period (Statistica, 2015).

LNE is thus the predominant player in the global market regarding the sale of tours, concert promotion, primary and secondary ticket sales and other related activities. As such, LNE's evolution marks a departure from the traditional structure and organization of the live industry in that it illustrates how the sector has become vertically integrated. Artists increasingly find that when touring, every filter or link in the live music chain is controlled by one corporate entity. Moreover, the 2008 acquisition of artist management company Frontline (which included WMG as a major stakeholder) by Ticketmaster meant that following the 2009 merger, LNE themselves have come to represent some 280 international recording artists (most of whom are distributed through networks under the control of the three major labels—Universal, Warner and Sony).

When we also consider its increasing encroachment into music festival ownership, LNE has become, as other authors have advanced, "the newest bogeyman of popular music culture" (Brennan, 2011, p. 72).

Summary and Concluding Remarks

The 21st century "reconfiguration" of the music industry has involved a continuing trend of acquisitions and mergers that keeps power highly concentrated across the music industry as the traditional major "record" labels have moved to reimagine themselves as broader "music" companies, encompassing a more diverse range of practices and activities designed to maximize the range of revenue streams from which it draws. Moreover, this reconfiguration brings with it the escalated commodification of music that has seen the relationship between music and other media sectors intensify in recent years as music as a "service" to be licensed grows in prominence relative to music as a "product" to be bought and sold.

Processes of market convergence offset many of the potential problems and challenges arising for the music industry from technological convergence. If we move our lens beyond the "technological," and consider contemporaneous innovations in, for example, the organizational and institutional realms, market convergence can be seen to more readily explain the nature of change in the 21st-century music business. In essence, this research shows that while digital innovations carry with them new and novel modus operandi for disseminating and using music and, the potential to undermine the roles and practices of established players, the music's industry's traditional power structures have been fundamentally maintained through the flexibility of its major actors to redesign their core structures.

Arguments relating to diminishing markets as a result of technological convergence are frequently used to justify such consolidation strategies. Such an approach to analyzing the evolving character of the music industry demonstrates how concepts such as concentration and commodification remain crucial to a more comprehensive understanding of the response of this particular media sector to the challenges posed by technological convergence.

Also, as ownership trends imply, the once dichotomous relationship that was perceived to exist between corporate and non-corporate actors has long since evolved into a more complex set of relations where major and independent companies increasingly integrate operations, with the three big labels coming to gain or share control of more and more independent distribution networks.

References

Barfe, L. (2004). *Where have all the good times gone? The rise and fall of the record industry*. Boston: Atlantic Books.

Baym, N. K. (2011). The swedish model: Balancing gifts in the music industry. *Popular Communication, 9*(1), 22–38.

Bettig, R., & Hall, J. L. (2012). *Big media, big money: Cultural texts and political economics* (2nd ed.). Lanham, MD: Rowman and Littlefield.

Billboard. (2011). Business matters: Former EMI exec says file-sharers are good consumers. *Billboard* [online], Tuesday 26 July. Retrieved from http://www.billboard.biz/bbbiz/industry/digital-and-mobile/business-matters-former-emi-exec-says-file-1005293592.story.

Blackburn, D. (2004). Does file sharing affect record sales? Cambridge MA: Harvard University, Department of Economics Working Paper.

Blackburn, D. (2007). The heterogeneous effects of copying: The case of recorded music. Harvard University, Cambridge, MA: Harvard University, Department of Economics Working Paper.

Brennan, M. (2011). Understanding line nation and its impact of live music in the UK. Situating Popular Musics—IASPM 2011 proceedings, pp. 69–75.

Business Wire. (2006). Vivendi Universal Reports Full Year 2005 Revenues Up 9 and 7% on a Comparable Basis. *Business Wire* [online], January 30, 2006. Retrieved from: http://www.businesswire.com/news/home/20060130005463/en/Vivendi-Universal-Reports-Full-Year-2005-Revenues#.Va5Rs_n4G5I.

CISAC. (2012). *Authors' royalties in 2010: An unexpected rebound—global economic survey of the royalties collected by the CISAC member authors' societies in 2010* (p. 2012). Paris: CISAC.

De Sola Pool, I. (1983). *Technologies of freedom: On free speech in the electronic age.* Cambridge MA: Belknap Press/Harvard University Press.

Dredge, S. (2016). Why is the music industry battling YouTube and what happens next? *The Guardian* [online], May 20, Retrieved from: https://www.theguardian.com/technology/2016/may/20/music-industry-battling-google-youtube-what-happens-next.

Dubosson-Torbay, M., Pigneur, Y., & J. Usunier, J. (2004). Business models for music distribution after the P2P revolution. In *Proceedings of the Fourth International Conference on Web Delivering of Music.* Retrieved from: http://www.researchgate.net/publication/4105198_Business_models_for_music_distribution_after_the_P2P_revolution.

Geisler, M. (2006). Consumer gift systems. *Journal of Consumer Research, 33*(2), 283–290.

Giletti, T. (2012). Why pay if it's free? Streaming, downloading, and digital music consumption in the "iTunes era." LSE Electronic Dissertation Series [online]. Retrieved from: http://www.lse.ac.uk/media@lse/research/media-workingpapers/mscdissertationseries/2011/71.pdf.

Google. (2016). How google fights piracy [online]. Retrieved from https://drive.google.com/file/d/0BwxyRPFduTN2cl91LXJ0YjlYSjA/view?pref=2&pli=1&curator=MediaREDEF.

Hughes, J., & Lang, K. (2003). If i had a song: The culture of digital community networks and its impact on the music industry. *International Journal on Media Management, 5*(3), 180–189.

IFPI. (2000). *The recording industry in numbers 2000.* London: IFPI.

IFPI. (2015a). The recording industry's ability to develop the digital marketplace is undermined by piracy [online]. Retrieved from: http://www.ifpi.org/music-piracy.php.

IFPI. (2015b). *The recording industry in numbers 2015.* London: IFPI.

IFPI. (2015c). Digital music report 2015: Charting the path to sustainable growth [online]. Retrieved from: http://www.ifpi.org/downloads/Digital-Music-Report-2015.pdf.

Ingham, T. (2015). Why Sony Music and Sony/ATV are on course for a big financial year in Music Business Worldwide [online]. Retrieved from: http://www.musicbusinessworldwide.com/why-sony-music-and-sonyatv-are-on-course-for-big-financial-years/.

Ingram, M. (2016). YouTube Pays Billions, But the Music Industry Says It's Not Enough. *Fortune*, [online]. July 13, Retreived from: http://fortune.com/2016/07/13/youtube-music-billions/.

Jenkins, H. (2006). *Convergence culture: Where old and new media collide*. New York: NYU Press.

Jin, D. Y. (2012). The new wave of Deconvergence: A new business model in the communication industry in the 21st century. *Media, Culture and Society, 34*(6), 761–772.

Kassabian, A. (2001). *Hearing film: Tracking identification in contemporary hollywood film music* (p. 2001). New York: Routledge.

Kassabian, A. (2002). Ubiquitous listening. In D. Hesmondhalgh & K. Negus (Eds.), *Popular music studies* (pp. 131–142). Oxford: Oxford University Press.

Kassabian, A. (2004). Would you like world music with your latte?: Starbucks, putumayo and distributed tourism. *Twentieth Century Music, 1*(2), 209–223.

Kelly, K. (1999). *New rules for the new economy: 10 ways the network is changing everything*. London: Fourth Estate.

Knopper, S. (2009). *Appetite for self-destruction: The spectacular crash of the record industry in the digital age*. London: Simon & Schuster.

Laing, D. (2012). What's it worth? Calculating the economic value of live music. Live Music Exchange, 2012. http://livemusicexchange.org/blog/whats-it-worth-calculating-the-economic-value-of-live-music-dave-laing/.

Leyshon, A., Webb, P., French, S., Thrift, N., & Crewe, L. (2005). On the reproduction of the musical economy after the internet. *Media, Culture and Society, 27*(2), 177–209.

Liebowitz, S. (2006). File sharing: Creative destruction or just plain destruction? *Journal of Law and Economics, 49*(1), 1–28.

Liebowitz, S. (2008). Testing file-sharing's impact on music album sales in cities. *Management Science, 54*(4), 852–859.

Mulligan, M. (2014). The Death of the Long Tail: The Superstar Music Economy [online]. Midia Consulting. Retrieved from: http://www.promus.dk/files/MIDiA_Consulting_-_The_Death_of_the_Long_Tail.pdf.

Music & Copyright. (2015). Recorded music market share gains for WMG in 2014, Sony/ATV is the publishing leader. Music & Copyright [online], April, 28. Retrieved from: https://musicandcopyright.wordpress.com/tag/market-share/.

Napier-Bell, S. (2008, January 20). The life and crimes of the music biz. *The Observer* – Music Monthly, p. 41.

Negroponte, N. (1995). *Being digital*. New York: Vintage.

Oberholzer-Gee, F. & Strumpf, K. (2010). File-Sharing and Copyright [online]. Retrieved from: http://musicbusinessresearch.files.wordpress.com/2010/06/paper-felix-oberholzer-gee.pdf.

Preston, P., & Rogers, J. (2010). The three Cs of key music sector trends today: Convergence, concentration and commodification. In D. Y. Jin (Ed.), *Global media convergence and cultural transformation: Emerging social patterns and characteristics* (pp. 373–396). Hershey & New York: IGI Global.

Preston, P., & Rogers, J. (2012). Crisis, digitalisation and the future of the internet. *Info, 14*(6), 72–83.

Resnikoff, P. (2014) The Music Industry Has Only Declined 3% Since 2000, Research Shows in Digital Music News [online]. Retrieved from: http://www.digitalmusicnews.com/permalink/2014/06/05/music-industry-declined-3-since-2000-research-shows.

RIAA. (2015). Who music theft hurts [online]. Retrieved from: http://riaa.com/physicalpiracy.php?content_selector=piracy_details_online.

Rogers, J. (2013). *The death and life of the music industry in the digital age.* New York: Bloomsbury.

Rogers, J. (2014a). The more things change, the more they stay the same: Where power lies in the 21st century music industry. *Civilizations, 13,* 33–50.

Rogers, J. (2014b). Canary down the mine: Music and copyright at the digital coalface. *Socialism and Democracy, 28*(1), 34–50.

Rogers, J. & Cawley, A. (2016). Striking a new note: Assessing the position, value and restructuring of the digital music industry in the context of Ireland's economic crisis. In A. Whelan & R. Nowak (Eds.), *Networked music cultures: Contemporary approaches, emerging issues.* London: Palgrave [forthcoming].

Rogers, J., & Preston, P. (2016). Crisis and creative destruction: New modes of appropriation in the 21st century music industry. In P. Wikstrom & R. Di Fillippi (Eds.), *Business innovation and disruption in the music industry* (pp. 53–72). London: Edward Elgar.

Rogers, J., & Sparviero, S. (2011). Understanding innovation in communication industries through alternative economic theories: The case of the music industry. *International Communications Gazette, 73*(7), 610–629.

Scholes, W. (2014). Piracy's ripple effect on the global economy. The Diplomatic Courier [online], January 14. Retrieved from: http://www.diplomaticourier.com/news/sponsored/2011-piracy-s-ripple-effect-on-the-global-economy.

Sony. (2011) Annual Report 2011. Retrieved from: http://www.sony.net/SonyInfo/IR/financial/ar/report2011/SonyAR11-E.pdf.

Statistica. (2015), Live Nation Entertainment's concert revenue from 2008 to 2014 [online]. Retrieved from: http://www.statista.com/statistics/193710/concert-revenue-of-live-nation-entertainment-since-2008/.

Sterne, J. (2012). *MP3: The meaning of the format*. Durham and London: Duke University Press.

Time Warner. (2003). AOL time warner agrees to sell its DVD/CD manufacturing and physical distribution businesses to cinram international for $1.05 Billion, press release, July 18, [online]. Retreived from: http://www.timewarner.com/newsroom/press-releases/2003/07/18/aol-time-warner-agrees-to-sell-its-dvdcd-manufacturing-and.

van Eijk, N., Poort, J., & Rutten, P. (2010). Legal, economic and cultural aspects of file sharing. *Communications & Strategies, 77*, 35–54.

Vivendi. (2008). Vivendi earnings, press release, February 29, [online]. Retrieved from: http://www.vivendi.com/wp-content/uploads/2012/03/PR290208_Results2007.pdf.

Vivendi. (2009). "Vivendi 2008 Results and 2009 Outlook" press release, March 2, [online]. Retrieved from: http://www.vivendi.com/wp-content/uploads/2012/03/EN-_090227_FY-08-final_ul-March-2-2009.pdf.

Vivendi. (2010). 2009 Vivendi Earnings, press release, March 1, [online]. Retrieved from http://www.vivendi.com/wp-content/uploads/2012/03/PR100301_Results.pdf.

Vivendi. (2011). 2010 Vivendi Earnings" press release March 1, [online]. Retrieved from http://www.vivendi.com/wp-content/uploads/2012/03/PR110301_resultats_annuels_2010.pdf.

Vivendi. (2013). 2012 Vivendi Earnings, press release, February 26, [online]. Retrieved from: http://www.vivendi.com/wp-content/uploads/2013/02/20130226_VIV_PR_R%C3%A9sultats-2012.pdf.

Vivendi. (2014). Investor Presentation March 2014 [online]. Retrieved from: http://www.vivendi.com/wp-content/uploads/2014/04/20140305_VIV_Investor-Presentation_March-2014.pdf.

Vivendi. (2015). 2014 Vivendi Earnings, press release, 27 February [online]. Retrieved from http://www.vivendi.com/wp-content/uploads/2015/02/20150227_VIV_CP_Annual_Results.pdf.

Warner Music Group. (2005). Investor Relations, press release, December 1, [online]. Retrieved from: http://investors.wmg.com/phoenix.zhtml?c=182480&p=irol-newsArticle&ID=791605.

Warner Music Group. (2007). Investor Relations, press release, November 29, [online]. Retrieved from: http://investors.wmg.com/phoenix.zhtml?c=182480&p=irol-newsArticle&ID=1082464.

Warner Music Group. (2008). Investor Relations, press release, November 25, [online]. Retrieved from: http://investors.wmg.com/phoenix.zhtml?c=182480&p=irol-newsArticle&ID=1229864.

Warner Music Group. (2009). "Investor Relations" press release, November 24, [online]. Retrieved from: http://investors.wmg.com/phoenix.zhtml?c=182480&p=irol-newsArticle&ID=1358713.

Warner Music Group. (2010). Investor Relations, press release, November 17, [online]. Retrieved from: http://investors.wmg.com/phoenix.zhtml?c=182480&p=irol-newsArticle&ID=1497315.

Warner Music Group. (2014). Warner music group corp. reports results for fiscal fourth quarter and full year ended September 30, 2014 [online]. Retrieved from: http://www.wmg.com/news/warner-music-group-corp-reports-results-fiscal-fourth-quarter-and-full-year-ended-september-3-1.

Zentner, A. (2006). Measuring the effect of file-sharing on music purchases. *Journal of Law and Economics, 49*(1), 63–90.

AUTHOR BIOGRAPHY

Jim Rogers is a Lecturer in Communications at the School of Communications, Dublin City University, Ireland. His primary research interests centre on the political economy of the media, with a particular focus in the music industry. His first book, *The Death and Life of the Music Industry in the Digital Age*, was published in 2013. Beyond this, his research has been published in international peer-review journals and various edited collections.

CHAPTER 12

Is Convergence the "Killer Bug" in the Media Ecosystem? The Case of Flemish Media Policymaking 2010–2015

Hilde Van den Bulck

INTRODUCTION

Taking key moments in media restructuring and policymaking in Flanders—the Northern, Dutch-speaking part of Belgium—between 2010 and 2015, this chapter analyzes how the Flemish government, regulatory agencies and stakeholders in the Flemish media system employ the "convergence argument" to formulate claims in media debates and policymaking processes. Convergence has been a buzzword in Flemish media policy and industry debates for several decades (Van den Bulck, 2008) but gained new momentum as it increasingly affects traditional functions and business models of old and new media. This increases pressures on policymakers, who need to disentangle the growing complexity of technology and of relationships between old and new policy actors that fight battles and forge coalitions across traditional boundaries. In turn, (commercial) media players ostensibly push a neoliberal agenda, yet

H. Van den Bulck (✉)
University of Antwerp, Antwerp, Belgium
e-mail: hilde.vandenbulck@uantwerpen.be

© The Author(s) 2017
S. Sparviero et al. (eds.), *Media Convergence and Deconvergence*, Global
Transformations in Media and Communication Research - A Palgrave and
IAMCR Series, DOI 10.1007/978-3-319-51289-1_12

241

increasingly turn to governments to protect their position in the media landscape.

Analyzing the merger of printing activities of multimedia groups Corelio and Concentra (the "Mediahuis" case), the struggle between Flemish broadcasters and operators (the "signal integrity" case), and policy discussions in the lead up to the 2016–2020 management contract between public service media (hereafter PSM) VRT and the Flemish government (the "management contract" case), this chapter explores how the (impact of) convergence argument is used by stakeholders to push certain policy decisions. It evaluates to what extent convergence is used as an argument sui generis or as a discursive tool to ensure decisive attention to, and impact of, market arguments in media policymaking. It further shows how this economic agenda behind the convergence argument is instrumental in pushing media policies that are reflective of controlled liberalization, favoring local interests.

The chapter starts from a theoretical framework that discusses key issues regarding technological–economic convergence and trends in contemporary policymaking processes, influenced by multistakeholderism and multilevel governance. Subsequently, it analyzes the three cases of media policymaking and their outcome. The study considers a "policy decision [as the] result of a process characterized by the formulation of views and interests, expressed by actors or stakeholders that adhere to a certain logic and that engage in debate and work towards a policy decision on relevant fora" (Van den Bulck, 2012, p. 18). The policy processes and outcomes are analyzed by means of a stakeholder analysis combined with an identification and analysis of key arguments.

With regard to stakeholders—that is, people, groups or organizations with a vested interest in (the outcome of) a particular policy—Hutchinson (1999, pp. 125–140) identifies politicians, regulatory institutions, media organizations and citizens. Other relevant actors include civil society, trade unions and the advertising industry among others. Stakeholders were identified on the basis of who they are or represent, their stake (or visibility), impact (or power), and attitude towards the policy issues. The latter regards their view on convergence and its technological, economic and cultural impact; on their position and that of other stakeholders; and on the role of the government. For the Mediahuis case, arguments were analyzed by means of a claims analysis (van der Burg & Van den Bulck, 2015; see also Koopman, 2002), while for the signal integrity and management contract cases, arguments were submitted to a discursive analysis. The data consist of written sources. In the Mediahuis case, this included the extensive (116 pages) report of the Belgische Mededingingsautoriteit (Belgian Competition Authority; hereafter BMA) (BMA, 2013) and a range of press publications. For the other cases, a range of published and internal policy documents of the core institutions (Flemish Government, Flemish Parliament), and documents of the main and peripheral stakeholders were collected and analyzed. Other sources include communications of stakeholders on relevant fora, including the Flemish Media Council and the Media Commission of the Flemish Parliament.

MEDIA CONVERGENCE: TECHNOLOGY MEETS ECONOMY[1]

Referred to as early as 1983 by de Sola Pool (1983) and an issue in media (policy) studies since the 1990s (McQuail & Siune, 1998), convergence gained new significance in discussions on media developments and policymaking in the past decade. Such a focus on convergence is contested by academics because, first, it suggests a strict media divide pre-convergence (Jin, 2013); second, it ignores changes in media relationships before digitization; third, it simplifies the complexity of media and technological change (Storsul & Stuedahl, 2007); and, fourth, it ignores the deconvergence taking place in some parts of the media industry (Jin, 213). However, criticism of convergence has not stopped its use by both academics and policymakers as a key term and argument in contemporary media debates. To analyze how it is used, media convergence here is conceptualized broadly as an increased connectivity and interaction between media activities, and an erosion of once distinct boundaries between media at the level of production, organization, content, distribution and consumption. As such it encompasses different types of convergence including network, terminal, service, market and regulatory (Fagerjord & Storsul, 2007).

Discussions regarding the benefits and dangers of convergence have been dominated by an implicit but powerful technological determinism—the idea that technology and the arrival of new forms of communication in and of themselves can change man and society, a claim apparently confirmed by the uptake of new technologies by consumers. The technical possibilities of converging media were influenced by a growing emphasis on interactivity and freedom of choice, further pushing the development and uptake of new media services (Galperin, 2004).

However, media convergence is not just about technology but affects relationships between industries and markets (Jenkins, 2004). Economic (or market) convergence thus refers to connections between media companies, their integration and consolidation.

Technological and economic convergence critically affects media value chains, that is the sequence of investing, producing, selling and collecting in the media industry. Different links in the chain generate a certain value and various media actors play a part in production, distribution or other relevant processes (Hartley, 2003). Convergence allows for formerly segregated sectors of production and distribution to (vertically) merge, thus changing the potential for value creation and the distribution of costs and revenue across actors. For instance, newspapers and broadcast news services, once distinct news providers, each can employ online and mobile media to distribute news, while services like video-on-demand, pay television and over-the-top (OTT) content provision allow distributors and other players to venture into audio-visual content distribution, once the exclusive domain of broadcasters. These services create new release windows and opportunities for value creation, undermining traditional business models.

These pressures have been exacerbated by returning and continuing economic downturns, most notably the Eurozone crisis that started in 2008. Although few studies examine the impact of economic downturns on media industries, the effect is considered obvious in academic and public debates. This seems confirmed, at first glance, by media-related events, ranging from layoffs and concentration waves in the European newspaper industry to the shutdown of the Greek public service broadcaster in 2013, all in the name of survival in times of crisis. Yet the precise relationship remains unclear (van der Burg & Van den Bulck, 2015).

As a result, Jenkins, (2004) observes a struggle over the search for a new digital media economy, that is, a need for old and new media players to find "new ways of co-existing in the digital reality, a natural need for new business models and new ways of structuring cooperative relationships, funding models, distribution platforms and marketing strategies" (Filmby Aarhus, 2011, p. 4). The latter may create the impression that all media companies work together, yet such interpretation overlooks the fact that convergence is a constant battle between media actors over (economic) power, competing in some areas while forging collaborations in others, in ever changing stakeholder coalitions (see Van den Bulck & Donders, 2014b).

Policymaking in an Era of Convergence

Since the 1990s, a "discourse of convergence" (Sampson & Lugo, 2003) has permeated media and Information and Communication Technology (ICT) policymaking in Flanders, as elsewhere, with battles being fought around the implications of convergence. This accelerated in the past decade, following waves of technological possibilities and their economic impact. Optimistic technological determinists in the field of media policy promote convergence and its innovative possibilities as they are convinced of economic growth as its ultimate goal. Pessimists, from an equally determinist position, see convergence as a threat to existing relationships and to the carefully established equilibrium in specific media markets, that is, to the so-called media ecosystem (see Van den Bulck & Donders, 2016). The concept of media ecosystem pays tribute to Darwin's idea of ecosystem as "interacting organisms in a constant process of change" (Fransman, 2010, p. 37) and has been used to refer to the relationship between the different players in a certain (inter)national, regional or local media landscape. The term can be considered highly ideological as it claims the authority and normality of natural cycles for man-made industrial-economic activities (see Gitlin, 1982, p. 216). What is more, while the original concept focuses on change as inevitable, there are studies suggesting a different use of the term in media policy debates, focusing on stability and balance (Van den Bulck & Donders, 2016). As such, media ecosystem thinking represents a particular view on the relationships between various (old and new) media players. This chapter analyzes, for the selected Flemish cases, how the media ecosystem argument, together with the convergence argument, are used by players in the media market as a tool to defend their "stake" in the media landscape against unfavorable changes.

Convergence has complicated media policymaking. First, policy makers need to unravel the complexity of technological developments and their legislative implications (Van den Bulck & Donders, 2014a). Second, convergence opens up traditional media markets to new players, including from the once distinct telecommunications sector, and creates new configurations between old and new players. This requires new stakeholders to be identified and understood in their attempts to influence media policy. Third, the growing economic importance of media and ICT industries results in new policy actors with a stake and therefore incentive to interfere in media policy decisions (Hendriks, 1995).

Fourth, media policymaking increasingly is characterized by multilevel governance. For one, European governments have been faced with the growing involvement of the European Union (EU), and the impact of the European Commission (EC) and European Courts in media and ICT policymaking (Sinclair, 2004). Adhering to a neoliberal "markets can cater for diversity" discourse, the EU has been instrumental in pushing convergence. Moreover, the EC has been responsive to complaints of commercial stakeholders against national media policymaking and legislation, especially with regard to public service broadcasting. This has led, among other things, to a growing multistakeholderism (Donders & Raats, 2012). In a multistakeholder policy situation, governments formally or informally consult a wide range of actors with a stake in the outcome of a certain policy issue. This chapter analyzes for the selected Flemish cases how multistakeholderism affects the use of the convergence argument in media policymaking and thus the media policy outcome.

These factors have led some to take a defeatist stance regarding the (im)possibility of regulating convergence: regulation may still be valuable to ensure socially agreed values, but has become obsolete because of its non-enforceability. However, there are indications that governments remain powerful actors in media policymaking, particularly in sectors like broadcasting (Sinclair, 2004). The diversity of media markets in Europe further suggests path dependency: choices made in the past impact the present and future (Brevini, 2013). For one, Lowe et al., (2011) suggest that small EU member states have adopted various models of "controlled liberalization," opening up their media markets but with due protection for domestic players, ostensibly to preserve national identities, culture and language but often for economic protectionist reasons. This chapter analyzes for the selected Flemish cases to what extent media policies demonstrate their own distinct path in Flanders in the selected cases.

In the subsequent sections, the three selected cases are explored with regard to these particular issues. Each case has been dealt with in greater detail elsewhere, either in its own right or as part of a wider project (for the Mediahuis case, see van der Burg & Van den Bulck, 2015; for the signal integrity case, see Van den Bulck & Donders, 2014a; for the management contract case, see Van den Bulck & Donders, 2016) but is analyzed here from the perspective of the convergence argument.

Convergence and Press: The Mediahuis Case

The Case. In late spring 2013, Flemish newspaper owners Corelio and Concentra announced plans to merge their (print and online) newspaper activities in the joint venture Mediahuis (Corelio 62% / Concentra 38% ownership, equal control). The third main Flemish newspaper group De Persgroep was not directly involved in the joint venture. The Corelio/Concentra joint announcement motivated the merger with "[t]he ability to create space for investments in product improvement and further development in digital activities… to remain competitive in a quickly changing media landscape characterized by advanced technologies" (Corelio, 2013a, our translation).

All mergers and acquisitions above a certain threshold based on operating revenue must be approved by BMA (Ysewyn et al., 2013). Moreover, the joint venture is a concentration as defined in competition law, as the notifying parties' business activities (partially) take place in the same market(s). BMA's determines whether the concentration creates a dominant position that threatens competition. It defines relevant product and distribution, audience and advertising markets to identify competition, and examines the merger effects for each relevant market, resulting in a decision—that is, prohibition, approval or conditional approval (Motta, 2005; De Streel, 2008). The latter implies that the notifying parties may propose structural remedies (for example, disposal of certain business activities) or behavioral remedies (that is measures preventing anti-competitive practices) to abate BMA's concerns. Ex post monitoring of media concentration is left to the Flemish Media Regulator (hereafter VRM).

Stakeholders. While the BMA is a crucial actor, the key informants are the so-called "notifying parties" Corelio and Concentra. However, the BMA report shows that an array of stakeholders and interested parties was consulted and thus had a say in the review's outcome. Document analysis (see Table 12.1) shows that almost half of all claims mentioned came from the notifying parties and most other claims from other market players. This is not surprising given the primarily economic focus on merger reviews, yet it is noteworthy that academics and legal authorities were much less quoted, confirming that market players become increasingly important in media policymaking.

Views on Convergence and Ecosystem. The case contained 574 claims which were identified as being focused on economic or socio-political

Table 12.1 Distribution of claims by types of stakeholders

Actors	N	%
Legal authorities (i.e. BMA, VRM, EC)	146	16.9
Notifying parties (i.e. acquiring and target firm(s))	366	42.3
Market players (e.g. competitors)	326	37.6
Scientists	28	3.2
Total (actors)	866	
Total (claims)	574	100.0

Source The author, based on van der Burg and Van den Bulck (2015)

issues. Interestingly, 92.2% of all claims were classified as economic welfare claims, 0.5% as socio-political and 7.3% as mixed. The main topics include the review process and definition of the relevant market, products and services and, to a lesser extent, consumer and citizen interests, merger effects and financial issues, and market developments. Very few claims (1.1%, N = 6) refer directly to convergence or synergy (2.3%, N = 12).

In quantitative terms, convergence, media ecology and synergy are addressed in a limited number of claims (N = 18). However, in a majority of other claims, convergence and a technological determinist stance are implicit assumptions. Of the 18 claims relating to convergence and ecosystem, most focus on economic issues, the others on both economic and socio-political issues. The latter refer, for example, to (qualitative) journalism, opinion formation and consumer choice. Half of the 18 claims are pro-merger, most others are against. The rare instances of a neutral stance are the discussions of the relevant market.

The notifying parties framed the merger in the context of media developments. Taking a technological determinist stance, they claim that digitalization has brought convergence, explained as multimedia brands distributed via different platforms, and that media use has changed owing to the availability of free content and new services provided by international market players. The latter are presented as external actors "undermining" the Flemish media ecosystem. They further maintain that the creation of (editorial and other) synergies generates new opportunities for journalism and for cutting costs. Taking over a media outlet that would otherwise not survive is thus presented as safeguarding consumer choice.

BMA recognizes that general developments in media, advertising or finances may deteriorate content. Its board of commissioners supports the notifying parties' viewpoint with regard to synergies. However, the BMA's auditor and six out of seven interrogated competitors take an opposing stance, arguing that synergy or other standardization strategies as well as the impediment of editorial autonomy lead to less content diversity (which means an indirect price increase) and less consumer choice (that is, a reduction of media outlets). These claims concur with criticism regarding (in)effectiveness of synergies (Jin, 2013).

Outcome. BMA's decision in October 2015 was an approval, on condition that behavioral remedies were applied. These were the notifying parties agreeing to retain all newspaper titles, each with a sufficiently strong editorial staff and led by its own head editor (BMA, 2013, p. 115, see Corelio, 2013b), and assuring for advertisers and readers the distribution of the regional newspaper Gazet van Antwerpen in the province of Antwerp, with sufficient regional reporting and advertising content. This was later confirmed by the announcement of a future plan for Mediahuis (Corelio, 2013c).

It appears that BMA has been responsive to the arguments of the economic impact of digitization and convergence and the necessity of concentration to prevent the demise of the Flemish press or a foreign takeover—in other words, to stop the Flemish ecosystem being fatally affected by convergence and globalization. At the same time the BMA has expressed a real concern over the diversity of content, as the conditions indicate.

CONVERGENCE AND COMMERCIAL MEDIA: THE SIGNAL INTEGRITY CASE

The Case. The "signal integrity case" revolves around relationships between, on the one hand, the Flemish commercial broadcasters Medialaan (then VMMa) and SBS Belgium and the public service broadcaster VRT—together representing an 80% audience share in the television market—and, on the other hand, distributors, especially the cable operator Telenet, a subsidiary of USA-based Liberty Global with an 80% share in Flemish television distribution. Until March 2014, Telenet had a contract with SBS and VRT to distribute their channels (that is signal) but no agreement with VTM, which nevertheless allowed distribution of its channels. Telenet provoked broadcasters by offering free additional consumer services, enabled by digitization and convergence, that allow for time shifting, ad-skipping and program recording, while maintaining an unyielding attitude in negotiations. Unable to resolve the issue, the broadcasters asked the Flemish government to intervene and protect their signal by recognizing them as the signal's owner.

Stakeholders. The key informants in this case are on one side the Flemish broadcasters, with the VRT, Medialaan and the SBS taking the lead. This was interesting as in many other policy cases (for example, the VRT management contract) public and commercial broadcasters hold conflicting positions. Opposing stakeholders were Flemish service providers Telenet and Belgacom, although the latter increasingly distanced itself from Telenet. International players like Google and YouTube had a potential stake in the outcome but acted like interested bystanders as they expected national legislation to pass them by. Interestingly, the signal integrity case proved an instance of government policymaking characterized by high levels of technical complexity, giving power to stakeholders' technical-legal experts who explained things to politicians.

Views on Convergence and Ecosystem. Relevant documents—that is the broadcasters' open letter to Telenet and reports on discussions in the Flemish parliament (Vlaams Parlement, 2013a)—reveal the broadcasters' claim that they are the owners of their signals. This claim contains two arguments: "content integrity" and "economic integrity." Content integrity refers to the broadcasters' demand that distributers do not harm the integrity of their signal's content, for example, with commercial lay-overs or pre-rolls for content (children, news programs), that is legally protected from commercialism. This point was most forcibly made by the public service broadcaster VRT.

Economic integrity refers to (commercial) broadcasters' financial well-being, as their business model was threatened by Telenet's digital services that allow ad-skipping, a system that bypasses the advertisers who finance the content and do not pay for audiences that skip advertisements. Until 2008, Telenet charged costumers a fee for these services and shared the revenues with broadcasters; after 2008, the services became for free. As owners of the signal, broadcasters demanded autonomy over decisions about the economic exploitation beyond free-to-air delivery of content.

The economic point was supported by a cultural argument, as broadcasters claimed that, while the Telenet profits mainly benefited the US holding Liberty Global, the key social-cultural functions performed by Flemish content—crucial in (re)articulating local culture and identity—were undermined. In particular, Flemish fiction production was seen as under threat as the television genre that is most expensive to produce, most subject to ad-skipping, and most difficult to exploit through pay television because of the limited size of the Flemish television market.

The broadcasters' claims were contested by Telenet and Belgacom, who claimed that they respected the content, that additional services were controlled by consumers, and that distributors could not be held accountable for changing viewing behavior. They further claimed that, at the time, ad-skipping in Flanders was still quite rare and that broadcasters' revenues from advertising and distribution had increased. They accused broadcasters of being averse to innovation and took the determinist stance that technological innovation is unstoppable and should be embraced rather than curbed.

Outcome. Urged by the broadcasters, members of parliament of the three government coalition parties (Christian-Democrats, Socialists and Flemish Nationalists) submitted a legislative proposal and, after fierce debate, the media committee of the Flemish parliament voted unanimously in favor. This led to an amendment to the Flemish media decree stipulating that distribution companies must transmit television broadcast signals without interruptions or alterations (art. 180, §1) and that functionalities that contravene this require prior consent from the broadcasters concerned (art. 180, §2). In the absence of prior consent, the Flemish media regulator must initiate a 3-month reconciliation procedure, after which it provides non-binding advice. Services that breach content integrity—that is, go against the editorial independence, autonomy and responsibility of broadcasters—can be refused outright by broadcasters (art. 180, §3). In return, any remuneration that broadcasters receive for allowing functionalities must be invested in Flemish content production (art. 180, §2). While these articles have been legally contested at national and European level, they survived to this day.

Convergence and Public Service Broadcasting

The case. The relationship between the Flemish government and the public service broadcasting institution VRT is organized through management contracts, renewed every 5 years, that stipulate responsibilities, demands and limitations, performance measures and financial means (Van den Bulck, 2008). The 2012–2016 contract was terminated prematurely after the Flemish government introduced financial cutbacks, making it impossible for VRT to fulfill its remit. Therefore, in 2014, negotiations for a management contract 2016–2020 were initiated.

Stakeholders. The key informants/stakeholders in this case are the Flemish government and the public service broadcasting institution, yet VRT's management contract negotiations are increasingly characterized by multistakeholderism. In part, this results from a complaint lodged by commercial players with the EC in 2004 against elements of VRT's public funding. This resulted in a request from the EC to formalize the steps involved in the management contract renewal and to explicitly take relevant stakeholders's views into account (Donders & Raats, 2012). As a result, the Flemish Media Bill stipulates that in the run-up to a management contract: "the Flemish Media Council organizes a public survey about the extent of the public service remit and the operationalization thereof" (art. 20 §1) and "evaluates the media market" (art. 20 §3). A key role is given to the Flemish Media Council, set up in 2007 as policy adviser to the media minister and comprised of independent experts and representatives of all the main stakeholders in the field of media (Vlaamse Gemeenschap, 2008). In the run-up to the new management contract, the Council commissions academic research into citizens' and stakeholders' views on the future role of VRT in Flemish society. These studies are to assist the Council in formulating its advice. The latter is communicated to the Flemish government and parliament, and the media minister must take it into account in contract negotiations with VRT.

Beyond this, the Flemish government increasingly engages more stakeholders in the policy process. Analysis of stakeholders invited to hearings of the media committee of Flemish parliament in preparation of the 2016–2020 contract (Vlaams Parlement, 2015; see also Van den Bulck & Donders, 2016) shows a wide range of actors, including, first, academic experts on public service broadcasting and on media evolutions in the small Flemish media market, as well as academics responsible for conducting the preliminary studies. However, the latter received limited attention compared to the money and effort that went into the studies. The parliamentary media committee invited, second, a number of organizations, such as the Flemish media regulator, the Flemish Media Council, the EBU and the EC's Audiovisual Media Services.

Most time and attention, however, went to companies and organizations believed to have an economic or societal stake in the eventual management contract. Distinction must be made between, third, organizations representative of socially relevant issues or minority groups such as the hearing-impared or ethnic minorities. These obtained much less time and attention than, fourth, companies with a commercial stake in what the public service organization can or cannot do. This group included print media, commercial broadcasters, the independent production sector and local and global distributors. Fifth, some time was reserved for VRT trade union respresentatives. Surprisingly little attention, finally, went to VRT as a public service institution (rather than an employer), as only the chairman of the board of directors and the CEO were allowed to present their views. No time was reserved for the general public.

So, multistakeholderism in this case appears quite one-sided, with commercial competitors dominating both the Flemish Media Council and the hearings in the media committee of the Flemish parliament, at the disadvantage of actors with a social stake and, indeed, of the public service broadcaster. Earlier research (Van den Bulck & Donders, 2014b) suggests commercial competitors also have direct access to the media minister and cabinet, further strengthening their negotiation power.

Views on convergence and ecosystem. While digital and convergence arguments dominated negotiations for previous contracts (Van den Bulck, 2008; Van den Bulck & Donders, 2014b), in this round important foci were the VRT's (diminishing) financial means—including the financial impact of VRT on its competitors—and the redefinition (that is, the limitation) of the VRT's key deliverables, favoring information, education and culture at the expense of entertainment. However, convergence was at the basis of many other topics. For instance, the advice from the Flemish Media Council concluded that the VRT, in the execution of its tasks, should be allowed on all platforms, reflecting the technological determinist stance that these evolutions are unstoppable, which justified the VRT's investment in them. Yet, it stated "that no consensus was reached regarding the exact nature of online content of VRT" (Sectorraad Media, 2015, p. 6), a reference to the printed press's contestation of the success of the VRT online news services. In the parliamentary hearings, commercial broadcasters (Medialaan, SBS) and publishers (Mediahuis, Persgroep) maintained that the online advertising market in Flanders was too small to allow the VRT to enter it in full force (Vlaams Parlement, 2015). This was an indirect reference to the impact of convergence on the traditional financing models of commercial media. The latter are increasingly dependent on online revenues and therefore see a need to "protect" that market from public service competition.

Stakeholders also made reference to the notion of an ecosystem where a public service broadcaster can disturb or sustain an equilibrium between players, for instance in the advice of the Flemish Media Council (Sectorraad Media, 2015):

> Within the Flemish media ecosystem, in which all players take up their position, the public service broadcaster functions as a hub, by engaging in partnerships and creating added value for other players in the value chain and in related sectors. As such, he is a motor for the Flemish audio-visual industry. (p. 6)

The impact of commercial players on the policy process is revealed by the fact that their complaints resonate in the arguments of the key informants (the media minister and the VRT). Their policy papers refer repeatedly to collaborating rather than competing with the commercial sector (Gatz, 2014, 2015), while the arguments of the other stakeholders are far less considered.

Outcome. The economic convergence argument, used by commercial competitors to avoid the VRT gaining a strong position online, partially resonates in the 2016–2020 management contract. It allows the VRT to be present on all platforms but prohibits generating commercial revenue via so-called online "long form" content (that is, entire programmes online) and stipulates that online content, especially information, must be predominantly audiovisual rather than textual/graphic. The "balanced ecosystem" argument, on the contrary, resonates clearly in the management contract, for instance in the following: "The changes in the media sector [that is, convergence] mean that VRT needs to prioritize sustainable development and anchoring of the media ecosystem. Therefore, this management contract focuses more on the collaboration between VRT and private media companies." (Vlaamse Regering, 2015,

p. 10) Most notably, VRT must spend 15% (eventually 25%) of its total income on crossmedia and, most importantly, on commissioning content from external (private) companies, especially fiction, a point strongly lobbied by that sector of the Flemish media industry that has thus managed to turn government policy in their favor.

CONCLUSION

The three cases provide interesting insights in convergence as part of discursive arguments that affect media policymaking. While heralding the potential of the new converging media market, at other times convergence is strategically presented as potentially the "killer bug" in the media ecosystem. First, technological and economic convergence is presented as inevitable—for better or for worse. All policymakers can and should do is to guide or curb it, to protect the local media landscape. The latter is portrayed as a (closed) ecosystem that needs protection from "attacks" by parasites, either from outside (Telenet as part of Liberty Global, the threat of foreign owners in the Flemish press), or from inside (public service broadcasting's success in online news provision).

Second, it becomes clear that, in the past 5 years, this ecosystem argument has come to dominate Flemish media policymaking. While it is not often explicit in the Mediahuis case, the two other cases very much revolved around this idea. The VRT management contract in particular uses the term frequently, defining VRT's responsibilities in relationship to other Flemish media.

Third, the media ecosystem argument, while sometimes clouded in a cultural discourse, is mostly an economic argument. This becomes clear, for instance, from the fact that BMA agrees (conditionally) to the Mediahuis merger, considered necessary to preserve the economic viability of the Flemish media ecosystem, yet it prescribes behavioral conditions that echo real concerns regarding the content diversity of that same system. Similarly, arguments regarding the importance of local productions in preserving culture and identity barely mask economic motivations behind VRT's requirement to invest in Flemish independent production companies. The economics are most explicit in the signal integrity case.

Fourth, convergence and its economic implications shake up traditional stakeholder coalitions: newspapers compete with each other, as the negative evaluation of the Mediahuis merger by its competitors suggests, but unite in criticizing VRT's success in the online (news) market. Commercial broadcasters fight VRT's dominance in the television market but they all join forces to fight distributors. Less than a year after the legal outcome of the signal integrity case, however, Telenet bought a considerable stake in commercial broadcasters SBS. All this suggests that convergence upends traditional coalitions and the shared, deep-rooted beliefs that are at the basis thereof, for instance about the relationship between the state and the media (see Van den Bulck, 2013), replacing it with pragmatic considerations regarding short-term economic gain. Policymakers seem to go along with these shifting coalitions, suggesting that media policies too are based on short-term economic considerations rather than considered and long-term views on the role of the media in society.

Fifth, the dominance of market arguments can be brought back to one-sided interpretations of multistakeholderism. Convergence has been an important impetus for governments to involve more stakeholders in media policymaking, yet each case shows uneven involvement of the theoretical range of interested parties. In each case, (commercial) mainstream media dominate while other relevant actors, including audiences, civil society and cultural institutions, are just nominally involved. Academics, too, remain at the margins of the policymaking process, even in cases where policy-enabling research is a formal part of proceedings, as in the management contract case.

Sixth, the complexity of contemporary media developments have further strengthened the power of market players whose technical and legal experts often have a better understanding than politicians or even academics of the complexity of the evolving media landscape. This becomes clear from the Mediahuis case, where much time went into understanding converging markets of various kinds and where most claims in that regard came from market players, and from the signal integrity case, where stakeholders' technical specialists gained indirect power through their knowledge of the complexities of converging digital broadcasting and distribution markets.

Seventh, despite the globalizing forces and the homogenization of transnational (EU) media policymaking, states maintain considerable power to shape their media systems and policies. The examples furthermore confirm Lowe et al.'s (2011) observation that contemporary media policymaking, at least in smaller European states and regions, is characterized by a controlled liberalization. In each of the analyzed cases, the Flemish policy decision makers have opted for a solution that acknowledges market forces while protecting local media actors.

NOTES

1. The theoretical sections on technological, economic and policy aspects are inspired by earlier work in this regard, most notably Van den Bulck & Donders (2014a).

REFERENCES

BMA (2013). Beslissing van 25 oktober 2013, nr. BMA-2013-C/C-03, inzake de oprichting van het Mediahuis door Corelio NV en Concentra NV. Accessed on 31 March 2014: http://www.mededinging.be/sites/default/files/content/download/files/2013CC03-BMA_pub.pdf.

Brevini, B. (2013). *Public service broadcasting online: A comparative European policy study of PSB 2.0. Basingstoke.* UK: Palgrave Macmillan.

Corelio (2013a). Persbericht van 26 februari 2013: Corelio en Concentra bundelen hun Vlaamse kranten en digitale uitgeefactiviteiten in Het Mediahuis. Accessed on Mar 31, 2014: http://corelio.be/2013/06/corelio-en-concentra-bundelen-hun-vlaamse-kranten-en-digitale-uitgeefactiviteiten-in-het-mediahuis/.

Corelio (2013b). Persbericht van 25 oktober 2013: Belgische Mededingingsautoriteit geeft Corelio en Concentra goedkeuring voor de oprichting van het Mediahuis. Accessed on March 31, 2014: http://corelio.be/2013/10/belgische-mededingingsautoriteit-geeft-corelio-concentra-goedkeuring-oprichting-mediahuis/.

Corelio (2013c). *Persbericht van 6 November 2013: Mediahuis stelt toekomstplan voor.* Accessed on 31 Mar 2014: http://corelio.be/2013/11/mediahuis-stelt-toekomstplan/.

de Sola Pool, I. (1983). *Technologies of freedom. On free speech in an electronic age.* Cambridge, MA: Harvard University Press.

De Streel, A. (2008). The relationship between competition law and sector specific regulation: The case of electronic communications. Reflets et perspectives de la vie économique, 1(Tome XLVII), 55–75.

Donders, K., & Raats, T. (2012). Analysing national practices after European state aid control: Are multi-stakeholder negotiations beneficial for Public Service Broadcasting. *Media, Culture and Society, 34*(2), 162–180. doi:10.1177/0163443711430756.

Fagerjord, A. & Storsul, T. (2007). Questioning convergence. In T. Storsul & D. Stuedahl (Eds.), *Ambivalence towards convergence. Digitalization and media change* (pp. 19–31). Göteborg, Sweden: Nordicom.

Filmby Aarhus, Alexandra Institute, and High Tech Accelerator Innovation Centre of the University of Lodz Foundation (2011). Report on business models, value chains and business development services in the audiovisual/ creative industries: Cases of the Łódź and Małopolska Provinces and West Denmark. First Motion and the European Regional Development Fund. Accessed Sept 2, 2014: http://www.firstmotion.eu/art/MediaCenter/FirstMotion/Results%20and%20Outcomes/BusinessModelsValueChains_DK_Poland.pdf.

Fransman, M. (2010). *The new ICT ecosystem: Implications for policy and regulation.* Cambridge: Cambridge University Press.

Galperin, H. (2004). *New television, old politics: The transition to digital TV in the United States and Britain.* Cambridge, UK: Cambridge University Press.

Gatz, S. (2014). *Beleidsnota Media 2014–2019.* Brussel: Vlaamse Overheid. https://cjsm.be/media/beleidsnotas-en-brieven.

Gatz, S. (2015). *Beleidsbrief Media 2015–2016.* Brussel: Vlaamse Overheid. https://cjsm.be/media/beleidsnotas-en-brieven.

Gitlin, T. (1982). Television's screens: Hegemony in transition. In M. W. Apple (Ed.), *Cultural and economic reproduction in education: Essays on class, ideology and the State* (pp. 202–246). London, UK: Routledge & Kegan Paul.

Hartley, J. (2003). The 'value chain of meaning' and the new economy. *International Journal of Cultural Studies, 7,* 129–141.

Hendriks, P. (1995). Communications policy and industrial dynamics in media markets: Toward a theoretical framework for analysing media industry organization. *Journal of Media Economics, 8,* 61–76.

Hutchinson, D. (1999). *Media policy: An introduction.* London: Blackwell.

Jenkins, H. (2004). The cultural logic of media convergence. *International Journal of Cultural Studies, 7,* 33–43.

Jin, D. Y. (2013). *De-convergence of global media industries.* New York, NY: Routledge.

Koopman, R. (2002). *Codebook for the analysis of political mobilisation and communication in European public spheres.* Accessed on Apr 30, 2014: http://europub.wzb.eu/Data/Codebooks%20questionnaires/D2-1-claims-codebook.pdf.

Lowe, G. F., Berg, C. E., & Nissen, C. S. (2011). Size matters for TV broadcasting policy. In G. F. Lowe & C. S. Nissen (Eds.), *Small among giants: Television broadcasting in smaller countries* (pp. 21–41). Göteborg, Sweden: Nordicom.

McQuail, D. & Siune, K. (Eds.). (1998). *Media policy: Convergence, concentration and commerce* (pp. 23–37). London: Sage Publications.

Motta, M. (2005). *Competition policy: Theory and practice*. Cambridge: Cambridge University Press.

Regering, Vlaamse. (2015). *Beheersovereenkomst 2016–2020 tussen de Vlaamse Gemeenschap en de VRT*. Brussel: Vlaamse Gemeenschap.

Sampson, T., & Lugo, J. (2003). The discourse of convergence: A neo-liberal Trojan horse. In G. F. Lowe & T. Hujanen (Eds.), *Broadcasting and convergence: New articulations of the public service remit* (pp. 83–92). Göteborg, Sweden: Nordicom.

Sectorraad Media (2015). *Advies over de beheersovereenkomst 2016–2020 tussen Vlaamse Gemeenschap en VRT*. https://cjsm.be/media/nieuws/advies-over-de-beheersovereenkomst-met-de-vrt-2016-2020.

Sinclair, J. (2004). Globalization, supranational institutions and media. In J. H. Downing (Ed.), *The Sage handbook of media studies* (pp. 65–82). London, UK: Sage.

Storsul, T., & Stuedahl, D. (Eds.). (2007). *Ambivalence towards convergence: Digitalization and media change*. Göteborg, Sweden: Nordicom.

Van den Bulck, H. (2008). Can PSB stake its claim in a media world of digital convergence? The case of the flemish PSB management contract renewal. *Convergence: The International Journal of Research into New Media Technologies, 14*, 335–350.

Van den Bulck, H. (2012). Tracing media policy decisions: Of stakeholders, networks and advocacy coalitions. In M. E. Price, S. Verhulst, & L. Morgan (Eds.), *Routledge handbook of media law* (pp. 7–34). London: Routledge.

Van den Bulck, H. (2013). 'Tracing media policy decisions: of stakeholders, networks and advocacy coalitions'. In M. Price, S. Verhulst & L. Morgan (Eds.) *Routledge Handbook of media Law*. London: Routledge.

Van den Bulck, H., & Donders, K. (2014a). Pitfalls and obstacles of media policy making in an age of digital convergence: The Flemish signal integrity case. *Journal of Information Policy, 4*, 444–462.

Van den Bulck, H., & Donders, K. (2014b). Of discourses, stakeholders and advocacy coalitions in media policy: Tracing negotiations towards the new management contract of Flemish public broadcaster VRT. *European Journal of Communication, 29*, 83–99. doi:10.1177/0267323113509362.

Van den Bulck, H. & Donders, K. (2016). Naar een nieuwe beheersovereenkomst. Multistakeholderonderhandelingen en politiek. In T. Raats; H. Van den Bulck & L. d'Haenens (Eds.), *Een VRT voor morgen of morgen geen VRT meer?* (pp. 179–200). Kalmthout: Pelckmans.

Van der Burg, M., & Van den Bulck, H. (2015). Economic, political and socio-cultural welfare in media merger control: An analysis of the Belgian and Dutch competition authorities' reviews of media mergers. *Information Economics and Policy, 32*, 2–15.

Vlaams Parlement (2013a). Verslag hoorzitting [hearing], 16/4/13, Stuk 1703 (2011–2012), Nr.4.

Vlaams Parlement (2013b). Voorstel van decreet van de heren Ludwig Caluwé, Bart Van Malderen, Kris Van Dijck en Philippe De Coene houdende wijziging van het decreet van 27 maart 2009 betreffende radio-omroep en televisie, Stuk 1703 (2011–2012), Nr.1 (July 4, 2013).

Vlaams Parlement (2015). Verslag hoorzitting [hearing], 7/5/15 morning, 7/5/15 afternoon, 21/5/15, 1/6/15, 11/6/15, 15/6/15 and 18/6/15— see https://www.vlaamsparlement.be/commissies/393772.

Vlaamse Gemeenschap (2008). Decreet houdende de oprichting van de Raad voor Cultuur, Jeugd, Sport en Media [Belgisch Staatsblad, 1165, N 2008— 110 (C—2008/37385)]. Retrieved at, http://www.cjsm.vlaanderen.be/raadcjsm/wetgeving/index.html#decreet.

Ysewyn, J., Van Schoorisse, M., Mattioli, E., & Van Keymeulen, E. (2013). *De Belgische mededingingswet 2013: een praktische en kritische analyse*. Antwerpen: Intersentia.

AUTHOR BIOGRAPHY

Hilde Van den Bulck is Professor of Communication Studies and head of the research group Media, Policy and Culture at the University of Antwerp (B), Belgium. She combines complementary expertise in media policies and structures—focusing on public service broadcasting and wider on stakeholder relations in media policy making—with expertise in media cultures and identity.

CHAPTER 13

Connected TV: Conceptualizing the Fit Between Convergence and Organizational Strategy Within a Contingency Theory Framework: The Case of Germany

Paul Clemens Murschetz

INTRODUCTION

Media convergence describes the merging of several formerly distinct areas like content formats, distribution channels and end-devices through the integration of functionalities. Moreover, it indicates the restructuring of the value chain, as players from formerly disparate sectors such as TV, internet and equipment vendors converge on the market; as well as the convergence of the industries as such (TV broadcast and internet broadband) (Carey, 2009; Daidj, 2011; Diehl & Karmasin, 2013; Dywer, 2010; Jenkins, 2006; Mello, 2009; Pavlik, 2013; Soun Chung, 2007). Similarly, convergence is seen as being invariably disruptive as it greatly challenges, among other things, traditional TV broadcasting. Driven by new developments in digital technology, transformations provoked by the convergence between television broadcast and internet broadband allow for the boundaries between television broadcasting

P.C. Murschetz (✉)
Alpen-Adria-University of Klagenfurt, Klagenfurt, Austria
e-mail: Paul.Murschetz@aau.at

© The Author(s) 2017
S. Sparviero et al. (eds.), *Media Convergence and Deconvergence*, Global Transformations in Media and Communication Research - A Palgrave and IAMCR Series, DOI 10.1007/978-3-319-51289-1_13

and the internet to disappear. This is mainly due to the likes of Netflix, an American provider of on-demand internet streaming of movies and TV series, Google's video-sharing platform YouTube, the market leader in Germany in free video-clips usage, the free video library services (Mediatheken) of the public-service and commercial broadcasters), and the new players offering paid-for VOD services (namely, Amazon Prime Instant, Apple iTunes, Maxdome, Watchever). Effectively, a variety of new and innovative TV services is being launched whose direction, scope and intensity, however, are being much disputed.

This chapter starts from the key idea of using "contingency theory" (in the following abbreviated as CT), a major theoretical lens in organizational studies (Lawrence, 1993; Lawrence & Lorsch, 1967; Kast & Rosenzweig, 1973; Donaldson, 2001), in an attempt to organize conceptual relationships between convergence and organizational strategy in digital TV broadcasting. It is argued that CT provides a useful heuristic and can fruitfully be applied to various questions surrounding the fundamental transformation of the television broadcasting sector towards what is called "connected TV." This argument is supported by evidencing the emerging "ecosystem" for connected TV services in Germany. By analogy of an ecosystem in biology, an ecosystem in the media applies to a community of economic agents interacting for the balance of all, in a framework favorable to positive or negative externalities. These externalities are considered a notorious type of market failure in broadcasting and occur when, for example, broadcasts are not offered according to the content preferences of consumers but may still be beneficial to society as such (Anderson & Waldvogel, 2015). By and large, the connected TV market in Germany is still immature and each provider is struggling with the challenge of developing an optimal strategic position and organizational form in this new ecosystem (Daidj, 2011).

The purpose of this chapter is to critically analyze the conceptual value of CT in modeling a hoped-for "convergence-strategy fit" of connected TV. This is deemed necessary as the television industry's convergence toward connected TV is a complex process of digital transformation which can only be understood when its dynamics of, and among, technological, industrial and organizational processes of change are taken into consideration. It remains to be analyzed whether developments toward connected TV are driven by the interplay of the industry's creed of "technology push" and/or the viewers/users demand for "application pull." This chapter emphasizes that connected TV is to be associated not only with technology but also with industrial and institutional struc-tures, as well as with social and cultural norms that shape and are shaped by converging media. If we believe in the boundary-spanning nature of convergence and emphasize that organizations interact with their envi-ronments by adopting their strategies (Amit & Zott, 2012), then much more attention to conceptual research and empirical analysis on the spe-cificities of managing the convergence of digital TV broadcast media becomes necessary. However, ambivalence towards convergence does not wane (Størsul & Stuedahl, 2007; Jin, 2012; European Commission, 2013). The problems are manifold, and the most pressing seems to be the nature of convergence itself, which remains multifaceted, difficult to operationalize and dynamic in nature. When looking into the driv-ing forces of convergence, for example, it becomes evident that the con-vergence process is better viewed as co-evolutionary in origin (Hacklin et al., 2009). This means that "its direction and pace is determined by the reciprocal interplay of technological innovations, corporate strate-gies, political-legal reforms and changes in media reception patterns" (Latzer, 2013, p. 7). It seems obvious that there is still a lack of critical analysis in media convergence research that would go beyond euphoric industry rhetoric and challenge notions of convergence as being a meta-process of media innovation whose outcome is at least questionable. For now, much of the rhetoric of media convergence contains no meaning-ful analysis of its potential perils, only the promise of market results that all actors benefit from equally. Recognizing this key paradox of media convergence—that is, showing its perils alongside its potential—will help us to better grasp the concept and the theoretical and empirical consequences.

This is where CT comes in. It has the potential to offer a larger-scale model for analyzing environment–system relations, thus poten-tially opening the convergence paradigm into new research domains. Generally, it assumes that environments create requirements for organi-zations that their managers need to address by adopting appropriate strategies and business models. These strategies in turn create contin-gencies—organizational size, decision on technology, level of diversifica-tion, or others—for which some organizational configurations are better suited than others. When managers of an organization find themselves with organizational practices and capabilities that do not match these contingencies (for example, because these contingencies have changed), their organization's performance suffers, and they endeavor to change

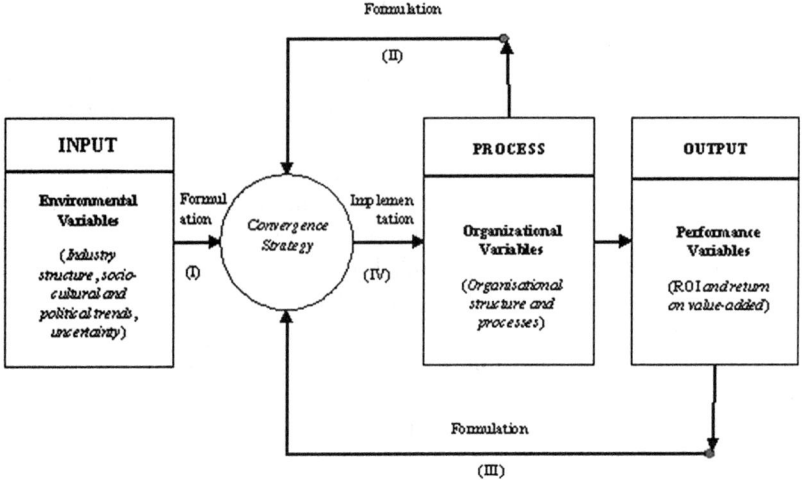

Fig. 13.1 A systems model contingency theory approach to convergence strategy. *Source* The author, based on Ginsberg & Venkatraman 1985

its structure and processes to one with a better fit, in order to improve performance. In other words, a convergence-strategy fit affects a company's performance, and if a change in one of the contingency variables (that is environmental, organizational and performance, see Fig. 13.1) causes a misfit, some adaptive change on the organizational level through adopting an optimal convergence strategy (that is by changing the convergence strategy) becomes necessary.

Hence, the following two research questions are posed:

1. What insight does CT offer in an organization's choosing an effective convergence strategy?
2. What empirical evidence can testify to contingencies in the transformation of digital TV broadcasting toward connected TV in Germany

To answer this, scholarly work was surveyed on the topics of digital transformation of television broadcasting toward connected TV. Further, a case study research design was used in order to look more deeply into the situation in Germany.

Research is based on reviewing the literature that explores convergence and its impacts on the industry's evolution and the strategic positioning of an organization within a new ecosystem. However, my own review of the literature below suggests that academia continues to wrestle with the substantial changes in the economics conducive to digital transformation and its application to television broadcasting economics and convergence management more particularly, albeit some notable attempts to reduce this deficit (Chan-Olmsted, 2006; Doyle, 2010; Hacklin, 2008; Hacklin et al., 2013a, b; Kind et al., 2009; Mierzejewska, 2011; Wirth, 2006). In my view, a clear picture of the relationship between media convergence, industry transformation, and the strategic options of TV companies under the aegis of digital disruption in the way broadcasting markets are currently transformed needs much more scholarly attention.

Germany was chosen as case study country because, in my view, the country reveals a best-practice model for understanding the challenges thrown up by the future of television broadcasting. Connected TV in Germany has now passed the threshold into rapid and sustained growth. In July 2015, 42% of all German TV households had connected TV sets (18 million), 70% of which were connected to the internet, but only 73% of these actually used it (gfu—Gesellschaft für Unterhaltungselektronik, 2015). Besides this, the television market in Germany is highly concentrated and one of the largest in Europe. Today, with almost 40 million TV households, Germany represents one of the biggest and most diversified TV markets in the world. However, there are three big media groups, which control the country's televisual market. The two biggest public service broadcasting (PSB) channels (ZDF—Zweites Deutsches Fernsehen with 13.3%, and ARD—Das Erste with 12.5%) together form the first big group and hold the dominant market position (in terms of national viewing share), followed by the two big commercial groups: the RTL Group SA and ProSiebenSAT.1 Media AG.

Contingency Theory Approaches to Convergence Strategy

In its most rudimentary form, CT refers to a class of organizational theories that contend that there is no one best way of organizing, leading or decision-making, and that, for example, an organizational strategy that is effective in some contextual situations may not be successful in others. In turn, as observed by Harvey (1982), "the contingency approach to strategy suggests that, for a certain set of organizational and environmental conditions, an optimal strategy exists" (p. 81).

Central to contingency theory is the concept of "fit" between structural and contextual characteristics of organizations (Donaldson, 1996a, b). Failure to attain such fit should result in inferior performance.[1] While traditional organization theories had failed to take into account many environmental influences that impacted on the performance of organizations, CT-based approaches posit that organizational viability is dependent (that is, contingent) upon a fit between the organization and its environment.

Over the years, CT research has brought forward a large variety of different variables on which organizational performance (or viability) is supposed to be dependent. Examples of contingency variables in the early CT literature are: organizational climate (Burton & Obel, 1998), size (Child, 1975), environment (Burns & Stalker, 1961; Lawrence & Lorsch, 1967; Duncan, 1972), information processing (Galbraith, 1973), task uncertainty (Burns & Stalker, 1961; Lawrence & Lorsch, 1967), task interdependence (Lawrence & Lorsch, 1967; Thompson, 1967), innovation (Hage & Aiken, 1969), technology (Aldrich, 1979; Burns & Stalker, 1961; Fry & Slocum, 1984; Thompson, 1967), and strategy (Chandler, 1962; Galbraith, 1973; Ginsberg & Venkatraman, 1985; Harrigan, 1983; Miles & Snow, 1978; Rumelt, 1974; Steiner, 1979). Over time, the following dominant schools of thought have developed under the umbrella of CT:

1. The structural contingency theory (SCT) school which first emerged in the 1950s and accepts that economic rationality, structural contingency theory argues that organizations will adopt structures that maximize efficiency and optimize financial performance according to the specific contingencies that exist within the organization's market environment (Donaldson, 1996a, b).
2. The contingency determinism school posits that a change in the contingency variable (for example, size, strategy) produces a change in the structural variable "directly and fairly immediately" (Donaldson, 1987, p. 2).
3. The SARFIT (that is Structural-Adaptation-to-Regain-Fit) model basically follows the contingency determinism model but additionally

claims that an iterative process of adaptation will lead organizations to grow, expand, innovate and diversify (Donaldson, 1987).

4. The strategic choice model rejects contingency determinism and claims that the match between structure and contingency can be restored by adjustment of structure to fit the new contingency (as in the SARFIT model), or by adjustment of the contingency to the structure (Child, 1972; Schreyögg, 1980).

5. The neo-contingency model which adopts criticisms of above more traditional views of CT, taking on board a series of revisions, particularly when it comes to analyzing the self-correcting dynamic processes through which organizations move from states of high performance to states of low performance and back again (Donaldson, 2001).

In order to delineate the domain of CT approaches to "convergence-strategy"-relations, I follow Ginsberg's & Venkatraman's (1985) systems model of contingency-theory-based strategic research and apply it to the issue of an optimal convergence strategy. As shown in Fig. 13.1, these convergence-strategy relations may be viewed with three components: (a) input, (b) process and (c) output. Input refers to environmental dimensions such as components of industry structure, broader environmental variables (socio-cultural and political trends) and environmental uncertainty; process refers to organizational dimensions such as structure and systems; and output refers to various performance criteria such as return on investment and return on value added. Four major links of contingency relationships can be identified in Fig. 13.1: (1) link (I) indicating the influence of external environment on strategy; (2) link (II) illustrating the influence of organizational variables on the formulation of strategy; (3) link (III) highlighting the influence of performance variables on the formulation of strategy; and (4) link (IV) depicting the influence of the chosen strategy on organizational arrangements such as structure, systems and style. Essentially, contingency variables are located in the organization's environment ("environmental variables"), the organization itself ("organizational variables") and the organization's performance ("performance variables").

Theoretically, connected TV delivers a good example for showing that a convergence-strategy fit is best seen in the way open systems theory views a system's elements, namely as units of dynamic exchange between input, process and output variables. CT has identified many different environmental contingencies which are critical to organizational viability. Three concepts are viewed as particularly important:

1. Dynamism, or volatility, is defined as the frequency of environmental change coupled with the unpredictability of market factors (Galbraith, 1973).
2. Complexity refers to the number and diversity of competitors, suppliers, buyers and other environmental actors that firm decision-makers need to consider in formulating their strategies (Duncan, 1972). The larger and more diverse the interaction set, the higher is the complexity (Aldrich, 1979).
3. Munificence refers to the resource-carrying capacity of firms, the extent to which environmental resources are available and accessible to firms (Aldrich, 1979).

Importantly, CT argues that organizational actors are constrained by these environmental contingencies which act as "situational imperatives" as follows (Tsoukas & Knudsen, 2005):

> In any situation actors eventually choose the structure that fits the situation, given the performance requirements for organizational efficiency. It is not that actors do not have subjective states of mind, but that these are explanatorily redundant—eventually the situational imperative tends to prevail, no matter what individuals think or feel. (p. 14)

Environmental variables such as regulation, "technology push" factors (for example, Hybrid broadcast broadband TV (HbbTV) technology, broadband infrastructure) and/or "demand pull" factors ("connection rates," household penetration) are usually exogenous drivers toward connected TV. As such, these are, by definition, outside of control by the focal organization or manager. In effect, they cause management to seize opportunities and reduce threats. Organizational contingencies, on their part, are seen as response variables to change drivers. These contingencies are managerial actions taken in response to current or anticipated environmental change factors. Traditional CT literature typically employs the following organizational contingencies more concretely: management style (organic vs. mechanistic; Burns & Stalker, 1961), organizational restructuring (centralized, functional vs. decentralized, multidivisional; Chandler, 1962), organizational redesign (tall vs. flat design; Woodward, 1965), or task uncertainty (differentiation vs. integration; Lawrence & Lorsch, 1967).

In this context, connected TV best exemplifies the generic uncertainty of organizations in formulating and implementing an effective strategy for managing digital TV broadcasting convergence. This strategy would serve as a linking pin between environmental pressures for change and an effective organizational design to cope with it. In fact, strategic alliances for content partnership and various concentration strategies in the market, notably vertical integration and horizontal growth, seem to be those strategies that reaffirm the CT approach of environmental conditions determining organizational response. On the one hand, some players in connected TV forward-integrate their businesses and thus increase horizontal supplier market power, while others become vertically integrated and differentiate out into key specialists in niche markets. On the other hand, these challenges open ways for new supply chain partnerships (Waterman et al., 2012). On top, innovation and product differentiation strategies are called for today in media convergence thinking (Habann, 2010; Størsul & Krumsvik, 2013). Traditional broadcasters, for example, may still operate as value chain companies, but enduring innovation in digital technology may change their plans for the delivery of information and entertainment content to the end consumer through connected TV. While holding rights and controlling access to a comprehensive range of desirable content, they may have to diversify their business model beyond linear broadcast TV and advance it into the new arena of on-demand TV, providing enhanced interactivity and enriched customer services through electronic program guides, video on demand, games, and information and transaction applications. Usually, performance is measured in terms of productive or allocative efficiency. In addition, innovation (that is the rate of technological advance) and quality are considered as further performance indicators.

All players seem to follow one meta-strategy: to become indispensable gatekeepers to the customer experience, which they do by using whichever competitive strategy leverage they have (Geser, 2012). They build up "portals" in order to gain control over customer relationships, organize the type of payment with the consumer, decide about the specific type of content and service offerings, and/or innovate on possible user interfaces. In their view, gaining market share and reach seems to be much more important than going for turnover or profit. Most generally, competitive rivalry is based on strategic choices (Hacklin et al., 2013a), that is market behaviors of aggressive marketing, product quality and differentiation, price discrimination and quality of service.

Finally, the CT systems model deals with the economic performance of an organization. Performance variables typically refer to the following concepts: economic efficiency (that is, costs necessary to deliver products and services), customer satisfaction, any financial performance measures (market share and gross margin), and, when connected to TV broadcast competition, social benefits and costs associated with broadcast–broadband convergence (Hollifield, 2006; McQuail, 1992; Wirth, 2006). For example, when looking into firm performance as an outcome variable of connected TV, research found that traditional broadcast strategies aim at trying to achieve a fit of the strategies with its internal organizational structure (specifically, divisional vs. functional form; Geiger et al., 2006). Offering both linear programming over traditional TV network channels and nonlinear services over connected TV infrastructure (for example, as with an "over-the-top" (OTT) subscription service whereby the delivery of broadcast content is done over the internet without the involvement of a cable or satellite broadcaster in the control or distribution of the content or, alternatively, as through a TV app) would be complementary strategies; the one would not cannibalize the other.

CONNECTED TV IN GERMANY

The German TV market is becoming increasingly "smart,"—that is, connected to the internet. Germany is the leader in the penetration for end-user technology in the TV home in Europe (Murschetz, 2015; and 2016). By year-end 2015, some 70% of all households owned a connected TV set (18 million). As for access, a broadband connection is a necessary precondition. In Germany, 70.9% of all German TV households now have a broadband connection to the internet, and, if equipped with connected TV hardware or other media streamers, can combine the strengths of broadcast and internet worlds on their large screens in their living rooms. At least 70% of these are connected to broadband networks; cheap media-streaming dongles and boxes also make physical connection an irrelevant issue (Gfk Retail and Technology GmbH, 2015).

However, while connected TV technology adoption has doubled every year, only 73% use connected TV functionality as such (with a "connection rate" of 70% in 2015). It seems that although consumers are inclined to buy and connect, they hardly use the connected TV apps and HbbTV services (that is, interactive TV services accessible via a "red button" service on the remote control) offered (with 92% of connected TVs supporting the HbbTV standard) to their full potential.

The industry structure in connected TV is typically determined by the size and number of buyers and sellers (that is connected TV application, content and service providers on the sell side) in the market. The market structure as such is mainly determined by the extent to which entry barriers are present. While the number of players may be a result of these barriers, product differentiation may ease and vertical integration between programming, aggregation and distribution may obstruct or facilitate entry (Chipty, 2001).

In Germany, there are a large number of players in various segments of connected TV and online video respectively. The big players for connected TV are (still) the incumbent commercial and public service broadcasters (that is, traditional broadcasters). They focus on services delivered through HbbTV technology which include services such as enhanced teletext, catch-up TV broadcasts, video on demand, electronic program guides (EPG), interactive advertising, voting, games, social networking and multimedia applications.[2] Their biggest competitors are Google's video portal YouTube and, increasingly, the VOD platforms of Amazon, Maxdome, Netflix, Apple iTunes, Telekom Videoload, Watchever, Sony Video Unlimited, Snap by Sky, and Microsoft Xbox Video, listed according to market share (PwC, 2015).

In mid July 2015, Germans consumed the following services most frequently:[3]

- Video libraries: TV shows, series, movies, documents and so on (Mediatheken) (for free and/or supported by advertising, usually 7 days' loan period) (58%).
- Videoclips on YouTube or Vimeo (to watch and comment for free) (53%).
- Video-on-Demand of films, TV series and so on (one-off transaction or sell-through[4] or on subscription) (41%).
- Online photo albums (31%).
- Social media networks (to share, participate and so on) (23%).
- Video telephony (to communicate) (19%).
- Online games (18%).

On an infrastructural level, the German market for connected TV sets (big-screen LCD TVs) is dominated by Samsung, accounting for by some 40% of all TV sets installed in the homes. This is about as much as the three runners-up, Philips, Panasonic and LG, combined. If we assume that most customers prefer built-in functionality with greater ease than connecting third-party devices (computers, tablets, set-top boxes) to the connected TV screen, the buying decision already determines much of their later viewing experience. In 2015, 20% of all TV households in Germany were equipped with connected TVs (die medienanstalten, 2015). The remainder of the services market is fragmented too, and disintegrates into various platforms that lack interoperability, but offer identical or highly similar content choices (for example, Amazon Prime Instant Video, Netflix, and Google Chromecast).

Indeed, when looking into the conduct of connected TV market participants, we find a variety of different pricing behaviors and specific product differentiation and advertising strategies applied. As far as pricing is concerned, free trials are combined with flat-rate penetration-pricing models, whereby consumers can chose between free offerings, one-off purchases or monthly subscriptions. Flat rates for film are becoming more and more popular (ranging from 4 to 12 euros per month) and allow for an unlimited access to the library of the provider (mostly by more than just one end-user terminal in the home). One-off services come as streams or downloads, and are priced according to quality (mostly servicing top-ranked movies). Having entered the German market in autumn 2014, Netflix has definitely driven up competition on pricing models among the rivals.

Content attractiveness and quality of service seem to be the important non-price strategy to control the value chain in connected TV. In Germany, the public service broadcasters (ARD/ZDF and regional PSBs), the private commercial free-to-air TV chains (RTL, ProSiebenSat1) and the pay TV (Sky) networks have positioned themselves firmly in the connected TV world in order to leverage their trusted brand names and their portfolio of content rights (that is, premium sports and TV shows). Their prime focus is on extending reach with their properties, whereby classic broadcast TV is enhanced with supplementary services (time shift, non-linear catch-up, trailers, additional background information), subscription video on demand (free and pay, depending on whether it is public or private broadcasting) and games. More sophisticated services such as payment systems, teleshopping, online betting and so on still remain underdeveloped (if they exist at all). By contrast, Amazon Prime Video, a new entrant in connected TV, for example, offers more than 15,000 videos on demand: blockbusters, TV episodes, some prior to free TV broadcast (English originals), and original productions, all to connected TV, tablet, smartphone; games consoles; or desktop computers). At the same time, most other content providers are opportunistic, jumping on any bandwagon (device, platform, app store) in the hope that the future market leader is among them. Sky Deutschland, for example, has secured the German rights to the second season of Netflix's original drama series House of Cards and will show it exclusively on its Sky Go mobile TV and Sky Anytime on-demand services. Sky started broadcasting the complete second season of 13 episodes from 14 February 2014 on Sky Go and a day later on Sky Anytime, parallel to the US launch on Netflix. Sky Go subscribers will be able to view the show on the web, iPad iPhone, iPod touch, and the Xbox 360, while Sky Anytime will make the show available via the Sky + HD DVR on-demand. Additionally, the consumer electronics giant Apple, very much a technology pioneer, leverages its competencies and market experience in order to establish a connected TV innovation platform aimed at complementary products and services.

German consumer electronics manufacturers such as Samsung, LG Electronics, Sony, Sharp, Panasonic and Grundig are the strongest opponents to traditional broadcasting in the connected TV era. Samsung, the market leader in sales of connected TV sets, is increasing its market share by way of an aggressive pricing strategy for TV sets. Becoming a connected TV services operator, Samsung aims at monetizing on its connected TV portal by integrating more interactivity (gaming, social media) into the viewing experience, a strategy called the "TV app store model." Hence, once being a downstream player, Samsung pursues a backward integration strategy by slipping into the role of a "portal," a convergence strategy also known as "platform strategy" (Doyle, 2010). Samsung is considered to be a best-practice example for this type of convergence strategy. It can even be thought of as a "platform leader" which derives advantages from their position within the ecosystem, while at the same time establishing content partnerships with other players. Scholars in internet and media economics call this model the platform model (Rochet & Tirole, 2003; Rysman, 2009). Likewise strategy is applied by internet protocol television (IPTV) and cable TV operators such as Deutsche Telekom, Kabel Deutschland, Unity Media and Vodafone.

Similarly, DVB-T(through Germany's largest distributor of audio-visual media Media Broadcast) and the satellite network operator ASTRA Germany, a subsidiary of SES, a world-leading satellite operator with a fleet of 49 geostationary satellites, also create portal offerings, hoping to exploit the market of web content on the TV set.

Further, for players who have adopted a positioning devoted to seamless access to content across all devices, the television is increasingly focused on becoming the central entertainment-delivery screen in the home, and is therefore the unified point of access for all digital content, regardless of provenance (be it broadcast stream, VoD, catch-up TV, Web and so on; WIPO, 2015). Ecosystem aggregators tend to be large companies that attempt to exploit the market opportunities resulting from a wave of emerging technologies. As explained by Hacklin et al. (2013a), "they leverage their competences and market experience to establish an 'innovation platform' aimed at complementary products and services. In doing so, they enhance the overall value of the core offerings, taking advantage of what is often called a 'network effect'." Google Play is a prime example of this strategy of being a typical "ecosystem aggregator" (Adner & Kapoor, 2010). There are thousands of movies and television shows available on Google Play Movies & TV, some in HD, including comedy, drama, animation, action and documentary. Movies can be rented or purchased and watched on the Google Play website or via an application on an Android device. Some titles are available only for rental, some only for purchase, and others for both rental and purchase. TV shows can be purchased by episode or season but cannot be rented. Alternatively, users can download movies and TV shows for offline viewing and view them later using the Google Play Movie app.

Conclusion

This chapter has explored the applicability of the contingency theory (CT) of organizations in ways that explain the current processes of the television broadcasting industry's convergence towards connected TV. Two research questions were raised: (1) What insight does CT offer to an organization's choosing an effective convergence strategy? (2) What empirical evidence can testify to contingencies in the transformation of digital TV broadcasting toward connected TV in Germany? Given the findings of this research, I can reasonably conclude the following:

First, notwithstanding the fact that since the mid 1980s contingency theory (CT) has been fairly dead within organizational theory, foremost because of what can be perceived as its lacking explanatory power, it is argued here that CT does help understanding and conceptualizing phenomena in TV broadcasting convergence toward connected TV. This is because CT looks at convergence more holistically and takes into consideration the dynamisms of, and among, the various and multidimensional drivers of convergence, that is the technological, industrial, organizational, political, and, last but not least, the socio-cultural factors. Essentially, I argued that research into the contingencies of convergence between television broadcast and internet broadband media can create valuable insights by seeking cross-fertilization with other aspects of change and innovation towards convergence. Certainly, CT does inspire thinking about the needs for redesigning broadcasting organizations as analyzed within frames of organizational studies and strategic management research when it comes to these legacy media having to transform their organizational structures and business processes into the era of media convergence. I believe that CT can deliver worthy contributions in this respect and, when applied to television broadcasting, helps to stress the need of an integrated socio-economic analysis of the TV industry's transformation.

Hence, this chapter has looked into ways to "reanimate" CT and tried to show that specific drivers for convergence in the television industry are contingent upon a variety of situational factors that shape and constrain organizational strategies towards connected TV convergence. While contingency theory seems to have lost some of its original luster over the years, the theory's early key idea of determinism in the causes-effects-relations and its basic evolutionary spirit in letting the "environment do the selecting, not the managers" (Whittington, 2001, p. 41) will not make it easier for an organization and its managers to find an optimal convergence-strategy fit.

By applying a systems model contingency theory approach to finding an optimal convergence strategy, I found that—on an organizational level—the broadcasting convergence towards connected TV is best observed through examining the co-evolution of the various factors as they are interrelated, the various patterns in innovation dynamics in a converging environment and the managerial responses that may be identified as being effective convergence strategies. What remains to be done is to analyze selected contingency variables in an effort to make causal inferences between contingency variables and convergence variables, and convergence performance and organizational performance, respectively. This could help to reduce some of the doubts as to CT's validity in applying it to issues of convergence in TV broadcasting. Technological determinism, one-directionality, linearity and monotonicity of causes–effects relations certainly needed to be looked at critically. Certainly, more research is needed in order to improve the validity of analysis by generating testable propositions for this study. This would imply establishing a full-fledged conceptual model which postulates effects between the different variables alongside the three larger CT variables and the observed strategies formulated by the players to achieve convergence-strategy fit (Schoonhoven, 1981; Van de Ven & Drazin, 1985).

And finally, of course, this study suffers from a range of other limitations. While the empirical case for convergence in TV broadcasting is rough and ready, the persuasive parts are pragmatic and qualitative rather than rigorous and quantitative. Simply, evidencing contingencies of the emerging connected TV ecosystem in Germany seemed to be confined to guesswork rather than rigorous academic inquiry. Although the strategic choices for a convergence strategy fit identified revealed some metaphoric quality, they nonetheless remained qualitative in nature and, hence, laden with a great deal of uncertainty as to the general outcome of convergence as such.

To conclude, I still see CT as a way for organizations to adapt to uncertainty by developing strategies with alternative scenarios. CT holds both the quest for an evolutionary understanding of convergence and offers a valid framework for deliberate managerial action. This gives insight into managing convergence for improved managerial performance. In contrast to the "rationalist school of strategy," which claims that strategy is the result of rational calculation and planning, CT approaches to organizational strategy belong to the "adaptive school of strategy" and address problems of how change unfolds and why. While rationalist approaches focus on the content of strategy, on the strategic plan, and seek to find a strategic position that will lead to optimal performance under specific environmental conditions through maximizing returns from resources and establishing competitive advantage, adaptive approaches see strategy as an ongoing process (Hoque, 2004). "Because environments are shifting constantly, strategic activity is a permanent process of reconciling and integrating an organization's external and internal worlds, by altering structure, people, and processes" (Küng, 2011, p. 49). In effect, managing convergence and formulating and implementing the "right" strategy (on various levels of competition, technological innovation, activities in mergers and acquisitions and so on) in a given situation needs alignment or fit according to various environmental and situational impacts, and as none of these situations is like the other, these alignments need to be flexible (Van de Ven & Drazin, 1985). In addition to other studies undertaken by this author on the broad issue of convergence and industry change (Murschetz, 2016, 2015), I am convinced that the CT model remains a strong heuristic tool in explaining a broadcaster's opportunities of developing an effective convergence strategy and this is mainly based on its key strength: to explain the dependence of an organization within its market context. As it stands, however, broadcasters will be faced with strategic uncertainty about the future.

Notes

1. Unfortunately, CT has used the term "fit" rather loosely. Although it is common for [contingency] theorists to postulate relationships using phrases and words such as matched with, contingent upon, consistent with, fit, congruence, and co-alignment, precise guidelines for translating these verbal statements to the analytical level are seldom provided (Venkatraman, 1989, p. 423).
2. Prominent examples are: ARD Mediathek, ZDF Mediathek, Arte + 7, 7TV of ProSieben, SAT1 Mediathek, and RTL Now.
3. Following a GFU online survey in May 2015 with 1000 respondents (gfu, 2015).
4. "Transactional video-on-demand" (T-VOD) is also referred to as Pay-per-View; the consumer pays on demand, but the title is not downloaded as with electronic sell-through (EST).

References

Adner, R., & Kapoor, R. (2010). Value creation in innovation ecosystems: How the structure of technological interdependence affects firm performance in new technology generations. *Strategic Management Journal, 31*(3), 306–333.
Aldrich, H. W. (1979). *Organizations and environments.* Englewood Cliffs, NJ: Prentice-Hall.

Amit, R., & Zott, C. (2012). Creating value through business model innovation. *Sloan Management Review, 53*(3), 41–49. http://sloanreview.mit.edu/article/creating-value-through-business-model-innovation/.

Anderson, S. P., & Waldvogel, J. (2015). Preference externalities in media markets (September 2015). *CEPR Discussion Paper* No. DP10835. http://ssrn.com/abstract=2663433.

Barwise, P., & Picard, R. G. (2015). The economics of television: Excludability, rivalry, and imperfect competition. In R. G. Picard & S. S. Wildman (Eds.), *Handbook on the economics of the media* (pp. 165–188). Cheltenham, UK and Northampton, MA: Edward Elgar Publishing.

Burns, T., & Stalker, G. M. (1961). *The management of innovation*. London: Tavistock.

Burton, R. M., & Obel, B. (1998). *Strategic organizational diagnosis and design: Developing theory for application*. Dordrecht: Kluwer Academic Publishers.

Carey, J. (2009). Convergence. In C. H. Sterling (Ed.), *Encyclopaedia of journalism* (Vol. 1, pp. 361–364). Thousand Oaks, CA: Sage.

Chandler, A. D., Jr. (1962). *Strategy and structure: Chapters in the history of the industrial enterprise*. Cambridge, MA: MIT Press.

Chan-Olmsted, S. M. (2003). Fundamental issues and trends in media strategy research. *Journal of Media Economics & Culture, 2*, 9–35.

Chan-Olmsted, S. M. (2006). Issues in strategic management. In A. B. Albarran, S. M. Chan-Olmsted, & M. O. Wirth (Eds.), *Handbook of media management and economics* (pp. 161–181). Mahwah, NJ: Lawrence Erlbaum Associates.

Child, J. (1972). Organizational structure, environment and performance: The role of strategic choice. *Sociology, 6*, 1–22.

Child, J. (1975). Managerial and organizational factors associated with company performance. Part 2. *Journal of Management Studies, 12*, 12–27.

Chipty, T. (2001). Vertical integration, market foreclosure, and consumer welfare in the cable television industry. *American Economic Review, 91*(3), 428–453.

Chon, B. S., Choi, J. H., Barnett, G. A., Danowski, J. A., & Joo, S. H. (2003). A structural analysis of media convergence: Cross-industry mergers and acquisitions in the information industries. *Journal of Media Economics, 16*(3), 141–157.

Crawford, G. S. (2015). The Economics of television and online video markets. Working Paper No. 197, Department of Economics, University of Zurich.

Daidj, N. (2011). Media convergence and business ecosystems. *Global Media Journal, 11*(19), 1–13.

die medienanstalten (2015). Digitalisierungsbericht 2015. Digitale Weiten, analoge Inseln—Die Vermessung der Medienwelt, Leipzig: VISTAS Verlag.

Diehl, S., & Karmasin, M. (2013). *Media and convergence management*. Wiesbaden: Springer.

Donaldson, L. (1987). Strategy and structural adjustment to regain fit and performance: In defence of contingency theory. *Journal of Management Studies,* *24*(1), 1–24.
Donaldson, L. (Ed.). (1995). *Contingency Theory.* Volume 9 in History of Management Thought Series, Dartmouth Publishing Company.
Donaldson, L. (1996a). The Normal Science of Structural Contingency Theory. In S. R. Clegg, C. Hardy, & W. R. Nord (Eds.), *Handbook of organizational studies* (pp. 57–76). London: Sage.
Donaldson, L. (1996b). *For positivist organization theory: Proving the hard core.* London: Sage.
Donaldson, L. (2001). *The contingency theory of organization design: challenges and opportunities.* Thousand Oaks, CA: Sage.
Donaldson, L. (2006). The contingency theory of organizational design: challenges and opportunities. In R. M. Burton, B. Eriksen, D. D. Hakonsson, & C. C. Snow (Eds.), *Organization design: the evolving state-of-the-art* (pp. 19–40). Heidelberg: Springer.
Doyle, G. (2010). From television to multi-platform. Less from more or more for less?. *The International Journal of Research into New Media Technologies,* 16(4), 431–49.
Duncan, R. B. (1972). Characteristics of organizational environments and perceived environmental uncertainty. *Administrative Science Quarterly, 9,* 313–327.
Dywer, T. (2010). *Media convergence.* New York: Open University Press.
Fry, L., & Slocum, J. (1984). Technology, structure and workgroup effectiveness: A test of a contingency model. *Academy of Management Journal, 27,* 221–246.
Galbraith, J. R. (1973). *Designing complex organization.* Reading, MA: Addison-Wesley.
Geiger, S. W., Ritchie, W. J., & Marlin, D. (2006). Strategy/structure fit and firm performance. *Organization Development Journal, 24*(2), 10–22.
Geser, M.-E. (2012). Strategieperspektiven für TV 2.0. Digitale Netzwerkmedien und ihre Auswirkungen auf Fernsehunternehmen. Wiesbaden: Springer VS.
Gfu Insights & Trends (2015). Begeistert oder abwartend? Was sich Konsumenten wünschen und wo sie skeptisch sind. Ergebnisse einer europaweiten gfu-Studie (by H.-J. Kamp). http://www.gf.de.
GfK Retail and Technology GmbH. (2015). Wachstumsmarkt Smart TV und HbbTV in Deutschland, 04/2015. http://www.tv-plattform.de/de/hbbtv-markt-2014.html.
Ginsberg, A., & Venkatraman, N. (1985). Contingency perspectives of organizational strategy: A critical review of the empirical research. *Academy of Management Review, 10*(3), 421–434.

Habann, F. (2010). *Erfolgsfaktoren von Medieninnovationen.* Baden-Baden: Nomos.

Hacklin, F. (2008). *Management of convergence in innovation.* Heidelberg: Physica-Verlag.

Hacklin, F., Battistini, B., & von Krogh, G. (2013a). Strategic choices in converging industries. *MIT Sloan Management Review, 3*(3), 283–298.

Hacklin, F., Klang, D., & Baschera, P. (2013b). Managing the convergence of industries: Archetypes for successful business models. In S. Diehl & M. Karmasin (Eds.), *Media and convergence management* (pp. 25–36). Berlin Heidelberg: Springer-Verlag.

Hacklin, F., Marxt, C., & Fahrni, F. (2009). Coevolutionary cycles of convergence: An extrapolation from the ICT industry. *Technological Forecasting and Social Change, 76*(6), 723–736.

Hage, J., & Aiken, M. (1969). Routine technology, social structure, and organizational goals. *Administrative Science Quarterly, 14*(3), 366–376.

Harrigan, K. R. (1983). Research methodologies for contingency approaches to business strategies. *Academy of Management Review, 8,* 398–405.

Harvey, D. F. (1982). *Strategic management.* Columbus, OH: Merrill.

Hollifield, C. A. (2006). News media performance in hypercompetitive markets: An extended model of effects. *International Journal on Media Management, 8,* 60–69.

Hoque, Z. (2004). A contingency model of the association between strategy, environmental uncertainty and performance measurement: Impact on organizational performance. *International Business Review, 13,* 485–502.

Jenkins, H. (2006). *Convergence culture: Where old and new media collide.* New York: New York University Press.

Jin, D. Y. (2012). The New-wave of De-convergence: A new business model of the communication industry in the 21 Century. *Media, Culture and Society, 34*(6), 761–772.

Jung, J., & Chan-Olmsted, S. M. (2005). Impacts of media conglomerate's dual diversification on financial performance. *Journal of Media Economics, 18*(3), 183–202.

Kast, F., & Rosenzweig, J. (1973). *Contingency views of organization and management.* Chicago: Science Research Associates.

Kind, H. J., Nilssen, T., & Sørgard, L. (2009). Business models for media firms: does competition matter for how they raise revenue? *Marketing Science, INFORMS, 28*(6), 1112–1128.

Küng, L. (2011). Managing strategy and maximizing innovation in media organizations. In M. Deuze (Ed.), *Managing media work* (pp. 43–56). Los Angeles: Sage.

Küng, L. (2013). Innovations, technology, and Organizational Change. Legacy Media's Big Challenges. An Introduction. In T. Størsul, & A. H. Krumsvik (Eds.),

Media Innovations. A multidisciplinary study of change (pp. 9–13). Göteborg: Nordicom.

Latzer, M. (2013). Towards an innovation-co-evolution-complexity perspective on communications policy. In M. Löblich & S. Pfaff-Rüdiger (Eds.), *Communication and media policy in the era of digitization and the Internet: Theories and processes* (pp. 15–27). Baden-Baden: Nomos.

Lawrence, P. R. (1993). The contingency approach to organization design. In T. Golembiewski (Ed.), *Handbook of Organizational Behaviour* (pp. 9–18). New York: Marcel Dekker.

Lawrence, P. R., & Lorsch, J. W. (1967). *Organization and environment.* Cambridge, MA: Harvard University Press.

McQuail, D. (1992). *Media performance. London: Mass communication and the public interest.* London: Sage.

Mello, B. (2009). Media Convergence. In W. F. Eadie (Ed.), *21st Century Communication. A Reference Handbook*, Vol. 1 & 2. (pp. 877–85). Los Angeles et al.: Sage.

Mierzejewska, B. I. (2011). Media management in theory and practice. In M. Deuze (Ed.), *Managing media work* (pp. 13–31). London: Sage.

Miles, R. E., & Snow, C. C. (1978). *Organizational strategy, structure, and process.* New York: McGraw-Hill.

Miller, D. (1986). Configurations of strategy and structure: Towards a synthesis. *Strategic Management Journal, 7,* 233–249.

Murschetz, P. (2015). The Changing Face of the German Broadcast Television Industry. *The Case of Smart TV. Medien Journal 3/2015, 39,* 44–58.

Murschetz, P. C. (2016). Connected television: Media convergence, industry structure and corporate strategies. In E. L. Cohen (Ed.), *Annals of the International Communication Association, 40*(1), 69–93. New York: Routledge. http://dx.doi.org/10.1080/23808985.2015.11735256.

Pavlik, J. V. (2013). Trends in new media research: A critical review of recent scholarship. *Sociology Compass, 7*(1), 1–12.

PwC—PricewaterhouseCoopers (2015). Video on Demand. Der digitale Wandel revolutioniert die Home-Entertainment Branche. www.pwc.de/media-trend-outlook.

Rochet, J.-C., & Tirole, J. (2003). Platform competition in two-sided markets. *Journal of the European Economic Association, 1*(4), 990–1029.

Rumelt, R. P. (1974). *Strategy.* Structure and Economic Performance, Boston, MA: Harvard Business School.

Rysman, M. (2009). The economics of two-sided markets. *The Journal of Economic Perspectives, 23*(3), 125–143.

Schoonhoven, C. B. (1981). Problems with contingency theory: Testing assumptions hidden within the language of contingency 'theory'. *Administrative Science Quarterly, 26,* 349–377.

Schreyögg, G. (1980). Contingency and choice in organization theory. *Organization Studies, 1*(4), 305–326.

Soun Chung, D. (2007). Profits and Perils. *Convergence: The International Journal of Research into New Media Technologies, 13*(1), 43–61.

Steiner, G. A. (1979). Contingency theories of strategy and strategic management. In D. Schendel & C. W. Hofer (Eds.), *Strategic management: A new view of business policy and planning* (pp. 405–416). Boston: Little, Brown.

Størsul, T., & Stuedahl, D. (2007). *Ambivalence Towards Convergence: Digitalization and Media Change.* Stockholm: Nordicom.

Størsul, T., & Krumsvik, A. H. (2013). *Media Innovations: A Multidisciplinary Study of Change.* Göteborg: Nordicom.

Tsoukas, H., & Knudsen, C. (2005). *The Oxford handbook of organization theory.* Oxford: Oxford University Press.

Van de Ven, A. H., & Drazin, R. (1985). The concept of fit in contingency theory. In L. L. Cummings & B. M. Staw (Eds.), *Research in organization theory* (pp. 333–365). Greenwich, CT: JAI.

Venkatraman, N. (1989). The concept of fit in strategy research: towards verbal and statistical correspondence. *Academy of Management Review, 14*(3), 423–444.

Waterman, D., Sherman, R., & Ji, S. W. (2012). The Economics of Online Television: Revenue Models, Aggregation, and 'TV Everywhere', http://ssrn.com/abstract=2032828. Accessed 1 April 2012.

Whittington, R. (2001). *What is Strategy—and does it matter?* (2nd ed.). London: Thompson Learning.

WIPO—Word Intellectual Property Organization (2015). Current Market and Technology Trends in the Broadcasting Sector, Standing Committee on Copyright and Related Rights, Thirtieth Session, Geneva, June 29 to July 3, 2015. http://www.wipo.int/meetings/en/doc_details.jsp?doc_id=307382.

Wirth, M. O. (2006). Issues in Media Convergence. In A. B. Albarran, S. M. Chan-Olmsted, & M. O. Wirth (Eds.), *Handbook of media economics and management* (pp. 445–463). Mahwah: Lawrence Erlbaum Associates.

Woodward, J. (1965). *Industrial Organization: Theory and Practice.* London: Oxford University Press.

Author Biography

Paul Clemens Murschetz is Lecturer on Media Management at the Alpen-Adria-University of Klagenfurt, Austria. His research focuses on strategic media and communication studies, media economics, media convergence and media innovation studies. He has published in journals such as: the *International Journal on Media Management*, the *European Journal of Communication* and ICA's *Communication Yearbook*, and is a frequent conference speaker on issues of media management and economics.

CHAPTER 14

Regulatory (de) Convergence: Localism, Federalism, and Nationalism in American Telecommunications Policy

Christopher Ali

On 26 February 2015 the American Federal Communications Commissions (FCC) voted to reclassify broadband internet provision under Title II of the 1996 Telecommunications Act. After a decade-long dispute that positioned the likes of Comcast and AT&T against those of Google and Netflix, this was the day that net neutrality became law in the US. While momentous indeed, it nonetheless overshadowed another decision made that same morning which may prove to have almost as much impact on American telecommunications: municipal broadband in North Carolina and Tennessee (FCC, 2015).

Municipal broadband sprang up over the displeasure of various municipalities with incumbent internet service providers (ISPs) and a strong belief that they could do better. By the early 2000s, several municipalities had begun offering broadband service to residential and business customers at a fraction of the price charged by cable or telecommunications companies (Santorelli, 2007). These services were generally

C. Ali (✉)
University of Virginia, Charlottesville, USA
e-mail: cali@virginia.edu

© The Author(s) 2017   285
S. Sparviero et al. (eds.), *Media Convergence and Deconvergence*, Global
Transformations in Media and Communication Research - A Palgrave and
IAMCR Series, DOI 10.1007/978-3-319-51289-1_14

superior to the incumbents', with download speeds upwards of 100 times faster (White House, 2015). This had major service providers (for example, Comcast, Time Warner Cable, AT&T, Verizon) nervous about the security of their oligopoly and they petitioned state governments to prohibit or inhibit these municipal activities through restrictive legislation (see O'Boyle and Mitchell, 2013). By 2015, 20 states had passed such provisions, based largely on the argument that municipal involvement in broadband distorted the free market and impeded competition (Brodkin, 2014). The range of these legislative acts went from prohibitive startup requirements (North Carolina) to outright prohibition (Pennsylvania).

In 2014, two municipalities (the Electric Power Board of Chattanooga, TN and Wilson, NC) petitioned the FCC to preempt their respective states' legislation on the grounds that it violated Section 706 of the Telecommunications Act of 1996, which compelled the FCC to promote advanced telecommunications services throughout the country (FCC 2015). The FCC agreed, and its decision may have set a precedent for the deployment of future municipal broadband projects across the country.

The municipal broadband case is significant for a number of reasons, not the least of which being that it allows these communities to offer competitive broadband services. It is also notable for marking the most recent event in a trend that has seen American states reinsert themselves into the communications policymaking process. This has sparked a battle between local municipalities, states, and the FCC in communication and constitutional law (Dunne, 2007). For decades, states have been relatively dormant with respect to communications policy, having largely outgrown their role as arbiters of local telephone rates and telecommunication interconnection (see Teske, 1995; Sterling, Bernt & Weiss, 2006). Their re-emergence on the national policy stage is therefore a significant development in American communication policy. To fully understand this re-emergence, however, it is wise to go back to the policy issue that brought states out of their near-quarter-century slumber: statewide franchising of cable television.

Traditionally, cable companies wishing to provide television service in a given state had to seek permission from each individual municipality. Statewide franchising, on the other hand, allows cable video providers (for example, Comcast) and telecommunications companies providing video (for example, AT&T) to bypass local municipalities and request franchises directly from the state. As of 2014 legislation has been passed in 26 states (National Conference of State Legislatures [NCSL], 2014). Like the legislation prohibiting municipal broadband, these actions reshaped regulatory jurisdiction in American telecommunications by giving states greater control over communication within their political borders.

Informed by the analytical framework of the critical political economy of communication (Mosco, 2009), I use this chapter to discuss how the case of statewide franchising reintroduces us to two actors in the communications policymaking process that have long been silent: local municipalities and state legislatures. The re-emergence of these actors exemplifies both convergence and deconvergence in American communications policy. Regulatory convergence—the shift from regulating communication technologies separately (for example, telephony, broadcasting, cable, internet) to regulating the industry holistically (Vick, Barr & Sandvig, 2008)—occurred through the deregulatory impetus of the 1996 Telecommunications Act that allowed multi-modal competition in cable, telephony and internet. Deconvergence occurs with a recognition of stakeholders and policy actors above and beyond those traditionally consulted (the FCC, major telecommunication companies, broadcasters, public interest groups, etc.). This is exemplified through the re-emergence of local and state authorities.

Separately, neither regulatory convergence nor stakeholder deconvergence are problematic. Indeed, more countries would do well to synchronize the regulation of communication technologies (broadcasting, cable, internet, telephony), and to broaden the roster of recognized policy stakeholders (Barr & Sandvig, 2008; Lunt & Livingstone, 2011). Taken in concert, however, regulatory deconvergence and convergence as manifest in the 1996 Telecommunications Act and exemplified in the case of statewide franchising, has led to a situation of what critical political economists of communication call "regulatory capture" and "policy failure" (Pickard 2015; Horwitz 1989). Regulatory capture occurs when the regulator favors the interests of the regulated over that of the public (Horwitz 1989). In our case, state legislation tends to mirror the interests of major telecommunication firms and the FCC has largely agreed. The idea of "policy failure" describes those instances in which policymakers have failed to protect the public interest (Pickard, 2015). This permits the further entrenchment of market fundamentalism and the propensity towards "discursive capture" in which policy options are "constrained by market-dictated imperatives" (p. 91). In the instance of statewide franchising, with the numerous legislative and regulatory bodies fighting for jurisdiction over this converged industry (cable television/broadband), we are left with a power vacuum that is filled by corporate interests. The public interest, most notably that of broadband rollout, pricing, and community television are often left unprotected. Given that this industry earned $116 billion in 2015 (Ibis, 2016) and that the market is effectively controlled by four companies (AT&T/DirectTV, Comcast, Dish Network and Time Warner Cable) —not knowing which level of government has ultimate jurisdiction has allowed companies to take control of the policy agenda and shape communications policy to their interests.[1]

This chapter begins with a brief history of the role of states in American communications policy, followed by a history of cable television regulation and the 1996 Telecommunications Act. I move forward with an explication of statewide franchising, its connection to municipal broadband, and a discussion of the failure of policymakers to adequately intervene in this matter.

THE STATE OF THE STATES IN TELECOMMUNICATIONS REGULATIONS

States have been intermittent actors in the development of American communication regulation. The apex of their power was at the turn of the century, when federal jurisdiction over the new medium of telephony was questionable. The 1887 Interstate Commerce Act gave the federal government authority over interstate commerce (for example, railroads), but intrastate commerce was left to the individual states (Teske 1995).[2] As the AT&T/Bell monopoly developed, this authority would be essential in keeping rates affordable and competitive for competitors and consumers alike (see Teske, 1995; Sterling et al. 2006). The division between state and federal oversight was cemented in the 1934 Communications Act which gave power over interstate communication to the FCC, while authority over intrastate communication remained with the states.

Once it was understood that intrastate telephony could not be divorced from interstate telephony, the role of the states declined and that of the FCC strengthened (Teske, 1995). This was particularly true during the monopoly era of AT&T from the 1930s to the 1960s. States emerged again as powerful players in communications regulation after the breakup of AT&T in 1984, when AT&T's regional telephone subsidiaries were forcibly spun off. States, through their public utility commissions (PUCs), were once again necessary to regulate the rates and interconnection of local telephone providers no longer under the aegis of the AT&T (Teske & Bhattacharya, 1995). Their power declined again after the passage of the 1996 Telecommunications Act, which deregulated telecommunication ownership and allowed for the recombination of AT&T's regional telephone companies (Sterling et al. 2006).

A Brief History of Cable Regulation

If states had a recurring role in the history of telephone regulation, they were largely absent in the history of cable television. In the 1950s and 1960s, the FCC was at a loss for how to regulate cable and even as to whether it had jurisdiction over the emergent medium. This question of authority was ultimately resolved in 1968 when the Supreme Court ruled that the FCC had "'ancillary jurisdiction' to regulate cable carriers under Sect. 2(a) of the Communications Act of 1934" (Rushnak, 2006, p. 48). Thereafter, the FCC began laying regulatory groundwork for cable. Emerging was a system of what the Supreme Court called "deliberately structured dualism" wherein franchising, construction and rights-of-way management fell under the purview of states or local municipalities through their local franchising authorities (LFAs), while issues of ownership and structure fell to the FCC [Rushnak, 2006, p. 48, quoting 440 U.S. 689, 708 (1979)].

This series of ad hoc regulations was finally codified by congress in the Cable Communications Policy Act of 1984—the first legislative foray into cable television in its then almost 40-year history. The 1984 Cable Act did six important things for cable regulation:

1. It modified the 1934 Communications Act to give the FCC explicit jurisdiction over the national regulation of cable television.
2. It codified into law the relationship between cable companies and local municipalities (through the local franchising authority) such that cable companies had to ask permission from LFAs to use the public rights of way. In turn, LFAs were forbidden to offer exclusive contracts.

3. It awarded the local municipalities the right to ask for compensation in the form of a "franchise fee" set at a maximum of 5% of the gross profits of the cable company for that municipality.
4. It codified into the law the existence and structure of public, educational and government access channels (PEG). PEG channels are community cable television channels, providing members of the public access to the tools and means of distribution of mainstream media (see Ali, 2017). Here, LFAs could request cable providers provide channel capacity for public access channels during franchise negotiations. They could also request capital expenditures in the form of building and equipment expenses. These expenditures were exempt from the franchise fee and therefore over and above it.
5. LFAs could require cable companies to install institutional networks (I-Nets)—separate networks often for public buildings.
6. It forbad telecommunications companies to enter the video programming distribution market beyond certain exceptional circumstances.

In sum, the Cable Act codified the dualistic structure of cable regulation, splitting jurisdiction between the FCC and LFAs. To be sure, states could always supersede the LFA and could in turn act as LFAs, since the definition of a franchising authority was not specifically "local" but rather "any governmental entity empowered by Federal, State or local law to grant a franchise." Before 1996, however, no state had actively pursued this course of action (US, 1984, §602 (9); Rushnak, 2006).[3]

The 1996 Telecommunications Act

The 1996 Telecommunications Act was the first major overhaul of telecommunications legislation in the US since the 1934 Communications Act. It was thus the first major act to deal with the emergence of digital technologies, most notably satellite and the internet (or "advanced telecommunications"). The Act is characterized by the relaxation of prohibitions on inter-modal competition. Henceforth telecommunication companies (for example, AT&T, Verizon) would be allowed to compete as multichannel video programming distributors (MVPD) and as broadband providers alongside traditional cable providers (for example, Comcast, Time Warner Cable) and digital broadcast satellite (DBS) providers (for example, DirecTV and Dish Network). It also removed numerous ownership restrictions on broadcasting and removed barriers that prevented the former subsidiaries of AT&T to recombine. The Act also deregulated cable rates, and tried to restrict internet pornography— a provision that was later thrown out by the Supreme Court (Pickard, 2007)

In short, the 1996 Telecommunications Act is the epitome of deregulation in American telecommunications (Aufderheide, 1999; Pickard, 2007). The promise, as Pickard (2007) writes, was that deregulation and the unshackling of market forces "would lead to enhanced competition" and, by extension, greater choice and cheaper services for consumers (p. 280). Adds Pickard, "the bill now suggests a mixed legacy," for it permitted an unprecedented level of corporate concentration, and confirmed a decade-long trend that equated the idea of the public interest with that of the market's interest (p. 280; Aufderheide, 1999).[4]

Statewide Franchising

The 1996 Telecommunications Act allowed telecommunication companies to enter the video distribution market and compete directly with cable companies for television and internet access (US, 1996). At the time, however, any telecommunications company wishing to provide these services through wires (rather than satellite) had to negotiate with each and every municipality for a franchise, just as cable companies had done for decades. In 2014, there were 33,000 LFAs, and telecommunication companies (most notably AT&T and Verizon) saw them as an impediment to competition and expansion (Goldfarb, 2008). As a result, they started lobbying statehouses to pass legislation superseding LFA authority through the sanctioning of statewide franchising. According to Verizon, statewide franchising allows it "to offer competitive video service to consumers much faster… instead of knocking on every city's door" (cited in Parker, 2011, p. 206). By the end of 2014, 26 states had passed some form of statewide franchising legislation (NCSL, 2014).[5]

The benefits to statewide franchising are lower barriers to entry, greater competition, and the potential for reduced rates and better service (Fealing 2009). The drawbacks are the loss of local control and autonomy and the potential loss of revenue for municipalities if the franchise fee is not redirected back to them. Redlining—the practice of offering broadband services only to wealthy areas (thereby avoiding building out services to lower-income areas, residents of which may not even subscribe)[6]—is also a concern, as is reduced customer service and reduced PEG funding (Fealing, Sakaimbo, Henry, McFarlane, & Kelley, 2009; Parker, 2011; Rushnak, 2006). To date, reactions have been mixed. While telecommunication companies and some legal scholars praise statewide franchising for encouraging competition and removing barriers to entry, local municipalities, cable operators, and PEG organizations perseverate over the reduction in local authority, local voices, and the survival of community television (Parker, 2011; Rushnak, 2006; Ali, 2017; see Table 14.1).

While legislation varies across states, comparison is possible using Parker's (2011) six categories of analysis of statewide franchising: (1) franchise fees, (2) PEGs, (3) public rights-of-way management, (4) regulatory oversight, (5) redlining and build-out provisions, and (6) pricing and broadband access (p. 211). I will not evaluate each and every case, but three illustrative examples—Texas, Kentucky and Vermont—will help to unpack the various iterations of legislation. I chose Texas because it is generally regarded as the first piece of statewide franchising legislation. Kentucky's law is unique in that it is not about franchising but rather about the franchise fee. Vermont is one of the few states to designate a specific portion of the franchise fee to PEG. I will focus particularly on the second of Parker's characteristics—PEG—for it became a point of significant contention between stakeholders (Ali, 2017).

The first statewide franchising law was passed in Texas in 2005 (Util. Code Ann §66.003). The franchise fee was kept at 5% and distributed to the individual municipalities. PEG channels are maintained, with new entrants required to match incumbents in terms of channel capacity and funding for "the duration of the franchise, then [contribute] 1% of gross" profits for PEG capital expenditures (Miller & Van Eaton, 2007). The revenue directed to PEG, however, does not include non-capital related expenditures. Previously, "many local franchise agreements had providers paying operating and staffing expenses" (Fealing et al. 2009, p. 13). The inability for LFAs to charge for these expenses represented a significant loss in PEG revenue and was directly responsible for the closure of a Dallas public access channel (Waldman, 2011). PEG channels in Texas (and Michigan) are also required to provide at least 8 hours of programming content daily. If this quota is not met then these channels may be taken off the air for an indeterminate amount of time (Fealing et al. 2009).

Table 14.1 Comparison of Stakeholder Positions

Stakeholder	Position on statewide franchising	Position on municipal broadband	Preferred level of regulation
Municipalities	Want to maintain control over the franchising of cable companies in their jurisdiction	(Many) want to be able to offer their own commercial internet service to residents and businesses	Local
States	Against federal/FCC control over the franchising process. In favor of statewide franchising or agnostic	Want to prohibit municipal broadband and leave internet provision exclusively in the hands of private companies	State
FCC	No firm regulatory decision but tangential actions and declarations suggest support for statewide franchising	Wants to cut down regulatory barriers to municipal broadband so as to promote greater broadband adoption in the country	Local and state
Telecommunication companies	Want cable franchising to occur at either the state or federal levels	Do not want municipalities to have the right to start their own ISP businesses—want to remain the exclusive providers of broadband connection	State and FCC
Public interest groups	In favor of local franchising	In favor of municipal broadband	Local and FCC

These are generalized categories and do not represent the position of all stakeholders.

Kentucky's law, passed in 2006 (KRS 136,600) is unique in that it focuses only on the franchise fee. The fee is actually larger than in most states, standing at 5.4% of gross revenues. Municipalities retain the rights to franchise MVPDs and the right to request PEG channel capacity, institutional networks, and build-out requirements. That said, Kentucky's law contains a provision forbidding any funds to be collected by municipalities, meaning that PEG organizations are effective de-funded (Pikeville, 2010). According to one Kentucky-based PEG organization, KRS 136,600 represented a "terrible blow for PEG funding in Kentucky" (Pikeville, 2010, p. 6). Wisconsin, Florida, Iowa, Georgia and Ohio also eliminated PEG funding, while Kansas, South Carolina, Missouri and Nevada do not require new entrants to provide any PEG support. In contrast with the sentiments about PEG funding, however, several Kentucky municipalities seem not to mind the provisions in KRS 136,600 as they retained their franchise authority.

In contrast to Kentucky and Texas, legislation in Vermont (also passed in 2005) allows municipalities the flexibility to allocate certain proportions of the franchise fee (for example, 0.25% or 0.5%) to capital expenditures. Many franchise agreements in Vermont also allocate the entire franchise fee to PEG organizations. On the other hand, the Virginia Public Service Board allows franchisees to set the build-out parameters of the cable system, something often taken as akin to redlining (see Table 14.2).

The point of this comparison is not to pit one state against another, nor is it to offer judgment on the merits of statewide versus local franchising. Instead, it is to demonstrate the positions of stakeholders regarding statewide franchise legislation and statewide franchising's impact on different aspects of the industry—from fees, to PEG, to build-out. This is also an opportunity to unpack the different discursive tactics marshaled by stakeholders. In the case of telecommunication companies, the arguments centered on lower barriers of entry, increased competition and lower customer rates. For incumbent cable companies, the arguments are about fairness, while for local municipalities the arguments center on authority and localism. Comcast (2006), for instance, argued the only reason "AT&T has been 'unable' to obtain local cable franchises is that *AT&T unreasonably refuses to apply for them*" (p. 4; emphasis in original). According to the cable giant, the Commission should avoid supporting statewide franchising and "reaffirm the bedrock principle— which is firmly established in Section 621 [of the 1996 Act]—that local communities must retain the primary role in managing the franchising process" (p. 3). Wanting to assure that telecommunication companies did not get a regulatory leg-up, cable companies thus sided with local municipalities against statewide franchising.

Table 14.2 Comparison of Texas, Kentucky, and Vermont franchising laws

	Texas	Kentucky	Vermont
Date	2005	2006	2005
Bill	SB 5	KRS 136,600	VT PSB 8000–8500 30 V.S.A. §501–517
Franchise fee	5% of gross or that paid by incumbent	5.4%: 3% tax on the retail MVPD service; 2.4% tax on gross revenues	5% of gross revenue
PEG channel capacity	Match incumbent; no case less than 2 channels	Municipalities can require PEG capacity	Up to three channels
PEG support fees	Match incumbent for duration of franchise, then 1% of gross	Municipalities may receive "donations" for PEG support but cannot request payment from cable providers	Some communities allocate the entire fee to PEG; others portion it out (e.g. 4.25% for operating costs and 0.5% for capital costs)
I-net	Provided at not cost until 1 Jan. 2006 and then is paid for by the municipality	Municipalities may request I-nets but cannot request payment from cable providers	By request
Right of way	Local government	Local government	Local government
Redlining/build out	No redlining; no build out	Redlining prohibited; build out determined by the municipality	Redlining prohibited; build out requirements determined by the franchisee

Source The author; the text of the Texas column and of the criteria is taken from Miller and Van Eaton (2007)

Local Franchising Report and Order

Eventually, the FCC was forced to intervene after receiving complaints from telecommunications companies accusing LFAs of overstepping their authority by making unreasonable requests of new franchisees. Companies like Verizon argued that LFAs were placing undue burdens on new entrants and were dragging their feet when awarding new franchises. To address these allegations, the FCC sought comment on activating Section 621(a)(1) of the 1996 Act which would allow the FCC to forbid a franchise authority from "unreasonably refu[sing] to award an additional competitive franchise" (Goldfarb, 2008, p. 4). As I write elsewhere: "This docket proved highly contentious, as it brought to light the FCC's jurisdictional powers and challenged the ability of LFAs to negotiate with cable companies on behalf of their constituents" (Ali 2017, p. 97). One of the major issues at stake, for instance, was if the FCC should become the "franchiser of last resort," with the power to preempt both local and state authority (FCC, 2005).

Another major issue was PEG funding. As we recall, the 1984 Cable Act allowed LFAs to charge a franchise fee of 5% from cable providers, and LFAs could exceed this amount when requesting channel capacity and capital costs for PEG. The Act, however, was ambiguous about whether non-capital-related costs were included in the franchise fee or if LFAs could exceed the fee for such expenses (for example, programming, salaries, and training). Ruling on what could be included in the franchise fee has obvious implications for PEG because if all non-capital funding were to be deducted from the franchise fee, PEG organizations would receive less money from the municipality (Goldfarb, 2008).

The National Association of Telecommunications Officers and Advisors (NATOA) vehemently opposed limitations on LFAs' ability to charge cable providers over and above the franchise fee to fund PEG organizations. It did so based on the importance of local authority and community responsiveness:

> Public, educational and governmental ("PEG") access channel capacity, facilities and equipment requirements, along with institutional network ("I-Net") requirements, are among the most vital elements of the local community cable-related needs and interests that the Cable Act was designed to preserve and protect. Because they are based on each community's own unique local needs, PEG and I-Net requirements vary considerably from community to community (2006, p. iv).

Such community responsiveness could therefore not be achieved through a statewide or federal system. Joining NATOA were numerous municipalities, along with the National League of Cities, the National Association of Counties, the United States Conference of Mayors, and PEG. As one municipality argued:

> Local governments represent their citizens' interests, and local officials are held accountable by their constituents. Thus, local governments promote their citizens' interests in (among other things) lower prices, better service, and choice among competitive video service providers. Their decisions and policies are geared toward enabling competitors to enter the market. (Arundel, 2006, p. 3)

Unsurprisingly, telecommunications companies such as AT&T objected. AT&T (2006) favored statewide franchising (citing Texas as an example), noting that LFAs impose "excessive demands for money and in-kind services and facilitates" (p. 10). It also argued for a uniform national franchise fee to speed along the licensing process. Lastly, AT&T interpreted Section 622 as meaning that LFAs could only mandate "'adequate' PEG facilitates—not duplicative or gold-plated PEG facilities" (p. 67). Verizon (2006) agreed:

> There is no question that the current local franchising process generates unwarranted delays and is engrained with overreaching practices—most of which are unlawful under the Cable Act and the First Amendment—and all of which are encouraged by incumbent cable operators in an effort to hinder competitive entry into the video market. (p. iii)

Clearly, this issue not only pitted local and state governments against one another, but also incumbent cable companies against telecommunications companies eager to enter the video distribution market.

It is telling that very few state governments filed comments with the FCC on this matter. Indeed, of the over 5000 comments submitted to the FCC only six came from state governments (the State of Hawaii, the State of Indiana Utility Regulatory Commission, the New Jersey Board of Public Utilities, the New York State Department of Public Service, the Public Utilities Commission of Texas, and the Vermont Public Service Board). This contrasts greatly with the over 400 comments received from towns, cities, municipalities and counties. Comments from the states supported statewide franchising and urged the Commission not to adopt federal regulation. Some, like New Jersey and Vermont, made the case that they are in the best position (compared with the FCC) to enact requirements for franchisees that suit the unique needs of the communities within the state.

Read together, the state comments were generally brief (Texas's, for instance, was four pages compared with AT&T's 305 pages), and were more concerned with the FCC's ability to enact nation-wide franchising regulations, than with defending their positions against local municipalities. This might suggest that states were reluctant interventionists with respect to this docket and the issue more generally.

Despite this lackluster participation from states, the FCC's final ruling was supportive of statewide franchising and the pleas of telecommunications companies. In its 2007 *Report and Order* the FCC found that the local franchising process "constitutes an unreasonable barrier to entry" and it therefore placed significant limitations on LFAs. LFAs were chastised for imposing "unreasonable demands" such as build-out mandates and I-net requirements, and for taking too long to award franchises. It also ruled "capital costs" to mean only "costs incurred in or associated with the construction of PEG access facilities" (FCC 2007, p. 51). All other costs—salaries, training, and facilities management—would be subject to the 5% cap. LFAs would heretofore have to deduct such costs from the franchise fee, and many PEG organizations saw substantial reduction in their operating budgets as a result.

The blow to PEG organizations and the loss of local control over cable franchising was not lost on FCC Commissioners Michael Copps and Jonathan Adelstein, both of whom dissented from the FCC's ruling. Not only was Adelstein convinced that this ruling "turn[ed] federalism on its head" but he was sure that the FCC's decision would be overturned in court (FCC 2007, p. 99). This did not happen, and the FCC's 2006/2007 ruling on local franchising authority stands. Today there is still much disagreement not only between the states that have and have not enacted statewide franchising, but even among those states—such as Texas, Kentucky and Vermont—that have statewide franchising regimes. The FCC has also refused to rule directly on statewide franchising one way or the other. This inconsistency becomes even more apparent when we reintroduce the case of municipal broadband. Here, the FCC seemed to favor municipalities while it chose to constrain municipalities in the franchising decision.

BACK TO THE PRESENT: MUNICIPAL BROADBAND

While the FCC refused to act on statewide franchising, a decade later it intervened to preempt state laws in North Carolina and Tennessee so as to encourage the proliferation of broadband through municipally owned systems. To be sure, some 20 states have enacted some form of prohibitive legislative against municipal broadband, but even still there are almost 500 municipal broadband organizations throughout the country. These include:

> 89 communities with a publicly owned fiber to the home (FTTH) network reaching most or all of the community, 76 communities with a publicly owned cable network reaching most or all of the community, over 180 communities with some publicly owned fiber serve available to parts of the community, over 110 communities with publicly owned dark fiber available, and over 40 communities in 13 states with publicly owned network offering at least 1 gigabit service. (Kruger & Gilroy, 2016, pp. 2–3)

These gains are not lost on opponents of municipal broadband, whose arguments broadly mirror those advanced by the advocates of statewide franchising (namely telecommunication companies, states, and deregulatory enthusiasts) (see Table 14.1 for a breakdown of stakeholder positions). The difference here is that the FCC opted to protect and in some cases enhance local control over broadband using Section 706 of the Telecommunications Act as legal justification.

In sum, the issues at stake in both statewide franchising and municipal broadband are akin: jurisdiction over telecommunications in the United States. The stakeholders are also the same: municipalities, state legislatures, telecommunications and cable companies, public interest groups, and the FCC. The outcome, as we know, could not have been more different.

CONCLUSION

The case of statewide franchising represents a tangible moment of policy failure in American telecommunications regulation. The responsibility, however, rests not solely with the FCC, but also on congress and stakeholders for failing to resolve these issues through compromise, legislation, or judicial appeals. Local municipalities, meanwhile, seem to have moved their attention away from statewide franchising and towards municipal broadband.

Comparing statewide franchising with municipal broadband demonstrates inconsistency at the FCC with respect to authority and jurisdiction over advanced telecommunications networks in the United States. Is this a local matter, as PEG groups and LFAs attest? Is it a matter of states' rights, as telecommunication providers attest? Or is this a federal matter, on which numerous attempts have been made to legislate in congress (Rushnak, 2006)? The tension between the convergence of technology and regulation on the one hand and the deconvergence of policy actors on the other has resulted in discord and disarray in a media system that is already heavily tethered to commercial interests (McChesney, 1999).

One of the major concerns of critical political economists in these moments of disjuncture is: Who gets to fill the power vacuum? In the case of statewide franchising, it is clear that major telecommunication companies succeeded in lobbying state legislatures and succeeded in convincing the FCC that LFA authority is circumspect. As we will recall, this exemplifies both regulatory capture and policy failure. We have seen how appeals to competition and lowered barriers to entry took precedence over arguments for local municipalities regulating public rights of way and for the ability of PEGs to operate as a public voice. While the benefit of regulatory deconvergence is that more voices are heard in the policymaking process, and the benefit of regulatory convergence is a more streamlined and technologically appropriate regulatory mechanism, the inability of the FCC to balance them has led to a piecemeal approach to the regulation of American telecommunications. The question we must ask now is: How do we balance a regulatory system that requires a converged technoscape but which allows for corporate concentration and monopolistic behaviors with a deconverged stakeholder system that rightfully permits the recognition of multiple policy actors, but which creates a power vacuum through jurisdictional disarray?

In her book, *The Entrepreneurial State*, Mariana Mazzucato (2015) argues for a greater direct role for the state in supporting innovation and risk-taking in the new digital economy. Noting that the state has always played a vital but unacknowledged role in fostering innovation, she argues that the state would be wise to assume the characteristics of venture capitalists to both fund and benefit from breakthroughs in everything from technology to pharmaceuticals. Her argument, however, stops short at investigating the need for greater and clearer regulation and public policy. I suggest, therefore, that the state needs to have a clearer regulatory role in telecommunications policy to stave off further instances of jurisdictional and commercial upheaval. This might happen, as some have suggested, through a rewriting of the Telecommunications Act (Heaton, 2014), or, less onerously, through a more proactive FCC, as was seen during the municipal broadband and network neutrality decisions.

Whatever course is taken, it is clear is that something needs to be done to correct for the jurisdictional battles that are plaguing telecommunications policy. "Policy coordination is needed," argued Megdel back in (1995), "[and the] state hearing rooms should not be used to determine national policy in a fragmented way" (p. 94). Until such coordination is achieved we need to be remain critical of those who seek to capture the regulatory process and capitalize on the moments when the intersection of regulatory convergence and deconvergence has led to policy failure.

NOTES

1. This is of course not a new concern (*see* McChesney, 1999).
2. The Mann-Elkins Act of 1910 applied this division to interstate and intrastate telecommunications.
3. PEG was a particularly important addition to the Cable Act in terms of local authority. While public access television had existed for a decade, its regulatory status was fraught until the Act, which permitted LFAs to request PEG channels from cable providers.
4. Examples include lengthening the license terms for broadcast stations from 5 to 6 years and making it more difficult to contest broadcast licenses (Common Cause, 2005).
5. The NCSL lists 25 states, to which we can also add Kentucky.
6. Redlining is also forbidden by the 1996 Act [§621(a)(3)].

REFERENCES

Ali, C. (2017). *Media localism: The policies of place*. Urbana-Champagne: University of Illinois Press.

Anne Arundel County. (2006). Comments of Anne Arundel County and Montgomery County, Maryland MB Docket No. 05-311. Retrieved from https://www.fcc.gov.

AT&T. (2006). Comments of AT&T Inc. MB Docket No. 05-311. Retrieved from http://www.fcc.gov/.

Aufderheide, P. (1999). *Communications policy and the public interest: The Telecommunications Act of 1996.* New York: Guilford Press.

Bar, F., & Sandvig, C. (2008). US communication policy after convergence. *Media, Culture and Society, 30*(4), 531–550.

Brodkin, J. (2014, February 12). ISP lobby has already won limits on public broadband in 20 states. Available at: http://arstechnica.com/tech-policy/2014/02/isp-lobby-has-already-won-limits-on-public-broadband-in-20-states/.

Comcast. (2006). Comments of Comcast Corp. MB Docket No. 05-311. Available at: https://www.fcc.govCommon.

Common Cause. (2005). The fallout from the 1996 Telecommunications Act: Unintended consequences and lessons learned. Washington, DC: Common Cause. Retrieved from http://www.commoncause.org/research-reports/National_050905_Fallout_From_The_Telecommunications_Act_2.pdf.

Dunne, M. (2007). Let my people go (Online): The power of the FCC to preempt state laws That prohibit municipal broadband. *Columbia Law Review,* 1126–1163.

Fealing, K. H., Sakaimbo, N., Henry, M. McFarlane, D, & Kelley, S. (2009). Statewide video franchising legislation: A comparative study of outcomes in Texas, California and Michigan. University of Minnesota. Retrieved from http://heartland.org/policy-documents/statewide-video-franchising-legislation-comparative-study-outcomes-texas-california.

Federal Communications Commission (FCC). (2005). Notice of proposed rulemaking MB Docket No. 05-311. Available at: http://www.fcc.gov/.

Federal Communications Commission (FCC). (2007). Report and order and further notice of proposed rulemaking MB Docket No. 05-311. Available at: http://www.fcc.gov.

Federal Communications Commission (FCC). (2015). Memorandum opinion and order WC Docket No. 14-115; WC Docket No. 14-116. Available at: https://www.fcc.gov.

Goldfarb, C. B. (2008). Public, educational, and governmental (PEG) access cable television channels: Issues for congress. Congressional Research Service. Available at: http://opencrs.com/document/RL34649/2008-09-05/.

Heaton, B. (2014, Jan. 15). Former FCC leaders caution altering telecom law. Government Technology. Available at: http://www.govtech.com/data/Former-FCC-Leaders-Caution-Altering-Telecom-Law.html.

Horwitz, R. (1989). *The irony of regulatory reform: The deregulation of American telecommunications.* New York: Oxford University Press.

IBIS World. (2016). Cable Providers in the US Market Research. Retrieved from http://www.ibisworld.com/industry/default.aspx?indid=2011.

Kentucky. (2006). KRS 136.660: Prohibitions—Local franchise fee or tax defined. Available at: http://www.lrc.ky.gov/Statutes/chapter.aspx?id=37644.

Kruger, L. & Gilroy, A. (2016). Municipal broadband: Background and policy debate. Washington, DC: Congressional Research Service. Retrieved from https://www.fas.org/sgp/crs/misc/R44080.pdf.

Lunt, P., & Livingstone, S. (2011). *Media regulation: Governance and the interest of citizens and consumers*. Los Angeles: Sage.

Mazzucato, M. (2015). The entrepreneurial state: Debunking public vs. private sector myths. New York: PublicAffairs.

McChesney, R. W. (1999). *Rich media, poor democracy: Communication politics in dubious times*. Urbana: University of Illinois Press.

Megdel, S. B. (1995). The benefits of state regulation. In *American regulatory federalism & Telecommunications infrastructure*, (pp. 85–94). Hillsdale, N.J: Lawrence Erlbaum Associates.

Miller & Van Eaton. (2007). Stable cable franchise laws at a glance. Retrieved from http://www.millervaneaton.com/content.agent?page_name=LEGISLATIVE%20FEATURE:%20State%20Page.

Mosco, V. (2009). *The Political Economy of Communication*. Los Angeles: SAGE Publications Ltd.

National Conference of State Legislatures. (2014). Statewide Video Franchising Statutes. Retrieved from http://www.ncsl.org/research/telecommunications-and-information-technology/statewide-video-franchising-statutes.aspx.

National Organization of Telecommunications Officers and Advisors (NATOA). (2006). Comments of the National Association of Telecommunications Officers and Advisors et al. MB Docket No. 05-311. Available at: http://www.fcc.gov/.

O'Boyle, T., & Mitchell, C. (2013). The Empire Lobbies Back: How Big Cable Killed Competition in North Carolina. Institute for Local Self Reliance. Retrieved from https://ilsr.org/killing-competition-nc/.

Pikeville. (2010). Comments of Pikeville, KY GN Docket No. 10-25. Retrieved from https://www.fcc.gov.

Parker, J. G. (2011). Statewide cable franchising: Expand nationwide or cut the cord? *Federal Communications Law Journal, 64*(1), 199–222.

Pickard, V. (2007). Telecommunications Act of 1996. In T. M. Schaefer & T. A. Birkland (Eds.), *The encyclopedia of media and politics* (p. 280). Washington, DC: CQ Press.

Pickard, V. (2015). The return of the nervous liberals: Market fundamentalism, policy failure, and recurring journalism crises. *The Communication Review, 18*(2), 82–97.

Rushnak, L. A. (2006). Cable television franchise agreements: Is local, state or federal regulation preferable? *Rutgers Computer & Technology Law Journal, 33*(1), 41–106.

Santorelli, M. (2007). Rationalizing the municipal broadband debate. *I/S: A Journal of LA Wand Policy*, *3*(1), 43-82.

Sterling, C. H., Bernt, P. W., & Weiss, M. B. H. (2006). *Shaping american telecommunications: A history of technology, policy, and economics*. Mahwah, N.J: Routledge.

Teske, P. E. (1995). Introduction and Overview. In Paul Teske (Ed.), *American regulatory federalism & telecommunications infrastructure* (pp. 3–18). Hillsdale, NJ: Lawrence Erlbaum Associates.

Teske, P., & Bhattacharya, M. (1995). State government actors beyond the regulators. In American Regulatory (Ed.), *Federalism & telecommunications infrastructure* (pp. 67–84). Hillsdale, NJ: Lawrence Erlbaum Associates.

Texas. (2005). Util. Code Ann 66.003. Public Utility Regulatory Act. Retrieved from http://www.statutes.legis.state.tx.us/Docs/UT/htm/UT.66.htm.

United States (US). (1984). Cable communications policy act of 1984. U.S. Code, *47*, 531–559. Retrieved from http://www.law.cornell.edu/uscode/17/

———. (1996). Telecommunications act of 1996. Pub. LA. No. 104–104, 110 Stat.56.

Verizon. (2006). Comments of Verizon MB Docket No. 05-311. Retrieved from http://www.fcc.gov/.

Vermont (2005). Cable Television Systems. Vt. Stat. Ann. tit 30, chpt. 13, §501.

Vick, D. W. (2006). Regulatory convergence? *Legal Studies*, *26*(1), 26–64.

Waldman, S. (2011). The information needs of communities: The changing media landscape in a broadband age. FCC. Available at: www.fcc.gov/infoneedsreport.

White House. (2015, Jan. 13). Broadband that works: Promoting competition & local choice in next-generation connectivity. Available at: https://www.whitehouse.gov/the-press-office/2015/01/13/fact-sheet-broadband-works-promoting-competition-local-choice-next-gener.

AUTHOR BIOGRAPHY

Christopher Ali is Assistant Professor in the Department of Media Studies at the University of Virginia, USA. His research focuses on communication policy and regulation, critical political economy, critical geography, comparative media systems, localism, and local news. He has published in numerous internationally ranked journals including: *Communication Theory; Media, Culture & Society*; the *International Journal of Communication*; and the *Journal of Information Policy*. His recent book, *Media Localism: The Policies of Place* (University of Illinois Press, 2017) addresses the difficulties of defining and regulating local media in the 21st century in the United States, United Kingdom, and Canada and the implications these difficulties have for the long-term viability of local news.

CHAPTER 15

The Triple-Network Convergence in China: Implementation and Challenges

Fei Jiang, Kuo Huang and Yanran Sun

INTRODUCTION: TRIPLE-NETWORK AS A FORM OF MEDIA CONVERGENCE

Internet protocol technology, which is based on multimedia applications and the popularization of broad data services, has made the internet an increasingly "omnipotent" medium. Nowadays, the internet can be used to transfer various types of data, including text, audio, images and so on; internet services such as electronic mails and online videos have become an indispensable part of media users' daily life, and media users' demand for multimedia services is also increasing. Moreover, traditional

F. Jiang (✉)
School of International Journalism and Communication, Beijing Foreign Studies University, Beijing, China
e-mail: fjiangmedia@yahoo.com

K. Huang
English Service of China Radio International, Beijing, China
e-mail: misshuangkuo@yahoo.com

Y. Sun
Graduate School of Chinese Academy of Social Sciences, Beijing, China
e-mail: sunyr25@163.com

© The Author(s) 2017
S. Sparviero et al. (eds.), *Media Convergence and Deconvergence*, Global Transformations in Media and Communication Research - A Palgrave and IAMCR Series, DOI 10.1007/978-3-319-51289-1_15

media such as telecommunications, newspapers, radio and television are applying digital technologies and are gradually becoming integrated into the internet. All in all, the development of information technology, the transformation of user habits and the evolution of the media industry have blurred the boundaries of telecommunication networks, broadcasting networks and the internet (Lu, 2015, p. 1), turning the convergence of these three networks from theoretical possibility into reality.

Media convergence is the last step of a multi-stage and multi-level process that starts from media interaction and then develops into media integration (Xu, 2006). In China, media convergence is carried out simultaneously at the three different levels: technology, services and institutional or conceptual (Ding, 2011).

This chapter studies "triple-network convergence" (or "triple-play") policy in China, known as San Wang Rong He (三网融合), which is essentially a top-down media convergence plan designed and driven by the Chinese government, which aims at promoting network technical innovation, combining the functions and services of the telecom network, the broadcasting network and the internet, as well as promoting the sharing of network infrastructures and other resources. In all, triple-network convergence consists of multilevel integration of techniques, business, markets, laws, regulations and regulators. The integrated network will provide various media services, such as data, audio and video transfer (Jin & Cheng, 2015, pp. 10–11).

China is not the only Asian country carrying out such a media convergence plan. For instance, the Japanese government initiated the "u-Japan" strategy in 2004, which aims at building a "ubiquitous network society"—an information-technological environment that can let people connect into the network anywhere and at any time (Wang, 2005). In order to achieve the goal, Japan has upgraded the information network facilities nationwide, which promoted broadband network construction, media digitalization and various telecom service platforms. As a result, nowadays, media convergence in Japan happens in media contents, forms and institutions (Piao, 2013). The government of Singapore has also realized the significance of the media convergence trend. Restrictions to the telecom and broadcasting industries were lifted at the beginning of the twenty-first century and various media supervision departments were merged into the new Media Development Authority (Zhao, 2011).

The main purpose of our research is to understand whether China's triple-network convergence plan is a real and important reform, or merely a political instrument. Based on sources such as government documents, reports, industry data, previous research findings and news reports, the chapter will first examine the progress of triple-play, then evaluate its implementation, and finally analyze future development trends.

DEVELOPMENT OF TRIPLE-NETWORK CONVERGENCE IN CHINA

In China, the idea of "media convergence" was not considered by media administrations until the end of the twentieth century. Cross-industry operations were explicitly prohibited by the General Office of the State Council: "[T]he Telecom Department should not operate services relating to radio and TV, while Broadcasting Department should not run telecom services" (General Office of the State Council, 1999, p. 1575).

After the USA's implementation of the "National Information Infrastructure" plan in 1993, many countries gradually became aware of the significance of the process of informatization. The situation in China changed in March 2001, when The 10th Five-Year Guidelines for National Economy and Social Development," approved by the Fourth Plenary Session of the 9th National People's Congress (NPC), announced the decision to "vigorously promote informatization," and officially mentioned "triple-network convergence of telecom, television and computer" (The 10th Five-Year Guidelines for National Economy and Social Development, p. 189) as a part of its plan. "Triple-Network Convergence" henceforth became a government policy, which promoted media convergence at various levels. Five years later, in the 11th Five-Year Guidelines, Triple-Network Convergence was described as a national information infrastructure plan. The document claimed that the government would actively promote the upgrades of the telecom and broadcasting networks and the internet infrastructures, and would also facilitate the interconnection among these networks (2006, p. 190).

Initialized as a top-down government strategy, the beginning of Triple-Network Convergence was relatively successful. After nearly 10 years of mulling and planning, the Chinese government's idea of Triple-Network Convergence was basically formulated, providing both a legal and a technical guiding framework. Moreover, the upgrade of the telecom network and the introduction of the Next Generation Broadcasting

(NGB) network laid the technological foundations of convergence, while the operators' initiatives increased the demand for media services.

Therefore, influenced by various factors, the process of China's Triple-Network Convergence was accelerated. From 2008 to 2009, a series of documents were issued by the Chinese government to promote it.[1] Besides their emphasis upon technical upgrades and popularization of digital networks, all documents focused on the media industries and had a strong market orientation. Moreover, for the first time ever, the NDRC proposed lifting the restrictions for industry operators and "realiz[ing] two-way access into radio and television and telecom industries" (China's State Council, 2009, p. 1). This shows that the Chinese government regarded media industry convergence, and the related development of a variety of new services, as a significant starting point for substantially promoting Triple-Network Convergence.

The implementation of the Triple-Network Convergence strategy only started in 2010. In January, a schedule for Triple-Network Convergence was finalized by the executive meeting of the State Council. It specified that the period between 2010 and 2012 was to be an experimental period aimed at exploring policies and approaches for convergence in pilot cities. Afterwards, between 2013 and 2015, a new industrial structure and system of supervision were to be formed.

Therefore, two lists of pilot cities and regions were announced by the State Council, in July 2010 and December 2011. A total of 54 cities and regions began Triple-Network Convergence, including Beijing and Tianjin. The state-level promotion soon triggered great enthusiasm. At the administration level, both MIIT and the former State Administration of Radio, Film and Television (SARFT, now SAPPRFT)[2] encouraged the enterprises under their jurisdictions to conduct product research. At the technology level, optical fiber technique was expanded in both internet and broadcasting networks, and data transmission networks were integrated and augmented while transmission speed increased. At the service level, various services and products emerged one after another, including Internet Protocol Television (IPTV), Video on Demand (VOD) and Over the Top (OTT).

Nevertheless, the departmental cooperation in China's Triple Network Convergence progress was rather problematic, and therefore the integration of technologies and services was hindered by the supervising departments. In the early 2010s, the process slowed down and even fell into stagnation. For instance, many integrated services could

not be launched because of conflicts emerging between different department functions, including SARFT and MIIT, which still took decisions
independently and only for their own respective benefits. Moreover,
despite the steady progress in optical fiber network construction, SARFT
and MIIT continued to build their own networks.

Three Levels of Triple-Network Convergence

This section evaluates Triple-Network Convergence at three levels: media
supervision, technology and business, following the tradition of the literature on media convergence (Cai, 2009, pp. 88–89).

Supervision and Management

In China, the broadcasting and television network, the telecom network
and the internet are under the direct supervision of two departments
subordinated to the State Council: the State Administration of Press,
Publication, Radio, Film and Television (SAPPRFT) and the Ministry of
Industry and Information Technology (MIIT). SAPPRFT supervises the
broadcasting and television network, and is in charge of network design,
license granting and supervision of production of domestic radio and TV
programs, while MIIT is in charge of the telecom network and the internet, and supervises operation of relevant enterprises.

Because of the divergent development policy orientation, broadcast
and telecom industries in China have each been fighting their own battle
and, as a result, their signals were incompatible. China Telecom, China
Unicom and the China Mobile Communication Corporation (CMCC)
are all state-owned businesses and independent legal entities, supervised
by MIIT. Each of the three major telecom companies adopted a distinct
wireless interface standard: CDMA2000 for China Telecom, WCDMA
for China Unicom and TD-SCDMA for CMCC. Meanwhile, the radio
and television industries are part of China's publicity system; therefore
they operate as public institutions and adopt multiple managements. The
nationwide cable network was divided based on administrative regions.
That is, China Central Television (CCTV) and China National Radio
(CNR) are directly subordinated to SAPPRFT, while local TV and radio
institutions are subordinated to local broadcasting offices. Before 2010,
more than 2000 cable TV network operators were running at the same
time, but after the provincial-level network integration of 2010, the

number of TV network operators dropped to 40 (Jin & Cheng, 2015, p. 173). Because both telecom and broadcasting industries have several operators and adopt incompatible signals, the convergence of networks has always been a great challenge. Nonetheless, the Triple-Network Convergence became China's state-level project in 2010 (China's State Council, 2010), and as a consequence SAPPRFT and MIIT both started to operate under the State Council's guidance.

Achievements: Top-Level Design and Policy Support
The implementation of the Triple-Network Convergence strategy faces lots of challenges since it causes interest conflicts among different ministries; therefore top-level design and supporting policies are needed to guide as well as secure the process. In China, various ministries set up administrative orders for their own sectors, but the State Council sits at the top of a complex bureaucracy of commissions and ministries and formulates general guidelines. When handling issues that are given high priority or are likely to evoke conflicts among ministries, the State Council usually establishes a temporary leading group led by the premier or a vice premier to strike a balance among interested parties. The National Triple-Network Convergence Leading Group is specifically designated to promote and enact the triple-network plan, and its achievements on a management level are the approval and release of policies and plans (Liu, 2013, pp 47–48).

The two-way access policy implemented by the State Council, China's top administrative authority, broke the long-standing barriers between the two industries. Broadcasting corporations are nowadays allowed to run added-value telecommunications businesses, basic telecommunications businesses, and broadband services based on cable TV networks. In the meantime, telecom companies have been given the green light for program production (except political news programs) and internet audio and video transmission (except the form of radio and television) (China's State Council, 2010, p. 6).

The State Council's top-level design for two-way access is to first conduct an experiment in pilot cities, then to expand the experiment's scale, and finally to promote it nationwide. In January 2010, the State Council issued the Overall Plan for Promoting Triple-Network Convergence. In June, 12 of the most developed cities in China became pilot cities to conduct the two-way access experiment (General Office under China's State Council, 2010). On 4 September 2011, the State Council published the latest Triple-Network Convergence Promotion Plan, which allowed cities and regions all over the country to adopt a two-way access policy. This document also urged administrative departments of all levels to "give permission to all qualified enterprises as soon as possible" (General Office under China's State Council, 2015).

In addition to two-way access policy for media service, in 2013 the State Council also issued a Broadband China Strategy and Implementation Plan. It proposed plans for upgrading the technology of the networks, including the construction of Next Generation Broadcasting (NGB) for the broadcasting and television industries, and the integration of the cable TV network nationwide. Meanwhile, copper cables were to be replaced by fiber ones for the telecom network in order to achieve high-speed internet access. Periodic objectives as well as general objectives for 2020 were set in the document: The number of fixed broadband (FBB) users would reach 400 million, and 70% of households would be equipped with broadband; the number of 3G/LTE users would reach 1.2 billion (a penetration rate of 85%) and the number of internet users would amount to 1.1 billion. Moreover, broadband bandwidth in urban and rural areas would be 50 Mbps and 12 Mbps, and for 50% of urban families FBB would reach the speed of 100 Mbps. The nationwide cable TV network interconnection platform would cover 95% of users (China's State Council, 2013). Meanwhile, given that upgrading broadcasting and telecom networks at same time would be a waste of resources, the State Council encouraged administrative departments and subordinate enterprises in both broadcasting and telecom industries to share network resources and plan for the reform together.

Challenges: Conflicts of Interest Between SAPPRFT and MIIT
Although the State Council has shown positive attitudes toward Triple-Network Convergence through various regulations and policies, disputes over conflicting interests between executive departments have emerged (mainly between SAPPRFT and MIIT). Differences appeared before the 2010 Pilot Plan for Triple-network Convergence was issued; this plan was in fact revised five times from April to June, mainly because of the numerous disagreements concerning some concrete measures proposed by the two departments named in terms of authority and business scope. Moreover, after the implementation of the pilot plan, both departments introduced protectionist measures to preserve their power.

One important reason for the conflict between SAPPRFT and MIIT was the fact that existing rules were outdated. Even nowadays, industry supervision is mainly based on two regulations issued by the State Council, the Regulation on Telecommunications (issued 25 September 2000, amended 15 August 2014) and the Regulations on Broadcasting and Television Administration (issued 11 August 1997, amended 7 December 2013). These regulations are outdated in the age of triple-play for two main reasons: Their definitions of subject qualification and division of rights and obligations are not applicable on today's broadcasting and internet industries; and, moreover, even the two amendments produced no advance, as they only simplified the administrative approval process for pricing and holding an event. Thus, there is still room for the two departments to enact their own regulations within the limits of their jurisdiction. In the meantime, SAPPRFT and MIIT play the role of supervisors as well as representatives and vindicators of interests, which determines their inclination towards industrial protectionism in the implementation of policies.

Technological advantages and supervision loopholes result from developments taking place outside the control of the authority. IPTV is one of the hotspots in the dispute between SAPPRFT and MIIT. Since October 2004, license-granting and platform management have been conducted by SARFT according to the Regulations on Audio-Video Program Service in the Internet and Other Information Networks (State Administration of Radio, Film and Television, 2004). However, using broadband lines and the technical advantage of the internet, telecom companies could bypass SAPPRFT and took the lead in the development and promotion of IPTV.

Consequently, in order to limit the business scope and market shares of telecom enterprises, SARFT issued Document No. 44 in April 2010, to reinforce its regulation on unlicensed IPTV services stating as the reason that these services were "severely impairing national network information security," while it forcibly stopped IPTV services in some regions run by China Telecom, China Unicom and other companies (21st Century Business Herald, 2010, p. 1). Licensing was discontinued until triple-play pilot work began in June 2010. With Document No. 344 and Document No. 43,[3] SARFT resumed the licensing process, but still held the permission of content integration and broadcasting tightly within its grasp.

The development of OTT Set Top Box (STB) also serves as an example. In pursuit of better integrating radio, TV and internet services, as well as for better marketization, OTT STB became key research projects for all internet and telecom corporations. Because at that time regulations were outdated and no specific rules applied to OTT STB, these companies operated their services without the supervision of SAPPRFT for some time and generated an income from their television services.

Thus, the radio and television industry suffered large losses, which resulted in SARFT's introduction of a series of documents, limiting internet and telecom enterprises' market shares. In October 2011, Document No. 181[4] was issued by SARFT and stipulated that STB could only be connected to seven licensed IPTV platforms, while all other internet software became illegal.[5] In July 2014, another notice required all STB products of cable TV network enterprises to install the TVOS1.0 system developed by SAPPRFT (State Administration of Press, Publication, Radio Film and TV, 2014). All these documents limited the STBs' content and technical structure, and impeded the internet and telecom enterprises' independent development of STBs. For instance, in 2012, Xiaomi[6] and several other companies were forced to stop their production of STBs because of their non-compliance.

Networks and Operators

The main infrastructure of triple-play is the broadband network, because the communication functions of cable TV and telephony can be achieved by computers and network communication technologies (Wang et al., 2012, p. 12). This network is optical-fiber-technique-based and has unified IP communication protocol. The "Broadband China" plan is implemented by the State Council. According to the overall layout, broadcasting operators are making great efforts to build the NGB nationwide, while telecom operators are promoting bandwidth upgrades and access to the optical network.

Achievements: Bandwidth Upgrades and Access to the Optical Network

Broadcasting and telecom industries have made some progress in the construction of network thanks to policy support. In 2008, Research Report on China Next Generation Broadcasting Independent Innovation was published by SARFT, which proposed three stages for the construction of the NGB network. Later, SAPPRFT also issued three broadband access standards for operators (State Administration of Radio Film and TV, 2014). Currently, China has achieved some success in the construction of the NGB. By the end of June 2015, cable broadcasting and TV services had 241 million users and a penetration rate of 54.7%; digital TV services had 195 million users and a penetration rate of 81%. Two-way broadcasting network services covered 123 million users, which accounted for 50.95% of the total amount of cable TV users. The two-way broadcasting network had 40 million users, which was 17.35% of the total amount of cable TV users (Xiao, 2015).

MIIT has implemented Special Operations on Broadband every year since 2013, which sets up goals for constructing the 3G and 4G communication networks as well as broadband internet. By the end of March 2015, the total length of optical cable lines in China reached 21.612 million km. The number of internet optical fiber access FTTH/0 ports was 186 million, and the proportion of optical fiber access FTTH/0 ports in internet broadband access ports rose from 40.6% at the end of 2014 to 43.8%. 94.696 million users had an internet access rate above 8 Mbps, which is 46.4% of the total number of broadband users, while 78.39 million users have optical fiber access FTTH/0, which is 38.4% of all users (Ministry of Industry and Information Technology, 2015).

According to the plan of MIIT, by the end of 2017, all cities of prefecture level and above will have access to the optical fiber network of 100 MHz bandwidth, 80% of villages will have optical fiber network access, and 4G communication network will cover the whole nation. With respect to broadband rate, the average access rate will reach 30 Mbps in China's major cities, such as municipalities and provincial capitals, and 20 Mbps in other cities (Chinanews Online, 2015). In addition, since 2013, in 10 cities like Beijing and Shanghai a backbone network has been built by MIIT (Xinhua New Media Center, 2014, p. 224). Cross-boundary operation is also in progress. For a long time, SAPPRFT and its subsidiaries did not have permission to operate telecom services. In May 2016, MIIT gave the "Business Certificate of Basic Teleservices" to China Broadcast Network (CBN), which is a subsidiary of SAPPRFT. The introduction of rivals from the SAPPRFT side is expected to bring some healthy competition into the telecom industry, but the result is yet to be seen (people.cn, 2016).

Challenges: Network Monopoly and Segregation by Operators
The convergence to optical fiber network hardly met any technological difficulties.

However, the separate operations of the broadcasting and telecom networks, as well as the long-existing "regional autonomy" of the two industries, made network convergence difficult to achieve.

Issues of network division exist within China's broadcasting and television industry. Local cable TV enterprises are mainly formed as joint ventures of local government and broadcasting companies. Thus, local cable TV networks are independent in terms of affiliation, operations and administration. Moreover, because local interests are involved, enterprises are constantly in competition and at odds with one another. In May 2014, China Broadcasting Network (CBN) was founded to integrate broadcasting and television cable network nationwide. Nevertheless, it only owns the cable's backbone network; hence, the goal of integration can be achieved solely by the acquisition of local radio and television networks. However, facing powerful public listed companies in the local broadcasting industry, for example, JiShi Media of Jilin Province, Beijing Gehua CATV Network, Shanxi Broadcast & TV Network Intermediary and so on, as well as its own shortage of funds and financial limitations imposed by market rules, CBN has found it a tough task to realize the goal of integrating nationwide radio and television networks into one.

One of the main problems within the telecom industry involves the existence network oligopolies. In the process of data transmission, broadband data first passes through the backbone network, then through the access network, and finally reaches subscribers' terminals. At present, China's backbone network is composed of nine networks; among them, the largest ones are UNINET (also called 169 net) owned by China Unicom, and CHINANET (also called 163 net) owned by China Telecom. Together, they carry 80% of China's total broadband traffic (He, 2013). The other operators have to rent broadband channels from them. Additionally, the two major operators put up barriers in order to increase their market shares. Hence, data transmission speed across UNINET and CHINANET has been very low. Given the situation, internet corporations have to set up servers in both networks to ensure fast access for users. The same situation applies to communication networks, where China Mobile acts as the main monopolistic power.

Moreover, there is still obvious segregation between the two industries. Although CBN has already got permission to run telecom services, the new permission only concerns the broadband market, but not the whole telecom industry. Given that the broadband market has already been taken up by the other three operators, little space to develop its own business is left to CBN.

Neither administrative departments nor subordinate companies in broadcasting or telecom industries have the intention of adopting the suggestions of the State Council—that is, using existing network resources and planning the reform project together. And because those "suggestions" were proposed in the notices issued by the General Office, they lack legal validity. Therefore, the State Council cannot force cooperation between SARFT and MIIT, and so they are both busy with construction of the "last mile" (the trade term for the final links to subscribers, which involve the most difficult upgrades to new technology). Their relationship is more one of competition than of collaboration: neither the NGB construction plan of SAPPRFT nor "Special Operations on Broadband" of MIIT envisaged cooperative developments.

Integration of Business

Based on broadband networks, the integration of media service is directly related to operators and users in the process of Triple-Network Convergence. Though China is still far from realizing one broadband line containing telephone, TV and internet services, integration of IPTV, OTT and other services is spreading on a large scale.

Achievements: Thriving IPTV and OTT Services

Five years after the introduction of IPTV in 2010, the number of users had already reached 36.3 million (Ministry of Industry and Information Technology, 2015). Different collaborative models of IPTV services have been formed between broadcasting and telecom enterprises. One successful example is the IPTV service of BesTV in Shanghai, also called the "Shanghai Mode." A work team was set up by broadcasting companies and telecom companies, to engage in research and in the promotion of IPTV. Shanghai Telecom undertook the work of constructing and upgrading the data transmission broadband network, providing operational support for terminal systems, user management and market promotion; while BesTV, a subsidiary of Shanghai Media Group (SMG), was in charge of content integration, management and broadcasting.

In addition to the various responsibilities, the profits of IPTV service are also divided between the two sides. In most areas of Shanghai, telecom operators take 60% of profit from value-added services and 40% from basic services, while the rest of the profits are attributed to radio and television operators (Hua et al., 2015, p. 92). Based on the stable, high-speed bandwidth (8–12 Mbps) optical fiber network built by the telecom operator as well as the comprehensive high-definition (HD) program provided by the broadcasting operator, BesTV now has 1.98 million IPTV users and 2.16 million HDTV and HD IPTV users (Shanghai Yearbook Editorial Committee, 2014). Shanghai has become the city with most IPTV users and with the most mature market. Besides the Shanghai Mode, there are also the Hangzhou Mode, led by a broadcasting operator; the Guangdong Mode and the Henan Mode, led by a telecom operator; the Harbin Mode and the Jiangsu Mode, which are collaborations of telecom operators and content providers like Xinhua News Agency, media and entertainment groups, and others.

Over The Top (OTT) is another integration media service, aggregating IP video and internet application. It transmits digital signals to TV terminals through the public network. Owing to its rising market position, some industry insiders predict that "OTT TV is the trend of development, while IPTV is only a transitional product" (China Information Industry, 2013). According to statistics from January to September 2014, shipments of OTT STB took up 30% of STB's new market, and had risen by 11%, compared with its market share in 2013, which was 18.4%. OTT became the second most distributed STB, following cable STB, but far more popular than IPTV STB (GL Research, 2014, p. 6).

At present, there are mainly four types of OTT STBs in China. The first are distributed by the original brands of broadcasting that have internet content service licenses—for instance, the "Red Cool Box" of BesTV. The second type is the result of collaboration between telecom operators and licensed enterprises: "Yue Me Box" of China Telecom is an example. The third kind is produced by a collaboration between internet companies, STB manufacturers and licensed enterprises; for example, Xiaomi Company's "Xiaomi Box." And the last type operates in the grey zone of administration, which illegally aggregates internet video resources. Among all these types of STBs, the one manufactured by enterprises with internet content service license has an edge because of its content, and develops more rapidly in the market.

Hunan Mango TV Company launched a commercial STB in 2012. It has now been cooperating with Hunan CATV Network Group, Shenzhen Telecom and Shenzhen Guangxin, and promoting OTT service in many provinces and cities. In addition, BesTV in Shanghai collaborates with Beijing Gehua CATV Network and Shanxi Broadcast & TV Network Intermediary and promotes DVB (digital video broadcasting) and OTT services in many regions. The number of potential users has reached 18.48 million (Shuyumenggongchang, 2015). The latest statistics from Wasu Group in Zhejiang (DVBCN, 2015) shows as many as 60 million people are using OTT TV services.

Challenges: Management Disputes and Vicious Competition
Although the number of IPTV and OTT STB users is constantly increasing, disputes over management and the distribution of benefits have become stumbling blocks in the development of integrated media services. SAPPRFT issued a series of regulations about STB content and technical specifications, but loopholes in their enforcement led to poor market standardization. For instance, in the first half of 2014, a large number of unlicensed STB applications emerged, but owing to SAPPRFT's slow response, Electronic Program Guide (EPG) programs in STBs were beyond the latter's control. It was not until the third quarter of 2014 that SAPPRFT got involved. SAPPRFT talked to the seven licensed enterprises to reiterate the regulation about internet content services stipulated by Document No. 181," and removed illegal applications from the market. Nevertheless, the lack of sustainable management, such as operation permission, media content censorship and so on, can hardly maintain a long-term, healthy competition among enterprises. When such management is relatively weak, companies quickly capture the market share with illegal services, which is really a vicious circle in the development of STB service. The sudden investigation of SAPPRFT caused abrupt "braking" and led to a volatile market. According to statistics, in the third quarter of 2014, STB shipments suffered a significant drop compared with the previous two quarters (GL Research, 2014, p. 16) because of the sudden check.

Because integrated services are still in an exploratory stage, the ambiguity in terms of the distribution of benefits also contributed to an unhealthy competition. Stakeholders are expected to operate and develop media services together, in order to utilize their advantages and, together, realize profits. However, currently, different industries and enterprises work against each other instead of cooperating. For example, in many places of China, partnerships between IPTV operators and local broadcasting and television enterprises have not been established. The charge for IPTV service is usually 20–50% lower than that for the local cable TV service. The price margin will certainly give IPTV service an advantage in grabbing market shares, and therefore the market share and profits of local broadcasting and television enterprises are likely to decline. For this reason, ever since the implementation of the Triple-Network Convergence plan in 2010, many local broadcasting enterprises have asked SAPPRFT to stop IPTV service. Even SAPPRFT itself has once demanded that non-pilot cities should not start IPTV service.

The same problems appear in the development of OTT services as well. In October 2014, China Telecom "Yue Me Box" bypassed local broadcasting and television departments and cooperated directly with the content integration company Aishang TV, damaging broadcasting and television companies. Beijing Television, Jiangsu Television and many other television stations boycotted this STB product. They sent a letter to Aishang TV Company before Yue Me Box was on the market, in which they refused to provide content for Yue Me Box on the grounds that this violated existing regulations.

FUTURE PATHS AND CHALLENGES TO TRIPLE-NETWORK CONVERGENCE

In accordance with the "Overall Plan" published by the State Council in 2010, the nationwide Triple-Network Convergence should have been completed by 2015. However, the development was not as smooth as imagined and triple-play was only partly successful in China. What is more, the key point of the overall informatization plan is gradually turning from Triple-Network Convergence to a new top-down strategy called "Internet Plus."

From Triple-Network Convergence to Internet Plus?

On the basis of the above analysis, in summary, we can draw the conclusion that the goal of "integration" advocated by the State Council has not been fully achieved, as divisions between the three networks still exist.

At the supervision level, despite the top-down convergence plan, China still lacks a unified network regulator and related legal provisions. Currently, SAPPRFT and MIIT are in charge of the approval of industry licenses and the related administrative power. Each department implements regulations that limit the access of their opponent and that favor the realization of profits for their own industries.

Though the technical difficulties have been solved, broadcasting and telecom networks remain fragmented. On the one hand, local broadcasting networks cannot be integrated easily; on the other, telecom networks are divided between four major operators, making interconnectivity hard to achieve. Despite the enormous market potential, the promotion of integrated media services has been impeded by an unhealthy competition arising from unlawful management and unclear benefit distribution. As a matter of fact, the most significant achievements are the various documents published by the State Council, SAPPRFT and MIIT, as well as local governments at all levels. In this sense, Triple-Network Convergence has come to be seen as a political slogan rather than a complicated, substantive construction plan.

In 2000, the chairman of the State Grid Corporation of China (SGCC), Liu Zhenya, proposed that Triple-Network Convergence should upgrade to quadruple-network convergence in which the smart grid will play a role. Although such a proposal has not been officially approved, in March 2015, the implementation of a new state-level strategy made Triple-Network Convergence and its failures gradually disappear from the public eye. At the end of the Triple-Network Convergence five-year plan, the National People's Congress announced a new convergence plan called Internet Plus (Xinhua News Agency, 2015, p. 1). According to the State Council's interpretation, this plan aims at "promoting deep convergence and innovative development of Internet and various fields" (China's State Council, 2015a, b, p. 11) and using the internet as a basic platform for informatization and industrialization (China's State Council, 2015a, b, p. 12). In this new plan, the focus of convergence expanded from the information network and media (in the former triple-play plan) to various industries, including agriculture, education, finance, logistics and transportation. Unlike the Triple-Network Convergence plan, which proposed cooperation and the joint development of the internet, the broadcasting network and the telecom network, the new Internet Plus plan has only one main character, namely the internet. All industries, including the media, have been encouraged to adjust themselves to a new mode of operation in the internet age.

Later, in July 2015, Guiding Opinions of the State Council on Actively Promoting "Internet Plus" Action was issued, which provided top-level design for the Internet Plus plan in three aspects: supervision, technology and services. An Internet Plus interministerial joint conference initiated by the National Development and Reform Commission (NDRC) is responsible for the supervision, while financial support is provided by the Ministry of Finance and the People's Bank of China. Market access limitation of integrated services will be further extended, and local governments will initiate a pilot project in cities and regions, to "break the policy barrier" and explore locally adapted strategies. On the technology front, the Broadband China strategy will be continued. The upgrade of the broadband network to optical fiber will be conducted jointly by NDRC, MIIT and other departments; such an upgrade aims at promoting inter-network connectivity, increasing networks transmission speed and reducing charges. In the service part, cloud computing, big data, internet of things, and other techniques will serve as the foundation. Integration between industries and the internet is encouraged in order to produce innovative products and services (China's State Council 2015a, b).

After the Internet Plus strategy was proposed, there were fewer discussions about Triple-Network Convergence between the administrative authorities, including SARFT, MIIT, and the industries involved, among which were various broadcasting and telecom enterprises. Less than a month after Internet Plus started, in a keynote speech at the 2015 China Content Broadcasting Network (CCBN), Chenxi Nie, the deputy secretary of the CPC Leading Group and deputy director of SAPPRFT, proposed the new concept of "Intellectual Broadcasting." In coordination with Internet Plus, this concept is aimed at furthering the convergence of the radio and television network with the internet, and to add an internet element to the production of content, the integration platform, the communication network and all parts of the broadcasting industry (Nie, 2015). Meanwhile, according to a document issued by the State Council in May 2015, the focus of the work of MIIT and telecom enterprises was shifted to a "Speed Acceleration and Expense Reduction" plan for improving the communications network and the internet. The telecom industry should not only enhance network construction, but also open the market to break the monopoly of state-owned capital and facilitate fair competition.

Both the Intellectual Broadcasting and Speed Acceleration and Expense Reduction plans aim at reinforcing network construction, raise the digitalization level and promote integrated media services. They are essentially an extension of the Triple-Network Convergence plan. However, this new rhetoric avoided mentioning the key problem of triple-play—the convergence of telecom, radio and television networks and industries. Network upgrades and convergence are considered separately, on the basis of the existing network structure and of industry chains.

Future Challenges to the Idea of Triple-Network Convergence

Despite its challenges and partial failure and despite the new Internet Plus plan, the Chinese government has not abandoned the Triple-Network Convergence plan, and has shown the intention of still pushing the process. In 2015, Premier Li Keqiang reaffirmed "advancing overall Triple-Network Convergence" in the "Report on the Government's Work" (Xinhua News Agency, 2015). Soon afterwards, in the Promotion Plan on Triple-network Convergence," the State Council emphasized "substantively carrying forward the convergence plan" (General Office under China's State Council, 2015, p. 48). Nevertheless, faced with institutional and industry barriers, the Chinese government is being forced to change some of the issues of the network convergence plan it stressed 5 years ago. For instance, compared with the 2010 "Overall Plan for Promoting Triple-network Convergence," the 2015 "Promotion Plan" refused the request of "telecom enterprises providing necessary communication facilities and services to broadcasting and television enterprises," which implied acquiescence in repeated network construction.

Nevertheless, the future of China's Triple-Network Convergence is uncertain for at least three reasons. First, there is no appropriate way of solving disputes among different departments. On the one hand, the government did not set up a compensation system for the sunk costs necessary for the provision of two-way access. If the cost of manpower, basic network construction and maintenance will not be compensated for, then neither telecom nor broadcasting and television industries will waive the right of control of their own fields. On the other hand, as

Jinzhou Zhu, research director of Informatization and Industrialization Convergence Research Institute, China Academy of Telecommunication Research (CATR) has said (Wu, 2015), "the crucial point of Triple-Network Convergence lies in finding a proper business model and a profit model" (p. 1). Given that triple-play cannot yield appreciable profits, and the profit distribution after convergence is still not reasonably resolved, neither telecom nor the radio and television industry would be actively engaged in triple-play, even it is a beneficial state plan for the people.

Second, there is a systematic problem with the efficacy of laws and regulations and with the delegation of the power of supervision. Both SAPPRFT and MIIT have the authority to promulgate regulations. Meanwhile, they each possess dual identities—both as representatives of interests and as supervisory departments. Therefore, they facilitate the profits of their own industries. In order to increase profits, they intend to occupy their competitor's market by upgrading their networks and services. From this point of view, the deficiency in regulations makes the Triple-Network Convergence plan merely a chance for both sides to enter the other's "territory."

Last but not least, the development of communication technologies is accelerating. As a latecomer, China's Triple-Network Convergence does not have many advantages, because, while the departments and operators are still arguing about the profit distribution, the internet technology is advancing so quickly that the overall design for triple-play should be changed accordingly. For example, the original design is based on non-mobile networks while the Chinese people have been stepping into a new age of mobile consumption. On the one hand, along with the participation of electronic networks, a pilot project of quadruple convergence was started and should be improved accordingly. On the other hand, Internet Plus has drawn the attention of government, industries, enterprises and even society at large. Compared with this new conception, Triple-Network Convergence appears to be an "old-fashioned" and difficult plan. Hence, it may fade from people's sight in the future.

In sum, an authentic, in-depth Triple-Network Convergence in China, as well as the expectation that "through technical innovation, the service provided by the three information networks will become more identical, and their infrastructure and resources can be shared to provide diverse services" (Jin & Cheng, 2015, pp. 10–11), remains rhetoric, a kind of perpetual vision of the future.

NOTES

1. The mentioned documents include *Several Policies of Encouraging Development in Digital Television Industry*, released by the State Council in 2008, *Announcement of Deepening Structural Reform in Telecom Industry*, released by the Ministry of Industry and Information Technology (MIIT) in 2008, *The 2009 Guidance of Deepening Structural Reform in Economy*, released by National Development and Reform Commission (NDRC) in 2009, and so on.

2. SARFT was merged with the General Administration of Press and Publication (GAPP) in spring 2013, forming the new State Administration of Press, Publication, Radio Film and Television (SAPPRFT).

3. *Document No. 334* refers to *Notice of SARFT on Issues of IPTV Integrated Control Platform Construction in Triple-network Convergence Pilot Regions*. *Document No. 43* refers to *Notice on Issues of IPTV Integrated Control Platform Construction*.

4. *Document No. 181* refers to *Regulation on Operation Management of Organizations with Internet Television License*.

5. The seven companies are: China Network Television (CNTV), BesTV, Southern Media, Wasu Media, China International Broadcasting Network (CIBN), Hunan Broadcasting Group and China National Broadcasting Network (CNBN).

6. Xiaomi is a Chinese mobile internet company, founded in 2010 to focus on hardware, software and internet services.

REFERENCES

10th Five-Year Guidelines for National Economy and Social Development. (2001). *Gazette of the Standing committee of the National People's Congress of the People's Republic of China 03*, 182–204.

11th Five-Year Guidelines for National Economy and Social Development. (2006). *Gazette of the Standing committee of the National People's Congress of the People's Republic of China 03*, 178–221.

21st Century Business Herald. (2010, April 24). *IPTV service checked by SARFT, Triple-network convergence faces obstacles again*. Retrieved from ifeng.com: http://tech.ifeng.com/special/guangdianfengshaiptv/detail_2010_04/24/842956_0.shtml.

Cai, W. (2009). Angle, prospective, path: On the researches of media convergence. *Journal of International Communication, 11*, 87–91.

China Information Industry. (2013, July 3). *Telecom Operators' OTT TV overall arrangement speeds up*. Retrieved December 8, 2015, from cnii.com.cn: http://www.cnii.com.cn/stock/2013-07/03/content_1176088.htm.

Chinanews Online. (2015, May 15). *MIIT: Penetration of mobile broadband will reach the level of medium-developed country in 2017.* Retrieved from Chinanews Online: http://finance.chinanews.com/cj/2015/05-15/7279199.shtml.

China's State Council. (2015a). Guiding opinions of the State Council on accelerating high-speed broadband network construction and advancing network acceleration and expense reduction. *Gazette of the State Council of the People's Republic of China, 16,* 26–29.

China's State Council. (2015b). Guiding opinions of the State Council on actively promoting "Internet plus" action. *Gazette of the State Council of the People's Republic of China, 20,* 11–23.

China's State Council. (2013). Notice of the State Council on issuing "Broadband China" strategy and implementation plan. *Gazette of Liaoning Province People's Government, 19,* 28–40.

China's State Council. (2009). Notice of the State Council on ratifying and forwarding the opinions of the National development and reform commission on deepening the reform of economic system. *Gazette of the State Council of the People's Republic of China, 16,* 9–14.

China's State Council. (2010). *Notice on issuing overall plan of triple-network convergence.* Beijing: Government Document.

Ding, B. (2011). Media fusion: Concept, cause, advantages & disadvantages. *Nanjing Journal of Social Sciences, 11,* 92–99.

DVBCN. (2015, July 2). *QIAO Xiaoyan: Wasu OTT TV has covered 60 million users. Future goal will be having 50 million active users.* Retrieved from DVBCN: http://www.dvbcn.com/2015/07/02-118230.html.

General Office of the State Council. (1999). Notice of the advice issued on improving radio and television cable networks' construction and administration. *Gazette of the State Council of the People's Republic of China, 35,* 1572–1575.

General Office under China's State Council. (2010, July 30). *Notice of the General Office under the State Council on issuing first list of triple-network convergence pilot regions (Cities).* Retrieved December 8, 2015 from www.gov.cn: http://www.gov.cn/zhengce/content/2010-07/01/content_1138.htm.

General Office under China's State Council. (2015). Notice of the General Office under the State Council on issuing triple-network convergence promotion plan. *Gazette of the State Council of the People's Republic of China, 26,* 48–52.

GL Research. (2014, December 12). *White paper on set top box 2014.* Retrieved from http://www.tmtbib.net/index.php?m=content&c=index&a=show&catid=41&id=310.

He, K. (2013, August 12). *Nine backbone networks form the foundation of China's internet and pave the "High way" for National Development.* Retrieved from China Quality News: http://www.cqn.com.cn/news/zgzlb/diwu/753986.html.

Hua, M., He, G., Yan, Z., & Xing, Y. (2015). *The theory and practice of the triple-play.* Beijing: Tsinghua University Press.

Jin, X., & Cheng, J. (2015). *In study of triple-play and development strategy of cable TV network.* Beijing: Capital University of Economics Business Press.

Liu, C. (2013). Examining China's triple-network convergence plan: Regulatory challenges and policy recommendations. *Government Information Quarterly, 30,* 45–55.

Lu, F. (2015). *In integration.* Beijing: China University of Communication Press.

Ministry of Industry and Information Technology. (2015, April 17). *Operation of Economy in Communication Industry on March 2015.* Retrieved December 8, 2015, from Ministry of Industry and Information Technology official website: http://www.miit.gov.cn/n11293472/n11293832/n11294132/n12858447/16548851.html.

Nie, C. (2015, March 27). *Build intellectual broadcasting, Enjoy digital life—Keynote speech at CCBN2015.* Retrieved from State Administration of Radio Film and Television: http://www.sarft.gov.cn/art/2015/3/27/art_57_24679.html.

People.cn. (2016, May 5). *CBN got telecom operation permission.* Retrieved July 4, 2016 from people.cn: http://finance.people.com.cn/n1/2016/0505/c1004-28328586.html.

Piao, Y. (2013). Analizing the difference of media convergence and convergence media—A case study of Japanese media. *Journal of News Research, 10,* 19–22.

Shanghai Yearbook Editorial Committee. (2014). *Chapter twenty informationalization.* Retrieved from www.shanghai.gov.cn: http://www.shanghai.gov.cn/nw2/nw2314/nw24651/nw33466/nw33491/u21aw1015617.html.

Shuyumenggongchang. (2015, June 17). *Behind dispute between Xiaomi and Letv, BesTV quietly started enclosure movement in broadcasting networks. Who is the OTT mighty.* Retrieved from Jiemian: http://www.jiemian.com/article/306318.html.

State Administration of Press, Publication, Radio Film and TV. (2014, July 22). *Notice of SAPPRFT on launching large-scale application test of smart television operating system TVOS1.0, and Promoting standardization and intellectualization of broadcast and television terminal.* Retrieved December 8, 2015 from China Netcasting Services Association: http://www.cnsa.cn/2014/07/22/ARTI1406002860869682.shtml.

State Administration of Radio Film and TV. (2014, July 4). *Notice of SARFT on accelerating application of next generation broadcasting standard, China State Administration of Radio film and television.* Retrieved December 8, 2015 from State Administration of Radio Film and TV Official Website: http://www.sarft.gov.cn/art/2014/7/4/art_36_1012.html.

State Administration of Radio, Film and Television. (2004, July 6). *Regulations on audio-video program service in the internet and other information networks.*

Retrieved from State Administration of Press, Publication, Radio, Film and Television of the People's Republic of China: http://www.sarft.gov.cn/art/2004/10/11/art_1583_26295.html.

Wang, W. (2005). Building ubiquitous network society in 21st century—An analysis of u-Japan and u-Korea strategy. *Information Network 07*, 1–4+8.

Wang, X., Jiang, L., Yao, L., & Liu, H. (2012). *Way of triple-network convergence*. Beijing: The People's Posts and Telecommunications Press.

Wu, J. (2015, September 14). Seventeen years of difficult path of triple-network convergence. Retrieved from Xinhuanet: http://news.xinhuanet.com/finance/2015-09/14/c_128227675.htm.

Xiao, J. (2015, August 26). Analysis of China cable TV development data in the first half year of 2015. Retrieved from TV Home: http://www.tvhome.com/article/20111.html.

Xinhua New Media Center. (2014). *China new media convergence report (2013-2014)*. Beijing: Xinhua Publishing House.

Xinhua News Agency. (2015, March 16). *Report on the work of the central people's government*. Retrieved from www.gov.cn: http://www.gov.cn/guowuyuan/2015-03/16/content_2835101.htm.

Xu, Y. (2006). Interaction, integration, comprehensive convergence: Three phases of media convergence. *Journal of International Communication, 07*, 32–36.

Zhao, J. (2011). Institutional innovation and practice of Singapore media supervision in media convergence background. *Modern Communication (Journal of Communication University of China), 06*, 28–32.

Authors' Biography

Fei Jiang is Professor and PhD supervisor in School of International Journalism and Communication, Beijing Foreign Studies University, Beijing.

Kuo Huang is Principal Researcher and Full Senior Translator (Professor) at English Service of China Radio International, Beijing.

Yanran Sun is a Ph.D. candidate at the Graduate School of Chinese Academy of Social Sciences, Department of Journalism and Communication. Her research focus is on intercultural and international communication, new media, and immigration issue.

Index

© The Editor(s) (if applicable) and The Author(s) 2017
S. Sparviero et al. (eds.), *Media Convergence and Deconvergence*, Global Transformations in Media and Communication Research - A Palgrave and IAMCR Series, DOI 10.1007/978-3-319-51289-1